DATE			
MAY [illegible] 1993			
AUG 26 1993			
DEC 14 1993			

BUSY BODIES

ALSO BY LEE BURNS

The Housing of Nations (with Leo Grebler)

The Art of Planning:
Selected Essays of Harvey S. Perloff
(ed., with John Friedmann)

The Future of Housing Markets:
A New Appraisal (with Leo Grebler)

Spatial Cycles
(ed., with Leo v. d. Berg and Leo H. Klaassen)

BUSY BODIES

Why our time-obsessed society keeps us running in place

LEE BURNS

with illustrations by

Shinji Isozaki

W. W. NORTON & COMPANY

New York London

Printed in the United States of America
First Edition

The text of this book is composed in Meridien with the display set in Baker Signet Oblique.
Composition and manufacturing by Haddon Craftsmen Inc.
Book design by Charlotte Staub.

Library of Congress Cataloging-in-Publication Data

Burns, Leland Smith.
Busy bodies : why our time-obsessed society keeps us running in place / by Lee Burns ; with illustrations by Shinji Isozaki.
p. cm.
Includes index.
1. Time management—United States. 2. Life style—United States.
I. Title
HN90.T5B87 1993
640'.43—dc20 92–20593

ISBN 0-393-03362-7

W. W. Norton & Company, Inc., 500 Fifth Avenue, New York, N.Y. 10110
W. W. Norton & Company Ltd., 10 Coptic Street, London WC1A 1PU
1 2 3 4 5 6 7 8 9 0

TIMETABLE

IV.

INTRODUCTION

How many times this week have you said, "Sorry, I just don't have time to . . . ?" You are not alone. Everybody seems to have the same complaint. Why time seems to be becoming so scarce, and how that perception of time's scarcity affects our actions, especially in late-twentieth-century America, is the topic of this book.

Because the book takes apart a puzzle—I call it The Paradox of The Good Life—I have chosen a paradoxical title. At one level *Busy Bodies* calls to mind people trying to jam too many activities into too few hours; more colloquially, it refers to people who try to be about the business of others. In this more idiomatic usage, busybodies pry and sneak into others' lives, perhaps out of a loneliness that forces their behavior into a vicarious mold, or perhaps out of a genuine concern for others. But the time required for such behavior is entirely incompatible with the busy bodies among us who are dervishly whirling, cramming and ramming activity into a fixed time allotment. For us time has grown increasingly scarce (which is what I mean by the *Busy Body*—or *BB*—factor), and dealing with our own affairs has come to take precedence over watching over others. How that paradox works out is one important theme of the book.

The central paradox of *Busy Bodies,* however, is that affluence—The Good Life—has brought us not more leisure, as one might expect, but instead has made late-twentieth-century Americans the most harried people on earth. Futurists once visualized an

Arcadian society of individuals who would spend their lives engaging in the most lofty and satisfying pursuits: thinking, improving the mind, cultivating the spirit. In fact, economic development has freed us from the grueling tasks of providing for life's basic needs. But as societies develop, somehow less and less time has remained for matters of mind and spirit. Daily schedules become congested with mundane activities and material goods that contribute precious little to the Good Life. Instead of freeing ourselves from the tyranny of enforced schedules, we have become The Harried Leisure Class, to borrow another economist's phrase.[1]

Busy Bodies attempts to show why time has become so scarce, and how this pervasive sense of scarcity changes the way we manage our lives. The first section demonstrates why—despite the fixity of the twenty-four-hour day—time has become more and more scarce, and how we manage our tighter time budgets according to rules much like those governing the allocation of our personal financial budgets. In deciding how to use time, we choose activities that yield the greatest rewards for each unit of time spent. As the rewards change, so does the time allocation. A chief factor driving these changes is technology and the gadgets, such as computers, produced at the inventor's bench. Change, in the era of the *BB* factor, is inevitable. Some activities gain in importance; others decline. That's the nature of trends.

Readers will see how the *BB* factor can account for many of the significant social trends of our time, in politics, education, our family lives, eating and exercise habits, etc. I trace these trends in the middle parts of the book. In the concluding section I look toward the future of the environment, the nation, and indeed the planet. I believe the future, if there is to be one, depends on a willingness to forego current pleasures even when the *BB* factor encourages making the most of the moment.

Canny readers will note that there are twenty-four chapters in all, the number of hours in a day, with the thirteenth left out (no, the omission is intentional) for reasons explained in the text. Read on, please.

In all of this, I have received considerable assistance. The John Simon Guggenheim Foundation provided resources to temporarily free me from teaching obligations at UCLA, and that institution's

Senate Research Committee furthered the work with funds for research assistance. The University of Cambridge's Department of Land Economy and the University of Tokyo's Research Center for Advanced Science and Technology provided me with places to work out ideas.

I am deeply indebted to tolerant colleagues who read manuscripts and contributed ideas, even when they had heard and read more than they cared to. Thanks too are due Naomi Carmon, Frank Mittelbach, Leo Grebler, Dolores Hayden, Archie Kleingartner, Ron Wakefield, and Martin Wachs for patiently listening to ideas and critically reading drafts. Roger Hahn and Melvin Webber gave productive encouragement. Patricia and Donald Shoup contributed more than they will ever realize. Librarian Anne Hartmere pointed me toward useful sources and Ryan Baum provided faithful research assistance. Henning Gutmann, my editor at Norton, gave expert help that ranged from untangling convoluted concepts to serving as an invariably well-informed sounding board for ideas. And Shinji Isozaki's cartoons sum up to the equivalent of thirty-five pages of text, if it is true that a picture is worth a thousand words. To each who helped, I owe a genuine "thank you for your time."

Finally, I owe a debt to the inventors of IBM computers and Wordperfect word-processing software who made it possible to write this book more quickly than by more traditional methods such as quill and foolscap, and the people at the Los Angeles Department of Water and Power who provided a continuous supply of very high quality electricity.

I hope that these helpers, as well as the readers of this book, will come to the conclusion that their efforts were time-worthy.

—Lee Burns
Los Angeles
May 1992

I.

1:00

GIFTS OF TIME

"I wasted time, and now doth time waste me."
—Shakespeare[1]

Everyone who lives in this world is either Class A or Class B. The Class As are those who are reading this book, and the Class Bs (some five billion people) those who are *not*. Two reasons motivate the non-reading Class Bs. Either they haven't heard of the book or they *did* know about the book but preferred to do something else with their time other than buying, borrowing, or stealing a copy to read. Now, dear reader, as a member of Class A, you are presented with the opportunity to decide for yourself whether reading this book is the best use of your time.

If you have better things to do with your time, immediately set aside this book and do whatever it is. Those who accept that generous invitation make a point which undergirds everything that follows: all of us are constantly reallocating time in our search for the balance that yields the highest total rewards per unit of time spent, for the now-non-readers (and members of Class B) are busy doing something else.

Those with the good judgment to read on (and who remain Class As) also prove the point: you have decided that there is no greater reward for a few hours spent sitting wherever you are, *when*ever you are, being illuminated with a robust new idea that promises significant consequences for your life and everyone else's. There *are* important immediate benefits—incidentally—of reading on, for we begin with practical methods for managing time more efficiently.

THE ART AND PRACTICE OF TIME MANAGEMENT

"You can never be too thin or too rich," someone once claimed. Others might add to that short list "nor have too much time." These others may not be altogether correct. Some, perhaps a diminishing breed, have time on their hands. For those in pain, in prison, in queues, time passes with a fitful slowness. One of that diminishing breed was the Duke of Windsor, who, in lonely exile with the Duchess, was a man with a surfeit of time on his hands (and who, incidentally, was too thin and too rich). "You know what my day was today?" asked the former King of England, "I got up late and then I went with the Duchess and watched her buy a hat."[2] Few can devote their days so sybaritically. In fact, most of us are engaged in a desperate search for ways to improve our time use. There is no scarcity of experts willing to aid the search and to map it out in the how-to books they insist on writing.

Published in big print and small words, these treatises which crowd the shelves of better bookstores everywhere claim to solve the mysteries of managing time. Delegate, delegate, delegate. Say "no" with conviction. Make lists of things to do. Set deadlines. Protect privacy. Learn how to end conversations. Each inscribes in stone a Ten Commandments of Management (something like these):

- Thou shalt prioritize all work, putting first things first, second things second.
- Thou shalt stop believing people who interrupt with a question that "will take only a minute to answer."
- Thou shalt position thy desk chair with its back to the door of thy office to discourage drop-ins from dropping in.
- Thou shalt maintain psychological control over visitors by standing up when they arrive and continue standing until they have the sense to leave.
- Thou shalt install a parking meter midway between thyself and visitors, and feed it several times (when you stop, the guest gets the point that it's now up to him to pay for your time).

- Thou shalt schedule meetings to start promptly at 4:43 on Friday afternoons.
- Thou shalt shorten the front legs of conference chairs by several inches to shorten meetings by several minutes.
- Thou shalt leave thy mail unopened for a year for, by then, most of it won't require answering.
- Thou shalt return telephone calls at the end of the day when long-winded callers are less likely to be talkative.
- Thou shalt hang up in the middle of a too-long conversation and, when the time-waster calls back, blame the interruption on the phone company's bad service.

"Thou shalts" such as these miss the point, for their advice deals with only half of the problem: minimizing the time required

to get something done. This fails to account for the other half: maximizing the satisfaction gained from the something that is being done in the presumably shorter time. If we took seriously the expert admonitions, so concerned would we become with spending no time doing something, that we would do nothing at all.

There are three methods to make time count for more. First, simply do as much as possible as quickly as possible. Second, get the most possible out of the time spent. Third (best of all), do both. Fame came to some of history's greats because they knew and practiced the art of time management.

History remembers Anthony Trollope as the author of many novels (forty-seven to be exact) and magazine and newspaper articles. A little-known fact is that he also worked full-time at the post office (and is the inventor of the mail box), arriving at his desk to start sorting the mail after a daily three-hour stint writing at the rate of a thousand words an hour to produce two novels a year.[3]

Thomas Alva Edison, the world's most prolific inventer, tallied up 1,093 patents, including the light bulb, phonograph, and movie projector. The wizard achieved his goal of producing "a minor invention every ten days and a big thing every six months or so," by working days on end and sleeping on the floor of his laboratory. Believing that "I am long on ideas but short on time," he coined and put into practice the aphorism that "genius is 99 percent perspiration and one percent inspiration."

John Wesley, founder of the Methodist Church, preached 42,000 sermons, wrote 450 books, and traveled on horseback an average of 4,500 miles each year, reading as he rode—a remarkable feat of balance and concentration.

The trio, please note, accomplished their tasks in a day long before Time Management became the art and science that it avers to be today. So did two equally prolific composers known for the great quality and sheer quantity of their work. Like Messrs. Trollope, Edison, and Wesley, Wolfgang Amadeus Mozart and Gioacchino Rossini knew how to make the most of their days.

Mr. Mozart turned out eighteen operas and more than fifty symphonies before he died at 35, an age when most of us have just gotten our engines going. Mr. Rossini was, like Mr. Mozart, a prolific composer but, unlike his precursor, indolent. Nonetheless he managed time well, but in his own way. Stendhal tells of an incident, occurring at the peak of Rossini's productivity, that shows the value the great man put on time spent composing versus the mundane duties of "getting organized":

> One cold day . . . he found himself encamped in a poor Venetian hotel room, and did his composing in bed to avoid having to make a fire. His duet finished, the piece of paper slipped from his hands and fluttered to the floor. Rossini cast his eyes about looking for it, but in vain, the paper had fallen under his bed. He stretched out his arm from the bed and bent over trying to seize it; at last, feeling cold, he wrapped himself once again in the covers and said to himself: "I am going to rewrite this duet, nothing could be easier, I should remember it well. . . . I cannot take the trouble to pick up the duets which fall."[4]

These were extraordinarily creative figures who, one can only imagine, had mastered the art of managing time, deciding what was important and what was not. Few among us are Edisons, Wesleys, Trollopes, Mozarts, or Rossinis. We need help discovering that rare art.

Those who work slowly, take heart: there are other ways to speed up. Many years ago, industrialists learned that technology was the engine of time efficiency. As wages rose, machine replaced man. The machine was quicker to produce, often more accurate, and cheaper over the long-haul. In much the same way, gadgets can shorten the amount of time required for an activity, by shifting the activity to a different and preferred time, or by piling activities on top of each other.

SHORTENING THE TIME REQUIREMENT

Was a new and successful machine ever invented that did not increase time-productivity, either by reducing the time required to perform a task or by raising the satisfaction gained from time so spent? Probably not. At any rate, I can find no examples of such technologies that have come into wide acceptance. In fact, the evolution of technological advance runs in tandem with time-efficiency. Each new gadget replaced an older one that took longer to do the job.

New waves of communications and transportation advances

hastened the delivery of words and people. Each communications innovation got the words on to the page faster, more accurately, and more attractively than the last. The quill pen gave way to the fountain pen, then to the ball point. The manual typewriter was superseded by the electric and electronic incarnations that the word processor has now made nearly obsolete. The telephone eclipsed the telegraph and letter writing. The postal system replaced the Pony Express, and the Federal Express revolution promises delivery of just about anything anywhere by 10:30 a.m. tomorrow; the now-ubiquitous facsimile machine, which instantly transmits words and images over phone lines, now threatens both. The automobile that replaced the horse-drawn carriage, and the airplane that replaced the railroad got their passengers more quickly and more comfortably to their destinations. In the quest for increasing computational sophistication, the pocket calculator replaced the slide rule that replaced the abacus. Transistors and microchips made the vacuum tube obsolete and paved the way for high speed computers that can estimate more equations in an instant than Einstein could in his lifetime, or churn out books like this one.

Innovations have also revolutionized housework. The food processor saves preparation time and effort by mechanically chopping, blending, scraping, and pulverizing. Toothpaste that comes in a pump container saves the time required to squeeze one end of the tube or the other, whichever is the correct one. And the Heinz people, who once took pride in "slow ketchup," now market the red substance in a fast-squirting squeeze bottle.

Other techno-toys only *seem* to compress absolute time. Variable-speed cassette recorders, for instance, trim the time it takes to listen to a recorded speech. One version plays back recorded sounds faster, and without Donald Duck–like distortion, by shaving a fraction of a second off each sound. Another collapses an hour-long lecture into one only half as long by editing out speakers' pauses. Nothing is lost from such abbreviations, and much is gained. Speech compression not only saves time, but increases comprehension. Radio commercials that fire off the message 25 percent faster are rated "more knowledgeable, intelligent, and sincere" than those played at normal speed, and listeners' recall rates average 66 percent higher.[5] Television viewers who watch commercials speeded up by 20 percent recall more brand names than those who watch the ads at normal speed.[6]

Some devices actually accelerate human performance. Restaurateurs have discovered that loud music raises profits by speeding turnover. Conversation is impossible and dawdling over dinner is discouraged when the diners are assaulted by music (?) played at 120 decibels, so they tend to hurry through the meal. Not only do noisy restaurants boost profits, but the hurried diners have more time for other matters. And they needn't worry about having anything to say, a significant problem in an age where good conversation seems to have met the fate of the sixth toe. The type of music, as well as its loudness, also influences the speed of consumption. Anthropologists who studied drinking habits in Missoula, Montana, and Minneapolis, Minnesota—sites chosen perhaps for their alliterative rather than representative properties—found that "slower songs went with faster drinking." During their *horas bibendi,* bar patrons swilled down the booze faster to wailing, lonesome, self-pitying music with lyrics about drinking, hard times, and lost love.[7]

Gadgets aside, straight-forwardness also economizes on time. "In search of someone to write the lyrics for his latest project, Andrew Lloyd Webber went to visit Alan Jay Lerner, lyricist for the musical *My Fair Lady.* 'I don't know why,' Lloyd Webber said, 'but some people dislike me as soon as they meet me.' 'Perhaps,' Lerner replied, 'it saves time.' "[8]

TRANSFERRING ACTIVITIES TO DIFFERENT TIMES

Writing and, after that, the printing press transferred the footprint of knowledge over time and space. In pre-Gutenberg days, reading anything worthwhile required scaling a mountain to a drafty monastic library and reading in a poorly lit room presided over by a rather bad-smelling monk. By making the spoken word portable, the most important invention in all of history allowed reading that book, and any of a thousand others, virtually at any time and in any place. Since then, methods for gaining access to codified knowledge (or, to use the more current term, information retrieval) have evolved rapidly. Today we buy books at the store or borrow them from the library. Tomorrow, when the compact disk has replaced bookstore and library, texts will be delivered via electricity, and all the books ever printed will be available on a compact disk 6 feet in diameter, instantly translated from any language, customized to the readers' personal tastes, and read from a hand-held video screen.

Records, tapes, and compact disks allow people to vicariously relive an event that occurred at other times and in other places, but at times and places convenient to *them*. Photography transfers visual images over time in much the same way as its cousin phonography transfers audio images. No longer must visitors to the Acropolis pause long enough to capture in their minds the images of major monuments. Cameras do it for them and transport the images home where they can be recalled whenever and wherever convenient. A click here and a click there is all it takes. By conserving valuable holiday time, tourists have more time left for cramming in visits to other places. Returning home, they have only to wait an hour—not overnight or a week—to see the fruits of their photographic endeavors.

Artificial illumination extended work and many other activities beyond the daylight hours. Gaslight first lengthened day into night but it was Thomas Alva Edison's invention in 1879 that stretched activity times around the clock's 360 degrees. Work could continue on into the night, when previously only sleep and sex had occupied the darkened hours. (Were it not for Mr. Edison's incandescent bulb, as comedian George Gobel reminded us, we might be watching TV by candlelight.)

Electronic time shifters move activities to times that fit our schedules, not someone else's. No longer must one be at home to see "Designing Women" or "Doogie Howser" at the times they are broadcast, for the videocassette recorder will electronically remember the programs and "retelecast" them at our convenience. Just as video recorders make us independent of the television's airing schedule, telephone answering machines and electronic mail make us independent of business hours and people who don't feel like answering the phone.

A more exotic, but surely no less practical, device frees petowners from the inconvenience of feeding or playing with or cleaning up after their Felix or Fido, at times being governed by the pet. Videotaped pets offer the satisfaction of pet-ownership "without the mess and inconvenience of the real thing." The tapes, available in leading catalogs and dogalogs, provide that time-transferring convenience.[9]

Time transfer is not without its faults. Lost forever in a transferred activity is the magic of the moment, regardless of the quality of the camera equipment, the stereo, or the VCR. Is five minutes spent viewing slides of the Parthenon the same as ten minutes spent on the Acropolis? Can hi-fi at home or in the disco reproduce the vitality of a live rock concert in the flesh?

DOUBLING-UP ACTIVITIES SYNCHRONICALLY

Will Rogers was once asked, if he had only forty-eight hours left to live, how would he spend them? "One hour at a time," he replied. All well and good, but in the era of the *Busy Body,* fewer and fewer are content to do things one at a time. As time costs rise, we find ways to double-up, triple-up, and quadruple-up activities. With *synchronic* time use, as with juggling, everything goes on at once.

Although Mr. Rogers may not have practiced synchronic time use, others did and do. Among them was Peter Paul Rubens, whose paintings and altarpieces fill museums, churches, and great homes throughout the world. A visitor to Mr. Rubens's Antwerp studio in 1621 filed the following report on the artist's remarkable work habits:

> While still painting, he was having Tacitus read aloud to him and at the same time he was dictating a letter. While we kept silent so as not to disturb him with our talk, he himself began to talk to us while still continuing to work, to listen to the reading and to dictate his letter, answering our questions and thus displaying his astonishing powers.[10]

Eric Gill, a celebrated British artist, also practiced the art of synchronic time management. During the four weeks in 1913 when he prepared himself for conversion to Catholicism, Mr. Gill continued to sculpt, reading from a catechism held in one hand, while polishing a bronze phallus with the other.

Technology had little to do with either artists' success in managing time synchronically, but it can aid lesser mortals materially. Set-it-and-forget-it technology has revolutionized housework by synchronically combining hosts of activities once performed sequentially. The modern washing machine that does the laundry faster, and does a better job of it, transformed an all-consuming, monochronic chore into one that could be done simultaneously with other things. Today, with the clothes churning away, the householder can prepare dinner in the microwave, watch a TV Julia Child for pointers, and, via closed circuit television, monitor the kids playing somewhere else in the house . . . all at the same time. Somewhat less successful, despite a synchronic capability, was the "Combined Grocer's Package, Grater, Slicer, and Mouse and Fly Trap," patented in 1897, that afforded cooks the rare opportunity of preparing food while simultaneously catching mice and flies.[11]

Dead-serious joggers probably jog and let nothing dilute the full masochistic joys of the experience. Less serious counterparts, decked out in the proper equipment, can be seen combining at least five very different pleasures. Besides jogging, they can simultaneously listen to a Walkman[12] that distracts the runner from the pain of the experience, and wear a Haro Hat Drink Helmet that automatically and constantly dispenses a favorite beverage via a tube to the mouth, leaving the hands free to squeeze fist exercisers. If that's not synchronic enough, a jogger can don a Japanese-made battery-powered headband that somehow cools to 15° below body temperature to improve mental acuity.

We have come to listen to music beamed over the airwaves as an almost inevitable background to many activities, whether the primary activities are jogging or working or something else quite unmusical. In fact, time-budget studies show that listening to the radio is the most frequent secondary activity of all.[13] Whether it is music, news, or the talk shows, the radio or the unwatched television generates white noise to keep our minds freed from important thoughts. Critic Walter Kerr leaves no doubt where he stands on such combinations:

> We have had Music to Read By, Music to Make Love By, Music to Sleep By, and, . . . Music to Listen to Music By. What is interesting about these titles is that they so candidly describe the position

> of the popular arts in our time. They admit at the outset that no one is expected to sit down, for heaven's sake, and attend to the music. It is understood that, while the music is playing, everyone within earshot is going to be busy doing something else. . . .[14]

So accustomed have we become to musical accompaniment that when the main object is a live performance, it is automatically suppressed as background for more "urgent" matters. Witness the increasing number of concert patrons who, during a live musical performance, find it essential to discuss with their neighbors whatever occupies their minds at the moment. Few anymore regard music as a solo performance. Except perhaps Marilyn Monroe who, it was rumored, spent her days at home with nothing on but the radio.

Smoking is another typically synchronous activity. Smoking usually accompanies another activity, like talking on the phone or drinking martinis before dinner. Smoking cessation programs commonly play on that fact, claiming that the associations with smoking are just as addictive as the nicotine. Forcing dedicated quitters to divorce smoking from bonded activities replaces synchronicity with monochronicity. As a result, the habit loses much of its pleasure.

Perhaps the most boring time of all is spent waiting in line. Synchronicity cannot shorten the queues, but may provide welcome distraction. Frustration, or the lack of it, may depend more on what happens while the waiter waits than on how long the waiter waits. To make waiting less onerous, pianists entertain the queued-up at a New York bank, providing white noise that mutes the sound of customers grinding their teeth. Another bank pays five dollars to those forced to wait in a teller line for more than seven minutes.[15] News screens installed over tellers' cages keep waiting customers abreast of local rapes, murders, and muggings. Video screens located next to elevators in Tokyo's dazzling department stores advertise the latest wares. Mirrors that adorn the elevators of some office buildings and hotels encourage people to primp rather than pout as they wait.

Creative genius, translated into innovative design, deserves much of the credit for exploiting the potential for stacking up activities synchronically. Three particularly notorious—and ultimately not-very-successful—examples are the piano bed, the bag bath, and the air-conditioned chair. Lucky owners of the piano bed, a nineteenth-century wonder, practice their scales at late hours or finger their passages while reclining in comfort on the mattress. *Science Siftings: A Chatty Journal* (1898) describes the India-rubber Bag Bath, invented by a Dr. Sanctorious of Venice, as follows:

> The bather can gradually subside into the recesses of the rubber sack, while he divests himself of his apparel. . . . Thus the hygienist may receive visitors, or write, or read the newspaper with decorum, while enjoying his matutinal lavation.[16]

No less innovative was the air-conditioned rocking chair, patented in 1869. The occupant's rocking compressed the bellows on which the chair was perched, forcing air through a tube aimed at his/her face, or any other anatomical part of his/her choosing. Elevated rails protected the rockers from "rocking on small children crawling on the floor, or strings scattered thereon.''[17]

Some activities beg for synchronic enjoyment. The business lunch and, more recently, the ''power breakfast,'' combine the pleasures of eating and working. A study of community organizations reveals that luncheon groups have far higher attendance records (88 percent) than average (51 percent).[18] Why? Because people who belong to such groups can use their precious time eating while conducting organization business. Perhaps the first ''power dinner'' was The Last Supper at which Jesus gave his apostles their marching orders as they supped on divine cuisine.

The immutable laws of supply and demand tell us that, when demand increases for a resource fixed in quantity, its price rises. Increasing the supply of that which is demanded mutes the unattractive effect on price. But the price effect is inevitable when the amount supplied is unyielding, as it is with time. Try as we might, there is no known way to expand the day to, say, 25 hours, not even to 24.1 hours. With time fixed in either objective or subjective terms, and an increasing array of ways to use it, the demand for time increases and up goes its price. A rising price encourages a more efficient use of the resource. The better the resource is used, the greater its value—time included.

We use surprisingly rational formulas, though perhaps unknowingly, for managing the twenty-four hours and giving that finite allotment added meaning and raising its value. We ''expand'' time by making each hour and minute count for more. We achieve that sleight-of-hand by speeding up activities without, of course, accelerating time itself. We transfer activities to a more worthy time. We pile activities on top of each other to use time synchronically. We seek and find and buy the goods that pack more satisfaction into every busy moment. For good reason, conspicuous consumption becomes the hallmark of a time-short society—indeed, of a society of *Busy Bodies*. Read on to find out how. . . .

2:00

MACHINERY OF TIME

"Eternity is in love with the productions of time."
—William Blake[1]

Most of us know *who* we are, *what* we are, *why* we are, and *where* we are. But knowing *when* we are is a different matter. What time is it right now? When was it that we told Nora and Norman Gnomon we'd be at dinner? Is this trash collection day, or is it next Monday? Time-keeping technology has helped answer those questions.

WHAT IS THE *TIME?*

Roughly 5.5 millennia ago, man and woman decided they had walked the earth long enough without knowing what time it was. A stick stuck in the ground—more precisely, a *gnomon*—harnessed sun rays and shadows and answered the question, "*when* are we?" Next came the sundial, the first portable gnomon and a precursor of the wristwatch. The later, advanced versions were Pharaoh-sized obelisks put up in public places for the benefit of those who had neither the resources to acquire their own sundial nor the strength to carry one on their wrist.

Telling time by sunlight still left the dark hours uncounted, however, since time refused to stop when the sun set. *Absque sole, absque usu* (without sun, without use) announced one sundial inscription. Mankind's response to this challenge was a gadget consisting of a string attached to an arm that calibrated time to the movement of stars. This device counted the hours at night but helped very little with time-keeping by daylight. The next generation of time-keeping devices—the water clock, the sand glass, and calibrated candles—would labor throughout the night and day and tell the time, albeit rather approximately, even in cloudy weather.

Then came clocks, but they had no minute hands. (One in Salisbury Cathedral, dating from the fourteenth century, and another in the sixteenth-century marketplace of Modena, Italy, have no hands at all.)[2] Never mind. Because time wasn't very valuable in those days, precise measurement was of little importance. Time could be measured in big chunks, or not at all. In India before modern times, for example, the shortest time interval for scheduling was thirteen minutes—the time it took to boil rice.

As the age of industrialization approached, the need ever increased for a more careful reckoning of the fixed resource. The big chunks would have to be broken up into little bits, and the notion of time elapse would have to become more concrete, visually aided by the "Snayly motion of the mooving hand"[3] crossing a dial. The minute hand arrived in the fifteenth century to divide the hour into sixty equal parts, and the second hand in the sixteenth century to divide the minute into another sixty equal parts.

But the "mooving hand's" precise description of seconds or minutes mattered little as long as the engine that moved the hands was inaccurate. Before the invention of the "escapement" in the fourteenth century, the average clock gained or lost about 1,000 seconds each day. Then appeared the reliable mechanical clock, first in weight-driven versions and later in spring-operated models. The great breakthrough in mechanisms for driving time-keeping devices, however, came toward the end of the sixteenth century when Galileo discovered the near independence between a pendulum's oscillation period and the amplitude of its swing. A few decades would pass before Dutch mathematician Christiaan Huygens introduced Galileo's discovery into clock-making, plunging the error of clocks astronomically, to only ten seconds a day.

Since then, the accuracy of time-keeping has paralleled the expansion of industrialism and urbanism, and the emergent needs for the accurate reckoning of time in a faster turning world. With the invention in the 1930s of the quartz crystal clock, the error dropped to .0001 second per day; with the advent of the hydrogen and the rubidium clocks, the error tumbled to a mere .0000001 seconds.[4]

If customers hadn't demanded more accurate measurement, the gains in precision might never have been made. As life grew in complexity and the opportunities for using time multiplied, the costs rose for not knowing exactly *when.* With the passing of every year, time became more scarce and—like any resource that shrinks in supply—gained in value and, as a result, came to be doled out with greater care. In the modern era, when minutes and seconds count, as well as hours and days, we need to know more precisely than ever before *when* we are, for a high price is paid for being late (or early).

THE "MOOVING HAND" OF TECHNOLOGY

It is the year 2000 and you are reading *Busy Bodies* on a computer screen rather than from the chemical mixture of black ink on white paper in the version published almost a decade ago. The book was electronically typeset using digital equipment that translated letters into 0s and 1s, then transferred onto an optical disk containing hundred of other books. You dialed up the book from a central information service in New York many miles away. If anything turns up that you deem worth saving, the push of one button produces a hard copy, the push of another transfers it to computer memory, and yet another incorporates it into your own book (with this paragraph deleted of course) and sends it directly to your publisher.

The force that makes this scenario a likely reality started in the 1980s with a revolution that rivaled the discoveries of other time-saving technologies, such as electricity and the telephone a century before. No longer are words transmitted as words, sounds as sounds, pictures as pictures, but as digits that travel anywhere, at low cost, almost instantly. Fast, yes, but speedier yet if the information could go directly into the human mind, via a brain-implanted cathode. That's perhaps twenty years down the road.

As technology accelerates the pace of life, the pace of technological advance itself accelerates. Humans have lived on earth for possibly 800 lifetimes, reckons Arthur Schlesinger, Jr. "Movable type appeared only eight lifetimes ago, industrialization in the last three lifetimes. . . . The last two lifetimes have seen more scientific and technological achievement than the first 798 put together."[5]

"The world did not double or treble its movement between 1800 and 1900," wrote Henry Adams in 1909, "but, measured by any standard known to science—by horsepower, calories, volts, mass in any shape—the tension and vibration and volume and so-called progression of society were fully a thousand times greater in 1900 than in 1800."[6]

From our vantage point near the close of the twentieth century, we can be equally sure that society has progressed another thousandfold. At the horizon, just waiting to be discovered, are a host of applications for high-temperature superconductor materials ranging from microelectronics, to high speed trains, to high energy physics research. Life with the superconductors—if they are not over-hyped, as some say—promises to be vastly accelerated over what it is today.

Yet, technology has followed an uneven history. Despite remarkable breakthroughs, many end-products from the scientists' benches never progressed beyond their registration at the U.S. Patent Office. Consider, for example:[7]

- **Eye Protector for Chickens** (1903)
  Protects fowls "from other fowls that might attempt to peck them."
- **Upper-Lip Shaper** (1924)
  Re-shapes a person's upper lip in the form of a "Cupid's bow."
- **Dimple-Producer** (1896)
  Produces dimples with a "drill-like device that massages the desired spot until the dimple appears."
- **Suspenders for Safety** (1885)
  "A suspender with a cord . . . easily detached therefrom, whereby, in the event of a person being confined to a burning building and having all of the usual means of escape cut off, the cords can be disengaged from the suspenders and lowered to the ground to receive a rope, and thus enable the person to effect his escape. . . ."
- **Chewing Gum Locket** (1887)
  Holds used chewing gum "with safety, cleanliness, and convenience. . . . Chewing-gum may thus be carried conveniently upon the person, and is not left around carelessly to become dirty or to fall in the hands of persons to whom it does not belong, and be

used by ulcerous or diseased mouths, by which infection would be communicated by subsequent use to the owner. . . ."

- **Saluting Device** (1896)
"A novel device for automatically effecting polite salutations by the elevation and rotation of the hat on the head of the saluting party when said person bows to the person or persons saluted, the actuation of the hat being produced by mechanism therein and without the use of the hands in any manner."

Alas, these inventions failed to find markets and to conserve time. The two faults are not coincidental. Most innovations gain broad acceptance by saving their users' time or at least by contributing to the enjoyment of time. Take, for example, the history of soap and other slippery matters.

DRIVING THE BLUE OUT OF MONDAY

Laundering, viewed in historical perspective, demonstrates the power of technological innovation to save time spent in the mundane necessities of household maintenance, and to make the chores a tad less onerous. From the wash days of antiquity, before the scrub board, even before soap, clothes were laundered by a merciless pounding against rocks in nearby streams. The scrub board, appearing in 1797, helped somewhat, yet launderers still had to heat rainwater, scrub and bleach the dirty wash, ring out the water, and hang up the wash to dry. The wringer, introduced fifty years later, eased one of the tasks but ninety more years passed before the chores became truly mechanized. Shortly after the turn of the century, the first chain-driven electric washing machine, Maytag's "The Hired Girl," appeared with both an attached wringer and the hope for yet better things to come. Hope became reality when the automatic washing machine debuted in 1937, stunning the home laundry industry and promising to drive the "blue" right out of Monday once and for all.

Soap, the number one cleaning agent for launderers, solved some cleaning problems but created others. A century ago, soap bars had to be sliced or flaked for easy dissolving. Lever Brothers ended that tiresome task when it introduced Lux Flakes to the home market in 1906. Then came faster-dissolving Rinso, a granulated laundry soap, and Procter & Gamble countered with quick-dissolving Ivory Flakes. By the 1930s, soaps were sold in varieties from chips and flakes to beads and powders, and widely advertised on afternoon radio melodramas, appropriately called "soap operas."

Soap, no different than appliances, required maintenance. Cleaning body or laundry with soap then required cleaning up a residue left behind. Soap in combination with mineral salts forms heavy insoluble scum that trims the tub with a notorious ring, and calcium precipitate that leaves its memento of "tattletale gray" on freshly washed clothes. The solution that swept away soap's "permanent presence" was a molecule that emulsifies grease and oils, and suspends them in water. In 1931, Proctor & Gamble introduced the surfactant (short for surface active agent) into Dreft, the first synthetic detergent, and the problem disappeared down the drain with the soap curd and the tattletale gray. Within a decade after World War II, detergents were outselling soap and "twenty years later, soap was all washed up."[8]

Technology in the form of synthetic fabrics also offered relief from the time-absorbing chores of ironing clothes, draperies, sheets, and tablecloths of "natural" fabrics. Rayon was first displayed at the 1889 Paris Exhibition and nylon, the first fiber synthesized entirely from chemicals, appeared forty years later at the Golden Gate International Exposition. The women who snapped up 64 million pairs of nylon hosiery believed that the time-saving features of the synthetic material made the price—twice the silk equivalent—well worth it. Acrylic, polyester, and others followed within two decades. In the early 1950s, "wash and wear," with its magic formula of 60 percent acrylic and 40 percent cotton, had become a household term synonymous with efficiency. Thus, synthetics joined indoor plumbing, gas hot-water heaters, mechanical washing machines, and detergents as innovations credited with lightening laundering chores that had once absorbed as much as one-third of a housewife's time.[9]

IN PRAISE OF THE PHONE

Little did Alexander Graham Bell know what would follow after that fateful day when he summoned his assistant down the hall with the first verbal message sent over a skinny little wire, "Mr. Watson, come here. I want you." In the century since, people have been addressing that desire directly to the telephone company.

History may rank the telephone, together with the myriad accessories that enhance its performance, as the great time economizer of history. By abbreviating time requirements, transferring activities to more convenient times, or expanding the possibilities for carrying on several activities synchronically, the revolution in telephone technology makes it easier, and quicker, to reach out and touch someone.

Accessories for your ordinary, everyday variety of telephone, like conference calling, call forwarding, automatic recall, group paging, and speed dialing save you time, if, of course, you have taken the time to have them installed. With conference calling, meetings are held over the wire, saving the time to set up and get to face-to-face meetings. Call forwarding follows you from place to place by routing calls to preprogrammed numbers, and saves the time of continually checking with the office or home for important messages. Automatic recall, which relentlessly dials a busy number, saves the time waiting around for the answerer's phone to be rehung. Group paging phones each party invited to an event, relays your pre-recorded invitation to each telephonee, and saves the time required to make individual calls. Speed dialing enables you to push only a button or two to reach your party, a large time saving compared to dialing complete numbers that may consist of as many as fifteen digits for an international call. Even upgrading dialing from the old-fashioned rotary to push-buttons saved about five seconds per local call.

Devices that conveniently shift time-use are among the most useful and the most used of all telephone add-ons. Answering machines and electronic mail allow us to talk on the phone when it suits us, rather than being at the caller's beck and call (if you will). Callers leave "Voice Mail" messages in "mailboxes," retrieved by receivers anywhere and anywhen. Computerized E-mail not only transfers time, but saves it. Messages are shorter because chatting time is eliminated. Callers get right to the point, omitting the usual throw-away lines about kids and weather.

The "Prega-Phone," a mouthpiece and funnel pressed to the abdomen, closes the distance between expectant mother and un-

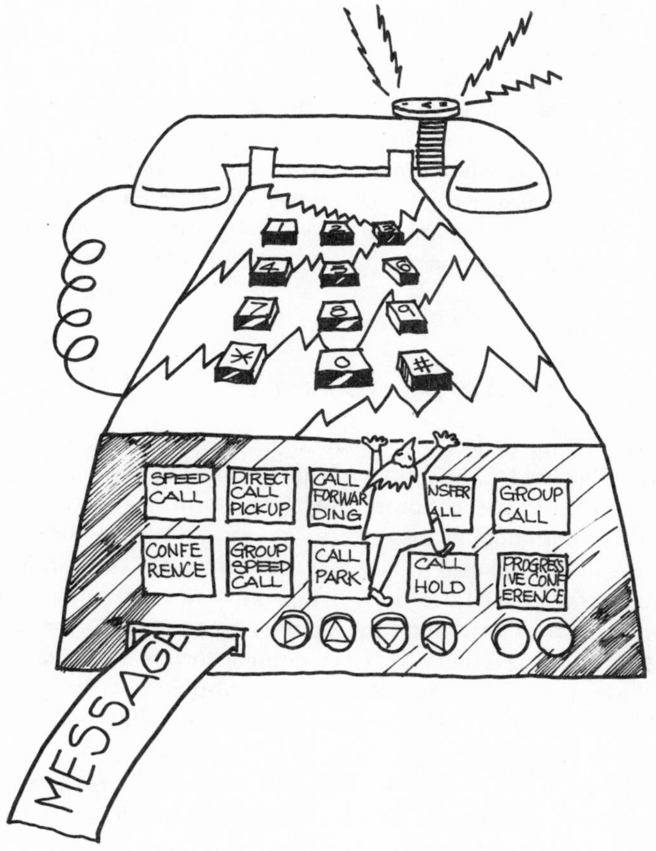

born infant. There are no installation charges and callee cannot put caller on hold. Properly used, the gadget gives the child a head start on life. While the child prepares for a dramatic emergence into this world, he or she can be taught to say "Mama" or "Papa" to surprise delighted parents, or "*Busy Body* factor" to delight the rest of us.

Not all phone technology saves our time. Want to know the balance in your checking account? Phone the bank and, if it has installed a system called "Automatic Attendants," a disembodied voice will read off a menu of options, instructing you to press the touch-tone button for the appropriate one. The message usually ends with, "If you wish to speak to a live receptionist, please stay on the line," an option that requires waiting until that receptionist is ready to take your call. If you choose to speak to a dead receptionist, however, have you remembered which button to push for the right number when the menu was listed? Although the system may save employee time, the savings are offset by the additional time it takes the customer to get what is wanted. All in all, this disastrous device is one phone "improvement" that deserves to be called off.

TECH-FIX OR TECH-FUTZ?

The 1970s introduced the microchip, the tiny device that transformed the work of telephones. The '80s introduced the robot, the human-like device that promised to transform work itself. Robots assemble automobiles, mix chemicals, cut up beef, and probe nuclear reactors and coal mines. But these tasks are kid's stuff compared to the possibilities now being explored for putting to work this ingenious effort- and time-saving invention. In Japan, a steel and plastic "guest organist," its ten fingers on the keys and its feet on the pedals, sight-read a Bach fugue without rehearsal. An Australian robot sheared 200 sheep. Its American and British counterparts played a ping-pong match.

Roboticist Hans Moravec of Carnegie-Mellon University predicts that within two decades robots will possess "human equivalence." They will have the same awareness of their own existence that human beings have, as much intelligence or more, and our kind of common sense.[10] Since the robot of the future apparently will have emotions, like children, they will require attention, at least until there are robot-care centers. When robots attain human equivalence, will they do everything that we presently do? If so, what will *we* non-robots do with *our* time? And what will robots do with *their* leisure time?

Although robots may someday qualify as the ultimate timesaver, costs well beyond the means of most of us currently prevent widespread application to routine uses. Yet, if history repeats, prices will fall perhaps even to levels where robots become adopted members of the family, taking over the more onerous jobs around the house. At least the price histories of household appliances raise that possibility.

Prices of most consumer goods and services have more than tripled in the past twenty years, yet, in a dramatic reversal of the usual spiral, the cost of most electronic equipment has fallen, oftentimes sharply. The first color television sets that hit the market in 1953 sold at $1,295 and compact disk players debuting in 1983 cost about $1,000.[11] Today, a color TV or CD player runs a few hundred dollars, and performance has greatly improved.

When the "cost" of equipping a complete kitchen is measured in terms of the number of hours worked in order to afford the gadgets, we can see just how dramatically prices of household appliances have fallen. In 1950, the average worker had to put in nearly 1500 hours of work to pay the bill for outfitting the kitchen with a new range, refrigerator, freezer, dishwasher, food disposer, clothes washer, and dryer. By 1989, only 376 hours of work bought that complement of appliances, and they were equipped with many more exotic, labor-saving features.[12]

An often-overlooked hidden expense of the new technology is the time-cost of mastering the presumably labor-saving features of television sets that can show nine channels simultaneously, videocassette machines that can be programmed to record shows a year in advance, and radios that can hop from station to station like fleas on a dog. Useful these add-ons *may* be, but who, except the most technically adept, can figure out how to operate them? How many of us, blindly flailing around with the array of identical buttons on the dashboard, have switched on the windshield wiper instead of the headlights? How many among us are fortunate enough to have at the ready the phone number of a computer-freak friend who can talk us through our computer problems? How many hapless business executives must depend on the secretary to format a floppy disk? How many have taken the time to read through the inch-thick instruction manual that gives directions for forwarding calls, or redialing? Manufacturers add accessory features because doing so is easy, but also to dupe the vulnerable consumer into believing that the basic device is glitzier than the competitors'. For those of us who must take the time learning to operate them, however, it's a very different lesson.

While the blessings of technological advance are mixed, one of its great advantages is not only in producing time savings but in raising the satisfaction gained from the ways time is spent. Technology "expands" time by saving it. By pushing back the limits on how we spend time, it also opens up new options (could anyone watch TV before the invention of television?).

Technology is in many ways democratic. With the high costs of development rapidly amortized by mass sales, once-exotic goods soon become affordable in ever broader markets. The wealthy few who are the first to buy a new gadget find that, indeed, technology confers the sought-after status, but the status is short-lived. With rising incomes and falling prices, the man and woman on the street gain the wherewithal to acquire the goods. Increased purchasing power and falling prices together push up the demand for technology, and make what was exotic yesterday commonplace today. A third factor, the increasing scarcity of time, further swells the demand for labor-saving technologies. As the *BB* factor raises time values—the subject of the next chapter—devices that save our time by taking over the burdens of work become more attractive.

U.S. Chief Justice William Rehnquist once noted that, "When you are young and impecunious, society conditions you to exchange time for money, and this is quite as it should be. Very few people are hurt by having to work for a living. But as you become more affluent, it somehow is very, very difficult to reverse that process and begin trading money for time."[13] Aha, Justice Rehnquist, if you had read this chapter, you would know that there *is* a way: buy time by buying time machinery.

3:00

THE VALUE OF TIME

"Men talk of killing time, while time quietly kills them."
—*Dion Boucicault*[1]

"As if you could kill time without injuring eternity."
—*Henry David Thoreau*[2]

Saiho-ji temple in Kyoto, Japan, ranks as one of the most sybaritic places anywhere. The temple garden, boasting dozens of varieties of moss, attracts as many as 8,000 visitors daily. At least that was the case until several years ago when it became apparent that the throngs of visitors to "the moss temple" threatened the very amenities that brought them to the place and gave it its justifiable fame.

Saiho-ji's enlightened abbot confronted the problem with one of those rare solutions that works both efficiently and equitably. The solution "priced" visitors' time, and did so fairly to both rich and poor. Today's visitor, on making an appointment to roam the wondrous garden, is first advised of a twelve dollar admission fee, and told to bring along an ink block. The effect of the hefty ticket price is clear: it discourages all but the well-off, for there are 7,000 other temples in Kyoto that offer free admission. The ink block discourages the wealthy—a more subtle effect.

Monks usher the arriving visitor into a Buddhist service, an hour-long ceremony that certainly satisfies many, including the participants' ancestors who are prayed for at length. Squatting awkwardly on a tatami, the visitor must devote a second hour to copying prayers onto parchment paper. Aha! the reason for the ink block.

The abbot exacted a large price, higher for the well-off who set a higher price on their time. Gaining that hour to wander through the garden requires the expenditure of two more hours, one praying and another working on the temple's behalf. The result: attendance has dropped to a few dozen a day.

Rarely has time been so explicitly priced; few are as perceptive as the good abbot whose knowledge of time costs may have saved *his* priceless treasure. One of the challenges that we must face in this era of rising time costs is how to save *our* priceless treasures.

TIME IS MONEY

All kids are told by parents, preachers, or teachers that Time is Money, as if it were a startling new concept. It is not, for it was one of Benjamin Franklin's bits of *Advice to a Young Tradesman,* rendered over 200 years ago. The equality that Mr. Franklin defined is more obvious than even he may have realized. Indeed we save money and save time, spend money and spend time, waste money and waste time, and we never have enough of either.

What Franklin failed to tell the young tradesperson, or us, was just how much money time is. But we have been finding out how valuable time is ever since. As time becomes more scarce and is used in more rewarding ways, time's value rises. And, as time gets more valuable, more join the ranks of the *Busy Bodies.*

Scarcity increases the value of time, as of gold and jewels. Yet, given the twenty-four-hour day (a reminder!), how can fixed time grow scarce? In the absolute sense, of course it cannot. As more options emerge for using time, however, the time available for pursuing any one of them decreases in relative terms. We are forced to pick and choose which options realize the handsomest rewards in the shortest time. As the value of their time rises, *Busy Bodies* constantly juggle things around until the allotted time has been filled with that best set of activities.

Wage increases also raise time's value, but for somewhat different reasons. Compared to those who labor at the minimum wage, workers paid ten dollars an hour are likely to value their time more highly and to choose their activities more carefully. Cultural anthropologists tell us that the poor and unemployed spend most of their time at leisure, gossiping, standing around, laying about, and all sorts of other activities that might be described as laziness. Because their earnings are low, the cost of their time spent fooling around is low. Among the employed, however, the clocks run faster. As wages rise, the pressures increase for putting their more valued time to better use. Higher wages, higher time values. That parallel emerges in a recent survey which shows that workers who earn more also value their leisure time more. The higher their income, the more anxious they are to "buy" free time by reducing paid hours at work. Seventy percent of those who earn $30,000 and up a year would give up a day's pay each week for an extra day off from work. But less than one-half of those earning under $20,000 would do the same.[3] That finding begins to answer the question that Mr. Franklin glossed over: how much money is time worth?

A survey of harriedness makes a similar point. Those in the age brackets when wages move up fastest are the most harried, and the busiest bodies. Middle-aged adults are the most likely to report "feeling rushed."[4] Earnings even affect the time spent sleeping. A worker whose wages double will spend a daily twenty minutes less in bed.[5]

"Zapping" practices also prove that the clock runs faster for the rich. Using their remote control unit like a semi-automatic weapon, viewers click from one channel to another, zapping one show in favor of a presumably better show. The practice is widespread. Nearly 20 percent of televiewers are heavy zappers, averaging a zap every two minutes, but the highest income households zap at a rate three times that of the lowest.[6]

Whether we admit it or not, we are constantly estimating the worth of our time and shifting what we do as the estimate changes. We price our time when we decide to take a day off from paid work. We price our time when we decide to accept the overbooked airline's offer of cash as a payment to wait for a later flight, for we have exchanged their money for our time. We price our time when we opt to go to driving school instead of paying a traffic ticket, for we have exchanged a fine for our time. We price our time when we cancel an appointment to take advantage of another that is potentially more rewarding. As value rises with scarcity, we try more vigorously to make time count for more. We *Busy Bodies* try to lower the time requirement, or heighten the satisfaction gained from the time required, or, better yet, tackle both at once. Each approach calls for valuing time either explicitly or implicitly. Take that all-too-familiar jungle, the supermarket queue.

Markets that advertise "we guarantee lines of no more than three shoppers" usually charge higher prices for groceries but, in the bargain, require their customers to wait fewer minutes. Shoppers willing to pay the premium prices in exchange for a shorter wait have consciously priced their time.

Once at the market of our choice, and having worked our way through the shopping list, the search is on for the check-out line that gets us by the cashier and out the door fastest. That may not be the shortest line. A longer line, or one with customers who have made fewer purchases, may move faster. We push the loaded cart from line to line, our gimlet eyes appraising each customer. Can the old lady in that one be counted on to present the cashier with a fistful of coupons after the bill is rung up? Or to write a check? Avoid that line. Is that a vegetarian with a cart full of unpriced unpackaged produce that must be weighed? Avoid that one. That cashier is notorious for chatting with customers. Look for another.

And so it goes. Whether it is the choice among supermarkets or among check-out lines, the decisions are based on the urgency of finishing up our shopping as quickly as possible, and that means putting a value on time.

Time-pricing, and the decisions that follow from it, can make or break a business. Until the laws of supply and demand are repealed, when the price of good A rises compared to the price of similar good B, more of us come to prefer B over A. Consider how well this works with the more subtle costs of time: we are constantly shifting our purchases toward goods which save time in consumption in the same way that our purchases shift toward cheaper items, without sacrificing quality. The *Busy Body (BB)* factor accelerates that shift.

- A turning point in the OJ market occurred in 1986 for, in that year, sales of ready-to-drink chilled orange juice passed sales of frozen concentrate. Why? "It's one less thing to hassle with in the morning," explains an industry spokesman.[7]
- Soft drinks are replacing coffee as the preferred beverage during the work break. Why? Coffee takes too long to cool. Carbonated drinks can be consumed the moment they are dispensed.[8]
- Power boats are outselling sailboats by a healthy margin. Why? People are too busy to rely on unpredictable winds.[9]

- Cats have become the favored house pets. In the latest whisker counts, Felixes outnumber Fidos by more than two million; as recently as 1983, it was the other way around.[10] Why? Cats require less time to care for. Cat owners don't have to spend time walking their pets.[11]

Whether switching from frozen to fresh orange juice, swearing off coffee for Coke, buying a boat powered by an outboard motor instead of a sail, or trading in a Fido for a Felix, *Busy Bodies* have made the conscious decision to save time, and to make life easier for themselves.

Sometimes others, like the abbot at Saiho-ji temple, price our time for us. Producers price consumers' time because they know that consumers price *their* time. Presumably "free" services are no exception. Remember the days when it was quicker and easier to call telephone information than to look up the number in the directory? It took the phone company several decades to discover that consumers were taking advantage of a free service that was costly to provide.

The company's first effort to discourage those too lazy to look up the number was requiring a one-minute wait to get information. The delay amounted to an indirect charge against the user's time. During the wait a recorded voice tried to make callers feel guilty for their laziness. But callers didn't feel guilty enough, so Ma Bell started levying a charge for information inquiries, a more direct and explicit pricing of time. And it worked just as theory would predict. After Cincinnati Bell began charging twenty cents per call made to directory assistance, for example, such calls fell off from 70,000 a day to 15,000. Customers, now forced to price their time, decided it was worth the twenty cents to look up the number themselves.[12]

Uncle Sam is also concerned about time-waste, believe it or not, and the consequences for the economy. Sam's concern led to a shorter 1990 census questionnaire. Filling out the form that the Census Bureau originally proposed would take forty-five minutes per respondent, according to the federal Office of Management and Budget. OMB's efficiency-minded staff eliminated about one-third of the questions to yield a half-hour time saving per respondent and a total monetary saving amounting to $450 million, calculated at $15 an hour for each respondent's time.[13]

PRICING TIME IN THE FAST LANE

Can time be valued too highly? Or too lowly? Because *Busy Bodies* come in many varieties, we could hardly expect everyone to value their time exactly the same. Of course, they don't. For workaholics, time is scarce, highly valued, and carefully rationed. Lazoholics, who seem to have too much time to do too little, place low values on time.

Columnist Alice Kahn reports on Lazoholics Anonymous, a California-based support group for people with too much time, and a shared desire to do nothing. Lazoholics use their vacations to plan the next one, discover that their sick leave is used up when they actually get sick, and find it hard to do even one thing at a time. "Lazoholism is on the rise in the downwardly mobile, low-achieving, slow-track communities where hundreds of young adults supported by inherited wealth live lives of quiet vegetation," reports Ms. Kahn. "Existing only on fries and nachos, they swim, surf and defy the ozone layer. The more intellectual among them sit at cafes and write haiku."[14]

At the opposite extreme are those who, like the early twentieth century novelist Thomas Wolfe, take time very seriously. A Harvard classmate claimed that, "He can do more between 8:25 and 8:30 than the rest of us can do all day." The celebrated author boasts about his obsession for reading: "The Widener Library has crumpled under my savage attack. Ten, twelve, fifteen books a day are nothing."[15]

Some types of jobs require such commitment. A senior senator advises a junior:

> If you want to really keep on a fast track, always have more than two things to do for any space on your schedule. Have people telling you about all the other things you should do. Go into politics, because there's always too much to do. And in politics, you can justify workaholism. After all, it's important for the country.[16]

Workaholism may be good for the country if the workaholic is a politician, or good for the pocketbook if the workaholic is a private professional. Hard work pays off for the lawyers and top managers who pull down jumbo salaries. But are these "paper warriors" enjoying their hard work more, in an increasingly complex set of rules and jurisdictions?

For corporate chief executive officers, who typically put in ten or eleven hour days plus up to five hours per weekend, life revolves around work and would be meaningless without it. They make time where they can find it—in cars and planes, in the shower, or by the pool. "Their hardest task: finding time for themselves." It's healthy, too, claims one chief operations officer. "Stress is caused by the things you haven't done—not the things you're doing."[17]

Lawyers seem less enthusiastic about the merits of hard work and long hours. Forty-one percent of lawyers surveyed believe that their career choice was a mistake and, if given a second chance, they would enter a different profession. The main problem for them is the time pressure of successful practice. When asked what aspect they most wanted to change in their working life, over half yearned for more time for family and leisure.[18]

Karoshi, officially defined as death from overwork, is the high price that Japanese executives pay for cramming too much work into too little time. In a country where employees work up to 500 more hours annually than their European and North American counterparts, it comes as no surprise that the number of *karoshi* cases are expanding at the rate of about 25 percent each year.[19]

Lawyers and CEOs may self-impose time requirements that do damage to themselves, but the work habits of other overworked and fatigued professionals, such as pilots and medical interns, may inflict harm on the innocent. For medical residents, laboring long hours has been the rite of passage into medical practice. The relentless hours of a three- to five-year residency have been justified as on-the-job-training that prepares novice physicians for a future of hard work. Residents' workweeks average seventy-four hours. One in ten surgical residents labors over 122 hours per week, frequently on uninterrupted thirty-six-hour shifts.[20] Interns on call average 2.4 hours of sleep a night.[21]

Such marathon training may have made good sense in a past when ministering to the ill or injured was relatively uncomplicated. Procedures have changed, however, from the days when "there were no medical intensive care units, no coronary care units, no respiratory care units, and no arterial lines, subclavian lines, Swan-Ganz catheters, pacemakers, Holter monitors, bedside monitors or cardioverters . . . no ultrasound, echocardiography, computerized axial tomographic scanning, and nuclear magnetic-resonance imaging."[22] In today's high-tech world of health care, the patient depends on the intern's alertness and skill to operate the complex life-saving machinery. When these doctors are sleepwalking, fatigued, stressed zombies, the difference for patients becomes one of life or death.

That simple fact became all too clear in a 1985 episode involving an 18-year-old Bennington College student who died of cardiac arrest within hours after she had been admitted to a New York hospital complaining of a fever and earache. After a grand jury attributed Libby Zion's death to errors made by exhausted, overworked residents and interns, states began to enact legislation that limited daily shifts to twenty-four consecutive hours and work weeks to eighty hours.[23]

This was not an isolated case. Supervising physicians at a major medical center reported that six out of seven surgical residents interviewed reported falling asleep "while driving to or from work during their internships and three were involved in motor vehicle accidents."[24]

Pilots too need sleep, and when they don't get enough, their actions, like those of interns, imperil others' lives. International air crews frequently spend as many as ten days away from home, on flights of over a dozen hours at times when their bodies believe it is the middle of the night. Tired crews stray off course, fly through assigned altitudes, improperly calculate fuel, land without clearances or on the wrong runways.[25] Pilots often nod off while the automatic pilot does the flying. Pilot fatigue was cited as either the cause or a contributing factor in sixty-nine plane accidents that claimed sixty-seven lives in a recent three-year period.[26] A pilot describes one of his life's more memorable moments:

> We were flying a 747 out of Houston at midnight with a load of freight. We were all dog-tired, so I asked the captain if I could take a nap. He said I could. When I woke up, the airplane was rumbling. We were on the verge of entering a stall. Everyone was asleep. We lost 2,000 feet before we got everything back to normal.[27]

Fatigued pilots risk their passengers' lives and overworked physicians risk their patients' lives. But there was a time, in the pre-anesthesia era, when speed in surgery had much merit. In the 1840s, the services of a certain British surgeon reputed as "the fastest knife in the West End," were much in demand. "Time me, gentlemen, time me!" Robert Liston would holler to the wide-awake students peering from the galleries of his operating theater. "Everyone swore that the first flash of his knife was followed so swiftly by the rasp of saw on bone that sight and sound seemed simultaneous."[28] In his quest to set new Olympian time-records, he removed in a spare four minutes a forty-five-pound scrotal tumor, whose owner had to carry it around in a wheelbarrow. One leg surgery, equalling the two-and-a-half minute record for which he was renowned, also lost for the patient his testicles. In another hastily performed amputation, the speedy Dr. Liston accidentally severed his young assistant's fingers, and a spectator's coattails. The patient died, so did the assistant, and the spectator, so terrified was he that the knife had pierced his vitals, dropped dead from fright. "This was the only operation in history with a 300 percent mortality," declared a physician specializing in medical disasters.[29]

THREE ROOT CANALS IN TWENTY MINUTES

" 'We were warned in dental school not to work in bad clinics because they would eat us up . . . that we'd have to work faster than we could imagine, that we'd be forced to do substandard work,' a Southern California dentist, now in private practice, told 60 Minutes last year. Still, after dental school he joined an assembly-line clinic built on convenient hours, heavy advertising, and high volume. Dentists were told they had to procure $50,000 in dental work a month, otherwise consider their jobs in jeopardy. One dentist did twice that much. 'I watched him shovel silver amalgam the consistency of soup into patients' teeth and carve the fillings with the tip of his finger. That's how he did fillings. I saw him do three root canals in twenty minutes.' "

—Robert Kanigel.[30]

HURRY SICKNESS AND EVEN WORSE DISEASES

Two other practitioners of the healing arts, Dr. Meyer Friedman and Dr. Ray H. Rosenman, contributed to our understanding of time-obsession in a way quite different from the celebrated Dr. Liston. The two San Francisco cardiac specialists coined the term "Type A" for people characterized by their neighbors, their work associates, their horoscopes, and their few friends as aggressive, assertive, belligerent, contentious, competitive, demanding, determined, driven, finicky, harassed, harried, hostile, irritable, nervous, self-involved, speedy, striving, superficial, and testy (thank you, thesaurus)—but otherwise, not bad sort of folk. More than anything else, this group is possessed of "a chronic sense of time urgency," in the very words of Drs. Friedman and Rosenman who, aided by their upholsterer, "discovered" the Type A personality.[31] The discovery came about in the detective work of solving The Puzzle of the Unevenly Worn Chairs. Here's how it happened.

The doctors decided it was time for a re-do of their reception room, which had become shabby. The workman called in for the job discovered that only the front edges of the seats were threadbare. Why? Apparently cardiac patients are prone to sit on the edges of chairs, possibly a sign of their stress and anxiety. Could there be a link between emotional state and heart condition? Geronimo! That was it! Heart patients suffering from "hurry sickness," as the two cardiologists first called it, "fidget on the front of the chairs, probably glancing at their watches every few seconds." Let's examine whether the connection has any truth in fact.

In the early 1970s, Drs. Friedman and Rosenman commenced a project that would become the keystone of research connecting personality to heart disease. Monitoring the health and behavior patterns of some 3,000 middle-aged men, they found, for example, that the serum cholesterol level of accountants rose sharply as the April 15 tax deadline approached. Moreover, "subjects *severely* afflicted with this type of behavior pattern exhibited every blood fat and hormone abnormality that the majority of coronary patients also showed."[32]

But perhaps everyone, heart attack case or not, exhibited the same pattern of behavior. So the researchers searched for subjects of polar opposite emotions—call them Type Bs—and found them on the rosters of the municipal clerks' and the embalmers' unions. Sure enough, the more phlegmatic and indolent Type Bs had lower serum cholesterol. Within a few years, the Type As were developing heart disease far more often than the Type Bs. The Type A men, in fact, faced 4.5 times the risk of developing heart disease. Certain sets of emotions apparently triggered chemical reactions in the body that, in turn, triggered heart attacks.

The Type A fails to perceive "the simple fact that a man's time can be exhausted by his activities. As a consequence, he never ceases trying to 'stuff' more and more events in his constantly shrinking reserves of time. It is the . . . everlasting *struggle* with time," wrote Drs. Friedman and Rosenman, "that we believe so very frequently leads to his early demise from coronary heart disease."[33]

Corporations actively seek out executives with Type A characteristics. They work hard. On the other hand, they drive everyone around them crazy. Although As climb the corporate ladder faster, rarely do they make it to the top. Ambition propels them into middle management, but a lack of creativity and questionable judgment leaves them there. Two management scholars cite the fact that roughly eight out of ten in middle management are As, but Bs dominate the top echelons.[34] Those invited into the highest ranks are advised to "slow down and take a longer time span. . . . Type A tendencies aren't compatible with what executive behavior calls for."[35]

The doctors' prescription for As' survival requires reducing personal time value. The advice has changed the life-styles of millions who had been committed to stressful work regimens and, given the results of the Friedman-Rosenman investigations, now suspected that they were candidates for a coronary. The clear choice was between getting too much done *now,* and having too few years ahead to get other things done.

Such fears may have been false alarms. Follow-up studies of the original Friedman-Rosenman group show that the uptight workaholic may stand a better chance of surviving a heart attack and of living longer than the more placid Bs.[36] Researchers examining subjects from the initial sample who developed heart disease discovered that surviving As had a lesser chance of a fatal second episode. In fact, the As faced only 60 percent of the risk of death faced by the Bs.[37]

Why? "In part by denying their illness and in part by taking control much sooner over their health status," explains Dr. Rosenman.[38] Researchers also speculate that the more compulsive As sought treatment earlier than Bs. Or, following a heart attack, the As may have more compulsively followed doctors' orders to diet and quit smoking.[39] Time's compulsion may not be so bad after all.

Take heart, Type As. Perhaps, when all is said and done, time can't be priced too highly.

PRICING TIME IN THE SLOW LANE

People seek pleasure and avoid pain, so it is said. Some, like Type As, seek their pleasure by maintaining furious schedules. Others find their pleasure via other routes. Some seek pleasure by instant gratification. Others find the deferral of pleasure a pleasure in itself.

Soap opera buffs are members of the latter group. The trick to keeping people tuned in, according to a soap opera producer, is "make 'em laugh, make 'em cry, but above all, make 'em wait." Draw out everyday happenings into "epics of voyeurism that can last months and even years."[40] For the rest of us, waiting is a bore and waiting is made tolerable only when the price is right.

Time spent pleasurably has its price, as the abbot of Saiho-ji temple demonstrated. As a rule, people must be paid for time spent painfully or, put differently, people will pay a price to avoid spending time in pain, for it has negative value. Of all of these—soap opera enthusiasts excepted—time waiting in line counts as one of the most familiar of all painful experiences.

Time is lost while we are stalled in traffic, or waiting out unintended delays in air flights, waiting for connecting flights, waiting at restaurants and barber shops, waiting at toll booths and traffic signals, waiting for busy signals on the telephone, waiting for latecomers to arrive at a meeting or for the meeting to end, waiting in queues at the post office or the Saturday night movies, waiting for those who repair our homes, or our bodies. We wait.

Four factors determine the amount of time lost in queues. The first two—the number of others lined up ahead of us, and how fast the queue moves—are pretty obvious, and follow from the first-come-first-served rule. The third factor is the importance of the person who waits. In general, richer and more powerful people can shorten the wait by buying their way out of the queue. Higher incomes and greater power, coupled with the higher value they place on time, give them the wherewithal and the incentive to do that. Their identification (the ID) therefore abbreviates the wait.

The fourth factor is the importance of the reason for waiting. People will wait longer, the greater the potential reward of the outcome. Knowing this, the person rendering the valued service can afford to keep clients waiting. Therefore, the more important the host's importance (the ego), the longer the wait.

The Ego and the ID

THE ID: The richer, because they value their precious time more highly, will spend less time waiting; the poorer, more. The host (the waitee?) for whom the waiter waits, knowing that the waiter is powerful, tries to minimize the length of the wait. With waiting time and power inversely related, deference is paid the powerful. How much time do Pope or President spend twiddling their thumbs waiting? Not much. The less privileged, however, must twiddle longer.

The rich and powerful also can reduce the time bandit's loot by using their wealth to buy their way out of the ordeal. They can hire a stand-in waiter, or take their business elsewhere. Those unable to pay for private medical services, for example, wait longer at public outpatient clinics because the poor have no alternative.[41]

There are exceptions to the rule. No stand-ins will do for court appearances or for obtaining visas, or certain licenses and permits, and for other situations that demand a personal appearance, because the service-provider presumably cannot take into account the waiter's importance. A public service operates as a monopoly, so there is no alternative.

THE EGO: Forcing others to wait—a commonly used device when power is unequally shared—is a means for wielding power. Highly placed persons, like the Popes and Presidents of the world, use their power to cause others to wait. "The ritual prostration of the devout; the rigid military stance of attention in face of a superior; the cessation of activity as a sign of respect for the lofty—these and other modes of deferential self-suspension, though they appear to have little in common with it, find their parallel in the still expectancy of the waiter."[42] To be kept waiting means that the waiter's time is less valuable, and presumably his or her social worth as well. Nearly two out of three high-level executives keep their clients waiting longer than six minutes, but only one in four low-level executives are guilty of that sin.[43]

The importance of the host—the person for whom we wait—and the importance of the reason for the wait also explain deferential treatment. The more important either is, the more waiting we tolerate. We wait to see the Pope or the President and are pleased to be granted the privilege of an audience, but are impatient if forced to wait for lesser beings like Nora and Norman Gnomon. "Thus, the waiting period that is taken in stride by the client of an internationally applauded brain specialist would give rise to seething if inflicted by the neighborhood dentist."[44]

The celebrated Dr. Liston's patients patiently (pardon the modest pun) tolerated long delays in his crowded waiting room for an abundant reward: an amputation that, under any other knife, would have been a far more drawn out and painful ordeal. (His butler circulated a decanter of madeira and biscuits to the patients in line, thus further enhancing the rewards of the experience.[45])

What to Dueue to Shorten the Queue

"The basic fact about human existence is not that it is a tragedy, but that it is a bore," wrote the sardonic H. L. Mencken. "It is not so much a war as an endless standing in line."[46] Lines seem to get longer all the time, as does the necessity for waiting in them. Were it not for a Danish engineer's fascination with congestion in Copenhagen's phone service, we would suffer even more distress from that endless standing in line.

A. K. Erlang's turn-of-the-century discoveries about queuing behavior not only helped unclog the local telephone network, but led to ways of designing everything from the movement of goods through factories (so that they didn't pile up at any one point) to figuring out how to schedule personnel at banks (so that customers didn't pile up in waiting lines). Thanks to Mr. Erlang's pioneering work, lines are shorter than they might have been.

Irksome waits nonetheless remain a ritual of daily life. To reduce delays, it is necessary to persuade people not to use fixed-capacity facilities like freeways, toll bridges, or supermarket cashiers at peak hours. Reducing prices at off-peak hours is one way to do this. Discounted movie tickets during the afternoon when theaters are half-empty, early-bird dinners at bargain prices for those willing to dine at unpopular hours, and cheap fares for the traveler who will fly at times when the skies are less crowded are among the incentives. How much money changes hands depends on how highly the parties to the deal value their time. The same reasoning underpins congestion-reduction programs that give ride-sharing drivers access to fast lanes while delaying solo drivers' entrance to the freeway.

As a person's earnings rise, it follows that their time value does too, and, with it, the worth of time-economizing alternatives. The response to worsening congestion of the airways illustrates the point. Every year the number of flight delays seems to grow. Congestion on both the ground and in the air costs passengers in lost time, and costs the airlines in lost revenues. The year 1988 was pivotal for it marked the reversal of the booming air travel business. The mounting number of delays drove people to cars, trains, and buses. In that year, Greyhound and Amtrak traffic rose by 10 percent; and traffic on rural highways was the heaviest it had been in years.[47]

Remember the gas lines of 1979, that painful example of "rationing by wait"? When Iran sharply curtailed petroleum supplies, less gasoline was available than consumers wanted at the established price. Since the government put controls on pump prices, service stations couldn't ration supplies by raising the price. Instead, they rationed gas according to how long customers were willing to queue up for it. The precious liquid cost more, not in out-of-pocket payments to gas station operators, but in terms of lost time. At first, the pegged price had an egalitarian effect. Rich and poor alike had to wait; no preference was given to drivers of Mercedes-Benzes over VWs. But the market quickly responded. Gas jockeys arrived to gas-up their customers' cars, exchanging their time at a price for their customers' time.

Although lifetimes can be, and have been, lengthened, the fact remains that daily activities must still be squeezed into a twenty-four-hour time quota. As opportunities expand, and the amount of time available for enjoying those opportunities does not, the value of each hour rises. As the *Busy Body (BB)* factor takes on more relevance more and more of us become *Busy Bodies* seeking ways of putting that higher-valued time to better use. We must get the most out of an instant's pleasure.

Who are they, these *Busy Bodies?* The prime market targets for the goods that make time more efficient are those whose incomes are rising the fastest: those employed in occupation groups like information technology, those in the age groups who are approaching their peak earning years; those living in dual-earner families, and particularly those families with women who have recently taken paid jobs. These are the *Busy Bodies* who, as their time grows ever more scarce, most frugally marshall that most fixed of all resources in their pursuit of the Good Life.

4:00

THE PARADOX OF THE GOOD LIFE

"We live in a world where time is becoming not less important but ever more so. Imagine a spacecraft running late! It might miss its orbit completely, and find itself wandering off into the trackless depths of the universe!"

—Michael Frayn[1]

"For the first time since his creation," observed John Maynard Keynes gazing into the future from the vantage point of 1928, "man will be faced with his real, his permanent problem—how to use his freedom from pressing economic cares, how to occupy the leisure, which science and compound interest will have won for him, to live agreeably and wisely and well."[2] Money problems would disappear, said the economic sage, eclipsed by the challenges of using newfound leisure wisely and well, in pursuit of The Good Life.

Arcadia pursued. Economic development seeks an Arcadian state where mankind, having satisfied basic needs, will spend its time in the most fulfilling ways, free to savor life to the fullest; freed, as John Stuart Mill put it, to enjoy "mental culture, moral and social progress . . . and the Arts of Living." The time would be passed thinking the great thoughts and reading the great books, writing poetry and singing songs, enjoying the arts and learning new languages, strolling in the park and swimming in the sea, watching the sun set and rise, or, in short, "listening to the birds sing." The Good Life offers the freedom and opportunity to pursue those interests and activities that matter, unfettered by the responsibilities of satisfying elemental wants.

Arcadia gained? But, as we have climbed the ladder of development, have we moved ever nearer the agreeable Arcadia envisioned by Messrs. Keynes and Mill?

Indeed, the standard of living for most Americans, Western

Europeans, and Japanese has risen by multiples of what it was in yesteryear, and rising affluence has freed the vast majority from worries about economic survival. Scarcely a half-century ago, President Franklin Delano Roosevelt declared that one-third of the American people were underfed, poorly clothed, and badly housed. Since that year from which Lord Keynes surveyed the future, the average American's disposable income has tripled, even after accounting for inflation. Today we ingest 38 percent more calories than our basic daily requirement, and many of us wish that we were closer to the minimum. Except for an emerging class of unsheltered, we are well housed. Affluence makes it possible for many of us to trash half our wardrobes at least once a year and to restock with the trendiest upscale duds. Consumer credit has expanded substantially—nearly quintupling since 1970—so consumers have more to spend for their ticket to Arcadia and more time to enjoy it once they arrive at their destination.

How have we used our greater abundance and leisure? For that range of activities running from thinking the great thoughts to cavorting with friends? In short, have we freed up time to pursue The Good Life?

Arcadia thwarted. It seems not. Instead of slouching steadily toward Arcadia, every dollar advance in the GNP seems to require working harder with fewer hours left to worry about "how to occupy the leisure, to live agreeably and wisely and well," and to savor "the Arts of Living." "Progress" has distanced us further and further from Arcadia. Therein lies the Paradox of The Good Life.

EXPLAINING THE PARADOX

There are two (and possibly more) approaches to explain how greater busy-ness goes with greater prosperity. One explanation is simple, the other is not. Both, fortunately, arrive at the same conclusion.

The simpler is this: the symbiosis of economic development and technological progress has produced a greater variety of ways to spend time. Because there are simply too many things to do in too few hours, the more attractive and rewarding opportunities crowd out the less attractive that absorb the fixed quantity of time available.

Here is the more complicated explanation: first, wages rise with economic development, and there are two consequences.

- There is an *income effect*. Higher wages increase purchasing power. We spend our larger earnings on the services and goods that enrich the leisure hours.
- And there is a *price effect*. Higher wages drive us to work more because, by working more, we earn more. But working longer hours leaves fewer non-work hours for enjoying the services and goods purchased with the larger earnings. Oops. Tilt!

The conflict leads to a dilemma: we want to spend *less* time working so that we have *more* time to enjoy the leisure-time goods bought with the fruits of our hard work, yet we also want to spend more time working in order to earn more. How can we reconcile these two desires which pull us in opposite directions?

THE HORRIBLE DILEMMA

One Possibility	*The Other Possibility*
Choices	
Working longer hours	Working fewer hours
Earning more income	Earning less income
Consequences	
Fewer leisure hours to enjoy a larger income	More leisure hours to enjoy a smaller income
More income to spend during fewer leisure hours	Less income to spend during more leisure hours

Different people will resolve the dilemma in different ways. Some will sacrifice leisure for more work at higher wages. Others will reduce hours at work to increase leisure. The *net* result of the pulls determines whether, on balance, people will work longer or shorter hours. Because the pulls are in opposite directions, the only answer is an empirical one. The statistics are revealing.

Over the past century, the average workweek has declined in

length and the average wage has risen. Pressures for shortening the workweek began as early as the 1830s when workers were governed by the rule, "eight hours for work, eight hours for sleep, eight hours for all the rest."[3] Because the production line required less work, Henry Ford argued that industrialization should free up time for leisure (and more leisure time would mean more spending on leisure products, like cars).[4] At the turn of the century, the average worker put in a sixty-hour week. His counterpart two decades later worked ten fewer hours. The Great Depression rapidly pushed that figure down by another twenty-five hours, but the return to normalcy led the New Deal to settle on the forty-hour week, a standard which has remained more or less unchallenged up to the present. In the meantime, average wages have moved up.

Based on the evidence of the long haul, the income effect has overwhelmed the price effect. As wages rose, workers resisted the opportunity to labor more hours for more pay, preferring instead to "purchase" leisure time for enjoying the benefits of their higher earnings. In this sense, the value of leisure time has risen more rapidly even than the value of work time. But, as George Washington observed when his portrait painter, Mr. Stewart, arrived with the unfinished canvas, there is more to the picture.

An abrupt turn-around occurred in the early 1970s, when the workweek began to exceed the forty-hour norm. All told, the average workweek has lengthened by more than eight hours (up 20 percent) since 1973.[5] A puzzled Bureau of Labor Statistics—the Government's official agency charged with reporting such matters—revealed that by 1990 more workers than ever were moonlighting, that the average factory worker was putting in four hours of overtime each week (the most in nearly twenty years), and that absenteeism had dropped to its lowest level since the early 1970s when the Bureau began collecting these data.[6]

Observers greeted the changes as a radical shift in work attitudes. Work was in; leisure, out. People had become bored with their free time. Work had taken on a new kind of "relevancy."[7] Speculations such as these grossly overinterpreted a far more straightforward phenomenon. What happened in the turn-around was simply this: salary increases had begun lagging behind inflation, and workers had to run harder just to stay even. This meant putting in longer hours that included overtime and moonlighting.

To pay the food bills, meet the mortgage payments, keep the children in college—in short, to maintain their standard of living—leisure time had to be sacrificed.[8]

The data show that, as wages fall, workers strengthen their work commitment; and as wages rise, workers "buy" leisure time by working fewer hours. In the trade-off of the twenty-four daily hours between work and leisure, the workweek shortens with rising wages as each additional dollar of earnings becomes less important than time spent in leisure; correspondingly, the workweek lengthens with declining wages as each additional wage dollar becomes more important than leisure time. Recent history has shown how lower real wages lead to longer hours on the job. As the number of leisure hours shortens, each of them becomes more valuable.[9] How we choose to spend those more valued nonwork hours is the last part of the theory. The Golden Rules of Time-Allocation govern those choices.

HOW TO ACHIEVE HAPPINESS IN ONE EASY LESSON: USING THE GOLDEN RULES OF TIME-ALLOCATION

All of us want to use our time in ways that yield the most satisfaction from the overall time allocation. Realizing it or not, we do this by opting for those activities that yield the greatest satisfaction (call it **S**) compared to the amount of time spent (call it **T**) pursuing the activity, all the while keeping in mind that everything must fit tidily into the twenty-four-hour day. No more, no less. In choosing what to do (and, of course, *when* to do it), we try to maximize the ratio of satisfaction received to time required (**S/T**). Dealing with **T** and ignoring **S**—or vice-versa—tells but half the story when both **S** and **T** matter.[10] What counts most of all is getting the largest possible **S/T**. That's the way to get more out of life.[11]

I will call the **S/T** ratio a "gazinta" (that's quick for **T** *goes into* **S**). Whether it's sleeping, shopping, cooking, working, helping others—whatever it is—each activity has its own gazinta that tells us how much satisfaction the activity yields compared to the time required. Some gazintas are larger than others. Walking the dog has one gazinta, and jogging has another, but walking (or running) the dog while jogging has a larger gazinta than either activity performed solo. If we choose to spend our time on the activities with the biggest gazintas, the sum of gazintas during our twenty-four-hour day will be as large as possible, which is what all of us want.[12] That is the first Golden Rule of Time-Allocation.

WHAT MATTERS MOST IN ALLOCATING TIME

Maximize the gazinta: **S/T**

The largest possible **S** and the smallest possible **T**:

S/T

The second Golden Rule of Time-Allocation is like unto the first, except whereas the first is static, the second is dynamic. The desired balance achieved under the first Golden Rule can only be temporary. Marketplace dynamics constantly challenge a balanced time-budget. Time-saving breakthroughs increase the overall satisfaction gained from the way time is budgeted. Some decrease **T**—leading toward the instantaneousness much sought after by *Busy Bodies*—and some increase **S** without affecting **T**. Best of all are those that both raise **S** and lower **T**. An electric toothbrush may or may not do the job faster than the old-fashioned nonelectric version, but it does a better job of it. The **S** of oral hygiene goes up and, with it, the **S/T** also rises.

Whether it is the purchase of an electric toothbrush or any of hundreds of other commodities, *commoditization,* the use of time-saving and satisfaction-enhancing goods, is a chief contributor to higher **S/T**s. In the world of business, when hourly wages rise, management boosts output by buying labor-saving (read: time-saving) equipment. The rest of us are no different. As the value of each hour of *our* time rises, we buy equipment—washing machines or answering machines, computers or cameras, bag-baths or piano-beds—to save our **T** and enhance our **S**. Time "commoditizers," mainly the products of ever-advancing technology, open up new vistas by reducing time requirements and boosting satisfaction.

LIMITING TIME-USE OPTIONS: EXCEPTIONS TO THE GOLDEN RULES

Every rule has its exceptions of course. The Golden Rules of Time-Allocation are no exception to that rule. Laws and institutional rules, custom or tradition, nature and climate, location, other peoples' decisions, and limits on the availability of goods and facilities constrain our freedom to choose activities as we wish, regardless of their **S/T**s.

Regulations, meant to preserve or enhance the public interest, prevent people from using their time to do-in friends and neighbors. For example, the law doesn't smile kindly on taking illicit drugs or shooting people, as attractive as those activities might be for some. Those who insist on pursuing these activities, if caught, "do time" in jail. The law also directly affects time expenditure by regulating speed on the road. With lower speed limits, driving to New Halcyon for the weekend with the Gnomons takes longer but presumably raises our chances, and others' chances, of getting to our destinations intact (if not in time).

Another set of institutional restraints enhances the social good. An educated electorate and national defense are common national objectives furthered by restricting individual options on time-use. Compulsory education laws require children to spend a certain number of their youthful years in school and, in many countries, conscription requires dedicating time to military service. Organized labor justified its successful battle for the forty-hour work week as necessary to allow workers the time to educate themselves in citizenship, civic culture, and literacy.[13]

Fortunately for the rest of us, the law prohibits unlicensed people from driving a car, dispensing drugs, or proffering knowledge. We cannot simply get behind the wheel, or don a pharmacist's white coat, or take the lectern unless we have passed examinations certifying our competence. Getting the license requires time in training.

In fact, most worthwhile activities require training and groundwork. No matter how much we might aspire to it, Olympic medals are reserved for the few who have trained most of their lives for a sport. Nearly everyone wants to direct a band or an orchestra, but those who fail to spend years getting ready for their Carnegie Hall debut must be content to satisfy their urges by waving their arms in front of a loudspeaker. Even fairly routine activities like cooking a dinner that evokes the much-desired Oohs and Aahs requires time to acquire the culinary know-how.

Custom limits certain time-uses by determining when certain things can and cannot be done. No matter how desperately we may want to go to the movies at 6 a.m., order a sherry in England at 10 a.m., or go shopping at midnight, we rarely can. Tradition and the custom of opening hours have determined that we will do those things at a different time.

Despite the gains in technology that have freed us from many natural constraints, nature does still constrain our freedom in allocating time and scheduling activities. Certain activities can be undertaken only at certain periods in life and hours of the day. Nature limits the amount of sleep we can get along without, at least in the long run, and how long we can go without eating or using the toilet. Procreation is limited to a range of years. Biological changes require ballet dancers, and professional baseball and football players, at some stage in their lives, to retrain for new careers. Most of nature's constraints are givens. The incubation period of a disease, the periodicity of hunger pangs, the interval of a sneeze (nearly 85 percent of the speed of sound), the blinking of an eyelid (24 times a minute), or the average length of a knee jerk (0.4 second), are all pretty firmly fixed in duration.[14]

Astronomers insist that the stars and planets orbit in regular ways and astrologers believe that those regularities, and the juxtapositions of such heavenly bodies, control what happens in daily life, and when. At least Nancy and Ronald Reagan's faith in such manifestations led them to an astrologer who came to rule the White House schedule. Joan Quigley's calculations arranged the optimal timing of press conferences, speeches, summit meetings, the Presidential debates, departure times for Air Force One, and congressional arm-twisting. If that weren't enough, the San Francisco astrologer set the time for Mrs. Reagan's mastectomy, Mr. Reagan's cancer surgery, and the confirmation of Anthony Kennedy for the Supreme Court at precisely 11:32:25 a.m. on 11/11/87, for those who care.[15]

In somewhat less metaphysical ways, nature governs the cadence of daily life by means of circadian rhythms—the biological clock whose set of alarms announce what to do when. The body's impersonal timepiece tells us when to get up in the morning with nearly the unflagging regularity of a conventional alarm clock, nags us into eating at certain times, and makes us sleepy. We become particularly aware of this mysterious clock (the least understood of all time-keeping mechanisms), and especially of its awful insistence, when we interrupt natural rhythms by moving quickly among time zones. All who fly long distances are familiar with jet lag, and all who have suffered its tribulations have their favorite tales to tell. One tale from the 1950s changed the course of history.

Negotiations on the Aswan Dam Treaty were set to begin shortly after the plane carrying Secretary of State John Foster Dulles touched down in Egypt. Because his biological clock was out of kilter, the secretary's bargaining skills failed to match the sensitivity of the task. The Soviet negotiators won the project, and, with it, their first foothold in the Middle East.[16] The moral is: failing to give nature her due can impose high costs, and not only for those who short themselves on sleep.

Winston Churchill knew this well. He needed his afternoon nap, no matter what. The Prime Minister's biological clock required a daily recess for a fifteen-minute snooze even when he was running a pitched battle in World War II from his operations room.[17] Mr. Churchill was not exempt from time's biological demands. He was bound by them. Apparently all of us are.

Besides the obvious rhythms like the monthly menstrual cycle and the daily sleep-wake cycle, even subtler rhythms govern the workings of body and mind. There are rhythms in blood pressure, blood levels of iron, levels of stress hormones, and body temperature, all influenced by so-called *zeitgebers* that, besides sunlight and day length, give time cues. A person runs three times the risk of heart attack at 9 a.m. than at 11 p.m. The suspected cause is the circadian rhythm that controls changes in hormones and other biochemical parameters.[18]

Nor are other creatures exempt from the rigid schedules that nature imposes. Felix wakes us up as punctually as an alarm clark, and Fido insists on his evening walk, even though neither cat nor dog has access to the technological marvels that humans have for clocking their daily routines. Animals mate at appointed times each year, lose their fur in anticipation of a seasonal change, and seem as regulated as we by seasonal and circadian rhythms.

This is not to say that such rhythms are infallible. Take the case of the swallows that take up summer residence each year on the Feast of St. Joseph at San Juan Capistrano Mission in California, 6,000 miles from their winter homes in Argentina. Tradition has it that the annual event reaffirms nature's rhythms because the migration has occurred each year since Father Serra built the place 200 years ago. The truth is that the swallows, who can't distinguish St. Joseph's Day from St. Josephine's Day, arrive over a period of many weeks, and, these days, more of them set up housekeeping at a department store across the street than under the Mission's eves.[19]

As oblivious as swallows apparently are to being in the right place at the right time, for human beings it's a different matter. Although the world is constantly shrinking, we still must travel to pursue many desired activities. Dedicating a certain amount of time to get where we are going remains part of the ritual. Commuting is a necessity for people who work in stores, offices, or factories, instead of their homes. Scaling Mt. Everest requires spending the time getting first to Darjeeling or some other convenient jumping-off place. Lunching at a sidewalk cafe on the Left Bank requires committing the time to transport ourselves to Paris.

Personal schedules depend in part on schedules made by others, as well as by Mother Nature. The kids must be driven to school at 8:15, the boss insists that we are at our desk at 9:00 sharp, and the family expects dinner on the table at 6:30, and that's all there is to it. Since people must drive the urban freeways at certain hours and create congestion, we must allocate more time if we insist on traveling at rush hour.

Most activities, but not all, require a component of goods and facilities. A bed isn't absolutely necessary for sleeping, but who can play tennis without a racket, a ball, a net, and a court? If the goods are unavailable or unaffordable, time won't be allocated to the activities. Lacking a television set, no time will be spent watching it, a rather obvious "fact" that explains why international time-budget studies show low average viewing times in some countries, such as the Balkans.[20] The quality of cooking no doubt explains why people in the socialist countries spend little time eating, but in France and Belgium, where the "goods" are most available and their quality is legend, considerably more time is spent enjoying the pleasures at table.[21] The availability of time-saving technology for preparing food, when taken with the affinity for quality cooking, also helps to account for variations in the amount of time spent in the kitchen. In France it amounts to an average of three hours daily, in the United Kingdom one hour, and in the U.S. only a half hour.

"DELIMITING" TIME-USE OPTIONS

Constraints such as the many noted above impose limits on free choice. But substantial flexibility remains for choosing what to do when. Rising consumer incomes, coupled with falling prices of technologies, have made a vaster range of gadgets available to a broader spectrum of the population. Many of the technologies also expand time-use options, and raise gazintas by increasing **S** and decreasing **T**.

Complicated technologies, like the computer, are high on the list. Plunging prices have made most of these magical time-savers almost as affordable as the ubiquitous "telly," and quality and capability have improved rapidly. It has been calculated that "if the aircraft industry had evolved as spectacularly as the computer industry over the past twenty-five years, a Boeing 747 would cost fifty dollars today, and it would circle the globe in twenty minutes on five gallons of fuel. Such performance would represent a rough analogue of the reduction of cost, the increase in speed of operation, and the decrease in energy consumption of computers."[22]

Far simpler innovations can do the same. Take the case of the lowly mail order catalogue, a time-honored device that facilitates convenient shopping at home. Shopping by catalogue saves the time traveling to shopping centers, is more comfortable, and can be done at any hour.[23] If the 142 ordinary catalogues stuffed into the average American household's mailbox each year are considered too rudimentary for a complex world, the shopping channels on television offer a higher-tech alternative.

The constraints imposed by limited shopping hours for many offices and stores are being relaxed, in part to accommodate the increasing pressures on consumers' time. Most banks are open beyond the once customary hours of 10 a.m. to 3 p.m., and if the bank is closed, the electronic teller will provide routine services. Stores have extended their hours, but when they are closed, the convenience stores welcome shoppers around the clock. And climate-controlled buildings have overcome the limitations on work imposed by extreme heat and humidity.

When to work or when not to work once depended entirely on others' decisions. The factory imposed time-discipline. No matter how desperately production workers preferred the night shift, if the assembly line operated only during the day, they must work then too. The assembly line split up work into specialized tasks that required coordination. And that meant dependency. A laggard could bring the whole production site to a grinding halt. A late-arrival could hold up the start of production for a team, perhaps an entire labor force. Management responded with threats that made those risks explicit. In about 1700, The Crowley Iron Works in England announced in no uncertain terms that "Every morning at five o'clock, the warden is to ring the bell for beginning to work, at eight o'clock for breakfast, at half an hour after for work again, at twelve o'clock for dinner, at one to work and at eight to ring for leaving work and all to be lock'd up."[24] During the centuries since then, the growth of self-employment and the shift from factory work in favor of service production have opened opportunities for more elastic work arrangements. Many workers today are experimenting with flex-time schedules that depart from the nine-to-five ritual. Ironically, machinery at first imposed a time regimen on work; now machinery has gone far in freeing us from enslavement to the clock. Transport technology, for example, has opened up the world in both its space and time dimensions. By giving greater access, jet flight has expanded the available options, bringing even the lunch in Paris or backpacking in the Himalayas into the realm of possibility. Conceivably, we can spend time in the morning swimming at the beach and the afternoon skiing in the mountains, confusing and exhausting as that may seem.

By relaxing many time-use constraints, technologies and institutional changes have increased time-use options, expanding the freedom to use time as we choose, and for living "agreeably and wisely and well." Yet, there are few bored affluent people today, living lives that suggest a surplus of time. To the contrary, *Busy Bodies* are frantically searching for the secrets of cramming more into a fixed time-allotment—the unyielding quotidian of twenty-four hours. Have those people who have discovered these secrets also found out what "agreeable, wise" living means?

LIVING "AGREEABLY AND WISELY AND WELL"

The dark threats of nuclear war, of environmental degradation, of soaring national deficits, of a worsening plight of the third world, and a host of other problems unknown in history, hang heavy. Yet, it appears that Americans are reasonably happy with their lives, and succeeding in the pursuit of personal happiness. At least the polls say so. Eighty-seven percent of those asked in 1988 said they are satisfied "with the way things are going" in their individual lives—a new high—up from 79 percent nine years before.[25]

Those who express satisfaction "with the way things are going" apparently have found out how to use their time in the most personally rewarding ways, despite their complaints that there is less than enough of it to do everything worth doing. In their time management calculus, that majority have found a balance in the set of daily activities which yields some optimum quota of happiness. But in a dynamic world where new time-using opportunities are always presenting themselves, today's equilibrium may not be tomorrow's.

As any new or improved activity presented itself, that majority asked themselves, "do I want to do this? And, if I do, what can give in a schedule already jammed full?" Television gets worse all the time, and films get better, so let's see movies more often and watch TV less. The sermons in church are the same ones we've heard for years, so let's play tennis Sunday morning instead. Keeping fit pays off in more years of better health, so let's enroll in an aerobics class even if it means working out during lunch hour. New kitchen gadgets have made gourmet cooking a breeze, so let's eat in instead of out. Electronic entertainment centers make staying at home more fun, so let's cocoon rather than going out so often. Paid work is more rewarding than unpaid housework, so let's look for a job and hire a maid. By continually shifting priorities to make way for new opportunities, constantly striving to find that ideal new balance in their time allocation, these *Busy Bodies* constantly moved to higher levels of satisfaction. By their adherence to the logic of the Golden Rules, that 87 percent found happiness in their lives.

Decisions such as these are the essence of analyzing and reanalyzing whether we are using our time to best advantage. In the unending balancing act that seeks to find the new and better time allocations, we constantly search for opportunities with ever higher **S/T** ratios. The *BB* factor, the mantra of this book, intensifies the search. A new opportunity, when found, can find space in the twenty-four-hour time allotment only at the expense of another activity, one with a gazinta that grows less rapidly.[26] The winners—*time-plus* activities that take on increasing importance in our lives—crowd out the *time-minus* activities. That's the way it is in this Darwinian world of time-use.

WINNERS AND LOSERS: TIME-PLUS AND TIME-MINUS

The parade of technology—or, more broadly, of innovation—helps to increase gazintas of activities by pulling up their **S**s (levels of satisfaction) and pushing down their **T**s (amounts of time spent). Rising time costs encourage buying the new products and services and increasing income provides the wherewithal: the innovations that economize on time, transfer it, allow it to be used synchronically, and boost its yield. In this way, the "rationalizing" of time becomes a reality. History has shown how prices of these innovations fall as sales grow. The rise in income and, with it, time costs, coupled with their falling prices, generates a triple-barreled demand for goods and services that lower **T** and raise **S**.

The impact of technology, however, falls unevenly. Technologically advanced goods and services can reduce the **T** or raise the **S** of some activities, and have little impact on others. The latter tend to become time-minus and recede into the historical background. The activities that emerge victorious in the competition are amenable to commoditization, and of course tend to be those with the faster rising **S/T**s.

Many of the time-plus are the *self-serving* activities of daily life, such as cooking, eating, shopping, housework, exercising, travel, and entertainment. In recent years, technological marvels have raised the **S/T**s of activities such as these, that have precious little effect on anyone except the individual himself or herself. They are the subjects of the chapters that make up the next section.

Other-serving activities, in contrast to self-serving activities, bear significantly on other people, in most cases on the commonweal. Caring for the elderly, for our children, and for our neighbors, discharging our duties as responsible citizens, making top-level decisions, and the other activities that serve others besides ourselves, are topics taken up in the third section. With only limited possibilities for either increasing the rewards, or making the activities more time-efficient, endeavors with a high content of otherness tend to get crowded out of the twenty-four-hour allowance. Squeezed out by the *BB* factor and lost in the shuffle, other-serving activities—part and parcel of The Good Life—become time-minus. In the bargain, society loses.

Glossary of Strange Terms:

Activities The ways we use our time. Anything we do—whether working, sleeping, eating, pestering others—that takes time. And that covers just about everything.

BB (Busy Bodies) *factor* There are more and more things to do—alas—in the same amount of time. Increasing time scarcity—the *BB* factor—presents the central challenge to managing our activities in the most rewarding ways.

Commoditization Using goods to increase an activity's **S/T**.

Gazinta **S/T** The rewards or amount of satisfaction **S** yielded from an activity per unit of time **T** devoted to that activity; any activity's gazinta (or **S/T** ratio) grows either when the **S** of the activity increases or the amount of time **T** spent on the activity decreases, or both. Commoditization often raises **S** or lowers **T**, and sometimes does both at the same time.

The Golden Rules of Time-Allocation First, choose activities with the highest gazintas; second, shift activities to those with the most rapidly increasing gazintas.

Self-serving and other-serving activities Self-serving activities affect primarily ourselves, and other-serving activities affect not only ourselves, but others, whether they are close friends or the society at large.

Time-use constraints Laws and institutional rules, custom or tradition, nature and climate, location, others' decisions, and the availability of goods and facilities put limits on our freedom to use time in the ways that we want. Although transport technology, expanded shopping hours, and elastic work schedules, for example, are reducing the importance of these exceptions to the Golden Rule of Time-Allocation, the twenty-four-hour day remains the ultimate constraint.

Time-plus and time-minus activities Time-plus activities will become increasingly popular as their **S/T**s rise; time-minus will lose out.

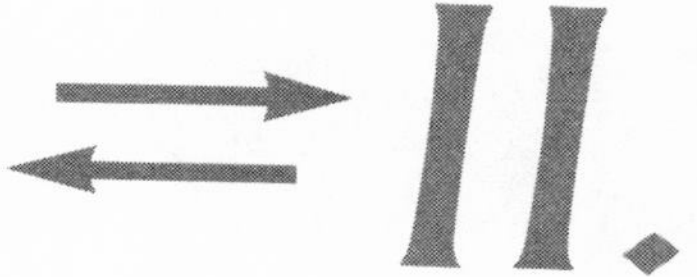

Now comes the fun. Which activities will win and which will lose in the game of substitution? Knowing the right answer can have significant consequences. Trends in the type of books that are selling are one barometer of how popular interests are shifting and how people are reallocating their time, and a particularly important one for publishers who want to stay in business. In the past couple of decades, statistics show that reading preferences shifted away from more traditional "heady" subjects like the arts, poetry, history, literature, and philosophy toward practical fare such as business, home economics, law, medicine, and technology.[1] So it is with our time-budgets. Practical pursuits that deal with day-to-day life are crowding out the more abstract, which engage mainly the mind.

But these are only speculations based on rather limited evidence. More convincing answers will be found in the chapters ahead.

5:00

RISING CURTAINS, FALLING ATTENDANCE

"There is no work of art that is without short cuts."
—André Gide

Sir Neville Marriner recognizes how time, and its increasing scarcity, shapes taste. The jet-set conductor attributes the remarkable record sales of his orchestra, The Academy of St. Martin-in-the-Fields, to working at "a particular moment in history (with) a turning point for technology." Marriner & Co. succeeded by finding a particular niche in listeners' time schedules: the commuting hour.

Programs aired during the traffic rush, Sir Neville believes, are the most heavily listened to. "Nobody wants to hear Mahler symphonies then," declares the conductor, "or Brahms so early. Besides, you can't get through a movement before it's time for the commercial." Baroque pieces composed during the seventeenth and eighteenth centuries are shorter, and easier to break up into fragments, compared to the longer-winded and more bloated opuses of the nineteenth-century Romantic period. "The longest movements we were playing broke down to three or five minutes. Handel, Bach, or Vivaldi all consisted of short movements, so you could advertise your toilet soap and move on to the next piece, or wait till the next to do your weather or traffic report."[1]

The increasing scarcity of time affects not only the type of music we listen to, as Marriner points out, but the whole range of cultural activities that enrich life. In fact, the very future of the performing arts may depend on the *BB* factor.

AMERICA'S CULTURAL REVOLUTION IN FACT AND FANTASY

Louis Harris, the eminent pollster who regularly inquires into what people do and believe, and why, has tracked the arts situation in the United States since 1973, and his most recent poll reports strangely contradictory results. In theory, Americans pride themselves on their support of culture, and the performing arts have attracted larger and larger followings. In practice, he has found, audiences are becoming smaller and smaller.

Culture has swept America. Nearly every major city across the land boasts a performing arts center to house a resident theater company and symphony orchestra. Professional ballet and dance organizations are springing up everywhere and playing to large audiences. The nation's 1,224 opera companies give 12,000 performances for 18 million people each year, and 1,572 symphony orchestras play 20,000 concerts to 24 million people who support them to the tune of over a half billion dollars in donations and ticket sales.[2]

The cultural revolution would not have occurred unless Americans were willing to commit themselves to a lively performing arts agenda. In announcing the results of his most recent survey, an amazed Mr. Harris said he found public interest in the arts "staggeringly higher than anyone ever dared imagine."[3] Well over half of those surveyed had attended live performances of plays and pop music concerts or visited art museums within the past year, about a third had gone to a live dance performance or classical concert, and a quarter went to the opera or musical theater.

Contrast the state of the arts today with what it was some years ago. Since the founding of the New York Philharmonic in 1842, an average of ten new symphony orchestras have been formed each year. Their gross income has skyrocketed by $26 million a year since 1970 and the number of concerts has tripled. Opera performances too nearly tripled and major companies grew five-fold. During the same two decades, Broadway's gross box office take quintupled to $253 million annually.

Again, according to the Harris survey, more Americans reported attending arts events than before. Whether it was art exhibits, plays, musicals, dance, or classical music concerts, more respondents believed that more was better.[4]

And public support *for* public support has blossomed. Larger proportions are willing to pay higher taxes for cultural activities and to dig deeper into their pockets for donations. No matter the type of arts organization, a rising share of Americans claim that they donate, and the size of the average contribution has swelled by about 9 percent each year.

The real picture is far less encouraging than these statistics reveal, however. Viewed through a glass darkly, the much ballyhooed American Cultural Revolution is exaggerated. Take an extreme case: theater's imperiled state of health.

American theater appears to have returned full circle to the perilous days of its birth. The first theatrical performance on American soil, given in 1665, ended in disaster, with the cast of "Ye Bare and Ye Cubb" thrown in jail—a portent of the future.[5] The problems of three centuries ago, however, pale in comparison to today's troubles.

Broadway, historically the creative center of American theater, has been in a long, steady decline. Forty new productions are staged on the Great White Way each year, a mere fraction of the number premiered during the 1927–28 season when the legitimate stage, then in its heyday, turned out 264 plays. Total playing weeks have dropped to half what they were in the '20s.[6]

How can this be? At first blush, the growth in box office receipts signifies great prosperity. Yet the figures contain distortions that magnify the real rise. Adjusting the figures for increases in prices, population, and income turns the growth rate negative.[7] While this relative drop in demand for tickets goes far in explaining Broadway's current and increasing financial woes, it does not explain why people are budgeting less of their larger incomes to attend the theater.

But how does this sorry picture square with Louis Harris's finding that the number and proportion of persons who attend live performing arts events is rising? Overall admissions are down, and the drop is accelerating.[8] The seeming contradiction is explained by the frequency of attendance: although larger numbers and proportions of people attend arts events, the number of events that the average person attends each year is way down.

In 1987, 114 million people attended a stage event—up 6.5 percent from 1980. But the number of events the average person attended annually dropped from 3.8 to 2.6, nearly one-third in only seven years.[9] As a result, total admissions were only 296 million patrons, down 27 percent from 1980.

The theater's predicament is not unique. Unable to meet their payrolls, symphony orchestras and opera and dance companies are asking their musicians and performers to accept hefty salary cuts or a package of other contract concessions, or are canceling parts of their seasons. Others, sinking deeper into seas of red ink, float on the verge of insolvency or go under altogether.[10]

EXPLAINING FALLING ATTENDANCE

How do we explain the shrinking number of admissions? Possible causes that come to mind are competition from electronic home entertainment such as television and videocassette recorders, increased difficulty in getting to venues, or the rising price of tickets. Shouldn't we add to the list patrons' shrinking time?

The miracle of electronics has generated enormous revenues to performers. But it has also created new competition for live performance and, for many, more convenient access to a medium formerly reserved for the concert hall or theater. The radio broadcast was the first intrusion into the domain of the concert hall. Then came phonograph records, tapes, compact disks, television, and the videocassette recorder. Low-cost electronics brought performances to any time and place, even in the commuter's auto during rush hour, as Sir Neville pointed out. Since nearly all households in the nation now own TVs, and a majority also have VCRs and cable services, performance-going has become a ubiquitous event, virtually unbounded by time or by space. So why be locked into a schedule? Why leave the comfort of home?

The electronic performing arts, as opposed to the live in-the-flesh performances, are bound to be time-plus activities, for they can be enjoyed synchronically with others. In concert hall or theater, few are the opportunities for doing something else during the performance. But at home, one can cook, work, or even eat popcorn while watching *Parsifal* or Michael Jackson.

The difficulty of getting to the concert or play or show or dance performance also could be a reason for poor attendance. In all performance categories, however, the most recent answers given by Harris Poll respondents show that getting there is easier than ever.[11] Because ready access encourages attendance, and accessibility appears to have improved, accessibility cannot be blamed for the attendance problem.

An obvious culprit would be high and rising theater production costs that squeeze profits and may force companies out of business. High-tech musicals like "Les Miserables," "Cats," "Chess," and "Starlight Express" today range up to $11 million to produce.[12] William J. Baumol and William G. Bowen, in their classic study of the performing arts, show how rising production costs translate into declining box office receipts. The "technology of live performance," or the resistance of the performing arts industry to factors that improve labor productivity and contain costs, are to blame, they say.[13] Technology introduced into manufacturing industries has saved labor and cut cost. In the labor-intensive arts, however, where the work is done almost entirely by the performers and backstage personnel, few opportunities exist for using technology in the same economizing way.

"It takes one and one-half hours of labor to execute a Schubert trio scored for a half-hour performance," assert the Baumol-Bowen team, "and that is all there is to the matter. Removing Judge Brack from the cast of Hedda Gabler would certainly reduce labor input to Ibsen's masterpiece, but it would also destroy the product."[14] Thus, if performers must do the things they have done for decades and centuries, and do them in the same way without the aid of technology, the performing arts seem destined to remain costly to produce and to attend.

As the costs of production rise, so must the prices of admission. And as consumers face higher ticket prices, say the immutable laws of supply and demand, the demand for tickets must decline. But have ticket prices, in fact, gone up?

A contemporary Rip van Winkle would be pleasantly surprised to find that equipping a modern kitchen—as we learned several chapters back—costs less than it did before he fell asleep many years before. The same holds true for theater ticket prices. After adjusting for inflation, the average top ticket sold today fetches a price 9 percent lower than it did sixty years ago.[15] If the decline holds true for ticket prices in general, the cost of admission disappears as an excuse for a price-conscious van Winkle not to attend. Or for the rest of us.

But a night at the theater can be costly in other respects. Attending is costly where it hurts *Busy Bodies* most: in time. If today's Rip van Winkle gets the same Schubert trio as in days of yore, and the length of the production remains unchanged, Mr. van Winkle's higher-valued time will discourage his attendance. Can't the three musicians save **T**ime without sacrificing the listeners' **S**atisfaction by playing the adagios allegro, and the allegros vivace? Unfortunately not. Although the players cannot adjust to the *BB* factor with faster tempos, the patrons can adjust by staying away and putting their time to other uses. Hence, patrons hold sway because it is their demand for the performance that is flexible and, depending on their willingness to attend, determines the fate of the event. That, in a nutshell, is what has been happening to the arts.

Is all of this mere speculation? To find out, speak for yourselves *vox populi*. Of all the reasons respondents gave when Mr. Harris asked, "why don't you go out more often to live performances?" which headed the list? It was—the envelope please!—"I don't have enough time to do it."[16] Time scarcity outranked the costs of tickets or of baby sitting, or the difficulty of getting to the theater, or any of a number of other excuses. Ticket prices were of course important but, in discussing his survey results, Mr. Harris hit the nail squarely on its head with, "time is much more important than money to the public nowadays."[17] People are diverting time, as it becomes more scarce, to activities that yield higher **S/T**.

SAVING THE PERFORMING ARTS

Threatening as these trends are for the future, they must also hold clues to boosting sagging attendance. Considering, for example, the basic **S/T** ratio, three basic approaches offer promise: raising **S**, lowering **T**, or doing both at once. Here's how.

Simultaneously Raising Satisfaction and Lowering Time

Few things are either/or matters, a generalization which also holds true for **S** and **T**. **S** can be augmented, or **T** shrunk, but a broad frontal attack on both may give the best result. Deliberately but delicately balancing lower **T** with higher **S** could save the theater for example.

American patrons flocked to see the Royal Shakespeare Company production of Charles Dickens's "The Life and Adventures of Nicholas Nickleby." What lured the crowds was publicity that asked, "What's got 432 lighting cues, 622 music cues, and 843 shoes? What's got 356 wigs, 751 props, and a humpbacked Glaswegian hag? What's got 150 characters, 350 costumes, 10 tons of scenery, and 99 muffins?" Clearly, an intensive experience was promised. Audiences, though commiting $100 per ticket and eight-and-a-half hours for the complete marathon, left the theater exhilarated rather than exhausted. Boosting **S** to offset a high **T** filled the houses.

Louis Moreau Gottschalk, one of America's first classical composers, also knew how to achieve just the right balance. To dispel any lingering doubts that his *Escenas Compestres* was suited to the occasion of its commission—the inauguration of Havana's new opera house—and to make obvious the fact that the production promised a high **S**, Mr. Gottschalk subtitled the opus, "An Opera of a Thousand." But from the first note of the overture to the final drop of the curtain, the entire work required all of eleven minutes to perform. So the piece, low in **T** and high in **S**, yielded a huge **S/T** (gazinta, remember?). But perhaps it was too disappointingly brief to the premiere's international audience, many of whom had traveled great distances to be on hand for the festive, but abrupt occasion.

Reducing **Time**

If audiences are discouraged by performances that are "too long," why not condense them? After all, books are condensed. Lengths of theater productions have indeed shortened as time has grown more precious. Performances in the Greek theater filled an entire day, and in medieval times dramatizations of biblical stories continued for several days, but in our day opportunities to see sustained theatrical performances are rare. We simply haven't time. (*Escenas Compestres* was perhaps just a tad short.)

Patrons are more likely to attend an event when they, instead of someone else, control the amount of time spent, and the ways it is spent. No matter how much we wonder whether the awful hours are worth the glorious minutes in an opera like *Parsifal,* leaving at intermission (if there is one) is an unappealing way out. This issue of time control may explain rising attendance at art museums, for patrons can spend as much, or as little time as they wish viewing the exhibits.

In the museum, technology eases the search for the best pieces. Electronic guides that offer prerecorded tours save the time and effort of fumbling around with catalogues to find out what is on view and where it is on display. Without such devices, discovering the treasures of a major museum can absorb many precious hours. Aided by one of those little black boxes that plug into the ear, the visitor who has budgeted only an hour for the Louvre will quickly discover that Mona Lisa and the Winged Victory of Samothrace are in residence, find out how to get to both without searching endless corridors, and still have time left for an aperitif on the Left Bank.

Another approach is to deal with the **T** of the activities surrounding a night out at the theater—activities like making reservations, parking the car, having dinner. If travel promoters have learned the merits of packaged tours, why can't packaging, with a twist, also work for arts promoters, and make the time required for an evening out total to less than the sum of the parts? The contents, instead of professional meetings combined with touring, are dining and shopping and the other events coupled to an evening at the theater. Package deals that include dinner at the theater save the separate trips to restaurants and to the theater for the show, reducing the overall **T** required.

Ernest Fleischmann discovered the wisdom of packaging cuisine with culture when, in the 1960s, he took over one of the nation's venerable concert venues, then in its nadir. To Mr. Fleischmann, attending the Hollywood Bowl's outdoor summer programs could be far more than easy listening under the stars on a balmy evening. Packaging the event to include picnicking al fresco, he doubled average attendance to 12,000 per concert.[18]

Saving time through packaging related events into a gala "mega-event" is one way to improve culture's gazinta. An alternative is dressing up packages more handsomely to increase the appeal of the contents. America's answer to concerts in England's stately homes, or opera at Glyndebourne, is a concert series sponsored by Los Angeles's De Camera Society. Scheduling concerts by leading chamber groups in buildings of historical importance or architectural merit has brought in full houses of patrons who simultaneously enjoy visual and aural pleasures. Similarly, the directors of countless festivals such as Santa Fe's opera, music at Tanglewood in the Berkshires, and Seattle's Wagner Ring cycle orgy have discovered the merits of combining a vacation with an intensive musical or theatrical experience. If growth in the number of such events is any measure, the results pay off handsomely. Better wrapping brings us straightaway to improving **S**, another way to save the performing arts.

Augmenting Satisfaction

John Wilkes Booth tried to liven up the experience of attending a show by assassinating President Lincoln. Mr. Booth failed to realize, however, that his one-shot effort was, at best, good for only a one-night stand. Other opportunities for enlivening theater have longer runs.

Museums, with the flexibility to change exhibits by buying and borrowing new works, can repackage and rewrap with relative ease. Considering the prices that masterworks currently trade for, museum patrons are in for an experience high in **S**—vicarious **S**, in any case. In the 1980s Rembrandts and Van Goghs brought from $10 million to $44 million at auction, topped only by the 1990 recordbreaker, Van Gogh's "Portrait of Dr. Gachet" at $82.5 million. The extraordinary prices speak directly to prospective patrons, declaring the importance of the works and the worth of time spent seeing them first-hand. After all, if the works exhibited brought such big bucks, the time spent looking at them must be worthwhile. So must the other great masterworks, even those not sold recently. Thus reasons the visitor, persuaded by the market. Such reasoning is boosting total attendance at U.S. art museums by 2.5 million visitors each year.[19]

Symphonies, facing the double challenge of falling attendance and an unresponsive repertoire, are in deeper trouble. Noël Coward once observed that "People are wrong when they say that opera is not what it used to be. It *is* what it used to be. That is what is wrong with it."[20] Ernest Fleischmann echoes that sentiment for the symphony. "The orchestra as we know it is dead," declared the articulate and knowledgeable executive director of the Los Angeles Philharmonic, "dead because concerts have become dull and predictable."[21]

As the musical repertoire has shrunk into a core of venerated masterpieces that each year recedes further into history, musical performance has become re-creative, not creative art. And audiences have registered their opinion of re-creative art by voting with their feet. Each year another one million long-haired music lovers find other ways to use their time.[22]

Modernizing the static repertoire by incorporating new works on the programs only seems to make matters worse. It is a Catch-22 situation. For one thing, performances of new fare are rare because composers are less prolific today than in the days of Bach, Beethoven, and Brahms. For another, audiences stay away by the thousands from premieres of new works.

This is because the symphony and opera cater to a remarkably conservative, unyielding audience for whom modern fare is an exercise in forbearance. Experiments in innovative programming show that patrons know what they like, and like what they know. A tally of attendance at different types of programming offered in London's Royal Festival Hall demonstrates the risks. "Adventurous programs," which included at least one piece that was not part of the standard repertoire, reduced attendance by one-fourth compared to programs devoted exclusively to war horses.[23] At New York City Opera, a company noted for innovation, a "contemporary" work (defined as one composed after World War I!) will fill the house only to 39 percent of capacity compared with the usual 65 percent. The corresponding decline at London's Covent Garden is from 83 to 67 percent.[24] Theater audiences, in contrast, seem in fact to crave innovation.

"Tell me and I'll forget; show me and I may remember; involve me and I'll understand." So says an old Chinese proverb that apparently works in the theater. **S** rises as audiences get involved in the action. Participation galvanizes the audiences' energies and enthusiasm by incorporating them as integral parts of the interactive drama, rather than as passive witnesses.

Participatory theater dates at least from Kurt Weill's Germany of the 1930s and debuted in the U.S. when theatergoers were invited onto the stage to dance with the cast of the wildly successful be-in rock musical "Hair." Matters theatric progressed another step when, in the late '60s, the cast of the Living Theater's "Paradise Now" talked the audience into shedding their clothes and marching into the street. More recently, "Nicholas Nickleby" audiences were encouraged to pelt the cast with muffins as the actors strolled through the audience. Audiences danced with the cast of "Tony 'n' Tina's Wedding" and played members of the entourage. In "Tamara," a mystery melodrama staged as a set of simultaneous events taking place in various rooms converted to miniature stages, each member of the audience followed a character through the action, literally pursuing the actor from room to room as a variety of convoluted plots unfolded. These were happenings that limited neither the audience's behavior nor the **S** they gained from the experience.

Whether the market will sustain the theater's future depends not only on the quality of performances *it* produces, but on the quality of entertainment produced in *other* arts areas, and on the quality of the large set of activities, performing and otherwise, that vie for the would-be or actual theatergoer's time. By "quality" these days, we really mean rising **S/T**. So perhaps extravagantly high-tech productions which promise high **S**, that can compete with other activities, will be the savior theater so desperately needs.

CAN HIGH-TECH SOLVE THE THEATER'S PROBLEMS?

There was a time when the staged musical ranked as America's major cultural export. In a dramatic reversal, the musical theater is now almost entirely dominated by composers, lyricists, designers, and directors from across the Atlantic. "The English have learned how to substitute spectacle for story," explains critic Robert Brustein. "They know how to exploit rock conventions on the stage; they understand the secret of substituting trance-inducing rhythms for a lyrical score."[25]

America had its chance to pioneer the high-tech show, for it was born here in the early 1960s with "Hair." No serious message to ponder, just pure simple enjoyment. Once launched, the successful high-tech musical could only get more high-tech. And more successful. Yet it took the Brits to make it happen; it was a chance for the Empire to strike back.

"Jesus Christ Superstar," "Tommy," "Joseph and the Amazing Technicolor Dreamcoat," and "Evita" arrived in the 1970s. Then came "Nicholas Nickleby," "Cats," "Starlight Express," "Les Miserables," and "Phantom of the Opera" in the '80s, and "Miss Saigon" in the '90s. High-tech commoditization had invaded the musical theater with a vengeance.

Andrew Lloyd Webber has scored (in both meanings of that term) most of Broadway's recent smash hits. He more than anyone else, and his high-tech musical froths more than anything else, earn the credit for keeping the theater afloat. In the following interview Mr. Lloyd Webber affirms the theory—readers will note—that raising the **S** of entertainment time is the avenue to success on the beleaguered boulevard of Broadway.

—A Conversation with Andrew Lloyd Webber[26]—

Busy Bodies: Perhaps it's the understatement of the year to say that the musical extravaganzas that you composed for London's West End and Broadway are smashing successes.

Mr. Lloyd Webber: Well, I wouldn't . . .

BB: Now, now. Critics, who variously dub you "musical theater's current genius," "a technological wizard," "founder of the megahit," credit you with tipping the musical's creative locus from New York to London, and for cornering the musicals market.

Mr. LW: Thank you.

BB: These hits have made everyone—your financial backers, your audiences, yourself—better off. Investors in "Cats," the musical that you based on T. S. Eliot's *Old Possum's Book of Practical Cats,* recouped their $4 million investment in a short thirty-nine weeks after its opening, and by 1990 had earned a 2,000 percent return on their money.[27] "Phantom of the Opera" set new Broadway advance-sale records with a pre-opening night take of $16 million in sales and the backers got checks in the mail for nearly half of their capital nine months after opening. "Aspects of Love" cost $11 million but took in $8 million even before the curtain went up. According to the press, your income runs to something over $200 million a year.[28]

MR. LW: Well, uhhh . . .

BB: Is it a coincidence that "Cats," "Evita, "Chess," "Starlight Express," "Phantom," "42nd Street," "Les Miserables," "Jerome Robbins' Broadway" were all very expensive to produce?

MR. LW: Yes. I mean, no, it was no coinci . . .

BB: Each musical, as it opened, set new records. "Starlight Express" cost $8 million to bring to Broadway. That's $3 million more than "Cats" several years earlier.

MR. LW: Right . . .

BB: Audiences queued up for tickets because they knew how costly these mega-musicals were to produce, and that they could expect to get a lot for their ticket dollars.

MR. LW: I . . .

BB: What audience wasn't awed by the huge casts and elaborate scenery of "Nicholas Nickleby," moved around by state-of-the-art electronic equipment, or by the roller skate gangs whizzing through that fantastic maze of moving bridges and ramps in "Starlight Express," or by Grizabella's ascent up the telescoping ladder to the top of the "Cats" stage, or by Old Deuteronomy's heavenward ascent on the enormous doughnut that flashed spotlights through fog effects like an object from outer space, or by "Phantom's" huge chandelier that rose over their heads to the throbbing rock beat of a human heart gone crazy? Is it great acting to a great script, or great singing to great music that brings in the audiences, or is it those mechanical marvels of a technological age?

MR. LW: Well, I wouldn't say . . .

BB: The musicals that you compose are far more than theatrical productions. They are events, they are mega-spectacles that demonstrate how much audiences want to be bombarded by imagery as intense and spectacular as in "Star Wars." Haven't the visual coups, rather than the sounds, oddly enough, saved the musical?

MR. LW: Ummm.

BB: You're not alone in transforming the musical into something more than a recital for soloists, backed up by a big orchestra and chorus. The Met's production of "Turandot" had the audience gasping, but they were prepared for they had seen or heard about Zeffirelli's "La Bohème" and "Tosca" and expected to be dazzled visually once again, even if it meant that Puccini's music played second fiddle, overwhelmed as it was by the sumptuousity of the sets.

MR. LW: . . . .
BB: What, besides phenomenal box office success, do they all have in common?
MR. LW: Glitz.
BB: Did I hear you say commoditization?
MR. LW: If you like.
BB: Thank you for your time.

Commoditization—using the latest high-tech innovations—is partly, perhaps largely, responsible for the musical theater's current good fortune, and Mr. Lloyd Webber is its commoditizer nonpareil. Another component of the *BB* factor also plays a complementary role in the theater's salvation. It is our penchant for instant gratification. The high-tech musical appeals by manipulation. Audiences have no time or urge to think, only to be overwhelmed by the commoditization of brassy scores, garishly stylized sets, vividly colored costumes, effervescent motion, electronic gimmickry, visual trickery, massive crowd scenes, and deafening music fused into an orgasmic whole (more and more about less and less?). Effects are comprehended easily and in a flash. Pondering takes longer. No time for that. That is what Broadway's musical theater has finally achieved, and it is devices such as these that serve it and will save it.

Oh well, there's nothing wrong with that. Susan Sontag said so. "High culture has no monopoly upon refinement," she wrote. "The man who insists on high and serious pleasures is depriving himself of pleasure." Accepting kitsch "makes the man of good taste cheerful, where before he ran the risk of being chronically frustrated. It is good for the digestion."[29]

THE DEATH OF THE LIVE PERFORMING ARTS?

Prone to rising prices and falling demand, performing arts organizations find themselves in a precarious state. Innovative programming carries its risks for forms such as the symphony and opera, and participatory theater perhaps has had its day. The well-kept secret for preserving the performing arts, as a form of entertainment that must bid for the patron's time, is to increase the attractiveness and intensity of the experience either by shortening **T** —for example by packaging related activities—or by increasing the **S**—as by high-tech commoditization.

Ironically, the theater, suffering the largest audience declines of all, offers the greatest opportunities for innovation. People go to the theater to be amazed, astonished that the celebrated stars are real people, and that life can be so gloriously embellished on the stage. But it takes much to amaze a society jaded by the tricks and gimmickry of a technological age. To succeed, it has to be awfully good stuff. Some innovators, among them Andrew Lloyd Webber, seem to have found the magic formula. That formula that has so enlivened theatrical performances might be the key to renewing and saving other varieties of the performing arts. Short of innovations, such events seem destined for the fate of the legendary tree that, for lack of an audience, drops to the ground unseen and unheard in an empty forest.

If prospects look dim for the performing arts organizations, matters are worse yet for the churches. Attendance is down, with only limited prospects for reversing the trend. That's next.

6:00
THE MYSTERY OF THE EMPTY PEW

"Blessed are the church-, temple-, and synagogue-goers, for they shall go alone."
—from "The Beatitudes" (approximately)

Religion offers people a means to confront the concept of time, as abstract as it may be. Yet the ways that people transform abstraction into reality may spell the death of organized religion. Jeremy Rifkin observes that "every religion holds forth the prospect of either defeating time, escaping time, overcoming time, reissuing time, or denying time altogether. . . . We come to believe in rebirth, resurrection, and reincarnation as ways of avoiding the inevitability of biological death."[1]

Faced with the practical problems of sagging attendance and rising defections, the institution that has provided that time-honored refuge from biological death seems doomed by its own pursuits. The church, at least the Protestant branch, trapped itself by equating time waste with sin. Daily life should be conducted methodically and efficiently, with particular care given to the use of time. "Not leisure and enjoyment, but only activity serves to increase the glory of God," wrote Max Weber in his gloomy definition of the Protestant Ethic. "Waste of time is thus the first and in principle deadliest of sins."[2] Ironically, people have come to regard churchgoing as a waste of time, hence the "deadliest of sins."

PLEASE, REV., COULD YOU PREACH THE SERMON A LITTLE FASTER? . . .

With an increasing number of activities competing for a fixed amount of time, the church fathers can only hang on to their followers by decreasing **T**, the time required for participation, or by increasing **S**, the rewards so gained.

Can **T** be reduced? Can the sermons be preached more quickly? Can the hymns be sung at a faster clip? Can the psalms be recited more swiftly? Can the collection be taken up more rapidly? Can the Sacred Word be read more speedily? No to all of the above.

. . . OR MAKE IT MORE INTERESTING?

If **T** can't be reduced, what are the possibilities for increasing the **S** of the churchgoing experience? In a word, limited. That depends on the organization's flexibility, on the message it preaches, and on its uses of technology to accomplish both.

Christian fundamentalists, by espousing the need for a total commitment to Jesus as Savior and the Bible as authority, seem to offer their adherents high "take-home value." On the other hand, the leaders of the traditional denominations adapt dogma, belief, or practice to the modern world only with considerable reluctance—a point I will demonstrate later. Those preachers who save worshipers' time by bringing church into the home are also having some success. According to the ratings, evangelists teaching and preaching over the airwaves have won a hands-down victory in luring viewers away from traditional churchgoing. The Rev. Robert Schuller's "Hour of Power" attracts the largest audience, with Jimmy Swaggart's weekly show beamed from Baton Rouge second, and Tulsa evangelist Oral Roberts next. Only one program produced by a traditional group, the Paulist fathers' "Insight," makes the list of the fifteen top favorites.[3]

Just as individual denominations compete with each other for members, churchgoing competes with other time-absorbing activities. In those respects and others, purveyors of religious services are no different from those producing and marketing more tangible goods and services. Consumers dissatisfied with one producer's product switch to another's. When enough customers make that decision, the maker of the inferior good must choose between turning out a better product or going out of business. Although churches can hang on longer than most conventional businesses, when their entire range of products fails to please, consumers will simply spend their time on something altogether different.

Crass and commercial the reasoning may be, yet church attendance data illustrate that people are making these crass and commercial decisions. The trends are clear: as some churchgoers switch to a more rewarding faith, others drop out altogether.

FEW IN PEW AND PULPIT

Americans are a churchgoing, God-fearing people. No wonder our money proclaims that it is in Him that We Trust. Ninety-six percent of Americans pray and 94 percent believe in God.[4] (Presumably the 2 percent in between address their prayers to whom it may concern.) Yet, of this vast majority of believers, fewer than half attend church or synagogue regularly.[5] Although they are giving less financial support to religions, and less time to organized worship, Americans in general are deepening their religious belief. A rising proportion of Christians believe, for example, that Jesus was either God or the Son of God.[6]

The up-trend in belief and the counter-trends in participation appear as contradictory as do interpretations of the Bible. How can belief intensify as membership, giving, and attendance wane? The *BB* factor answers the question. Avowing a belief in God takes no time, and not much more is required to pray to Him/Her. But regular churchgoing—the chief overt act of worship—is a very different matter. It requires the greatest time commitment of all, and it seems to be dropping off fastest. Continuing a membership requires neither time nor effort and many once-active members see little reason to terminate an affiliation even when their interest wanes. That downtrend is the slowest. Many continue to make donations, another measure of commitment, although when they attend church less frequently, the urge to continue financial support also diminishes.

The churches that once were the cradles of American religion and culture are the religious organizations currently suffering the worst crisis. Once known as the old-line, the traditional liberal Protestant congregations are now more aptly referred to as the sideline. In an average year, the Episcopal Church loses 2,800 members, the United Church of Christ 11,000 members, the Presbyterian Church (USA) 44,000, and the United Methodist Church a whopping 70,000. The fraction of population embraced by the largest religious group in America, the Roman Catholic Church, has dropped to one in five.[7]

The polls show that, contrary to widespread opinion, members are not leaving to join the conservative, evangelical faiths. They are leaving, period, to join the ranks of the nonaffiliated, the dropouts who no longer drop-in on Sunday morning. They still may be "believers," but they are no longer "belongers"—a distinction drawn by pollster George Gallup, Jr. Gallup reports that a rising proportion of adults fall into the "unchurched" category, up five percentage points from a decade earlier. Three out of four believe that "a person can be a good Christian or Jew without attending a church or synagogue," and their belief has saved them considerable time.[8]

Institutional loyalty is also indexed by the number of dollars contributed. Two surveys cast light on the subject. A study of Protestants' generosity, undertaken by empty tomb, inc., showed a sizeable reduction in the proportion of their income that churchgoers dropped into the collection plate. Giving fell from 3.1 percent in 1968 to 1.8 percent in 1985.[9]

The Rev. Andrew Greeley, whose studies of Catholicism established him as a sociologist well before he became a best-selling novelist, comes up with somewhat different figures, but the trend is the same. From his survey, Catholics and Protestants alike dropped 2.2 percent of their incomes in the collection plates in 1960, but twenty-five years later, the Catholics' donations had fallen to 1.1 percent.[10] And the loss in contributions has been monumental: by Fr. Greeley's estimate, an astonishing $6 billion per annum.[11]

The Empty Pew . . .

As the collection plates become empty, so do the pews. Although people seem to have deepened their commitments to the concept of religion, as they have to the importance of the perform-

ing arts, they are less willing to give their time to either. Membership, giving, and belief make no claim on time. Attendance does.

When there was little competition from other activities, churches, temples, and synagogues were full. When more compelling activities won out in bidding for fixed time, church attendance suffered. That seems to have been true for a long time. The 1851 Religious Census of Britain, taken at the peak of the Industrial Revolution, called attention to the problem of low church attendance.[12] People were too occupied with their work and the struggles of adjusting to city life to go to church. Yet, attendance boomed in America during the Great Depression when a lack of jobs made time available for more spiritual exercises.

Since then, the *BB* factor has taken its toll. In 1958, when people were asked whether they had gone to a service during the past week, half said they had. That proportion has eroded to 40 percent, with the old-line traditionalists registering the lowest attendance and the fundamentalists the highest.[13]

To put the explanation in now-familiar terms, the traditional religious organizations have failed to increase the rewards of churchgoing, compared to the amount of time the activity takes, and compared to the rewards gained from other activities. If a great religious revival is sweeping the country, as the telepreachers claim, the statistics fail to show it.

. . . And the Empty Pulpit

The vacuum appearing in pulpits mirrors the vacuum appearing in pews. The number of U.S. clergy per capita has fallen steadily since the turn of the century, leaving fewer shepherds to tend smaller flocks.[14] As a result, the major Christian traditionalists—Lutherans, Methodists, Presbyterians, Disciples of Christ, and Roman Catholics—face the predicament of a steadily aging ministry approaching retirement. From 1970 to 1985, the typical priest, for example, "aged" statistically from 47.6 to 53.4 years old.[15]

As the number professionally committed to God's work falls, so do enrollments in theological studies, the source of new personnel. For every three priests who resign or die, there are only two in the pipeline.[16] Due to the shortage, seminaries that once admitted a fraction of applicants are now inclined to take nearly all comers. Quality falls as admission standards fall, a sore fact that became apparent in a study of seminary admissions which found that the top tenth intellectually has been lost and the type now admitted is more dependent, sexually indifferent, and conservative.[17]

Priests and nuns, too, are exiting the religious life by the thousands, and the Catholic Church—not coincidentally the most doctrinally dogmatic and unyielding of all—is suffering a decline of crisis proportions. Overworked, sexually troubled, demoralized, and frustrated, 42 percent of priests now resign within twenty-five years of their ordination, and the rate is higher among the younger clerics. If the high attrition continues, a common greeting among bishops in the future may well be "long time, no see."

Defections among nuns and the reduced number of novices entering convents illustrates how the **S/T** of religious vocations—like everything else—is influenced by the **S/T**s of alternative callings.

Nuntheless . . .

The veterans who returned from the battlefields of World War II displaced the Rosie the Riveters who had womanned the assembly lines. Religious vocations boomed as many ex-Rosies took the veil as the best way to use time that, for many, was now in surplus. But the movement of women into the labor force in the mid-1960s multiplied the opportunities for gainful employment at salaries many times the subsistence wages nuns received, and bid them to leap over the wall. And many took the leap.

The number of U.S. nuns has tumbled almost 40 percent since 1966 when the flood of women's vocations reached high tide. With only a trickle of new vocations, convents had little new blood; in a dozen years, the median nun's age rose by eleven years, from 55 to 66.[18]

What of the future? If defections and attrition continue at current rates, it will not be many decades before the pews and pulpits—at least those of the traditional faiths—will be empty. The mystery of the empty pew is solved, but that revelation tells little about ways to refill it. Streamlining the service by shortening **T** seems a near-impossibility. Raising the **S** of the experience by boosting the rewards of attendance offers more promise.

INCREASING REWARDS ETERNAL AND TEMPORAL

In the sixteenth century, the established Church rose to the challenges of the Protestant Reformers by enhancing the rewards of faithful attendance. Rome's counterreformers, searching for ways to mend the tears in "the seamless robe of Christ," plumbed Genesis, the Book of Revelations, and the Song of Songs for the graphic descriptions of the heavenly Jerusalem that would soon decorate their ecclesiastical real estate. Great Baroque edifices sprang up in city and countryside. Construction began in earnest on the masterpiece of them all, St. Peter's. The severe, somber Gothic structures built five centuries before were flamboyantly "Rococoed." The humblest village churches were adorned with images of angels and saints. Incense, lavishly brocaded vestments, and choirs chanting propers in Latin, gave olfactory, visual, and auditory meaning to St. Paul's words, "Eye hath not seen, nor ear heard, neither have entered into the heart of man the things which God hath prepared for them." The heavenly Jerusalem was right here at home, in church. The Counter-Reformation arrested the heavy-handed moves of the Reformers. Change won out.

Today's compensations for being religious cannot hold a candle to the rewards available in days past. Many back then came to believe that eternal bliss rewarded temporary misery. What happened on earth mattered little compared to what must happen thereafter. "The world was but an inn at which humans spent a night on their voyage to eternity, so what difference could it make if the food was poor or the innkeeper a brute?"[19]

St. Catherine of Siena (1347–80), for example, subsisted only on raw vegetables, water, and bread, flagellated herself thrice daily, and, as an act of self-mortification, sucked the pus from the breast sores of a woman. Her mortification was surpassed perhaps only by St. Veronica Giuliani (1660–1727) who, it is reported, would dine on a plate of cat vomit and top off her lunch by licking the refectory floor clean.[20] Traditions have changed, to be sure, and most of those committed to the religious life today at least have less peculiar eating habits.

Although Christian manifestations of fervent zealotry are far rarer today, the modern church is trying in its own ways to keep going in the face of declining donations, membership, and attendance. Retrenchment has been the traditionalists' response to decline: fewer church services and disemployment of the clergy, and a resistance to modernization. It is this reactive stance that prompts theologians like Harvey Cox to criticize traditional Christian belief as outmoded and functionally stagnant. "How often I have been tempted to jettison this all-too-human little freckle on the Body of Christ,'' he writes, ''and stay home on Sunday with better music on the hi-fi and better theology from the bookshelf.''[21] By voting with their feet, many reared in the traditional faiths cast ballots with Dr. Cox.

The evangelicals opt for an active response, and their expanding membership roles show it. A million Hispanic Americans have defected from the ''native'' Catholic faith that once claimed virtually the world's entire Hispanic population, and converted to fundamentalist and Pentecostal Protestantism.[22] Although hardly modern in outlook, the evangelical Protestants take pride in their missionary fervor and emotional power, public declarations of religious faith, stern pronouncements on religious truth, conservative interpretation of Biblical teachings, sing-along choruses, and emphasis on self-help. All this offers Latinos something different and apparently more appealing. A committed Roman Catholic writes of his astonishment at what he witnessed from the back rows of evangelical churches: ''kids with tattoos, tough kids, kids who testify to having been on the streets as recently as last week, kids who spent their childhoods on drugs, in gangs, in trouble; kids now in suits and ties, singing hymns to Christ. They are not converted to holy milksops. They are aggressive men who have discovered spiritual empowerment.''[23]

Eastern faiths, applying layers of exotica to the religious experience, have multiplied like the fishes and loaves of Biblical fame. The followers of Park Chang No Kyo's Olive Tree Movement drink Mr. Park's bath water to cure their physical ills, and number two million worldwide. Japan-based Denshin-kyo (''Religion of Electricity'') worships electricity, manifested in the light bulb, as the form of deity, and ranks Thomas A. Edison, not surprisingly, as a prophet.[24] (The late Anglican Bishop James Pike explained the rise of exotic Eastern religions and the parallel decline of Western Christianity in these *BB*-like terms: The Islams have it right; three wives and one God are better than one wife and three Gods.)

With their offer of something new, nontraditionalists hang on to their own followers and recruit bored members from the major faiths. Take the cases of religious groups that cater to dual markets, that look to past and future, and that exploit miracles to merge abstract faith with contemporary reality.

The Assembly of God, in an earlier day the ''church across the tracks,'' thrives on educational, economic, and cultural diversity by operating two very different churches in every town. At one, Oldsmobiles fill the parking lot and handbills advertise weekend retreats on how to make money. At the other, pickup trucks are lined up outside and bulletin boards announce square dances. The result: in ten short years, membership has surpassed the growth rate of every U.S. mainline religious organization, and the Assembly of God now ranks as the largest Pentecostal group in the world.

In a few brief years, the Unarius Academy of Science has grown from a small base in southern California to 10,000 members worldwide (including Poland and Nigeria). Known by the modest acronym URIEL (Universal, Radiant, Infinite, Eternal Light), the founder holds that in fifty-five previous lives on earth (''a kind of General Motors proving ground for the cosmos'') she was, among others, Bathsheba, Buddha, Charlemagne, Mary Magdalene, Mona Lisa, and Socrates, and that her late husband was none other than Jesus Christ himself. Her devotees prepare themselves for ''the dawning of the age of Unarius'' by practicing past-life therapy, a process that requires investigating former lives as ''the angels or devils they used to be.''[25]

The announcement of a miracle—or an *apparent* miracle—is the invitation that curious and devout alike wait for as an excuse to ''go'' to church. Fellini-esque scenes like weeping pictures and blood-squirting statues can always be counted on to attract a good crowd. In recent history, a statue of Jesus bled in a Pennsylvania church, leading the vicar, by some mysterious logic, to reason that he was the Pope. It was standing room only at a California mission when someone discovered that Jesus appeared in photographs taken of a weeping statue. Thousands of pilgrims flocked to a house near Montreal to view a weeping-bleeding Madonna although the statue's owner later admitted to smearing the figure with after-shave lotion and his own blood. A painting of the Virgin Mary appeared to weep at a Chicago church across the street from a supermarket; many of the 5,000 visitors who made pilgrimages synchronically combined venerating with shopping.[26]

Coast-to-coast, traditional faiths are putting untraditional devices to good use. Although the eucharist remains the centerpiece of worship, the liturgy at New York's mammoth Cathedral of St. John the Divine has been enriched with African chants and Zen

Buddhist meditation, liturgical dance, an Earth Mass accompanied by the sounds of birds and whales, and an aerialist's high-wire acts. On the west coast, Pasadena's All Saints Episcopal Church blends spirited social activism with solid spiritual leadership. The parish takes strong liberal stands on issues ranging from racism to disarmament. Ninety activities offer something for everyone. Immigrants are relocated from skid row and the homeless are provided with food and shelter. Musical fare ranges from the classics to black gospel. Membership is booming and the budget has doubled in five years. Both edifices are jammed not only every Sunday but on weekdays and, since All Saints is located in southern California, so is their parking lot.[27]

Madison Avenue to the rescue? Some religious institutions are not above using the slick, professionally managed marketing campaigns that the commercial world finds so effective. After all, the churches sell a product too. An enterprising Hasidic group, trying to woo inactive Jews back into the fold, maintains a fleet of "Mitzvah Tanks," large vans that roam the streets of New York City offering on-site prayer and literature. The Episcopal Church's Ad Project welcomes back lapsed worshipers "regardless of race, creed, color, or the number of times you've been born." One ad shows pallbearers lugging a casket down the steps of a church, with the tagline, "Will it take six strong men to bring you back into the church?" and another, featuring Henry VIII, is captioned, "In the church started by a man who had six wives, forgiveness goes without saying."[28] It will take more than advertising, however, to reverse the exodus, no matter how clever the catch-line.

THE DECLINE AND FALL OF ROME II

While Protestants and Jews seek new directions to rekindle the fires of their faiths, the Roman Catholic hierarchy stands as a bulwark against change. The intractability of the institution that has extended its hegemony over 841 million people worldwide is of long standing for, in taking its title seriously, Catholicism seeks a universal dogma, the same to everyone, everywhere, and every *when*. In a world where the only constant is change, steadfast adherence to the last criterion has gotten the Church into the most trouble. Their commitment to a monolithic and unyielding faith waning, Catholics are discovering that the Church no longer has Mass appeal, so to speak.

It is not that, over the years, the Church has refused to countenance change. Charging interest on loans was condemned as usury in the Middle Ages, for usury contravened natural law by "selling time."[29] The Church no longer condemns usury. Nor does the Church hold to a once-unqualified preaching that there is no salvation outside its walls. Priests, bishops, even popes have married in the past, but no more. On some matters, Rome seems willing to bend. But not very far.

In the most far-reaching set of ecclesiastical changes undertaken in the current century, Vatican II reformed ceremonies that had remained unaltered for 400 years. Out the chancel window went the smells and bells, long-winded sermons, and Latin as the official language of the Mass. In the narthex door came an unadorned order of service featuring swingy folk Masses, relevant homilies, modern language, and, in theory, a pluralism that promised tolerance for new ideas.

The changes in liturgy, though well-intentioned, only seemed to erode the quality—the **S** of the experience. Take sermons for example. Before Vatican II, a spare two-in-five gave "excellent" marks to preaching but, in a post-Council survey, that figure fell to an even more embarrassing one in five.[30] Church scholar Michael Novak perhaps speaks for the majority when he recommends thinking about "preachers whose lips are like a hen's ass blowing air. That makes me smile, and sermons become tolerable."[31]

Liturgical revision was only one aspect of change, for the Church also entered the arena of activism by taking statesperson-like positions on an array of social and political issues. In Poland, the Church promoted the only free trade union in the Communist world. In East Germany, the Church demanded far-reaching democratization. In the Philippines, it helped topple a decadent dictator. In Latin America, liberation theologians breathed the gospel into the lives of the powerless and politically oppressed. In the U.S., the bishops went on record rejecting nuclear arms and condemning "privileged concentrations of power, wealth, and income."[32]

All well and good, but most American Catholics find such noble efforts at best irrelevant. Few American Catholics lose much sleep worrying about a new world economic order, Solidarity in Poland, former President Marcos of the Philippines, Christian-based communities in Latin America, or even the clergy's right to teach and preach what theological research leads them to believe. Those matters are all too abstract—too far away geographically, and too far away conceptually—for the people in the pew who are wondering, is the **S/T** of being here worth it? What they seek is concrete guidance that helps them cope with life's daily struggles and affects the practice of their faith. Those are the bread-and-butter issues like family, and getting a good education for their kids. Will they get the advice in church? Will it be acceptable? Will it make the weekly hour on Sunday worthwhile?

The gap between what Rome *says* is right, and what Rome's adherents in pulpit and in pew *believe* is right, steadily widens. As the Chinese say, "Same bed, different dreams." But for Catholics, going to church and hearing things they do not want to hear transforms those dreams into nightmares. Catholics' patience has grown short. So has their time.

For the record, here are the positions the Church takes on issues of concern to its members: The Church opposes abortion, artificial birth control, in vitro fertilization, remarriage after divorce, sex outside of marriage, active homosexuality, a married clergy, and women's ordination. In all cases, save one, poll after poll confirms the fact that popular Catholic judgment fails to accord with those rules. The reasons will become clear after reciting the Vox Romanum/Vox Populi litany:

On the Church's position against birth control:
People: O Holy Church, with thee we disagree.

Two-thirds of Catholics disagree with their church's stand on birth control.[33] They could hardly believe otherwise for eight in ten American Catholic women of childbearing age and their spouses rely on the pill or other contraceptives to limit pregnancies.[34]

On the Church's position against abortion:
People: O Holy Church, with thee we disagree.

Although the Church and its members are seen as a dominant

force in the groundswell of support for the pro-life movement, only a bare 14 percent of Roman Catholics agree that abortion should always be illegal[35] and 56 percent support in vitro fertilization in the context of marriage, a proportion not far removed from the 60 to 74 percent of all Americans polled on the subject.[36]

On the Church's position against remarriage after divorce:
PEOPLE: O holy Church, with thee we disagree.

Three in four Catholics favor allowing remarriage.[37]

On the Church's position against premarital sex:
PEOPLE: O holy Church, with thee we disagree.

Surprisingly, fewer than one in three believe that premarital sex is always wrong.[38]

On the Church's position against active homosexuality:
PEOPLE: O holy Church, with thee we agree, sort of.

Only on the issue of homosexuality is there a popular consensus with the Vatican position. Two in three Catholics believe that homosexual acts are morally wrong; still, over half favor legalizing gay relationships.[39]

On the Church's position against a married clergy and the ordination of women:
PEOPLE: O holy Church, with thee we disagree.

Majorities of priests and laity favor optional celibacy for the ordained clergy.[40] As for the alternative means for dealing with the clergy crisis, two out of three Catholics maintain that women priests are OK.[41]

To approximate the proportion of Catholics at odds with Church teachings, add to the 80 percent who regularly practice birth control, the homosexuals, the couples living together without ecclesiastical blessing, the women alienated by the church's misogyny, and very quickly 100 percent (or close to it) of the people who are (or were) in the pews are accounted for. Ah! Another clue to unraveling the mystery of the empty pew—but only a clue.

God, the Scriptures claim, said "My ways are not your ways." In that respect, the Pope seems to be echoing the Creator. It is little wonder that a recent Gallup Poll found that more than half of

Catholics (compared to 38 percent of Protestants) were not convinced of their religion's relevance in their lives.[42] And what relevance the Church has, has eroded steadily since the Gallup organization began asking people about the importance of their religion. In 1952, eight in ten Catholics responded "very important" but, in 1985, under half gave that response.[43] For the rest, there was little reason to devote much time to an activity that had come to be unimportant or peripheral.

Those who see it otherwise tend to be the older and more accepting parishioners raised to believe that to miss Mass on Sunday or to eat meat on Friday was to face eternal damnation. That generation will eventually die off, leaving behind a younger cohort of the disenfranchised and detached who can hardly be expected to carry on in the ways of their elders. The trouble is, instead of planning for a twenty-first century, writes John Deedy in a tightly reasoned analysis of the future of American Catholicism, "the church is looking back, preoccupied with codes and disciplines that belong to another age."[44] When asked why the mainline churches are experiencing decline, the dean of management experts, Peter F. Drucker, put it simply and bluntly: "People are turning to a church that asks 'What do these people need that we can give?' rather than 'How can we preserve our distinctive doctrines?' "[45] Elizabeth McAlister also worries about the priorities. The Church did not excommunicate war criminals, notes the former nun, yet "sins" involving narrow moral issues, such as marriage and sexuality, seem uppermost. "Eating meat on Friday was much more important than feeding the hungry—one was a sin, and the other was just a nice thing to do."[46]

The "nice things to do" are important to today's Roman Catholics, who are better educated and earning higher incomes than ever before. They are making rapid progress up the socioeconomic ladder, and doing so faster than the members of most other religious groups. Since the mid-1960s, when the Church's "business" started dropping off, Catholics' incomes have equaled or surpassed every Protestant denomination except Presbyterian and Episcopalian. The fraction of college-educated Catholics has doubled in twenty years, and the proportion currently enrolled exceeds the national average.[47] As the demographics of rising affluence signal an in-tandem rise in time costs, time is allocated more carefully, and in favor of activities that matter: those with high and rising **S/T**s. Church involvement, alas, is not one of those.

As their time becomes more valuable, why should Catholics continue to support an institution with which they disagree, and disagree so violently? Quite a different matter it would be if they believed that dissent was productive of change, or even if their disagreement was countenanced. But neither seem any more likely than a ruling that disallows the use of Amen in church.

With barely half of Catholics showing up at Sunday Mass, compared to three-fourths in 1958,[48] and 38 percent attending less frequently than a decade ago,[49] is it any wonder that most believe that the time has come for the Pope to take his dogma for a walk?

WHO'S CORRECT, EDWARD BURNETT TYLER OR LENNY BRUCE?

Over a century ago, Edward Burnett Tyler observed that from the beginning no society, as we ordinarily define it, has been without some form of religion. If by "religion" the founder of cultural anthropology meant organized groups that meet together in time-consuming rites of worship, future societies may prove Mr. Tyler wrong!

As comedian Lenny Bruce put it, "Every day people are straying away from the church and going back to God."[50] Spending time in church, temple, or synagogue in an earlier era of lower time costs was easy. The *BB* factor makes that long-standing practice more difficult.

The challenge the Church faces, to put it simply, is to find ways to make spiritual engagement a valued use of personal time. Even if Catholics do not subscribe to the logic of the Protestants—that wasting time is the "deadliest of sins"—they can still find good reason for choosing not to devote time to an institution that requires strict adherence to unacceptable teaching and has apparently forgotten its historical attempts to compete in the religious marketplace, when challenged.

Religion may always be with us, just as anthropologist Tyler insisted it always has been, but belief may be practiced, as Lenny

Bruce said, by staying away from church. Active involvement in traditional religious organizations seems destined to disappear as a use for time unless regeneration includes accommodation to changes, among them ever scarcer worldly time.

Amen.

7:00
CHASTE BY TIME

"[Americans are] better at having a love affair that lasts ten minutes than any other people in the world."
—Stephen Spender[1]

There are some things better than sex, and some things worse," observed W. C. Fields, "but of one thing we can be absolutely certain, there's nothing quite like it." Unique sex may be, but the activity shares one attribute with all others: it takes time. Not a lot, to be sure, but it *does* take time. That bare fact leads prominent time-concerned specialists (read: timeologists) to forecast the Waterloo of this necessary and, according to widespread reports, pleasurable activity.

Fortunately for the future of the race, their predictions are wrong.

Those who have pondered the subject carefully reason as follows: Sex takes time (no surprise), and there is no way of reducing the **T** required for the act. Nor can technology enhance its **S**. With other activities increasing their **S/T**s, and no increase in the **S/T** of lovemaking, the imperiled activity is destined to appear on the time-minus list. So the argument goes.

Sex probably takes as much time today as in those halcyon days of Adam and Eve's coy experiments before the cataclysmic apple-and-snake incident. Because the **S** of sex can't rise, so to speak, the only solution is to cut down on the total time given to it. Apparently that is happening. One informant reports that, "the French institution of the *cinq-a-sept*—two hours for which love-seeking husbands do not always feel bound to account—is disappearing in the increased hustle of life."[2]

Three unhappy consequences follow. First, because affairs are very time-consuming they "become less attractive." Second, "the time spent on each occasion of lovemaking is being reduced." And third, "the total number of sexual encounters is declining."[3] Each proposition warrants careful consideration. Note, however, that the sex act constitutes only one part of a more complex set of events surrounding the time-consuming projects of courtship and love. The aspects of the sexual encounter—romance and "doing it" (henceforth, simply "it")—must be distinguished, for each responds differently to the *BB* factor. Romance, for the record, consists of the preliminaries, starting with wooing. "It" is anatomical conjunction.

We begin with romance.

CALLING, DATING, COMMITTING, WEDDING, AND BEDDING—DOES ANYONE STILL BELIEVE IN ROMANCE?

We have come a long way since the times, recalled by salty old Alice Roosevelt Longworth, when "people were always having love affairs with their poodles and putting tiny flowers in strange places."[4] Today, flowers and poodles take too much time. At the turn of the century, however, the rigid structure of etiquette circumscribing courtship insured that romance could not be rushed.

Courting in those days brings to mind visions of earnest beaus wooing downcast-eyed young women with tokens of affection (like "tiny flowers"?) and proposing on bended knee. A boy who had "called" on a girl had taken the first in a series of measured steps the well-bred took in a ritual that might or might not end in marriage. Calling was a formal but leisurely occasion, the response to a written invitation advertising the girl's availability "at home." The anxious beau could expect to be received in the girl's family parlor, served hot chocolate and cookies, entertained by her piano playing, and meet (read: be examined by) her mother. If all went well on all sides, she could expect a later appointment to be taken "out" somewhere. He issued that invitation, at a place and time convenient to him, for everyone knew that his time was more valuable than hers.[5] So time-consuming was the process that it was ripe for streamlining.

Beginning in the teens of the new century, dating began to supplant the older, more complicated ceremonial. Dating rather than calling now became the first step in the middle-class rite. Historian Beth L. Bailey traces those changes in her aptly titled book, *From Front Porch to Back Seat*. Dance hall or restaurant or theater replaced the parlor as the venue, Coke replaced chocolate, and "parking" replaced the walk in the park. A quarter of the way into the century, calling had all but disappeared, too extravagant of time, to be replaced by dating.[6]

DATING DEFINED

"A date, at this juncture in history, is any prearranged meeting with a member of the opposite sex toward whom you have indecent intentions. . . . One does not have to sleep with, or even touch, someone who has paid for your meal. All those obligations are hereby rendered null and void, and any man who doesn't think so needs a quick jab in the kidney."

—Cynthia Heimel[7]

The *BB* factor would ultimately doom dating too. World War II marked the turning point. Before the war, the number and variety of dates indexed a youth's competitive success. Variety, though perhaps the spice of life, was too time-expensive when working seriously on one conquest could short-circuit the courtship ritual. On the one hand, going steady with a "fixture"—the parlance of the day for the date who was right to be seen with—was deemed inferior to playing the field. As one critic poetically put it,

Going steady with one date
Is okay, if that's all you rate.[8]

On the other hand—and sour grapes aside—going steady was so much more time-efficient that commitments to a single suitor soon supplanted dating many potential conquests, and it worked "as long as you don't get tied up with an impossible gook."[9] Going steady meant not having to initiate a new routine with each new partner or to spend time shopping around for a date for the movies or major functions like "the hop." There is "no competition and no impression to be made," with Steady Freddy, recommended *Datebook's Complete Guide to Dating*. "If you didn't have Freddy, you'd be spending a lot more time in front of the mirror—deciding how to bring out your best features. . . . Without Freddy, you'd be putting your best foot forward and there wouldn't be an old sneaker on it.''[10]

The best foot to put forward was the left one, and it was clad in a Puppy Love Anklet, the symbol for fidelity to a single suitor. If the rule was faithfully observed, by the late '40s fully 80 percent of teenagers qualified for wearing Puppy Love Anklets on the left foot.[11]

But dating, even with a steady (like Freddy), was destined to oblivion. A *Mademoiselle* survey published in 1963 described the ideal date as an event beginning with cocktails, then dinner at an elegant restaurant, theater or a concert, and then dancing.[12] Courtship, the ritual ''crushed by an amazingly fast-paced world . . . dying in America because there isn't time for it,''[13] was ripe for further streamlining.

At the turn of the century, parents worried greatly about the dangers of holding hands and kissing. It was not what the practice would lead to. Something just seemed wrong with it. Ditto necking, or in the earlier vernacular, spooning, snuggle-pupping, and fussing, that became the conventions to worry anxious parents.[14] By the mid-1960s, parents had new grounds for concern. Whereas in the late '30s only a minority of high school girls expected a good night kiss, mores shifted spectacularly in three decades. At the dawning of the sexual revolution, a *Look* survey reported that nearly half of teens approved of a boy and girl ''living together'' if they were in love.[15] Premarital intercourse had become the convention.

''Sex appears to be the normal, if not unproblematic, medium of contemporary courtship,'' writes Ms. Bailey, for it is a time-hungry society's method for short-circuiting courtship rites. As virginity lost importance and strictures against premarital sex vanished, ''intercourse replaced petting as a convention of youth.''[16] And the time-efficient version of romancing, now merged with sex, has come to involve little more than meeting a stranger at a singles' bar, hopping into bed, and out of it the next morning uncommitted, and presumably guilt free (even in the knowledge of how lethal sex has become).

Romancing, if practiced at all these busy days, has come to resemble a business arrangement. "No frills, few flowers, no time wasted in elaborate compliments, verses, and lengthy seductions, no complications, and no scenes please," is how Sebastian de Grazia describes the modern incarnation.[17] With increasing time-pressures and disappearing gender differences, "whateryadointonite?" elicits the desired response that the invitation delivered weeks in advance once did, and the female is as likely as the male to set the schedule. Conveniences like singles bars have abbreviated the time-elapse between Dating Contact and Anatomical Conjunction, from DC to AC, so to speak.

For romance to be on the decline, the partners to the liaison must be *comparatively* less happy spending time and effort in their collusion than in "competitive" activities with more rapidly rising **S/T**s. If that is indeed true, romance will lose out in the competition for fixed time. Apparently it is, for the "Hite Report" concludes that 79 percent of women doubt whether their love relationships are worth the energy required, and a sparse 19 percent put their relationship first in their lives.[18] Other time-uses have assumed greater importance.

In an investigation billed as "the most eye-opening survey ever!" Deidre Sanders and her staff at *Woman* magazine questioned a sample of 5,000 men about their love lives and discovered, to no one's surprise, that women are more committed to romantic preludes than men, and more willing to commit time to it. Husbands are three times as likely as wives to believe that intercourse surpasses kissing or cuddling in importance. Hubby wants to get right down to business and avoid the time-consuming prelude that wifey enjoys. Men are more likely to be employed for wages—at least in England where the survey was conducted—hence to "rationally" value time (even bedtime) in money terms, and be impatient with romancing. Moans one respondent, John, 21, "the pace of modern life is so detrimental to creating that relaxed climate in which lovemaking flourishes."[19]

So fragile a thing is romance, so easy to postpone, so easy to forget about altogether when something else intervenes. "Our relationship generally fluctuates from good and innovative to poor and mundane," says Ewan, 27, a production manager, who blames the poor and mundane aspects on "work, family problems, holidays, and so on."[20] It is little wonder that "Dinks"—the acronym for bustling couples who boast double incomes and no kids—rely on secretaries to schedule their time together. Perhaps Ewan should do the same.

Increasing numbers see the single life as one way to minimize the time devoted to romance. In the last twenty years, the proportion of young men and women who have avoided middle-aisleing has doubled.[21] The trend can be attributed in part to postponing marriage, and partly to a desire to avoid marriage altogether, with its time-consuming responsibilities. Increasingly, Americans seem to prefer the single life with its greater freedom to do their thing without having to worry about others. The "Hite Report" again furnishes evidence, this time that one can be happy though single.

Though not particularly profound, Ms. Hite's respondents' of the I-love-doing-what-I-want-when-I-want mentality are illuminating: "I like being single—I like to check out the merchandise." "(I'm) not tied down emotionally." "If on Saturday I look like a witch, and don't get dressed all day, it's my choice." In sum, "I'm too busy right now for romance," say the 93 percent of single, never-married women who apparently prefer the freedom of being on their own.[22]

Women are not alone in their apparent aversion to taking on the time-consuming tasks and responsibilities of the connubial commitment. Many men also seem to favor traveling life's paths solo. Journalist Trip Gabriel interviewed a cross section of bachelors to discover what prevented them from marrying. They were, in a word, "scared." Scared of the time required to make a marriage work. "Dating . . . is a hassle," said his informants, "relationships seem very stifling." Sports were a better use of time and apparently yielded a higher **S/T**. "Some bachelors seem to have effected a simple exchange between the vicissitudes and uncertainties of a single man's sex life," writes Mr. Gabriel, "for the known payoffs of athletics."[23]

Bruce Weber, another journalist, crossed the nation asking tough questions about marriage, relationships, and romance. In the answers, he heard about "life equations already written, doubt banished. . . . They are self-preoccupied." Let them speak for themselves. Peter, 25, is "down on romance" because it requires neglecting "other things." If time is spent in romance, it is used as parsimoniously as possible. "We don't need much time together to confirm our relationship," says Clark, 24. Hard work guarantees a secure future. No time for fooling around. For making love.[24]

If romance appears to be time-minus, how about sex?

THE URGE TO MERGE: ANATOMICAL CONJUNCTION

Comedienne Dame Edna Everage writes that sex can be "fairly beautiful, if you are extremely lucky and have no other interests in life."[25] In the age of the *BB* factor, rising **S/T**s of those other interests threaten activities even as important as the acts required to perpetuate the race. Sex tends to get lost, for example, in the daily routine of home and work obligations. Generalizing from the results of her penetrating *Woman* magazine survey, Ms. Sanders notes how "a woman with, say, the housework and dinner on her mind is fairly unlikely to drop everything at the sign of her husband in his underpants. If he walks into the bathroom and finds her bending over cleaning the bath, with her bottom in the air, however, he may well feel roused and make a pass."[26]

> "Sex is by no means everything. It varies, as a matter of fact, from only as high as 78 per cent of everything to as low as 3.10 per cent. The norm, in a sane, healthy person, should be between 18 and 24 per cent." —James Thurber and E. B. White.[27]

The excitement about sex seems fleeting. Once the honeymoon is over and the novelty has vanished, diminishing marginal utility—to use the economist's rather hygienic term—apparently sets in fairly rapidly and gives meaning to the cliché that a man wants a wife in the home and a mistress between the sheets.[28] A marriage counselor puts it more visually: "sex tends to go out the window when moonlight and roses turn into daylight and dishes."[29] When problems arise, as often they do, family stands in the way of finding the times to work them through. Kids sitting around the table eliminate breakfast as one of those times. "It's no good just after making love saying, 'Well, that wasn't much good,' even if you're feeling it,'' laments Leslie, 39, a civil servant. ''And it's hardly the time over the cornflakes in the morning.''[30]

If taking on the routine chores of a household distracts from the pleasures of the boudoir, new impediments turn up when the kids arrive. Among men who have no children or whose children have left home, 40 percent report being happy with their sex lives, compared to just 29 percent of fathers with children in the house. Children may threaten even a happy marriage, as Len, 54, believes. ''Their constant presence makes it difficult to have any sex life at all and the stress of bringing them up made us much more bad-tempered.'' Perhaps Len and his mate would be happier playing with dogs. Jonathan, 33, a garage owner, has it all figured out: ''My wife is 27 and as yet not bothered about kids. We have two dogs and they are our family. A lot less trouble and time-consuming than kids. I think I may be too selfish for children but time will tell.''[31] Right. Time *will* tell!

Although economists view ''sex as a conceivable obstacle to economic growth,'' one of them sees the increasing time scarcity that accompanies ''economic growth as a conceivable obstacle to sex.''[32] Homeostasis works that way and keeps the system in balance.

Yet if the routine of household duties, child care, work, and other claims on ever-scarcer fixed time interfere, it follows that the *BB* factor is one of the obstacles to sex. Whether sex can survive requires a tidier empirical answer.

> ''An opthalmologist who studies two thousand similar eye ailments can come up with dependable conclusions, but the scientist of sex, completing his investigation of two thousand persons in love, is just about where he was when he started out.''
>
> —James Thurber and E. B. White[33]

Sadly, the statistical compendia shed little light on the question. The record is mute. Even the Kinsey Reports, with their 1,646 pages of cold statistical facts (and, alas, no illustrations) fail to tell us whether people were doing it more or less than ''before.'' Still, there are scattered reports from here and there, and changes can be inferred in evidence drawn from other sources.

Perhaps because it is less embarrassing to watch animals couple, more is known about how long they take in sexual congress than their human counterparts. Let it be known that they too involve themselves in complicated preludes. Chimps' "couplings last only a few moments, but much chatter and flirting precede them. . . . Even the boar, which has a reputation for being direct, sings a mating song, in baritone grunts, until he is out of breath and foaming at the mouth."[34] Humans are more complicated and take longer. But not much.

The late Bhagwan Shree Rajneesh, for example, was able to boast that he "had more women than any man in history," perhaps because the flashy Indian guru who spread a message of free love and mysticism was too busy to spend but a very short time with each. "A couple of minutes on top, and then it was over." The quality of couplings apparently matched the quantity of time given to each, for a former disciple laments that he "was not much of a lover."[35] The Indian mystic may not have been unusual for the Kinsey Report cites a very low time expenditure for the exchange of fluids, a couple of minutes at most.[36]

OPPRESSED BY THE *BB* FACTOR

A school-marm at an Eastern girls school ended her favorite instruction with the provocative challenge, "Girls, is an hour of pleasure worth a lifetime of shame?" A wee, small voice from the rear queried, "How do you make it last an hour?"

Aside from the amount of time consumed per event, what about the frequency of events? The evidence, again limited, points to *more* rather than *less* frequent sex, contrary to the timeologists' dour assertions. The Kinsey Report on women found that the typical frequency for marital intercourse by 40 years of age was 1.5 times per week. A bare 5 percent in this age group made love more than three times a week. Some thirty years later, *Redbook* asked the same question and got dramatically different results. One in four 40-year-olds had sexual intercourse three to five times weekly (weakly?).[37] If the amount of time spent per event has remained unchanged, and the frequency of events has increased, then more time overall is being spent in conjunction.

We also know that the soothsayers who base their gloomy predictions only on **T** overlook the possibilities for enhancing satisfaction. With frequency on the rise, the **S** of sex must have increased for, contrary to the timeologists' contentions, the activity *can* be, and indeed *has been,* enhanced, oftentimes with the aid of technology. The markets for boudoir accessories have responded to raise the productivity of reproductivity, since all enterprising manufacturers, barring those motivated by a healthy amount of altruism, are out to make a buck. Like everyone else.

RAISING THE PRODUCTIVITY OF REPRODUCTIVITY

Sex-wise, things are getting better. Of 26,000 women surveyed, 43 percent report being "very satisfied" with their sex lives as against only 33 percent polled 13 years before. And 22 percent, compared to an earlier 15 percent, happily report that they reach orgasm every time.[38]

The aphorism Necessity is the Mother of Invention apparently still applies. If the *BB* factor jeopardizes sex, and if sex is necessary, then necessity has mothered inventions to save sex. The daisy-chain of innovations that have increased **S**, if not reducing **T**, ranges from marriage manuals (as they used to be called) or the sex manuals (as they are more aptly called today) to whips and chains for those less inclined to read. Some are products of the marketplace. Others, like changing partners, changing position, and changing environment have little to do with the marketplace. Some, like birth control devices, and most notably the pill, introduce safety by removing the fear of an unwanted pregnancy. Others introduce variety to alter a time-honored activity that has grown dull through repetition. But all share the common goal of making sex a more uplifting experience.

The sperm-of-the-moment decision to fool around with another may provide the needed variety. Swapping has certain advantages over promiscuity, aside from the fact that it's easier to spell and pronounce. Either may rekindle passion's flame. And rekindling may be necessary with the routine of bedding down night after night with the same partner. Two New York Yankee players answered Dorothy Parker's lament, "Woman lives but in her lord; count to ten, and man is bored,"[39] by exchanging wives, and also their children, homes, and dogs. "This wasn't a wife swap," both men emphasized, "it was a life swap."[40]

In an age when deadly sexually transmitted diseases are running rampant, promiscuity is not likely to be a favored option for increasing variety. Less risky, less harmful, and less expensive alternatives can also introduce new excitement into relationships and loosen inhibitions. Fantasy, whether it involves changing the situation in reality or in imagination, meets those criteria.

"She does like making love in public risky places," reports Dominic, 24, unemployed, about his wife's preferences for fantasy. "We also use love beans, inserted anally, and a vibrating dildo (somewhat more impressively proportioned than myself)." However, he adds reluctantly, "She still balks at aids such as duo balls and love eggs." (The mind runs wild!) All well and good for Dominic and the Missus, who seem to be on the right track, but not just any old fantasy will do. Good fantasy requires more than dreaming about things at hand, or *in* the hand. Consider the nocturnal admission of, Wesley, 32, a bank clerk, "Nothing destroys an intimate atmosphere quicker than realizing she is closing her eyes and thinking of England."[41]

Change the venue for the event or alter the circumstances surrounding it. Usual things can be used in unusual and economical ways as libido enliveners, proves Marabel Morgan. The marriage counselor and born-again Christian suggests baking a sweet potato soufflé for dinner and sticking a candle in it. Frolic in an unusual place, like a hammock, diving board, or trampoline.[42]

The movies suggest some other unusual places. Jacqueline Bisset and Hart Bochner played out their love drama on an airplane in "Rich and Famous." A Chicago commuter train was the preferred scene for Tom Cruise and Rebecca De Mornay to frolic in "Risky Business." For Warren Beatty and Julie Christie in "Shampoo," it was a Nixon campaign dinner.

Fix the bedroom up real nice. "Drape a red nightie over the lamp shade to give a diffused, warm, soft glow," purrs Mrs. Morgan. "Twist rolls of red crepe paper into streamers from ceiling to bed frame. After the big event, leap out of bed and applaud your husband."[43]

Try variety in dressing. Dressing is as important to sex as it is to salad. Meet your hubby at the door wrapped only in Saran wrap, she recommends.[44] Costumes that are less astonishing to the kids and the neighbors add no less spice to the event. Terry, 24, a student teacher, adds that "We make use of lingerie, vibrators, magazines, scarves, net curtaining, and so on [that] succeed in arousing me no end."[45]

If Ms. Sanders's survey is representative, in Britain it seems as if suspenders turn on every Tom (21), Dick (32), and Harry (25). They are not alone. Soldier Dudley, 28, self-employed Bob, 38, financial rep Gareth, 36, center lathe turner Phil, 43, roofer Tim, 23, and investment consultant Simon, 25, also volunteer the news that suspenders hold up more than their trousers. Simon volunteers more specific detail on that aspect of his partner's raiment. "We have a varied sex life," says he, "but I prefer her dressed up in some flimsy thing when we make love. Suspenders are best."[46] Suspenders? Is there something the Brits know that we should find out about? "It's more exciting if she uses these clothes coyly, without being brashly sexual," ejaculates (note clever use of synonym for "says") chartered engineer Gordon, 46, "for example, if I catch a glimpse of suspender when sitting normally at home."

And then there's the case of Harvey, 46, an explosives engineer. . . .[47] Oh well . . . never mind.

Cross-dressing appeals to more than might be expected—at least among our neighbors across the Atlantic (where kinkiness may be more prized than on local shores). The Sanders survey discovered that a number of Brits regularly don female attire, fitting themselves out in wigs, make-up, dress, bra, panties, suspenders (there it is again!), stockings, and—for extra kicks—camisole tops and French knickers. A quarter of all men have cross-dressed at some time.[48] The remainder apparently consider it a drag.

Many mechanical devices increase sexual arousal, particularly in women, notes satirist P. J. O'Rourke. "Chief among these is the Porsche 911 Cabriolet."[49] The market also offers less-pricey alternatives that promise ever higher **S**s through commoditization: aphrodisiacs, pornography, gadgets, and—yes—the telephone.

For soloists, there's telephone sex. For the phone company,

their ad come true: you *can* reach out and touch someone, but with anonymity and hygiene as plusses. Telephone sex saves the time spent romancing and fixing oneself up in costumes (including suspenders). Sex telephonists have found dial-a-porn more fun than dialing the Gnomons in New Halcyon especially when, according to the ads, veritable stables of Nubile Nudies and Handsome Hunks are awaiting a call to send *you* on transports of joy. The time-saving business of hearing someone talk dirty has grown so rapidly with time scarcity that, in four short years, revenues have multiplied by a factor of twelve![50] Other time-savers have longer traditions. One of these dates back to Aphrodite, Greek Goddess of love.

Ever since Brangane, Isolde's maid, gave her and her enemy Tristan a magical love potion with aphrodisiacal properties that not only neutralized their mutual hate but threw them into passionate embraces on hard rocks in dark places, people have searched for elixirs to heighten their interest in sex. Among the old-fashioned variety were certain tree barks, crushed beetles (aka "Spanish fly"), bears' gall bladders, human sweat, olives, powdered rhinoceros horns, oysters, and sundry sexual apparatus removed from hares, hyenas, and weasels. An updated list would include green M&Ms and vitamin E. Some moderns have found Cupid in a medicine bottle. Drugs, many discovered in the '60s, operated as moodshifters. The right chemical combinations sent their users to new highs of orgasmic pleasure by boosting fantasy and stretching out time. Psychoactive drugs, ranging from "uppers" like cocaine and amphetamines to "downers" like barbiturates and methaqualones, are commonly believed to spark sex drives by raising testosterone levels, by prolonging male "staying power" (for those with time to spare), and by lowering the higher brain center's control over inhibitions and anxiety.[51] Like Brangane's love potion, the search for chemical love may produce unpleasant, even dangerous, side effects, and still fail to yield the alleged and hoped-for advantages. Never mind, there are other possibilities.

One of these is pornography. While porn is as old as aphrodisiacs, studies suggest that today's product is less subtle, better in quality, and *certainly in focus.* Moreover, few regard porn as the evil that Mr. Meese's inquiry made it out as. More Ameri-

cans than not believe that "explicit renderings of sex . . . can help improve the sex lives of some couples, . . . provide entertainment . . . (and) information about sex."[52] Porn video and films, available at the Easy Come Porn Shop, have become big business, stimulated by the movement to hygienic sex and by the time savings they offer. Each week 4.3 million pornographic videocassettes are rented. Annual porn sales range up to an estimated $1.5 billion, compared to the $8 billion that mainstream Hollywood grosses from theatrical rentals and video sales of its films.[53] And why not, when video offers the chance to watch "Becoming Orgasmic" or to enroll in a video-*assisted* course in fantasy called "The Sexual Attitude Restructuring Guide"? For those of more specialized bent, who may want to look into the possibilities of bondage & discipline, for example, "Spankmasters" is a definite possibility—the first in a series, "Spanking, Paddling, and Hairbrushing."[54]

Technological innovation has made it an easy matter for anyone and everyone to equip their homes in the bizarre and exotic ways that add novelty to the experience. With the aerosols, gels, lotions, ointments, salves, rubbery devices, and other novelties currently and readily available, any couple considering themselves well-endowed with sex toys could easily transform the ordinary bedside table into a hybrid between a well-equipped laboratory, the local pharmacy, and the cosmetic case at Saks. The greatest challenge of all is to figure out how to use them, post-acquisition but pre-coital, for many of the toys require the talents of a graduate engineer, the skills of a gynecologist, the deftness of a Yoga master, and the patience of a Job.

Whether tech-fix or tech-futz, innovations have increased the productivity of reproductivity. A rising **S/T** has saved sex from the fate of time-minusness. Not the least, although sex may not last an hour, the goods that commoditized it demonstrate that the time can be well spent.

Before our eyebrows have been raised permanently, consider less intimate personal relationships: the attention that we give to the pleasures of the table.

8:00

TAKING CARE OF OURSELVES

''Diets are for those who are thick and tired of it.''
—Anonymous[1]

Entertainment and enlightenment meet in happy collision at the frequent evenings spent in the company of our good friends, technologically upscale Nola and Nolan Gnomon (who prefer that the ''G'' of their surname remain silent ''to add to the alliteration''). There is the setting, their electronically advanced home in New Halcyon, and a ''technologically enhanced'' dinner (as Nolan puts it) prepared by the latest state-of-the-art kitchen aids, and the string of instructions on useful ways to improve our ''life quality'' (again Nolan's term). We always leave well fed and well informed. Who could ask for anything more?

En route to one of these bi-weekly events, our speculations meandered between the general and the specific. Generally, what new electronic wonders would the Gnomons unveil during the evening ahead? Specifically, why had Nola been in the hospital?

''Well, here we all are again,'' chirped Nola at the door, and frankly looking quite different somehow. ''What do you think of the face-lifted, body-sculpted Nola?''

(This answered our second question.)

''Youth regained. Quicker than all those oily gels, nightly ointments, mildewy packs, scratchy sleeping straps, carcinogenic wrinkle creams. Nolan's been ribbing me with that jibe that some oaf made about poor Wallie Simpson—you know, the Duchess of Windsor—after her third lift-off. Something like how 'her mouth stretches from ear to ear.' But there's more to the story. . . .''

''Anyway . . . NOLAN! . . . I nearly forgot. NOLAN, THEY'RE

HERE! TURN OFF YOUR MACHINE AND POUR THE CHARDONNAY. You know, I hardly see my other half anymore. He's always on his exerciser. (Ah! a start at answering the first question.) It's stage one of his new at-home fitness program. No more puffing and panting running down the street scaring the neighbors into thinking he's about to combust right there in front of their house. It's all set up in Nolene's old room that Nolan's dubbed Nolene's Nautilus Nook. You'll never believe what technology can do until you see his time-saving torture contraptions.

"NOLAN, TURN IT OFF. THEY'RE HERE. ON TIME AS USUAL. RIGHT ON THE BUTTON. BUT YOU'RE NOT. IF YOU HAVE TO SHOWER, I'LL SERVE THE CHARDONNAY. You *do* want chardonnay, don't you?"

"Well, here we are. On time as usual. Right on the button. Nola, show off your new kitchen gadgets while I clean up, will you?

"I'll do my best, but I'm hardly up to date. A new one arrives every day. Come on in and I'll show you the latest arrivals. With this little electronic egg candler we can decide for ourselves, rather than relying on someone else to tell us, an egg's gender. I think that's what it's for. This new model food processor grinds, grates, pulls, mashes, smashes, squashes, squeezes, squirms, squirts, shoves. Even rolls filter-tip cigarettes. No, ugh, I don't mean that."

"Wait until you sample the joys of capuccino made in our espresso machine. It's a superior Italian model of course. I'll show you the catalogue from the importer. Nolan just assembled this electric butter slicer from a kit, didn't you dear, and only half the price for those who can figure out how to put it together. I didn't want it, but he insisted. 'Electronically relevant,' he said. It won *When Magazine*'s time-saver gadget-of-the-month award for February. You do subscribe, don't you?

"Nolan . . . THE CHARDONNAY PLEASE. By the way, if he hadn't forgotten to charge its batteries, the Omnibot 2000 would be serving drinks for us, right now. That's Nolan's toy from Christmas and you should see its cute little robotic arms pick up objects and hand them to you—OBJECTS LIKE GLASSES FILLED WITH WINE, NOLAN! And he's ordered an ecologically relevant solar-powered can opener just on the market, haven't you love? Oh yes, I nearly forgot. Next time you're here we'll all be treated to a real Japanese fiesta made in the electric sushi-maker. Right, Nolan?"

"Right, dear. Just $99.50, plus tax and shipping of course. Nola, do you have the address handy? What about THE CHARDONNAY? But don't let me interrupt."

"That mysterious black thing where the burners used to be is a halogen cooktop. Just a wipe cleans it up; no muss, no fuss, so they say. What a wonder to see with all its tiny red lights flashing, but we won't be using it tonight. Actually, dinner's right here in this little bag. It's one of the new prepless entrees: a pre-prepared, pre-washed, pre-chopped, pre-sliced, pre-diced, pre-peeled, pre-shrunk, pre-measured, pre-combined, pre-whipped, pre-steamed, pre-tested, pre-everythinged turnip soufflé that's just dying to be microwaved before making us ecstatic. But you probably know about prepless-everything already, don't you?"

"Did we show you our 10-K food analysis computer last time you were here? No? Punch in the menu for each meal and at month's end it prints out a list of the calories, carbohydrates, cholesterol, fat, sodium, and protein so that we'll know what we shouldn't have eaten."

"Say, what do you think of Nola's face lift? Mouth from ear to ear, just like what's-his-name said about . . ."

". . . Lay off, Nolan. If you use that tired old line again, I'll tell everyone about your electronic denture cleaner. OK? A deal?"

"You do that, hon, and I'll describe every little detail about lipectomies during dinner. OK? A truce!"

It was quiet for the first time since we arrived and we hoped they wouldn't forget the chardonnay offer, however . . .

"Come on and let me show you the new home gym. Just what you need. Just what *everyone* needs. When it's all equipped I'll be able to do all the routines right here that I do at the health club. Saves time that way. And I can use the time getting fit for reading the *Times* or drinking a chardonnay, all synchronically . . . Nola, love, WHERE'S THE WINE? . . .

"This little number is a multifunctional digitally controlled exercise machine, designed just for home use, with a treadmill, bench press, slant board, and rowing machine. Only $399.95. Whips and chains extra—ha, ha. And next to arrive by freight is a stair climbing machine that firms up the legs and buttocks, if you'll pardon the expression, and a pushup stand that turns ordinary pushups into super-charged exercise. According to *When*

Magazine, each one is tested continuously for 1,000 hours by twenty-five marines in boot camp to make sure it holds up. By the way, you do subscribe to *When,* don't you? I suppose not, but we'll give you a subscription for Christmas. How about going out shopping next Saturday? I can get you discounts."

"Nola, it's time to start fixing dinner. Ready for the fifteen-second countdown? On your mark! 15 . . . 14 . . . 13 . . ."

Such is life among the time-conscious moderns.

The Gnomons aren't your ordinary run-of-the-mill, just-down-the-street-and-around-the-corner sort of friends. They're too obsessed with efficiency for that. Nolan once explained his (their) passion for electronic thingamajigs. "Suppose Nola and her liberated house-husband—that's me—could prepare dinner in half the time, if they were helped along by modern electronics," he explained. "Wouldn't they do it? Of course they would, and so would you."

"If she uses the 'technology-aided alternative,' as I would put it, Nola can fix a fancy dinner for the four of us in only one hour, where scraping and chopping the veggies by hand, baking in a conventional oven rather than microwaving, and all the other fooling around would require two hours. The gadgetry doubles efficiency without lowering quality. An hour is saved for something else like entertaining both of you. The time saving is valuable and translates into demand for the technology."

"Let me put it another way. Because we have the technology to help us, people cook more fancy dinners than they would if we didn't have the gadgets to help. Hot dogs and sauerkraut don't get more important because there's no way to prepare them in less time or make them taste better. But the wonders of technology have made it time-efficient enough to try the more complicated and toothsome cuisines that experts like Julia Child and Jacques Pepin teach us how to fix. That explains why, even in this time-scarce era, some of us home chefs won't settle for less than gourmet cooking."

Now this is one of those rare times when Nolan's recipe blends a little of the wrong with a little of the right. Correct he is in arguing that gadgetry from the food processor perhaps even to the solar-powered can opener has saved the amount of preparation time that cooking requires (**T**), produced a better meal (**S**), and helped sustain America's interest in cooking the gourmet way. But, as we shall see, home cooking technology has not advanced fast enough to maintain **S/T** in competition with other ways of getting the meal on the table. For perspective, let's turn back the clock and look at cuisine preparation a few years ago, and then demonstrate the way that the *BB* factor affects how we cook, where we eat, what we eat, and how much time we give to those activities. Look where we've come from.

THYME ON MY HANDS

Remember the menu board, welcoming us to the school lunch cafeteria line, and announcing a repast that promised to nourish, refresh, and strengthen us through an afternoon of educational horrors like chem lab, trig, and English comp? Who can forget the excitement of choosing among such temptations as soup avec crackers au saltine, toasted Velveeta and Spam melange with a soupçon of Durkee's dressing, marshmallow topped confit of chow mein, fish farci, and potatoes mashee? Or climaxing the gustatory orgy with dessert choices that ranged from ice cream cube and fish mints to jello surprise? What challenging decisions! Fortunately, we had never heard of Brillat-Savarin nor had we heard his threat made in 1825, "Tell me what you eat, and I shall tell you what you are."[2]

What we "were" was nutritious and balanced, but it was never altogether clear whether "skool food" was meant to be eaten or whether it was supposed to eat us. These lunch hour feasts offered the perfect excuse to drop out and find a decent job to support our hamburger habits, but those of us who stuck with it swore that never, ever would we eat like this again. Skool food was the engine that drove us to search for more satisfying cuisine, the foods with higher **S**s. For many, that meant learning to cook.

The search for basics, coupled to ambitious naiveté, led us straightaway into French cooking and expert tutoring by Julia Child on TV. As our courage built, we took on the challenges of more specialized courses of instruction that promised to reveal the secrets of nouvelle cuisine, Thai specialties, Bulgarian regional fare, spa cooking for healthful living, and the ubiquitous pastas. We stocked up on cookbooks and discovered that a kitchen library without Alice B. Toklas on the shelf was like a day without sunshine, or a salad without feta cheese. We raided the cooking appliance shops and upscale markets for everything from arugula to zesters, learned to read basic Italian, Spanish, and French to understand recipes that called for *prosciutto, mascarpone, shiitake* mushrooms, and *aceto balsamico,* and discovered that nasturtiums (organically grown, of course) could be used to garnish the salad, not the nose. We summoned the courage to serve *carpaccio* as an appetizer once we learned that it wasn't a disease. We learned at first hand the real meaning of salad days. We began to wonder, what's left to discover for the table besides eye of newt and toe of frog?

Fancy fare, rewarding as it was, took too much time, and the search was on for new and more efficient ways to prepare new and more efficient victuals. Technology, as it had done in the past, responded with time-economizing alternatives that also raised satisfaction. But, back to history.

One of the biggest-scale technological breakthroughs was frozen food. World War II gave the impetus. A quarter of the nation's housewives worked in defense plants and had precious little time to cook from scratch. Freezing not only speeded up preparation time, but made seasonal fare available throughout the year: **T** fell and **S** rose. In 1920, when produce was shipped, sold, prepared, and eaten "fresh," the average American ate 110 pounds of vegetables a year. Thanks largely to food freezing, the per capita consumption of vegetables doubled by 1980.[3]

Fast foods (or "standardized dining" as it is more kindly referred to in the trade) offered another solution to the cooking time problem. "Fast foods will never be haute cuisine," predicted *Consumer Reports* in 1979, "but we have paid more and waited longer for a lot less."[4] Fast food sales are climbing at the rate of 8 percent a year, and fast food restaurant sales tripled in only ten years, while sales for the rest of the restaurant business only doubled.[5] So much for the *statistiques gastronomiques.*

Quick to produce and quick to consume, the hamburger is and always has been the king of fast foods. And if hamburger is king, chicken is queen. Emblazoned on the walls of the fast food hall of fame, right beside Clarence Birdseye, are the names of heroes Howard Dearing Johnson, who perfected the art of franchising hamburgers as the quintessentially American cuisine for the masses; Harland Sanders (later commissioned Colonel), who combined eleven spices and herbs in just the right proportions for baking chicken; and Ray Kroc, who stumbled on Mac and Dick McDonald's tiny, tidy burger-and-fries stand in San Bernardino, named his company in their honor, and the rest is history.

The Quick-Fix Icons of the '80s

Two out of three American households own a microwave oven, cooking technology's icon of the '80s. "It's no coincidence that during the '80s—the decade in which time has come to rival money as the commodity people crave most—the appliance moved from the realm of the novel to the necessary," announced the *Wall Street Journal*.[6] In fact more families own microwaves than dishwashers, food processors, toaster ovens, or VCRs.[7] The microwave, perhaps more than any other innovation in the home appliance market, has minimized the **T** of cooking without compromising the **S** of the final product. With the culinary possibilities running the gamut from popcorn to hot fudge sundaes (and the ice cream stays cold) to steaks that look charcoal broiled but aren't, microwaving hastens getting to the table a meal that would rival the abilities of a French chef.

In the era of the *BB* factor, the bandwagon support for microwaving comes as no surprise. Those most keenly pinched by time scarcity have most quickly made the transition from conventional cooking. In four years, the use of microwave cooking by "Dinks"—childless double-income couples under age 45—rose by a striking 11 percentage points, the highest growth rate of any group, and the percent of dinners they cooked on a conventional range dropped by the same proportion.[8]

Besides time-shorteners like microwaves, the marketplace has supplied the quick cookbooks that teach shortcuts and quick-to-fix fare, and prepless cooking that brings to the kitchen products that are nearly ready for the table. Altering the menu in favor of quicker-to-prepare foods is another time-economizer. And if all else fails, the harried cook can leave the task to others either by dining out at a restaurant or dining in on take-out cuisine.

Alice B. Toklas's invaluable instructions to the striving cook make it clear that the chief requisite for achieving gourmet status is time. Lots of it. Her celebrated recipe for clear turtle soup proves that. "Soak ½ lb. sun-dried turtle meat in cold water for four days," writes Ms. Toklas, "changing the water each day." And that's just the first step. Preparing *Gigot de la Clinique* requires an eight-day head-start. Mutton is done after a mere seven hours of fiddling around over the stove, and the time-bargain of all is dulce, which requires only "about an hour" of *continuous* stirring.[9] Gone are the days—in fact, gone are the hours—for attempting such culinary feats.

Less adventurous modern cooks want to be taken by the hand, assured that time consuming mistakes can be avoided. They want to know how long it takes to prepare the meal, and do it fast without sacrificing quality. Their salvation is found in the quick-cookbooks with time-tested techniques and recipes that speed up cooking without diluting the diners' gustatory pleasures.

Classics, such as *The Joy of Cooking* and *The Good Housekeeping*

Cookbook served the home cook well for many a decade. But, as time scarcened, they were eclipsed by quick-cookbooks that trumpeted time-efficiency in their titles. *60-Minute Gourmet,* published in 1979, quickly made the best-seller list. Sales were so staggering that author/chef Pierre Franey went back to his kitchen to cook up a sequel, entitled (you guessed it) *More 60-Minute Gourmet.* Greased with success, the market then produced dozens more with titles, revealing of the times, like *Quick Cook, Fast and Flavorful, Fresh 15-Minute Meals, Fast Italian Meals,* and *Quick, Healthy Recipes from Japan.* Some carried assurances that half the recipes in the book will take only thirty minutes to prepare, "start to finish."[10]

"Prepless cooking" saves even more time. The upscale version of take-out promises a way to eat out at home. Preparers in restaurant kitchens or behind the supermarket take-out counters bag up all of the ingredients, ready to be taken home, combined and warmed up as prescribed on the instruction sheet, and put on the table ten minutes later.

With the time factor as prepless cooking's chief appeal, eating out at home has become a near-national custom. In 1977, a third of American adults bought take-out food at least once a month. In ten years, that proportion went up to one-half, and there is reason to believe that, soon, one in four meals eaten at home will have been cooked somewhere else.[11] The franchises for quick-chicken increase by more than 300 a year, for burgers by over 900, and for pizza by 1,100.[12]

As the market has expanded, so has quality. Cuisine-to-go items like lemon chicken and shredded duck salad are replacing the traditional deli fare of fried chicken and potato salad faster than you can say burger and fries. A Los Angeles eatery specializing in Chinese take-out, advertises "Wok-Away Chinese Home Cooking Kits."

And it's all because of the *BB* factor.

Eating Out Is In

Which jobs will grow most in the years ahead? Computer services? Nursing and medical services? Building trades? Timekeepers? The correct answer, alas, is none of these. Government projections estimate that new jobs in eating and drinking establishments will top 2.4 million by the year 2000, or nearly double the number created in the second ranking industry.[13] There is good reason. The demand for waiters and cooks, sub-chefs, dish-washers, restaurant accountants, and for all the others who back them up, will increase as more and more people give new meaning to that old line, "the best things to make for dinner are reservations."

The ultimate in delegating cooking tasks is simply to eat out, the dining alternative that reduces to zero the time spent cooking. The fraction of incomes spent on food away from home is rising, just as the proportion spent for home-cooked food is on the decline. Restaurants now capture more than forty cents of every food dollar, up from less than twenty cents in the 1960s.[14] Moreover, spending for food away from home rises to a peak between ages 35–54, just when time scarcity approaches its zenith.[15]

Hungering for better nutrition . . . or more time?

The *BB* factor even has a role determining what types of food go into our stomach, and goes far explaining the shift in our culinary preferences from red meat to white. Each year the average American consumes 1.4 pounds *less* of beef and two pounds *more* of chicken and half a pound *more* of seafood than the year before. Chicken consumption has now passed beef consumption.[16]

Health consciousness is part of the explanation for the shift. Worried about cholesterol and calories and their links to heart disease, hypertension, diabetes, and cancer, people are abandoning the cornucopia of fats and sweets that once graced the table. With nearly six times the amount of saturated fat per pound of a T-bone steak compared to a chicken, birds are perceived as more healthful.[17]

The quicker preparation time of chicken also encourages the cook to make the timely switch. Chicken parts that have been boned, skinned, marinated, breaded, and injected with salt and spices—the versions that have replaced the now near-obsolete "feathers-off, guts-out" whole bird—are, surprisingly enough, quicker for the gourmet chef to prepare than red meat. The support for this claim is found in one of the better cookbooks, better partly because it alerts the cook to the amount of time required for each recipe. Chef Jacques Pepin's[18] cookbook tells how much more speedily white items, compared to red, are prepared. The typical fish recipe takes a mere twenty minutes to prepare and cook, chicken takes forty-two minutes, and meat takes seventy-five minutes. Thank you, Messr. Pepin.

We know that serving chicken or seafood is more time-efficient than serving red meat. We also know that chicken and fish are more healthful. So the question is, which fact better explains the shift toward white "meat," diet-consciousness or time-consciousness?

And the answer is time-consciousness. The evidence points to the *BB* factor winning out over the much-ballyhooed healthful and nutritious protocol. It works this way. If people took nutrition seriously, wouldn't we expect consistency in their dietary preferences? Right. That means, doesn't it, that people will stick to those preferences whether they eat in or out? Wrong.

Fish and fowl may be preferred at home but not in restaurants. A recent poll asked people what they wanted more than anything else in the whole world when they ate out. It was (hang on tight for this one): a big, juicy T-bone steak! Beef, the first choice, ranked head and shoulders, loin and flank over the presumably healthier alternatives. Apparently people are willing to pay a pro to cook the fare that takes too long for them to cook themselves, even though the fare the pro cooks may be the dietary inferior.[19]

The nutritional craze may in fact be on the wane, particularly for *Busy Bodies*. The Food Market Institute Survey recently found that only 58 percent of shoppers were "very concerned" about the nutritional content of what made its way into their stomachs, down 6 percentage points from three years earlier. Nutritional concerns dropped the most among those aged 25 to 39, the years when both incomes and time pressures multiply rapidly. Worries about food's chemical additives, preservatives, freshness, purity, harmful ingredients, and food coloring all fell by large proportions. Apparently, this is a price that consumers willingly pay for the convenience that busier schedules require.

The nation, in fact, has embarked on a junk-food binge, and a high-calorie one at that. In surveying eating preferences over the past ten years, pollster Louis Harris discovered that the proportion of adults who crave all-you-can-eat specials in restaurants rose markedly and those looking for "dieter's specials" inched down. More and more *Busy Bodies* are blowing their diets and relying on junk food throughout the day. Over half admit to grazing all day long on nuts, grains, popcorn, ice cream, fruit, chips, pretzels, baked goods, candy, and "Vegi-snax" ("the celery with no strings attached").[20] Snacks have in common three time-saving features: they require no preparation time by the consumer, they can be consumed synchronically while the snacker does something else and, because they keep the stomach filled, no time need be wasted preparing and eating regular meals. Such constitutes the fare of the time-conscious.

The greater importance of time over diet, as explanation, is further supported by a deeper probing of the pleasures of the table, the other side of the coin from cooking, and the ways that the *BB* factor has compromised those delights.

FOOD FOR FUN OR FUEL?

Conversation and dining have long been nearly synonymous. Jesus instructed his disciples at the Last Supper. Roman orgies featured grapes-and-chicken-legs while other things went on, and King Arthur's chums reveled around his well-stocked round table. For centuries, the ritual of the evening meal fed soul as well as body, a time for gathering the family together and recalling today's activities and planning tomorrow's, for gossiping about Aunt Ida's latest escapades and chiding the kids for their low grades. TV doomed that. The Six O'Clock News preempted family conversation.

Americans' penchant for fast eating and synchronic dining also doomed a movement that promised to lift standards of good health to new heights. Horace Fletcher, a turn-of-the-century businessman, made the startling discovery that an invisible filter-like something-or-other at the back of the mouth was responsible for digesting food. All that was required for the "filter function" to work at its best was thorough chewing. According to his careful instructions, to Fletcherize was to chew each morsel until no taste remained. After something on the order of one hundred masticacations, the food was involuntarily swallowed and any residue of unchewed food would be automatically regurgitated.

Mr. Fletcher's supportive physician, an enthusiastic convert to the cause, declared that the religious practice of Fletcherizing had cured him of "gout, incapacitating headaches, frequent colds, boils on the neck and face, chronic eczema of the toes, . . . frequent acid dyspepsia (and) worse still (a loss of interest) in life and in my work."[21] Tests made at Yale University noted the absence of odor in Mr. Fletcher's excretions, a discovery that prompted the elated excreter to mail personal stool samples to a growing coterie of admirers.[22] Recipients of Fletcher's largesse included many well-known personalities of the day, among them Henry and William James, Upton Sinclair and Bernarr McFadden.

Despite success in adding years to its follower's lives—and *quality* to those years—the movement faltered. The hundred-chew rule interminably stretched out the time it took to finish a meal, and eliminated many possibilities for dining synchronically. Conversation, at least, was futile. Fletcherizing "added a new horror to dining out," wrote a leading arbiter of good taste, because "these strange creatures seldom repay attention. The best that can be expected from them is the tense and awful silence that always accompanies their excruciating tortures of mastication."[23] Fletcherizing was ahead of its day. Were it not for the time required to practice the technique, Fletcherizing could enjoy a current vogue for the lack of conversation at dinner would in no way compromise the pleasures of the hundred-chew rule.

The once-joyous social occasion of "the table" now ranks together with tooth brushing and sleeping as indispensable, but hardly pleasurable. Lost is that precious opportunity for communication. Indeed, we have become what Rupert Brook called Americans, "A country without conversation."[24] Yet Mr. Brook could say the same about his own country, England, where a TV graces the dining table of the best-regulated of households. Reports a London correspondent: "After a day spent working with Lord Snowdon, I was riveted to discover that in Kensington Palace, a television sat squarely on the dining table. Even with a guest present, the Snowdons shamelessly watched the news in the middle of dinner."[25]

Synchronicity aside, time scarcity has shortened the quantity of time most *Busy Bodies* are willing to spend simultaneously nourishing body and mind. As food became fuel, eating became maintenance. Fueling up the body now takes little longer than fueling up the car. "Those families that do eat together do so in approximately twenty minutes, with minimal interaction,'' notes a trend-watcher.[26] People read or watch television as other members of the family come and go, grabbing a bite and moving on to something else. Many would rather do away with the mandatory twenty minutes, and an astonishing number would prefer taking a pill to eating.[27]

If we spend so little time at formal meals, when do we feed ourselves? Synchronic dining remains, but it has taken on new forms. Fueling-up has become far more efficient in the contemporary junk-food era, for most have already ''grazed'' more or less continuously throughout the day. The secretary-typist synchronically enjoys a power-snack, guzzling and munching while typing, a bowl of Fritos and a can of cola at the ready. Never mind the greasy finger prints decorating the letters, she/he is saving the hours that more traditional types would waste at table. The CEO downs a bran muffin for breakfast. The busy lawyer gulps a something-or-other sandwich on the way to court. The commuter picks at a snack balanced on the dashboard. We know them well.

The *BB* factor has radically changed the central figure responsible for transforming things raw into things tempting. Yesterday's cook is today's facilitator who stocks cupboard, refrigerator, and freezer, and keeps at the ready the number of the nearest take-out pizza. An exaggeration? Perhaps, but let a food giant, and one whose very future depends on the *BB* factor, have the last word on the subject.

Monitoring by the Pillsbury Company of eating behavior since 1971 makes it clear that the traditional family meal will be all but dead by the year 2000.[28] ''Happy Cookers'' and ''Down Home Stokers,'' as the Pillsbury people dub them, are traditionalists who accounted for the vast majority of the cooking population in 1971, but are now fading from view. ''Happy Cookers'' are career home makers who nurture their families with three full meals a day, rely on fresh ingredients, make casseroles from scratch, and bake cakes just like mother's. Their distant cousins, the ''Down Home Stokers'' are women who work out of economic necessity and, because of it, carefully ration their precious time. These old-fashioned types fix old-style but quick-to-cook meals like homemade fried chicken, cornbread, meat, and potatoes.

And who will fill their shoes (and kitchens)? Upward-bound,

young urbanites known as ''Chase and Grabbits'' will have more than tripled in proportion by the year 2000. To dine in is to sup on that inevitable pair, hamburgers and carryout pizza, and, when variety demands it, microwaved popcorn. To dine out is to eat fast food and, when variety demands it, sushi. Coming in second among the growth groups are the ''Careful Cooks'' who focus their diets on skim milk, yogurt, salads, and fresh fruits and vegetables, for they crave an understanding of what goes in their mouths and stomachs. If they appear an aberrant case, caring much about what they eat but caring little for how long it takes to prepare, they are not. Because many of them are retired, the Careful Cooks are under considerably less time pressure than their juniors. Blessed as they are with the time to translate their knowledge into healthful diets, they represent a last bastion of cooking in time-expensive ways.

The food of the future will consist of easy and portable things that require minimal time for cooking or consuming. Little wonder then that the new edibles cater to the tastes and time constraints of the fast-growing Chase-and-Grabbit mentality. The big sellers consist of quick-and-easies like bagels, muffins, breakfast sandwiches, snack cakes, veggies packed in single portions, frozen soup-and-sandwich combinations for easy microwave thawing at office or home, ice cream bars, ice cream sticks, and ice cream bonbons. Tomorrow's cuisine is of the ''don't-sit-down-with-the-family'' variety.

THOUGHT FOR FOOD

Time scarcity has fomented a revolution at the table. Altering the how, what, where, and when of cooking and eating has yielded time premiums, and seems to be an inevitable consequence of the *BB* factor at work. Woe to the Chase and Grabbits, and the others whose dining habits have yielded to time pressure. For them, it is an easy return full circle to Skool Food, the toothsome repasts that were as distinctive as they were unforgettable. It is to them, in their earlier incarnations, that the celebrated gastronome, M. F. K. Fisher, spoke when she listed the bases of various national cuisines. For the French, it was butter; for Italians, olive oil; for Germans, lard; and for Americans, it was tin cans.

The most obvious casualty of eating on the run is the evening meal; the less obvious casualties are the joys that once accompanied that nearly defunct event. With dinner's demise, lost is one of the surviving opportunities for social communication between parents and generations younger and older. Sharing food, and the rituals that went along with it, brought the family together in a unique experience. That experience will be sorely missed in a time-scarce age when—to preview a point elaborated in an upcoming chapter—individual activity seems destined to displace social activity.

We now know all about the invasion of technology into the Gnomons' gastronomic life (and we know perhaps more than we want). But the details surrounding Nola's face-lift-body-sculpt remain a mystery. The secrets are revealed in the next chapter.

9:00

CLEANLINESS, FITNESS, AND BEAUTIFULNESS

"It's the old problem, of course—that one that makes life so tough for murderers—what to do with the body."
—P. G. Wodehouse[1]

Whether it is bathing, brushing (and flossing) teeth, shaving, making-up, or using the toilet, most personal maintenance is just downright b-o-r-i-n-g. Some activities have been unaffected by the parade of new time-saving technologies. Machines can wash our car in five minutes, but there is no gadget to help *us* come clean in less than the ten minutes it takes to shower. However, innovations ranging from quick cosmetics to exotic surgeries that can radically and almost instantaneously transform our appearance have enhanced the **S** and reduced the **T** for some aspects of personal maintenance. And exercise devices—like those in the Gnomons' home gym—promise the fitness that "manufactures" time by saving days lost to illness and adding years of longevity. Events centered on the bathroom demonstrate how other innovations can exploit synchronicity as a time-economizer.

BATHING

Bathing habits illustrate how time value influences hygiene. Those who place a higher premium on time seem less inclined to devote expensive time to washing.

An investigation of Tokyo residents' post-toilet habits concludes that 54 percent of men wash their hands after using the toilet, as against 93 percent of women.[2] In a nation where most males but few females work for pay, the perception of higher time costs may account for the men's more cavalier attitude. And in Britain, a higher proportion of male adults than of housewives—49 percent compared to 41 percent—never take baths at all.[3] Different values placed on time could explain the gender difference, with employed British males, like their Japanese counterparts, valuing their time higher.

Given Americans' reputation for time economy, is it any wonder that the shower wins hands down over the bathtub? Most of our homes have a shower, but only 10 percent of U.K. households can boast the same.[4] Although tub bathing has rewards over the more utilitarian shower, it takes longer.

Minimizing higher-valued **T**ime is but one factor determining the habits of the bath. **S**atisfaction gained from the experience is no less important.

Contrast the bathing propensities of Germans and Japanese, peoples widely separated both geographically and in terms of the attention given to the pleasures of the bath. Germans, little obsessed with the ritual and gaining little satisfaction from it, have little time for bathing. According to Alexander Kira, who has dedicated himself to understanding the art and practice of bathing, over half the German population take a bath only once a week and brush their teeth rarely and, for about 10 percent, bathing is a monthly ritual. The West German Baths Society reports that there are forty-one television sets for every bathtub in the country. Professor Kira maintains that some people, including many Germans, have a particular affection for seasoned clothing. For them, laundering merely compromises life's rewards. "The average German changes his shirt every other day, his socks and underwear every three to four days, and his bed linen every four weeks." Moreover, "when the East German army tried to persuade its troops to change underwear more frequently, the men simply sent the fresh underwear to the laundry and continued to wear their old underwear for weeks at a time."[5]

The Japanese, not at all as unobsessed with such matters, bathe at least daily. The western tradition of taking long hot baths, immersed in dirty water, is frowned upon. A small bucket is used for washing, followed by a plunge into a large tub filled with hot water that is rarely changed. The soothing and calming bath offers escape from the day's high-voltage tensions. The showers that Americans prefer are generally described by their users as an in-

vigorating form of hydrotherapy that refreshes and revitalizes, and certainly the faster alternative. Summarizing the options, authority Kira comments that "Persons who have a choice say that they take a shower bath when they are in a hurry but a tub bath when they have the time and are tense and wish to relax."[6]

In an earlier day, bathing was bathing, a procedure intended simply to rid oneself of the dirt, waste, and grime accumulated since the last one. Then came the discovery that under the right circumstances and given the amenities of a heated bathroom, an abundance of hot water, and a supply of sweet-smelling soap, bathing could serve multiple purposes ranging from the utilitarian one of simply getting clean to the hedonistic one of pleasure. "Asked to explain their motives for bathing," concluded one survey, "few of the victims of this inquisition seem to have admitted ever to being so dirty as to *need* a bath. . . . Most of them mentioned relaxation."[7]

As hedonism replaced utilitarianism, the outhouse underwent a radical transformation to the indoor, functional, white toilet-tub-and-basin bathroom, to the colorful, glamorized, and spacious salons of today. And salons they are, or will be with the realization of novel possibilities forecast for raising the **S** of bathroom activity. The World Future Society envisions throwing parties in bathrooms as one of its "Most Thought-Provoking Forecasts." Like the Roman baths, the bathroom will be transformed to a social center, a next evolutionary step made possible by larger multiple-occupancy tubs. At the party of the future, the hostess may invite guests to "join us in the tub."[8]

The evolution of the water closet serves as an inspiring example of how technological advancement has upgraded one set of bathroom functions, but has done so slowly and unevenly since its invention in the sixteenth century. Except for its relocation from the privy to the indoor bathroom, not a great deal happened for many years in perfecting the loo. It has to be the bathing-obsessed Japanese who deserve credit for mothering the more remarkable innovations of recent years. Bravo to them for bringing new excitement to the easing of nature, one of the most tedious—albeit welcome—of the day's events.

Japan has enthroned the toilet, so to speak.

- The Etiquettone generates toilet-like sounds wherever and whenever its user wishes. A survey found that Japanese women flush an average of 2.7 times a visit to mask more natural noises. The practice wastes about 15 liters of water per visit and millions of liters daily, a problem of particular concern in a country that faces a chronic water shortage. Fuji Bank, by installing these sound-disguisers at its 1,600 branches, has chalked up annual savings of $500,000 in water bills.[9]
- A device unfortunately called the Moover automatically coats the toilet seat with a thin layer of plastic, guaranteeing each new user a clean surface to sit on.

- At the touch of a button, the "paperless toilet" produces a nozzle below the heated seat that, bidet-like, squirts water on the part needing attention, dries it with a blast of hot air, sprays a scent, and finally washes the bowl clean.

A prominent toilet-use expert has calculated, for our enlightenment, a parameter called "toilet occupation time." Years of patient research distilled by Professor Nishioka at Koio University established the fact that Japanese men spend an average of 31.7 seconds in the lavatory on each of their 5.5 daily visits. Women, to no one's surprise, take more time. Japanese women visit the loo seven times a day, for an average of 97 seconds per visit.[10] With time in the lavatory summing up to nearly two months in a male's lifetime and seven months in a female's, there is good reason why the Japanese lead the pack in toilet technology that trims the time requirement **T** or enhances the **S**. Because each episode on or at the toilet is often of short duration, however, neither the efficiency nor the pleasure of the experience is easily increased. But adding to it another activity—synchronicity, in our parlance—helps.

Reading is commonplace (40 percent do so) while defecating,[11] and a library of sorts is a useful adjunct to that basic function. The relationship is not symmetrical however for, as Mr. Kira points out, it is more usual to put a library in the toilet than to put a toilet in the library.[12] History furnishes other notable examples of how toilets have been used synchronically.

- Plumbing historians have noted Louis XIV's love-hate relationship with the objects of their study. Although he never bathed, the Sun King had 264 toilets installed in Versailles Palace. Those searching for better ways to combine activities in novel juxtapositions will honor him for the public audience he held to announce *ex cathedra* his forthcoming marriage to Mademoiselle de Maintenot—while perched on one of the 264 thrones.[13]
- Saints were not exempt from the bodily function of elimination, nor from the tedium surrounding it. St. Gregory, for instance, commended this "isolated retreat" for "uninterrupted reading."[14]
- Lord Chesterfield in his celebrated *Letters to His Son,* advised that he "knew a gentleman who was so good a manager of his time that he would not even lose that small portion of it which the call

> of nature obliged him to pass in the necessary-house; but gradually went through all the Latin poets, in those moments."[15]

Others have externalized the call of nature from the necessary-house without sacrificing synchronicity. James I was one. The monarch, according to reports, "regularly and splendidly beshat himself while in the saddle since he refused to pause in the hunt for any reason."[16]

Modern technology has continued the tradition of introducing synchronicity into toilet functions with Japan again at the forefront. Using built-in sensors, "Asa Ichiban" ("First in the Morning") offers special appeal to *Busy Bodies,* for the new "intelligent toilet" analyzes body waste *in situ* with a liquid-crystal display that reads out the user's blood pressure, pulse, and weight.[17]

And beyond that? A major Japanese plumbing manufacturer is at work analyzing the social merits of moving toilets out of the bathroom and putting them right in the living space (perhaps even in the library, Prof. Kira?).[18] And just at a time when people are moving into the bathroom for socializing. We must make up our minds what happens where.

EXERCISING: THE WORK OF WORKING OUT

Biology and society compel us to use the toilet and bathroom. Neither Mother Nature nor friends, however, compel us with the same urgency to exercise. Coming as it does under the heading of boring "personal care," exercise would seem to be doomed as a potentially time-minus activity, easily crowded out by others that give more pleasure. Yet, fitness has not only survived the competition but has become a craze. Why?

Exercise was once seen as something of a necessity. It had to be done because of the good it somehow did you. Today, however, the typical committed exercisers, whether male or female, devote about five hours per week to their routine.[19] Each year no less than seven million people pay the health club membership fees that buy them access to equipment for twisting their bodies into desired shapes. Expenditures for equipping home gyms with weights, exercise bikes, treadmills, and other exercise paraphernalia have mounted by 100 times in ten years. Manufacturers of major brand athletic shoes raked in $6 billion in 1987, alone—triple their revenues of a decade earlier.[20]

So there must be good reason for the exercise craze, time consuming as it is. There are, in fact, several: to lose weight, to feel fit and healthy, to live longer, to look glamorous . . . and perhaps even to meet others with the same peculiar set of values. What of the relationship between these benefits and time scarcity? Time spent exercising, if it increases healthiness, may save the time required to recover from illness and, if the fit live longer, the effort extends time on earth. Exercise, a short-run time-absorber, may translate into a long-run time-generator.

The Healthiness of Exercise

Taking better care increases time measured either in days of good health or in days of life. For example, experts maintain that six to eight hours a week given to a program of vigorous exercise can add as much as a year to a life.[21] A vigorous exercise regime stimulates the heart to pump blood through the body in only a few seconds, whereas a minute is the usual time required to make the complete circuit. Running not only exercises the heart but lowers blood pressure, increases levels of the desirable cholesterol carrier HDL, and reduces the incidence of coronary disease. These connections are fairly well known, but recent research adds to the athletes' list lowered risks of diabetes and certain types of cancer.[22]

Former Surgeon General C. Everett Koop, the "nation's doctor," dismayed and insulted one-fourth of the nation's population by labeling 34 million Americans obese. It is little wonder, then, that slimness topped the wish list of those who were asked what aspect of their physical appearance they most wanted to change. Weight was the target of 56 percent of the men queried, and waistline came in at 49 percent; weight and waistline garnered 78 and 70 percent of the women's vote.[23]

Exercise, a favored method for achieving the number one ambition, temporarily speeds up the rate at which the body burns calories. Dieting, another method, plays a complementary role. The Framingham Heart Study, which has monitored the health of some 5,000 people over two generations of their lives, discovered that trimming 10 percent off body weight lowered by 20 percent the chances for coronary heart disease.[24] Successful weight-loss programs lower blood pressure and cholesterol levels, deal with diabetes by controlling blood sugar, and help people feel better about themselves and how they look. Weight-loss programs that include exercise get rid of fat and build muscle, and reduce the likelihood that the exerciser-dieter will regain the weight. In short, synchronically merging dieting with exercise is dynamite for *Busy Bodies!*

The High-Tech of Exercise

Increasing health-consciousness has boosted the **S** of exercise, and the new technology that has both raised its **S** and lowered its **T** has elevated exercise to time-plus status. In fact, it is doubtful whether any other personal activity has been commoditized so rapidly and extensively, or been more thoroughly justified in medical research as a means for positively modifying human behavior.

Up through the 1960s, the venues for achieving the body perfect were the figure salons, fitted out with motorized vibrating belts that jiggled fat and presumably disposed of it somehow, and the musty gymnasiums where Mr. and Mrs. Americas-to-be pumped their way to trophies, and boxers trained for their next Golden Gloves bout. In the 1970s, the keys that unlocked the door to fitness were a good pair of running shoes and a subscription to *Runner's World* magazine. Technology and computers, plus a healthy dose of aggressive salespersonship, moved exercise from those dark ages of odoriferous gyms to the high-tech world of the 1980s, built the $50-billion-a-year fitness industries, demonstrated that thinning people fattens profits, and motivated the millions of Americans who huff and puff to tone muscle, trim fat, and incinerate calories.

Gadgets that fairly shout fitness and health have pointed the way to the perfect pec, bicep, tricep, quad, and armpit. The glamorous gear that so intrigues the Gnomons ranges from miniaturized monitors to state-of-the-art computer-driven behemoths affordable only by the super-rich. Complete weight-training systems, costing up to $50,000, substitute silent magnetic fields for clanging weights, tailor the workouts individually, test strength, count repetitions, measure calories burned, and, with a computerized voice like C3PO, cajole users into pumping away. Treadmills, stationary bikes, and rowing machines bring walking in the park, cycling on the street, and rowing at the lake right into the home and save the time getting to those locations for the workout, the time required to find a parking place for the car in the lot and for the body on the exercise floor, or the time waiting for machines and showers.

A working knowledge of the anatomy is almost essential to understanding what the exotic machines do, or are claimed to do. You're ready for a Home Rotary Torso Machine when "love handles" start sagging over your belt. "Insufficient hip rotation is the cause," taunts the promotional material, and at the root of that frightening diagnosis is "a gradual weakening from age of your external and internal obliques."[25] A less-than-modest payment to the Nautilus people who manufacture the machine starts the debilitated on the road to recovery with a "scientifically engineered workout that will restore power and tone to your waistline."

While they walk to nowhere, cycle to nowhere, row to nowhere—except toward the goal of fitness—users of electronically souped-up reincarnations of the treadmill, the stationary bicycle, and the rowing machine are distracted from the pain and agony of the experience, and motivated to keep at it by audio-visual add-ons. A glass of scotch in hand, and astride a Videocycle, the committed home-exerciser can vicariously whiz down a German *autobahn,* across the Place Concorde, or along Rodeo Drive, inspired by a built-in, large-screen television plus appropriate travel tapes. A 13-inch color computer screen shows exercisers who work out with Liferower the progress of their racing sculls competing against pre-set pacing crafts, and a built-in sound system transmits roars of approval from an electronic crowd. Monitors with electronic feedback calculate calories burned, take blood pressure, estimate pulse rate, measure stress, and figure "fitness scores." Most useful are digital pulse monitors that periodically read out the status of the heartbeat and reassure their users that they are still among the living.

High-tech equipment, though unnecessary for building the perfect body, provides exercisers with the incentive to undertake such strenuous labor and to keep at it. Because of its cost and complexity, the high-in-**S**-low-in-**T** machinery *must* be doing some good and doing it fast. So it is believed among the dues-paying *Busy Bodies* who belong to the fitness cult. The electronically glamorized treadmill must be worth the five-hundred dollar outlay even if it only takes the home-based exerciser for a long walk in a short room. Dedicated exercisers, like Norman Gnomon, can be comfortable in the knowledge that the yield on exercise is on the upswing.

Yet, all it takes to duplicate many of the fanciest strength-builders is a bag of sand hooked up to a couple of pulleys by a few feet of rope, and a stopwatch. An old bicycle, wheels-removed and propped up on a stack of bricks, does the work of an aerobics machine. Old-fashioned calisthenics, like the couple of stretches in bed and shaping up in the shower that Barbara Pearlman recommends in *Workouts that Work for Women Who Work,*[26] can handily substitute for an investment of a few thousand dollars in computer-driven alternatives. Although the virtually costless substitutes don't flatten the wallet, they're no fun at all and fail to distract users from the pain of the experience. In short, low-tech is a low-**S** substitute.

Exercise commoditization has also invaded the great outdoors, the third major venue for carrying on the activity.[27] Be they fisher-persons, golfers, joggers and runners, skiers, skaters, or swimmers, every outdoor athlete can find equipment to enhance the quality of the experience, and perhaps to save time. Available in small, medium, or large sizes, equipped at high-, medium-, or low-techs, and priced at the low, middle, or high ranges, there are exercise gadgets that offer something for everyone.

Joggers and runners can select any of roughly eighty models of shoes, with accessorized supercushiony models at the top end. One version comes equipped with built-ins that record how far and how fast its wearer runs: shoes that time men's tries, so to speak. A pedometer not only reads out distance but, with a snooze alert, instantly startles dozers back into alertness. An angler searching for a new angle will discover a vestpocket computer that suggests the perfect lure—whether grub, worm, or lizard—to fit every condition. All else failing, it tells the hapless fisher to change locations. Another, the "Automatic Fisher," hooks its prey with an unattended rod and sounds an alarm signifying the exact moment to reel in the catch, thus freeing the busy fisher-person to do something else (like going fishing *without* an Automatic Fisher).

Some devices "save" time by synchronically combining exercise with another activity. Skaters who want to strengthen knees and ankles as they glide around the rink will want to doff a pair of aerobic roller shoes that promote "flexibility of tendons and ligaments as it develops the cardiovascular system and muscular strength and simulate the motions of cross country and downhill skiing."

Other gadgets "buy" time by making exercise feasible when bad weather or darkness would have ruled it out. Electrically heated mittens and socks add to the number of days that runners and skiers can enjoy their sport. For especially warm days, solar-powered helmets with built-in fans give welcome relief from the heat. A search light and a nylon umbrella attached to the Automatic Fisher extends sporting time into the night and rainy weather. Illuminated night golf balls are available to those who insist on playing a round in the dark.

And finally, for the male who can afford neither the equipment nor the time for exercise, there's an easy and inexpensive (thirty-five dollar) path to *apparent* fitness. It's a pullover polyester and cotton shirt with built-in foam falsies that reveal the "male torso with pure definition . . . bulging at the chest pecs, through the shoulders, and down both arms," according to its vendor.

If diet and exercise prolong life, then exercising is **T**-effective. On the other hand, if vanity is a chief motivator, then exercising and dieting are also high in **S**. Other paths to beauty, however, merit consideration for they may be far more time efficient.

BEAUTIFYING

The Duchess of Windsor recalled that, on the day she was to meet the Prince of Wales, "I got up and spent the entire day on face and nails."[28] In the era of the *BB* factor, few women can afford such extravagance.

Like so many other paths to personal perfection, the time spent beautifying is, at best, a bore. The cosmetic industry has caught on quickly to that fact and now "instant" has become one of the magic marketing catch-words in this realm. Major producers market products with names like Instant NailColor ("one application dries in about two minutes''), Rapide Instant Beautifier, or Instant Action Rinse-Off Cleanser. Artificial tanning lotions, that promise quick-tintings in an hour or two, save days working on a tan at the beach, and are probably safer.

Cosmetics such as antiageing creams obscure time's ravages by cutting the appearance of years off life, and one manufacturer claims for its product that skin ''looks more clear and a little more taut almost *instantaneously.*'' For the really impatient, an instant skin spackle can hide wrinkles, fill crow's feet, and conceal taught lines, by somehow changing the way skin reflects light. Prepainted stick-on fingernails provide instant manicures.

None of these options, however, offers the quick path to beautification that cosmetic surgery does. ''Aesthetic'' surgery has become a booming business in a market that has expanded threefold in a spare five years. By one estimate, three million Americans a year choose a bagbob, boobbob, browbob, bumbob, nosebob, tummybob, or your usual, everyday facelift or hair transplant.[29] Credit more sophisticated procedures, safer anesthetics, and a narcissistic society's vanity and fear of aging with causing the boom in ''body sculpting'' (to use the more polite term).

THE PRICE OF BEAUTY

Hair-replacement surgery	$250–$10,000
Face lift	$1,200– $8,000
Eyelid tuck	$1,000– $5,000
Nose job (rhinoplasty)	$300– $6,000
Breast augmentation	$1,000– $5,500
Breast reduction	$2,000– $7,000
Tummy tuck	$1,200– $8,500
Liposuction	$500– $5,000[30]

Procedures such as these don't always work as intended. Facelifts can make people look more surprised than younger, cause nerve damage that results in a crooked smile, or eventually droop like a failed soufflé. Silicone implants sometimes produce rock-hard or square-shaped breasts, or breasts that list in one direction but not the other, and even worse, the possibility of auto-immune disorders, and even death.

We were haunted by Nola's pregnant "there's more to the story" after the revelation about her face-lift. Did the unfinished bit have something to do with body contouring? It had!

Nolan graciously gave us the story on the phone one evening when Nola was out of their electronically integrated home, apparently to return merchandise. "Well, she was all upset about her 'love-handles,' and a few bags and bulges here and there. We had heard about something called 'liposuction' and how 'lipectomies' had won the Grand Slalom for speedy diet-for-beautification."

"So, we investigated. We were worried at first. You heard the story about the woman who had her belly button fixed and the plastic surgeon left it an inch-and-a-half off center. Well, she sued and won $650,000. Do you realize that comes to $433,333 per inch, or over $15 million a yard?[31] Lipectomies do carry some danger of damaged nerves and discolored skin, but the American Society of Plastic and Reconstructive Surgery gave the procedure its blessing, and only eleven deaths have been reported since the technique arrived from France in the early '80s. The price tag was hefty, but we thought, why not?"

"You would have been impressed. We didn't wait a minute in his office. He ushered us right into the operating room. Our lipectomist knows that his patients value their time highly, otherwise they would have opted for more leisurely weight-reduction methods. He allowed me to watch the whole procedure. Here's the behind-the-scenes report."

"He sedated Nola, then made a tiny half-inch slit near her stomach, and poked in a drainage tube connected to a suction apparatus. Then he used such advanced surgical procedures as brute force to thrust the thing around deep inside her to dislodge as much fat as possible. This goes on for maybe twenty minutes as the fat cells, that are now separated from fiber, come gurgling out."[32]

"It took so much effort that it wasn't clear whether he or Nola lost more pounds. Anyway, out came the remnants of her good life and now she's pounds lighter. The last step is a cashectomy, then we're back on our feet, ready for a meal, and getting the whole sequence going again. How about that?"

And all in the name of time saving!

10:00
HOUSEWORK

"Home life as we understand it is no more natural to us than a cage is natural to a cockatoo."
—George Bernard Shaw[1]

The windows were heavily shrouded, the drapes heavily fringed and tasseled, the floors heavily carpeted, the furniture heavily upholstered in chintz and embroidery, the walls heavily papered in crimson and gilding, and heavily hung with Japanese fans and family portraits recalling generations. It was filled with "pretentious uselessness," exclaimed a certain Mrs. Orrinsmith in describing the Victorian home furnished with objects that "seem as if chosen on the principle of unfitness for any function."[2] But the furnishings and decorations *did* serve a function. They provided heavenlike sanctuary from an unheavenly world.

BE IT EVER SO HUMBLE

Writers of the era portrayed the home as an inspirational retreat from an inhospitable world, a bright haven from the dark outside. Mrs. C. A. Riley exulted in *The Family Circle and Parlor Annual* of the "hours of sweet and holy communion in this blest retirement from a cold and calculating world."[3] Even dispassionate de Tocqueville joined in the paean of praise, extolling the home as no less than a "cherished sanctuary of earthly happiness."[4] Innocent and uncorrupted, home served as both haven and heaven.

The home was a sanctuary in the liturgical and nonliturgical sense of the word. The little pointy Gothic arches crowning the windows and doorways of the quintessential Victorian house were just like those at St. Clement's down the street. With the housewife reigning as grand high priestess of the Temple of Earthly Happiness, home served as a source of religious sentiment.

Fortunately, there was little competition for the time and energy of this priestess. The social norms of the age effectively kept housewives at home, for it was believed that feminine qualities, such as virtue and purity, disqualified women from gainful employment. So lively was the topic that the Shakespearean Club of Osage, Iowa, was prompted to feature a debate, "Resolved: that the work of the outside world unfits a woman for home duties," at its April 18, 1893 meeting.[5] There is little doubt which team emerged victorious.

A wife's enforced idleness reflected her husband's success and position. It was a proud husband who, gesturing grandly to his well-maintained residence, could announce to the world—or to a meeting of the local Shakespearean Club—that his wife did not "work." She spent her days keeping the house to keep him happy . . . and to keep him. "It is not, however, merely in his wife that a husband should look for and expect beauty," asserted *The Family Friend* in 1867. "It should, as far as possible, be made to appear in everything with which he is surrounded."[6] The keeper of the surroundings was more than a husband's wife; she was, in the truest sense, a *house* wife, as married to her dwelling as to her mate. In an odd way, time spent in housework had a high **S**.

The fantasy of home as heaven could survive only so long as able and willing servants were available to care for the children, to prepare the meals, to preserve the food, to carry the water, to wash the dishes, to dust the furniture, and to launder and iron the clothes—the day-to-day operations that protocol excluded the proper middle-class housewife from performing in the proper middle-class household. Lacking that help, managing home-*cum*-heaven could be hell.

All this was destined to change as the twentieth century approached. The Servant Problem, the movement toward egalitarianism, and a lifting of the social and economic barriers to the gainful employment of women converged to alter the Victorian view of household management. Technological advance furthered these changes and heightened the opportunities for housewives to allocate their **T**ime without losing a measure of the domestic **S**atisfaction gained.

THE DAWNING OF A NEW CENTURY AND A TIME FOR CHANGE

Continuing a trend that started in the 1890s, the household servants who played such central roles in the drama of the well-regulated Victorian household began to vanish. The country girls who once performed the onerous chores came to prefer industrial jobs, for factory work gave them a type of independence lacking in domestic work. Yet, without their help it was left to the mistress of the household to take on the responsibilities and learn the skills abandoned by the departed servants. Housework had to be simplified.

The dawning of a technological age began the transformation of the home, making housework more tolerable and, it was hoped, less time-consuming. There also came the realization that a wife's time in housework might have value in much the same sense as her husband's time in "real" work. And there came the parallel realization that if his time at factory or office could be made more efficient by the use of machinery that served "real" production, so could hers. If only the time-saving machinery of the factory could be harnessed for the home. In fact, it could.

The sewing machine, first manufactured during the 1850s, was "exported" from factory to home as soon as mass production drove the price within reach of householders. Penetrating the domestic market required promoting the merits of the industrial machine in domestic application. Isaac Merrit Singer found the key that unlocked that market, by demonstrating how the sewing machine could both lower the **T** of housework, and produce a healthy dose of **S**.

In advertising his machine, Mr. Singer called attention to "the countless hours it has added to women's leisure for rest and refinement" and went on to enumerate "the numberless opportunities it has opened for women's employment" (presumably at home). The machine also increased opportunities "for that early training of children, for lack of which so many pitiful wrecks are strewn across the shores of life." If those virtues weren't enough, Singer credited the device with "the comforts it has brought within the reach of all which could formerly be attained only by the wealthy few."[7]

None of this would have been possible were it not for the invention of electricity. Since this fuel of the future powered the gadgets that promised domestic users freedom from toil and drudgery, "our homes will be transformed to operate smoothly with the aid of electricity," predicted A. G. Whyte, "so that the labor involved in cleaning, in heating, in cooking, and in washing and other domestic tasks will be performed by an electrical deputy. The energy thus released can be devoted to the enjoyment of home life, to education, to the cultivation of music and art, and the other beneficent recreations for which a measure of freedom is essential."[8] It was a proud housewife indeed who, by the turn of the century, could boast a range, a sewing machine, a vacuum cleaner, and even a dishwasher. She needed the "deputies" to do the work done by the now-absent human equivalents.

"Home economy," a term that fairly snaps, crackles, and pops with the idea of **S/T**, was another innovation to offer hope for confronting the servant problem. The home economics movement, beginning over a century ago, sought ways to save time spent in home maintenance and to make chores more tolerable. Scientizing homemaking prevented a woman from becoming "too solicitous a housewife, too anxious a housekeeper," as Elizabeth Banks straightforwardly put it, and "too contented a drudge."[9] Demonstrating to housewives how they could plan and carry out domestic duties as if they were industrial tasks promised them salvation from the tyranny of housework, and from the sobering prospect of becoming too-contented a drudge.

First things first. Cleaning ladies were still available but the live-in maid who arose at dawn, kindled the fire in the stove, stirred the porridge, and fried the bacon and eggs was gone. For good reason the reformers urged targeting first those operations centered in the kitchen. Kitchen labor could be streamlined to yield time savings without sacrificing the **S** of homemaking, urged Catherine E. Beecher and Harriet Beecher Stowe, mavens of the home economy movement.[10]

Lay out the kitchen better, locate everything within easy reach, organize goods and utensils on built-in shelves and in drawers, make work surfaces more compact, and get the proper equipment. Those who carefully applied the principles of home economy could prepare food more efficiently without sacrificing wholesomeness. And those lacking the time for food preparation could leave it to industry to do so at larger scale and lower cost, and at no apparent loss of nutrition. Ex-cowboy and real estate promoter Charles W. Post discovered how to do that, first with a quick coffee substitute, then with a ready-to-eat breakfast food. "Postum," the cereal-based beverage that he lent his name to, met the multiple objectives of time-efficiency and nutritional value. So did Grape-Nuts, the "brain food" that was advertised not only as a quick source of nutrition but as a cure for consumption, malaria, and loose teeth.[11] To be sure, Postum and Grape-Nuts were quicker to prepare, but somehow they sacrificed the quality of the fare they replaced. So did canned foods.

Canned goods dealt handily with **T** but was the convenience worth the sacrificed freshness, taste, and nutrition? Consumers answered with a definite "yes," and sales of canned and other prepared foods soared.[12] Time conservation won out. As it usually does.

Much of this had happened by the year 1900, the turn of a century and a turning point in the evolution of household management. The appliances, canned goods, and electrically powered machinery that arrived to commoditize domestic production in the "modern" home left no room for Victorian trappings. Out went the overdraping, overcarpeting, overfurnishing, overupholstering, overdecorating, overknicknacking, overstuffing. Like so much detritus. Out it went, but destined to return in concept less than a century later.

BACK TO VICTORIANA

Although the furnishings and accessories differ, today's home marks a return to the Victorian villa of yore. In place of the Baroque clocks, figurined candlesticks, gewgaws, and excrescences, the totems of the *nouveau* Victorian dwelling are the computers, stereos, video recorders, and other trappings of the electronic age that fill the fully amenitized "smart homes" of the decidedly upscale. All promise to save time traveling for services that can be brought right into the home: the electronic home entertainment center that saves trips to the cinema and theater; electronic shopping that saves trips to the store; the home gym that saves trips to the athletic club; the teletex that saves trips to the airline, library, and singles bars to shop for tickets, information, and mates; the electronic home work station that saves telecommuters' time traveling to work; and the electronic butler that holds the promise of resolving the irksome servant problem.

Privatizing Domestic Life

The contemporary counterpart of the piano, as the entertainment nucleus of the Victorian home, is the glimmering, buzzing, flashing, glitzy electronic pleasure-givers that have transformed living rooms into the primary showplaces for the performing arts. Besides providing at-home entertainment and education, and saving the time and effort of traveling to the more traditional venues, the electronic home entertainment center has become the status symbol of the *nouveau* Victorian Age.

Bringing Fun Home. The increasingly ubiquitous TV-coupled video recorder, has profoundly altered the distribution of venues for popular entertainment. As video stores spring up, movie theaters close. As growing numbers of home televiewers watch the performing arts, the live versions on stage decline. By a margin of 46 percent to 28 percent, Americans prefer staying at home over going out for their entertainment. Of specific home activities, renting a movie wins the most votes.[13]

Movies brought the whole world into the neighborhood movie house. Now, with the TV and VCR bringing the whole world into the home through an electronic window, videotime is replacing movietime. In fact, watching videocassettes accounts for the 50 percent increment since 1965 in time spent watching the tube.[14] Why go out to the movies when the best seat in the house is often at home?

Wouldn't most of us prefer watching movies in cinemas equipped with wide screens and Dolby THX sound instead of viewing video-taped movies at home, with the big images squeezed down to fit onto small screens and the big soundtracks funneled through squeaky three-inch speakers? On the other hand, wouldn't we prefer home over those shoe-box multiplexes that boast all the ambience of a dentist's waiting room and screen images that look like eight-millimeter home movies projected on bed sheets? Yes the merits of the at-home alternative are winning out.

For one thing, microwaved popcorn made at home has real butter.

For another, with just about every movie ever made available on video tape, the options are nearly unlimited. Tapes offer children's films, classics, martial arts, nostalgia, self-improvement, cult films, and X-rated shows, with fare ranging from how-to's like "Appalachian Clogging," "Goose Calling," and "Picking Up Men," to exotica like "Dracula Sucks," "Hercules Goes Bananas," "Space Sluts in the Slammer," and "Surf Nazis Must Die."

Vidiots, as they are unkindly called, decide what and where they want to watch and, most importantly, *when,* without being locked into a rigid schedule imposed by someone else. In a world of unpredictability and pressure to perform on time, it is little wonder that flexibility in scheduling leisure time becomes important. The cinemagoer is more or less stuck if the movie is bad, but if the taped movie at home disappoints, the viewer simply zaps it into oblivion and starts over with another. Polls show that many prefer "renting movies to watching them in a theater mainly for the chance to control the viewing experience" and "TV viewing is the ultimate controllable experience," says timeologist John Robinson.[15] The fastest-growing group of vidiots consists of working women, stressed by the *BB* factor, yet wanting to be masters (sorry, mistresses) of their time.[16] After all, the value of their time is increasing, and the amount of leisure decreasing, perhaps the fastest of all groups.

Besides greater freedom of choice, home viewing offers the privacy lacking at the bijou. The enclosure of home gives the same security from intrusion as the plain brown wrapper in which "those" magazines and books arrive in the mail. No need anymore to sneak off to the dingy little movie theater, the sleazy book shop with all of those cellophane-wrapped magazines. Thanks to the VCR, videotaped porn is available for viewing at home where people are free to be a tad wicked. With the porn film/video industry booming and annual sales running at eight billion dollars, the sex emporiums, bookstores, peep shows, strip joints, and sleazy little movie theaters are vanishing from the map. Nationwide, the number of such outlets (so to speak) has dropped to half what it was a decade ago.[17]

Teletex and videotex, another electronic component of the "smart" home, couples information with entertainment. At the touch of a button, viewers can summon up airline schedules, bank balances, home management hints, local events calendars, phone numbers, recipes, shopping guides, stock market quotes, television newspapers, traffic information, and weather forecasts. Home-based teletex users can dial up Jewish jokes, book hotels, shop for groceries, leave messages in electronic mail boxes, make blind dates and theater reservations, question politicians, trade sexual messages, get holistic medical advice, and engage prayer services ("Our Lady's Workers" offers "an urgent message for America from the Virgin Mary").[18]

And if this electronica weren't enough, the robo-butler promises to once and for all solve the servant problem. The electronic butler with a microchip brain will express compliance with a (frankly, rather sexist) "yes, master." Although master or mistress may be miles away, the electronic servant dials the police or fire department when he/she/it senses the presence of an uninvited guest or a high temperature, transmits sounds from nursery or sick-room, switches on (or off) lights or hi-fi in response to a spoken command (like *Fiat Lux*), draws the bath water, adjusts the thermostat, starts the oven, and announces when the mail has arrived.

Bringing the Goods Home. The Duchess of Windsor had embroidered on one of the pillows in her Waldorf Astoria suite, "If you're tired of shopping, you're using the wrong shops."[19] These days, shopping fatigue is more likely to come from using the wrong television channels. Mail order, home delivery, and electronic shopping are booming in an age when more working women than ever are pressed for time and an aging population prefers remote-control shopping to fighting crowds in the mall.

Sales statistics show how effectively the mall has moved into the home. Mail-order sales are spiraling upward at twice the rate of store sales.[20] Home delivery more or less disappeared in the '50s for just about everything except newspapers, but this happy alternative to pushing shopping carts through clogged aisles has returned with a vengeance. Sales of restaurant-prepared, home-delivered food quadrupled between 1985 and 1990.[21] Video-valets offer door-to-door video rental service, and various-valets pickup just about anything and anyone from dry cleaning to friends at the airport.

With everything from Oral Roberts to oral hygiene huckstered through the tube, electronic home shopping has become the most exotic of all remote-shopping possibilities. Whether teleshoppers seek cubic zirconium brooches, porcelain bouquet centerpieces, stomach tighteners, Veg-O-Matics, X-rated anatomically shaped chocolates, or other necessities of life, the TV tube has become the shop window. Teleshopping offers the quick, clean, and painless alternative to the trip to the mall, the wait in line, and the uninformed clerk. The demographics of shopper-viewing have made time scarcity the engine of the electronic market, for typical TV shoppers are higher income people and, not surprisingly, women who work in the labor force.[22] These are the couch-bound.

Bringing Work Home. Home entertainment centers and remote ordering save time by bringing home goods, services, and leisure activities, and telecommuting saves time by bringing work home. As others commute to offices, millions of workers transmit the fruit of their labor over phone wires from their dens, spare bedrooms, or converted attics and garages. Telecommuters are members of a new class of "invisible workers" employed in a "Network Nation" created by advances in technology, by the growth in jobs that exchange information, and by the unceasing quest for new ways to economize on time.

About 25 million workers, by one count, have chosen home hearth over corporate office, and the group expands each year by about 15 percent.[23] Stay-at-homes include advertising directors, consultants, designers, engineers, planners, researchers, stockbrokers, and writers. Potentially about half of the work force could telecommute, according to estimates, and given the rapid growth of jobs that deal with numbers, pictures, or words, a majority of all workers soon could discover that work is not limited by the walls of an office.[24] Prisoners in California and New York State, for example, answer telephone inquiries and make reservations for the Department of Motor Vehicles and for TransWorld Airlines.[25]

Setting up shop at home, or in prison, requires only a word processor or computer connected to a data source by modem and phone line. With only the basics—computers, cables, and connections—the home professional is ready to go to work with bosses or clients. Hook these up in happy electronic collusion with an electronic mailbox, fax, photocopier, and teleconferencing, and the "electronic cottage" (to use Alvin Toffler's term for the home-based work-station) is fully equipped.

Telecommuting claims many advantages of the **S**-type. Fewer interruptions boost work efficiency, and fewer commuters on streets and freeways cut air pollution, congestion, and energy consumption, and save transportation costs. And if everyone telecommuted, we would save having to pave over the whole country so that people can get to their offices.

Of all the blessings, time production is the bottom line. Telecommuters can devote the daily hour or so they formerly spent in nonremunerative work on the road either for paid work at home or for added leisure. Telecommuting does for work what the VCR does for entertainment: it provides scheduling flexibility that was previously never thought possible. Workers toiling at a home computer can choose their hours of work and shift work times to any hour of any day or any day of any week that best suits them. Telecommuting opens up new work opportunities for mothers and the handicapped, for flexibility in the *when* of work is advantageous to parents with young children, and flexibility in the *where* of work is important to those with handicaps.

Work can be done virtually anywhere via electronic hook-ups with far-off high-amenity places like, for example, Bali. In this way, the telecommunications that have transformed information into a weightless commodity also raises the possibility of restructuring the world settlement pattern. On a smaller scale, electronically equipped householders save time by bringing home activities formerly enjoyed only in other places.

This has given rise to a new trend (as if we needed another) first identified in the late '80s. Whether called "cocooners," "couch potatoes," "nesters," or (in old-fashioned parlance) "stay-at-homes," the followers of the trend decidedly prefer the barefoot comforts of home. The "very complex" phenomenon, says Faith Popcorn, the trend-watcher who first identified cocooning and named it, "basically involves building a shell of safety around yourself, so you're not at the mercy of the unpredictable world."[26] The self-incarcerated cocooner has "a fascination with time management" and an "interior obsession," both of which can be satisfied by acquiring the basics for internalizing activities into the private sphere of home.

THE BASICS FOR EQUIPPING THE COCOON FOR A NIGHT ON THE HOUSE

- Barcalounger with stereo headphones
- Electric popcorn popper
- Fax
- Gourmet frozen foods
- Home computer with modem
- Home delivery for everything from milk to videos
- Hot tub
- Massage equipment
- Microwave oven
- Phone with at least two lines, and answering machine
- Shopping catalogues
- Stereo sound system
- TV with cable access
- United Parcel Service's phone number
- VCR
- Workout equipment

People have been driven to cocooning as a way to insulate themselves from what they perceive as a harsh, unpredictable outside world. They inhabit that commoditized inside world alone together.

A CENTURY OF HOUSEWORK IN RETROSPECT

The Victorian home, isolated from a world viewed as hostile, offered domestic sanctuary with all of the requisites for survival and enjoyment. The nouveau Victorian home of today marks a full-circle return to that "ideal." With declining environmental quality, the urban world outside is once again seen as hostile and dangerous. Today's electronically equipped fortresses provide modern sanctuary, and many urban dwellers have opted for self-incarceration. The evolution of housework from one Victorian form to its reincarnation recounts an action-filled tale of the search for ways to conserve time and increase the satisfaction gained from its use.

Satisfaction or Time-Use Efficiency?

The Victorian home represented the terrestrial metaphor of heaven, a retreat from an unfriendly world outside, minded and made heavenly by a totally dedicated housekeeper. Then, the emerging view of a less cold and cruel world outside, furthered by relaxed social codes, presented opportunities for escape, if only housework could somehow be done more quickly without compromising quality. Time-saving technology and scientific management, domesticized from office and factory, helped increase efficiency but did little to guarantee that housework was truly rewarding.

With love of family gone as the dominant theme that underpinned the satisfaction gained from housework in the Victorian times, what was left to motivate the hard-working housewife in performing her dirty, isolated, unending chores? Mainly, the satisfaction that came from doing those onerous jobs better. Westinghouse, in 1945, advertised its line of appliances as "friend(s) in need to harassed housewives," and some years later an electric broom manufacturer declared, "New! Have a *'Company-Clean'* home every day . . . in minutes." Strange as it may seem, housework was meant to be fun and easy; at least that was the way to make the **T** commitment seem high in **S**. So the advertisers would have their readers believe, and it seemed like an appropriate concept for a post-war society that deserved to have a good time.

Still, the **T** of the gazinta, not the **S**, was the squeaky wheel that got more attention. Food preparation, for example, came in for particularly careful scrutiny, and hints abounded in ways to fix quicker meals. "Quick 'N Easy" became the cook's new watchword. Cakes could now be made from a mix. A recipe for "emergency tomato soup" called for immersing three teaspoons of catsup in a cup of heated milk. Each chemical breakthrough promised a new time-saving advance in the culinary arts, and most of them were marketed in cans. With convenience apparently mattering more than taste and freshness, canned goods came to replace fresh produce on the supermarket shelves. "Quick Stunts with Hunts" could be performed with tinned tomato sauce. The unmistakable odor of cream of mushroom and cream of chicken permeated the many homes that relied on canned soups as the bases for hundreds of recipes that could be turned out with the twist of a can opener.

It fell to a new movement, however, to place housework into proper perspective. Feminism emerged to join ranks with scientific management and domestic technology in the struggle to free those still trapped in the role of housewife trapped in the shell of home. Time saved in housework was better put to use in other ways and in other places, sagely reasoned an appliance manufacturer's ad of the 1930s. "Time wasted in a kitchen is gone forever and with it goes the opportunity to do many things that make life more complete," counseled the Elgin Stove Co. "Every woman is entitled to her share of social life, companionship, and recreation, and she should not be robbed of time and energy by the drudgery of kitchen duties."[27] Betty Friedan and other feminists of the 1960s echoed that reasoning three decades later. Contrary to the accepted wisdom of decades, and perhaps of centuries, only the most masochistic of housewives could find true pleasure in housework, and to expect housewives to continue to perform such dreary tasks as a voluntary expression of love was as exploitative as it was naive.

Besides, there was a real irony in the type of chores a post-war wife had to do. Despite the assistance that innovations rendered, the modern housewife did much the same work done by the now-absent nineteenth-century servant. Child rearing, cleaning, and cooking, which had been regarded as sufficiently dignified only as the hired helps' work, were the contemporary middle-class housewife's duties, for a major part of these tasks resisted automation. Phrased in mundane, though now familiar terms, although the **T** of housework *may* have declined, the **S** was hardly worth it. Housework as a glorious activity was a myth.

Time Savings or Higher Standards?

Feminists suggested yet another myth. At issue was whether inventions like the sewing machine, vacuum cleaner, synthetic fibers, and detergents, or the improved design of living and working space, or the application of management techniques saved the *overall* time spent in housework or simply made *individual* chores more time-efficient. Put simply, were the alleged time savings reality or illusion, fact or fancy?

Innovations unquestionably lightened burdens and saved time, but the greater ease of carrying out the daily chores of the household also encouraged the dedicated housewife toward higher performance standards (to phrase the argument in the cold-blooded vocabulary of the business firm). Instead of devoting time savings to leisure, she did the job more frequently or did it better. As Hazel Kirk put it in 1933, "The invention of the sewing machine meant more garments (to sew), . . . of the washing machine more washing, of the vacuum cleaner more cleaning, of new fuels and cooking equipment, more courses and more elaborately cooked food."[28]

Thus, household technology raised **S**, the quality of tasks performed, but like a sort of Parkinson's Law the amount of **T** that housework required seemed to remain unbudgeable.[29] Appliances helped get the tasks done better, though apparently without yielding the housekeeper much in time savings. Truly the work was never done. Joan Rivers got it about right when she remarked, "I hate housework! You make the beds, you do the dishes—and six months later you have to start all over again."[30]

Our good friends the Gnomons had been suspiciously quiet but we knew they were up to something, in their up-scale way, when they started turning down our dinner invitations. At first we thought it was their distaste for our terribly low-key non-state-of-the-art living style, although everything became clear when Nola called to announce that they had traded their up-scale home up-state for an even-more-upscale version. The new place was "electronically integrated," as Nola explained it, with her usual deferent asides to Nolan, and would we care to come for an evening of dazzlement?

Images from our last visit to a home show whizzed through our minds as we made the trek up to New Halcyon. For the health-fanatic, there was a coughing ash tray; for the space-conscious, a vertical fishbowl; for the music-lover, a doorbell to announce guests with any of thirty-two tunes; for the laundry-phobe, underwear with three leg holes in it that needs washing only once in six days (providing the user scrupulously follows the manufacturer's detailed schedule for rotating the garment and turning it inside out).[31] Knowing the Gnomons, we also knew that the possibilities were unlimited.

We arrived about 6:29:31. At the touch of the bell-button, "Home Sweet Home" chimed in the distance (a first hint that our fantasies were right on track; but could it play "Time on My Hands"?), followed by a muffled shout, "Nolan! It's them. On time as always. Right on the dot. Wouldn't you know?" followed by dogs barking (but they're a dogless couple!).

"Darlings! So good to see you. Right on the button. And speaking of button, what do you think of the electronic door chime? It plays thirty-two pre-programmed tunes and we could program in any favorites if we weren't so tone-deaf. (Good grief: they *were* music-lovers.) And did you hear the electronic dogs? The latest in burglar-proofing. Right, darling?"

"Right, love. Well, welcome to the electronic age, the dwelling of the future, 'Electrome', the developer's combination of 'electronic' and 'home,' but you guessed that anyway, didn't you? Can't put anything over on you two. Look at the Supa-frambus over there. . . . "

Truly the Gnomons live today in the home of tomorrow, their Nirvana. To us, as we headed home, it seemed downright Victorian.

11:00

TIME IN MOTION

"Time travels in divers paces with divers persons."
—Shakespeare, "As You Like It," Act III.

The plane, the pencil, the telephone, the paper plate, Saran wrap . . . the automobile? Which innovation was meant to become the greatest time-saver ever invented? Your answer, if the automobile, may be wrong. First, the main purpose of the automobile has not been to save time. Second, many people's behavior suggests that the automobile is not used to get between two points as quickly as possible. Instead, the automobile is used as a means—and quite a splendid one—to *spend,* rather than to *save,* time. Read on, for another paradox looms on the horizon.

FUNCTION FOLLOWS FORM

From the earliest days of automobility, it was the form of the auto that caught the public attention. The **S** of the experience mattered more than functionally reducing **T**. The automobile's form bestowed status on owner and passenger alike, contributing to their enjoyment over and above the function of merely saving travel time. In 1893, when the Duryea brothers of Springfield, Massachusetts, hooked up a one-cylinder engine to a second-hand carriage and succeeded in making the contraption move on its own, the car became "a much admired luxury, identified with country living and adventure."[1] Although the time-saving qualities of automobility soon became obvious, what persisted from then until now has been the image of the auto as a symbol of adventure and the good life.

"Once at the wheel of our car we declare our territorial independence," exults historian J. B. Jackson. "We give notice to the world that we alone are going to choose where we go and even where we want to work and enjoy ourselves."[2] The auto, by removing the shackles of foot-, bicycle-, and train-travel, created a class of mobile consumers who were free to go *where* they wanted to, *when* they wanted to, whether the destination was the store or the movies, and the time was the morning or late at night.

Motor cars extended their owners' social and territorial reach. The car, winning successive victories over the horse-and-buggy and the train as the vehicle in favor, brought countryside to city, city to city, and city to countryside. As concrete interstate highways replaced the dirt roads cars once sputtered along, the Pullman compartment gave way to the luxury car as the American elite's favored mode of long-distance travel. The large unified school district replaced the little one-room school house, the A&P and Safeway replaced the mom-and-pop grocery, Montgomery Ward and Sears Roebuck replaced the old-time general store. Nearly everything expanded in scale.

In synergistic relationship, new services both accommodated auto transport and were accommodated by it. Drive-to's and drive-in's sprang up across the country. The auto spawned time-saving developments such as the drive-in movie, drive-in restaurant, drive-in church, drive-in bank, and later the minimall and take-out. There's even curbside undertaking. A Florida funeral home boasting a "serenely lighted" drive-in window gives mourners the opportunity to view the deceased without leaving their cars. One in ten clients chooses the window service that "includes a pull-out tray with a register book for mourners to sign."[3]

Lower prices and technical improvements won the substitute for the horse-drawn carriage new friends and users. A price of $2,000, the equivalent of nearly four years of a typical worker's annual take-home pay, put the first version of Henry Ford's legendary Model T (1908) beyond reach of all but the very rich. Within a decade, however, mass production on the moving assembly line pruned prices to $290, or three months' earnings, and made the Model T affordable to the middle class.[4]

Because women generally had the final say in selecting the family car, many improvements were targeted especially at them. The first of these to put women into the drivers' seats was the self-starter, or "ladies aid" as it was called in 1912, that replaced the cumbersome crank. Later, air conditioning, automatic transmissions, heaters, plush upholstery, and other comfort and convenience options were introduced with women particularly in mind. Women now drove cars in droves. Each additional creature comfort not only expanded markets but boosted the auto as a symbol of luxury for male and female alike, and as a means for its owner/driver to distinguish himself/herself from nearly anyone else.

All these options led to market segmentation. When he became GM chairman a half-century ago, Alfred P. Sloan successfully bid markets away from Mr. Ford's Model T, which had achieved fame for its standardization. "A car for every purse and purpose," proclaimed Mr. Sloan. The motto has remained durable right up to the present. So durable in fact that by the end of the '80s Americans could choose among 572 different models of cars, vans, and trucks, 164 more than when the decade began.[5]

And there was an option for every purse and purpose to boost **S**. The purposes of some—like dual-overhead-cam balance-shafted engines with rack-and-pinion steering and double-wishbone suspension—are not easy to discern. But everyone knew that the automatic transmission, power steering, and the electric cigarette lighter were meant to increase the **S** of automobility.

Not all of the innovations—whether new-model cars, or new add-ons—have enjoyed the success of the automatic transmission and the electric cigarette lighter. The fate of Ford's Edsel is well known. Others, less so. Take for instance the automatic color-changer, a device invented in the 1950s to alter an automobile's hue. Colored liquids could be pumped into the car's hollow top, molded in clear plastic. Yesterday, a green-topped car; today, red; and a blue one tomorrow.[6]

As for the car's *function* as a major time-saver, increased speeds lowered the **T** of getting from here to there and back again. Radar detectors that confronted the fuzz with a buzz were invented to circumvent the inconvenience of cops and speed limits, so at least some drivers can lower their **T**, zooming down the road immune from detection.

Although innovations such as these do little to boost maximum automotive speeds, some raise *average* speeds. And with good reason, for congestion on the roads and highways is increasing and the costs of waiting are high and rising. Transportation experts put the cost of traffic delays nationwide at over $73 billion a year in lost productivity, and the two billion hours lost annually to traffic jams are projected to increase five-fold by the year 2000.[7]

While the automobile is undeniably a time-saver, it has not saved *enough* time, and the call is out for proposals to further reduce travel times. Solutions include building new motorways or rapid transit systems, or better maintaining existing ones. All proceed from the assumption that motorists want to spend the least time getting from one place to another, and are willing to pay a price for speed. Those who value their time at, say, ten dollars an hour will pay something approaching a ten-dollar toll to take a faster road that saves the hour. After all, an hour saved in transit—if it serves no positive purpose (a big "if")—is freed for an activity with a higher **S**.

The heroic assumption that people want to spend the least time getting from one place to another underpins the traffic experts' equation, Time In Transit = Time Wasted.[8] The "Constant Travel Time Law" demonstrates how wrong that assumption may be, for the "law" illustrates how people prefer spending, rather than saving, time traveling.

THE PUZZLING CONSTANT TRAVEL TIME LAW

If motorists regard the hours and minutes on the highways and byways as "up" time spent pleasurably, instead of as "down" time wasted, solutions that speed drivers to their destinations are misguided. Contrary to the experts' assumptions, the evidence shows that not all travelers want to minimize time on the road. For them, that time is a benefit, not a cost.[9]

Some years ago, researchers turned up an amazing statistic. Data showed that the average commuter, no matter where that person lived, took the same amount of time traveling between home and work.[10] In New York, New Orleans, or New Halcyon (where the Gnomons live), the average home-to-work trip consumed twenty-nine minutes, just two minutes short of an hour a day for the round trip.[11]

Even when transport improvements speed up the traffic, the average travel time seems to stay right where it is. Surveys taken by Pittsburgh planners some years before and after the metropolitan freeways were put in place revealed that the number of minutes it took to get to work remained unchanged, even though commuters traveled faster and farther. The proportion who spent fifteen minutes, or the average of thirty minutes, or an hour remained just the same before and after the system opened.[12] To the planners' surprise, commuters evidently set aside a certain number of minutes for the daily trip, and that target remains fixed.

The discovery of the Constant Travel Time Law baffled traffic experts who believed their job was to accommodate commuters' desires to shorten transit times. Yet what the experts believed commuters wanted, and what commuters actually wanted, apparently were quite different.

The response to upgraded transport systems takes several directions. First, as might be expected, most drivers can cover the distance faster. Second, commuters can move further from work without adding to travel times.[13] Both happened. People tend to choose a longer work journey rather than a shorter travel time when traffic speeds up. Right to this day, the statistical regularity remains unexplained. But those steeped in the mysteries of the *BB* factor will find that the answer to the riddle comes with dazzling simplicity. Elementary, Dr. Watson.

Commuters like to commute! Or at least, substantial proportions who do so by car don't dislike commuting very much. When polled, over half disagreed with the statement "I spend too much time commuting."[14] For surprisingly large numbers of drivers, commuting time is not wasted time: it is high in **S/T**!

The comfortable, entertaining, private interlude spent on the road offers benefits to be enjoyed, not costs to be avoided. One of those rewards, claim six out of ten, is its buffering effect.[15] To historian Reynor Banham, commuting embraces the "calmest and most rewarding hours of [motorists'] daily lives."[16] Those presumably unstructured hours offer refreshment, a welcome pause in the hectic day between work at the office or factory and social life at home, a chance to shift gears (so to speak) while screening out the pandemonium of home from the pandemonium of work. Framing the work day, the time spent enclosed in a technologically advanced device has become the most precious leisure time many have, and one of the few forms of privacy left.

Encapsulated in our mobile container (and barring a car telephone), we are isolated from the hustle-bustle of our world. The car allows us to partake of the pleasures, among others, of getting in touch with ourselves or doing those things we might not do in public. In our private world, our refuge, we can do and say and think whatever we want. (Surely the therapeutic value of this time alone, just when we need it most, contributes to our stubborn penchant for solo commuting.)

Aside from the therapeutic merits of privacy and buffering, many value commuting by car as pleasurable in its own right. Commoditization of the automobile has catapulted to new heights of enjoyment those fifty-eight minutes, starting each workday at 6:50 a.m. So advanced has become the technology that upgrades the **S** of those blocks of time that many regard the auto as the place (indeed the palace), and the commute as the time, of ultimate joy. Do I exaggerate?[17] Consider how those traveling life's fast and slow lanes pile up activities.

''AUTOMOBOLUS SYNCHRONUS''

Of all activities, few are so well suited to synchronic time-use as the home-work trip and, of all transport devices, few are so well equipped for synchronic use as the automobile. To be sure, for many years commuters by train and transit have read the papers, played cards with friends, or even had a drink while en route. But the gadgets that equip today's automobile—gadgets that make those which helped James Bond catch Goldfinger a generation ago look like children's toys—have facilitated the doubling up of activities as never before and transformed the daily commute from wasted time into valued time. In the process, the car has come to be used synchronically . . . and *synspatially!*

The car of today has become a multipurpose, synspatial center: a mobile office, a telephone booth, a reading room, a classroom, a breakfast nook, a dressing room, a gymnasium, a beauty parlor and—for those with sunroofs and amenable climates—a place to get a sun tan. It has become an ideal place to do many things, even things that might prove embarrassing or irritating in the presence of others.

Gadgetry as mundane as lighted vanity mirrors or as sophisticated as briefcase-size lap-top computers have made on-the-road synchronicity a reality. Technological advance has also made in-transit cooking possible. Near the turn of the century, one Robert Martin patented an automotive stove consisting of an insulated compartment installed under the driver's seat. The exhaust pipe, routed around and through the stove, provided the heat. Pop something into the oven, claimed the inventor, and after an hour's driving, it was ready to eat. The contraption never caught on, but has found a current incarnation in a book describing the how-to-do-it of in-transit engine-top cheffing. *Manifold Destiny*[18] reveals the secrets of cooking with gas, so to speak. Nothing to it: wrap the food in foil, place it on the exhaust manifold (hence the title), and drive off. How long to cook the item? That depends on how far you're driving and when you expect to be hungry. Hyundai Halibut and Provolone Porsche Potatoes each require about fifty-five miles; Speedy Spedini and Poached Perch Pontiac need forty miles. The method works particularly well in Mazdas with rotisserie engines. In the future, the less-adventurous will be able to synchronically heat up snacks, as they ride or drive, in microwave ovens installed in glove compartments. Side-by-side with the oven, a tiny refrigerator keeps frozen foods and completes the on-board built-in mini-kitchen.

Alas, not all household chores are as portable as cooking. Doing the laundry, for example. Like the first cooking gadget, an automobile washing machine invented in the '20s was intended to save both the car's fuel and the user's time. The curious contraption, bolted to the running board, consisted of a tub outfitted with paddles. Simply fill it up with soiled clothes and add soap and water. Bouncing along over rough roads agitated the contents to squeaky cleanness.[19] There were plenty of such roads to give the needed bounce. Sinclair Lewis described them in his 1919 novel *Free Air* as made of "prairie gumbo—which is mud mixed with tar, fly-paper, fish glue, and well-chewed, chocolate covered caramels."[20] Eventually, roads surfaced in dried prairie gumbo would disappear and, with them, the automobile washing machine.

Technology alone is not responsible for the synchronic utilization of automotive travel time. Chanting and romancing require no technology at all.

Chanting, as a form of "moving meditation" advocated in K. T. Berger's *Zen Driving,*[21] offers relief from the tensions of the daily routine at home or at office. Knowledge of the technique is the only prerequisite for transforming a car into a temple. Practitioners maintain that chanting a mantra makes the passage of time seem shorter, relaxing and calming drivers, and—so it is claimed—improving their driving ability.

"Cars fulfilled a romantic function from the dawn of the auto age," writes historian David L. Lewis. By extending courtship from "the five-mile radius of the horse and buggy to ten, twenty, and fifty miles and more," not only did the territorial market for a mate increase, but the auto distanced couples from "parlor sofas, hovering mothers, and pesky siblings." That it worked is revealed by the fact that two out of five marriages have been proposed in an automobile,[22] and unknown numbers of virginities lost.

TRANSPORTS OF JOY

Of all forms of built-in automotive entertainment, audio amusement seems to be the type drivers most crave. Although sound-making devices have enjoyed the most certain future, matters were a tad unsure in the beginning. One of the earliest of these, devised in the first decades of the century, was a pipe organ patented for automobility. Passengers played on a keyboard attached to the back of the front seat, entertaining not only themselves but those within earshot. Unfortunately, the same rough roads of the period which agitated the clothes in the auto washer also threw the instrument out of tune. According to reports, the results were anything but musical.

In the years since, the back seat organ has given way to radios, cassette or compact disk players, stereos, and other mobile electronics that no road, no matter how bumpy, can knock out of tune. At a price that may exceed the cost of the car itself, motorists can equip their autos with a sound system that presumably increases the **S** of motoring not only for themselves, but for entire neighborhoods. Amplifiers delivering 5,600 watts of power, hooked up to a battery of thirty-six Godzilla-like speakers of sound-stage quality, can crank out sound at 140 ear-shattering decibels (distressables?), 15 more than a jet produces at take-off.

Less entertaining but more useful for managing time synchronically, the cellular telephone permits placing calls en route to family and friends, clients and secretaries. Cellular phoning can save up to six weeks a year for those who spend an hour a day on the road, making their business calls as they drive. Following its appearance in 1982, the cellular phone quickly became a status symbol that established its owner-hotshots as an especially busy and important breed. Now, with cellular phones installed in over three million automobiles,[23] the prestige value of dealing while driving has dipped somewhat. However, those ever in search of the latest and chic-est will soon be able to equip their mobile phones with answering machines and call waiting.

In the past, the car driven by a uniformed chauffeur was the front-seat symbol of a wealthy back-seat passenger who put a lower **S/T** on time driving than on time spent doing something else en route. In the future, the electronic chauffeur—the ultimate in synchronic time-management on the road—will offer those services. ''Smart'' cars gliding along ''smart'' roads will fairly shout ''leave the driving to us.'' With drivers no longer driving, but chauffeured along the roads electronically, time spent in transit can become as productive as time spent at home or work.

Get in the car, push a button, and the electronic chauffeur takes over. Motorists glide along, unconcerned with steering, accelerating, dodging in and out of traffic, and freed of concerns about which route is fastest, or where is the nearest parking lot, gas station, motel, or hospital. The electronic chauffeur is paid to do that. All occupants, including the driver, are passengers who can use their time in higher **S/T** pursuits.

All this may seem unnecessary, but gadgetry once seen as frivolous has become commonplace. At first, sun/moon roofs, electrically operated windows, power locks, adjustable steering wheels, radios with cassette players, air conditioning, and coffee cup holders were disdained as superfluous. As cars became surrogates for homes and offices, however, they were deemed worthy of being equipped just as comfortably. Frills become necessities when they increase the **S** of motoring.

Frivolous may be the features that do little more than increase a car's gee-whiz quotient, but no one will doubt the worthiness of devices intended to increase safety and maneuverability. Automobile mishaps take over 50,000 lives every year in the U.S., more fatalities than are caused by all other accidents.[24] The courts have defined the automobile as a deadly weapon, and from the earliest days, the search has been underway for the means to reduce accidents caused by the "weapon."

Although most safety devices are intended to protect drivers and passengers, one of the earliest served to protect others (and, perhaps for that reason, it failed). Hanz Karl's amazing apparatus, invented in 1932, minimized the injury to pedestrians hit by a car. When triggered by an impact, a bar installed across the front of the vehicle automatically slammed on the car's brakes. A blanket stored behind the bumper quickly shot forward to catch the falling person "so the clothes will not be spoiled," as Mr. Karl explained, and "his fall will be softened."[25]

The discovery of ergonomics, the science that attempts to ensure painless interaction between man and machine, furthered the acceptance of safety features. Switches on sticks that can be reached without taking hands off wheel (rather than placed in the dash), color-coded controls, fitted bucket seats on thinner frames, and glare-reducing tinted windshields are among the newer user-friendly design features contributing to the art and science of accident-avoidance. A sleep-driver alarm, powered by a microcomputer with an optical sensor mounted in sunglasses worn by the driver, will set off a wake-up alarm when the eyelids droop. Instant alcohol testers will allow users to monitor the alcohol level in their system before they get caught. Personal Security Vehicle Kits which cater to the neuroses of the marginally paranoid consist of 007 gadgets like bullet-proof glass strong enough to stop a .38-caliber bullet, door lock systems, survival kits for those locked in involuntarily, and inside-outside intercoms that permit speaking to unfriendly outsiders without rolling down windows. Such are the design improvements and technology meant to raise the **S** of motoring, chiefly by adding to the creature comforts and transforming the auto into a home on wheels.

To return to an earlier point, some regard the automobile as the world's greatest time saver; others, as one of the world's greatest time users. The statistics tell the success story of the automobile in raising the **S** of motoring. The growth of car ownership is outpacing the growth of licensing so rapidly that, if current trends continue, in forty years there will be more automobiles than drivers.[26] Twenty percent of households today have at least three of them, double the fraction from fifteen years ago. The automobile not only performs valued functions, but confers status and enjoyment on its users. Technology has contributed to the enjoyment of time on the road, and to perfecting the art of synchronous time management. With its rising **S**, travel time earns its designation as a time-plus activity.

As we have seen, self-serving activities like personal fitness and eating well are booming mainly because innovations have increased their appeal and bettered their position in the competition for the daily twenty-four-hour time quota. But innovations have hardly left a mark on activities like helping family, friends, neighbors, and indeed the commonweal. As a result such other-serving activities are increasingly casualties of the *BB* factor.

Despite new information-processing technologies, the same can be said for the process of careful thinking, required of our leaders in politics, the professions, and elsewhere. The implications, as I show in the next chapters, are troubling.

12:00

DOING UNTO OTHERS

"Eternity looks grander and kinder if Time grow meaner and more hostile"

—Thomas Carlyle

> The family takes its mauve and cerise, air-conditioned, power-steered and power-braked automobile out for a tour [and] passes through cities that are badly paved, made hideous by litter, blighted buildings, billboards. . . . They pass on into a countryside that has been rendered largely invisible by commercial art. . . . They picnic on exquisitely packaged food from a portable icebox by a polluted stream and go on to spend the night at a park which is a menace to public health and morals. Just before dozing off on an air mattress, beneath a nylon tent, amid the stench of decaying refuse, they may reflect vaguely on the curious unevenness of their blessings. Is this, indeed, the American genius?[1]

So John Kenneth Galbraith described the contradiction of public squalor in the midst of private affluence in the 1950s. Blessings are no more evenly distributed today, with a natural landscape lavishly decorated in a debris of wrappers here and beer cans there. The coasts and rivers have become sewers of floating trash, the roadsides littered with cans, bottles, and tires. These man-made, man-discarded artifacts, unlike those of nature, found their place by the conscious decisions of graduates of the just-heave-it-out-the-window school, who are indifferent to the consequences on others. They are the users' means for putting their mark on the landscape in the least time-consuming way, a statement of contempt for nature and a visible symbol of the *BB* factor.

Littering is but one example of how individual actions, governed by the principles of time economy, impose costs on the larger community. It works this way.

Nearly every individual action mixes personal and social consequence. Take, for example, personal care, primarily a private activity, yet one with a social element. The grouchiness that follows spending too little time sleeping hardly makes others happy, and failing to bathe or brush the teeth often enough may drive them away in disgust.

Many individual actions, however, have larger elements of "publicness." Helping our neighbors and taking care of elderly relatives, of children, or of the handicapped, are largely selfless endeavors, for the immediate personal rewards are minute compared to the amount of good they do for others. As time becomes more scarce, these actions lose out in favor of actions that accrue chiefly personal benefit. **S/T** helps to explain why.

The **S/T**s for activities with large social ingredients—"other-serving" activities—have grown sluggishly, if at all. They are losing out in the competition for time because either the satisfaction **S** gained from engaging in activities that benefit others has increased very little, or the time **T** required to carry them out has not dropped, or both parts of the **S/T** ratio have stayed about the same. The problem is this: the personal rewards of "doing unto others" remain little changed, while the personal rewards of "doing unto ourselves" have usually changed in a positive direction. Technology has raised the satisfaction gained from many of the self-serving activities, like the musical theater or exercise, but has failed to raise the **S** of the actions that serve family, friends, and more anonymous others somewhere "out there." With the twenty-four-hour day as a fixed quantity, people favor activities with rising **S/T**s—for the most part, easily commoditized self-serving activities.

Before exploring the evidence, let us return once again to America's littered highways. Tossing the empty Fritos bag out the car window gets rid of it quicker than the alternative of stopping by the roadside and dropping it into a waste bin. Indeed there are social and legal sanctions against opting for the more time-efficient solution. Our neighbors, if they saw us littering, would point their fingers in shame. The highway patrol, if it caught us, would impose a fine. But we rarely meet our neighbors on the open road, and the chance of being caught by a patrolman is slight. Judging by the roadside evidence, these sanctions have failed to deter us from the personally more time-efficient, but socially more damaging, choice.

Two homely examples illustrate how the *BB* factor easily swings the decision to act for ourselves rather than for others. In one case, our time is abundant; in the other, our time is short.

We have a half-hour to kill while walking from the parking lot to the doctor's office for a 1:00 appointment, a distance that normally takes about five minutes. As we leisurely stroll down the street, window-shopping on the way, a stranger stops us to ask for directions. With time to spare, we lavish great care on a detailed reply that, we trust, will be helpful. The benefits to the stranger are large, the costs to us are small.

Now, suppose instead that, due to traffic delays, we arrive at the parking lot with only five minutes to spare. We hurry, knowing full well that doctors don't wait for us, even though we wait for them. The same stranger who interrupts our gallop down the street gets a short answer to his question, if any at all. The benefits to the stranger of a *complete* answer would be the same regardless of whether we were rushed or not, but the costs to us of providing that answer are far higher when we risk being late, for we have something more important to do than to be helpful. A scarcity of time

makes keeping on schedule matter more than a stranger's welfare.

A surplus of time allowed us the "luxury" of being helpful, but our concern for the others' welfare vanished when time was at a premium. When scarce time inflates the value of each minute and hour, we begin the search for higher **S/T** alternatives. The analogy works the same way over the long haul: increasing time scarcity leads to the gloomy conclusion (and prediction) that rewards measured in personal terms will increasingly take precedence over rewards measured in social terms, and self-serving activities will crowd out "living for others."

The logic explains why we have come to take less seriously our social obligations to people "out there," whether the stranger on the street or anonymous others half a world away. And the same with our civic duties. With every election, a smaller proportion of registered voters goes to the polls to discharge their obligations as members of a democratic community. With every decennial census count, a smaller proportion of the population returns the questionnaires.[2] Willingness to serve on juries or to volunteer for work with community organizations is on the wane. Rudeness is becoming a national sport, mainly because courtesy takes time. The quality of personal services is in decline.

None of this would have happened if a key point made by the eighteenth-century philosophers like Adam Smith had had a longer half-life, one stretching into the far more complex world of the twentieth century. Prof. Smith and his crowd maintained that people, when maximizing their own material well-being, inadvertently enhanced the common good. An invisible hand benevolently translated private gain into social benefit. Smith *et al.* got it right for the world in which they lived, but for ours it is a different matter. Given the interdependence of the modern world, my actions affect you (and your actions affect me) even though you live on the other side of the globe. When the *BB* factor drives my actions, for better or for worse, you too may reap the benefits, or pay the costs. All too often the private gains from those actions, instead of enhancing the common good, further the common bad. As *Busy Bodies* shift their twenty-four-hour time allotments toward the self-serving activities, doing unto others may become doing others in, inflicting harm that can even explode into disaster on an international scale.

A gloomy little three-act melodrama, each act with seven parallel scenes, will set the stage for following chapters that document these true-to-life events in greater detail. When we foresake low **S/T** activities (in Act I) for higher **S/T** activities (in Act II), others may get hurt (in Act III). The mercifully shortened synopsis of "Stranger than Fiction" runs as follows.

"STRANGER THAN FICTION"

*Act I: When We Foresake Low **S/T** Activities . . .*

Scene 1: *(a street)* A stranger stops us, asks for directions; we ignore him and hurry on to a doctor's appointment.

Scene 2: *(a child's study-space in a middle-class home)* A parent once again ignores her latchkey child's bid for help with his homework.

Scene 3: *(a politician's study)* A Senator, pondering an appropriations bill, puts down his notes, picks up the telephone, and calls a lobbyist to set up an appointment.

Scene 4: *(a drafting room)* A structural engineer, having decided that it is a waste of time to recheck his calculations for a new bridge, sends them off to the contractor.

Scene 5: *(a medical laboratory)* A technician hurries through his analyses of Pap smears, erroneously rating twenty-nine of them positive.

Scene 6: *(the bridge of an oil tanker)* The captain abandons the bridge just as his ship enters perilous waters.

Scene 7: *(the control room of a nuclear power plant)* An operator overrides safety controls to speed up a test of the reactor.

*Act II: . . . For Higher **S/T** Activities . . .*

Scene 1: *(the doctor's office waiting room)* We are seen reading a rather dated magazine and looking pleased that we have arrived for the appointment on time.

Scene 2: *(a parent's work-space in the middle-class home)* The parent is seen, bathed in the blue-white light of a word processor, writing a business report.

Scene 3: *(the interior of a restaurant near Capitol Hill)* The Senator is seen downing breakfast while listening intently to a group of lobbyists plead for funding favorable to their special interests.

Scene 4: *(an electronic home entertainment center)* The engineer is seen "plugged in," passively listening and watching.

Scene 5: *(the workout room of a gym)* The lab technician is seen working out at a Liferower.

Scene 6: *(the captain's quarters below deck)* The skipper is seen downing his third scotch and soda as the fog swirls outside.

Scene 7: *(again, the control room)* As the test of the reactor proceeds, the operator is seen gazing at his watch, counting the hours until he can go home.

Act III: . . . Others May Get Hurt.

Scene 1: *(again, the street)* The hapless tourist wanders aimlessly. . . .

Scene 2: *(again, the child's study-space)* Textbooks, papers, etc. thrust aside, the dejected youth ponders the possibility of saying "yes" to drugs . . . just once.

Scene 3: *(the Senate floor)* The Senator defends a bill that is favorable neither to his constituents, nor to his colleagues' constituents, nor to any . . . except the political interest group.

Scene 4: *(a river)* Surrounded by the debris of a collapsed bridge and half-submerged automobiles, lifeless bodies float in the darkness . . .

Scene 5: *(the admissions unit of a hospital)* Twenty-nine women are being admitted for hysterectomies . . . all unnecessary.

Scene 6: *(somewhere in coastal waters)* Steel grates against rocks, and an oil slick begins to move ominously in all directions . . .

Scene 7: *(the globe, seen at great distance)* From far away, the wail of emergency sirens, followed by a quick flash; a tiny plume of radioactive dust emerges, grows larger, and slowly encompasses the northern hemisphere. . . .

As the curtain falls on Act I, the principal characters have forsaken certain duties for activities with greater appeal. In Act II, they enjoy the more personally rewarding, self-serving, higher **S/T** activities that won out. Finally, in Act III we discover the unhappy outcomes. The characters in scenes differ, the events differ, the outcomes differ. But the commonalities are more important.

Whether it is aiding a stranger, helping offspring, drafting legislation, ensuring the safety of a structure, performing medical tests, piloting a ship, or testing a nuclear reactor, all are activities that benefit others. The responsible characters, from parents to power-plant operators, driven by the *BB* factor, forsook tasks beneficial to others for one that apparently yielded greater personal rewards. The results: the stranger lost on the street, the latchkey lad contemplating drugs, constituents who must foot the bill to support special interests, the dead floating beneath the collapsed bridge, women who will never again bear children, wildlife killed by the oil slick, people killed or contaminated by nuclear radiation. All are innocent "bystanders" who must bear the burdens of decisions that rewarded *Busy Bodies* who, perhaps unwittingly, were doing unto others by doing others in.

In the chapters that follow, I trace the real-life aspects of these dramas. At this point, we skip from Chapter 12 to Chapter 14, omitting Chapter 13 not only as a concession to the neuroses of triskaidekaphobic readers, but as an ominous signal that the narrative style shifts suddenly, as does the nature of the discourse. Both style and substance move to the more serious. One can afford to be more cavalier, and even silly, about events and activities that affect only ourselves. But the topics ahead of us, dealing as they do with the effects on others of *Busy Bodies'* decisions, are more somber and menacing, for the consequences of time-pressed behavior on the larger community, the nation, and indeed the world around us is pretty serious stuff.

14:00
UNDOING OTHERS

"So many pedestrians,
So little time."
—a bumper sticker

Declining social relationships and commitments to neighbors, the decline of volunteering and voter turnout, dedication to employers and employees, increasing selfishness and rudeness, the rise of "me-ism" and insularity—all bespeak what the *Busy Body* factor predicts. All appear to be the emergent hallmarks of a time-scarce society bent on undoing others. All are activities essential to the quality of life, yet in terms of the *BB* factor they are time-minus.

Lest assertions become orthodoxies, consider the evidence.

DOING UNTO THY NEIGHBOR, OR DOING THY NEIGHBOR IN?

George Bernard Shaw has defined middle-class morality as "to live for others and not for myself." Because the *BB* factor makes living for myself more attractive and living for others less so, Mr. Shaw's middle-class morality must be in jeopardy.

Social commitments require time, and lots of it. Social relationships are time-intensive and, as time grows scarce, they are likely to become increasingly superficial. Economist Roland McKean predicts that the deleterious effects of increasing time scarcity will reach beyond those nearest and dearest to us, and permeate the whole fabric of society. The *BB* factor, in his words, leads to "weakened commitments to aged parents, friends, spouses, children, and perhaps reduced cohesiveness in general (with) spill-over effects on the loneliness of the aged, on the emotional stability of children, and on the quality of life for almost everyone. . . ."[1] The evidence supports his contention.

Few truly enjoy going to weddings, bar mitzvahs, family reunions, and funerals, when time can be spent in so many other interesting ways. A sense of duty prompts us to appear at ceremonial occasions that honor others in flesh and spirit. Personal enjoyment is secondary. Yet, governed by the *BB* factor, and by the fact that there are few ways to boost the **S/T**s of such "other-serving" activities, we will increasingly convey regrets, whether for real or feigned reasons.

That we are willing to spend less time memorializing the departed, for example, is clear in a survey which reports a declining proportion of funerals that are traditional "complete" affairs. Attendance at even the streamlined versions is down.[2] Poor attenders should be warned, however, that if you don't go to other people's funerals, they won't come to yours.

Commitments to next-door neighbors are also at risk. Take the case of neighborhood watch groups in which local residents take responsibility for patrolling their neighborhood, looking for suspicious characters, and reporting them to the police. The groups spring into being when neighborhood crime erupts, but enjoy only short-lived success because organizers fail to take account of the volunteers' time costs. Two realizations destine failure. First comes an awareness of how unequally the burden is shared. Not all neighbors agreed to participate, though all stand to benefit from the hard work of the valiant few. Second, when the participants come to realize how much time their dedication requires, and how many other activities are foregone, the cooperative effort peters out. Putting an explicit price on participants' time is one solution. Offering rewards for patrollers who provide the authorities with the information they need to arrest an "unfriendly visitor" prices the benefits of hard work and rewards those who earn them. "Thank you for your time," the reward says.

Increasing indifference to our family's and neighbors' welfare is bounded neither by home nor by neighborhood. Indifference has spread even into the work place. William Whyte portrayed *The Organization Man* of the 1950s as a rigid conformist who had his priorities straight: organization came ahead of self. Some three decades later, management consultant Paul Leinberger "redid" Whyte's pioneering work, asking whether children of Mr. Whyte's junior executives held the same personal values. Things have changed, discovered Mr. Leinberger from his interviews, and they have changed radically. The reincarnated executive is more cynical, more self-reliant, and less willing to sacrifice personal life for the corporate good. "I'm in it for me; I see a company as a vehicle," sums up the feelings of many, perhaps most.[3]

Because so many are "in it for me," the business establishment garners few favorable votes among the public. Greed has driven out ethical behavior, claims people surveyed on the subject. Seventy percent polled by Louis Harris indict business for failing to see to it that "its executives behave legally and ethically."[4] Pure greed drove the Yuppies into the Wall Street scandals of a few years ago, or at least 56 percent of those polled thought so. But Yuppies aren't the only guilty ones; given tip-offs, the majority also would have engaged in illegal insider trading on Wall Street. Furthermore, over half of all young professionals admitted to doing their own income taxes so that they could cheat on their IRS returns. The Harris organization concludes inevitably that "make it fast, make it now, get it all" adds up to nothing less than a dominant theme of the moment.[5]

Getting it all for *me* paves the way to happiness. The trend toward personal gains, away from the social good, is not only on the upswing but seems destined to continue. A bellwether of long-term trends is the increasing numbers of young folk who proudly cite the individual ambition of making it for themselves, rather than helping others to make it. Every year entering college students are asked about their life goals. Over the years, clear and consistent patterns have emerged. *The* emergent goal over the last twenty years has been "to get rich." In the early '70s, accumulating wealth was important to about 40 percent of the Fern and Freddie Freshmen, but nearly twice the proportion cited the goal by 1991. As getting rich ascended on the scale, helping the less fortunate receded into the background.[6] A young entrepreneur assessed the balance between personal and social reward in this very-much-to-the-point way: "If you've worked hard for your money—and this will sound greedy—it's yours," says the teener, who founded a computer business. "There should be no pressure or obligation to give it up."[7]

Not so many years ago it was the greedy "me" generation that inflicted itself on the American scene, a mentality of people who sought ego involvements and ego fulfillments as life's ultimate rewards. Rampant self-indulgence replaced the sense of a larger community and an obligation to help one's fellow human beings. Yuppies have taken up where the "mes" left off, and seem to take the *BB* factor even more seriously.

MAKING IT FAST, YUPPIE STYLE

Some of us knew them, some of us were them, but all of us knew the Yuppies as the young-upwardly-mobile-professionals who took pride in being on first-name terms with self-centeredness and material possession. The Yuppies' major life goal was to make as much money as possible, as quickly as possible. Some 73 percent of the general public believed that, and so did 81 percent of the Yuppies themselves! Moreover, more than half of all people, including Yuppies, found this quality singularly unappetizing.[8]

Yuppies were not always like this. Earlier, before their lives grew more harried as they climbed the ladder of success, Yuppies were different. University of Michigan researchers who followed a panel of high school seniors graduating in 1965, interviewing them again in later years, showed how they changed. Even though the Yuppies attended college during the Vietnam era and strongly protested America's continued involvement in Southeast Asia, age and success softened their liberalism. More and more they opposed, for example, the government's responsibility to provide public services and a guaranteed minimum living standard. "The speed with which those formerly liberal economic views were erased," exclaims project director Gregory B. Markus, "is nothing short of dramatic."[9]

Then there are the Yuppies' near-cousins, the Dinks—double-income-no-kids couples. Dinks wear the badge of the *BB* factor proudly and, like Yuppies, are self-centered, concerned with material possessions, well-off, and not much concerned with aiding others. The Dinks' life is their fast-track jobs (read: making money). Realizing that kids are time-expensive, they have chosen to remain childless. With responsibilities only to themselves, and high and rising incomes, they are free to spread around their time in the most fulfilling ways. Time spent in the service of others ranks low on the priority list, if it's there at all. Time-minus activities only get in the way of the time-plus alternatives, and most of those are spelled j-o-b. What matters most are the basics, like keeping ahead in their high-profile careers and keeping their marriages together, while allowing time to breathe now and then. Dinks tend to be cavalier in their spending habits, and spend "too much" for housing and food because they refuse to spend time shopping around. Never mind, given their incomes, does it really matter?

As time-poor people, Dinks must carefully manage their schedules. Actually, *they* don't manage the schedules. That's too time-consuming. Secretaries do that for them by coordinating the couple's overstuffed work agenda and somehow finding time for the marriage. Keeping in touch via cellular phones, the secretaries arrange appointments so that the Dink couple can see each other for dinner or drinks, even if the venue is the airport between flights, and schedule the other events that couples enjoy in blissful combination. They live out their lives alone together.

ALONE TOGETHER: THE SOCIAL CONSEQUENCES OF TECHNOLOGY

With the same aggressiveness and effectiveness as the troops that stormed the beaches of Normandy, technology has invaded home, neighborhood, and work place—indeed, nearly every aspect of life. Not only have the new technological guests among us shifted our activities toward the self-serving, but they have widened the social distance between people, whether they are the family across the dining table, the neighbors across the alley, or the fellow-workers across the hall.

Gadgets ranging from the now nearly standard personal computer and electronic home entertainment centers, known to most of us, to the latest exotica, known only to the truly up-scale like the Gnomons, have of course simplified, and even taken over many of the dreary tasks of domestic life. Technology keeps track of the family accounts and helps restore our financial position from complete impossibility to its usual level of merely imminent disaster. Technology transfers office jobs to the home and helps write books like this one. Technology entertains the children and distracts them so that parents can be about other activities. Praise to you, O Technology! However, the technology that displaces routine domestic chores sweeps with it other domestic responsibilities, including social interactions (to use the voguish term).

By making it possible to work at home, to shop at home, to be schooled at home, to be entertained at home, the time-saving electronic alternative displaces opportunities for face-to-face contacts with other workers, other shoppers, other children, and other movie-goers and sports-fans. Social intercourse, once a central feature of home life, has given way to social isolation.

What can rival the arrival of a new gadget that simplifies life and perhaps entertains in the bargain? A study of 300 recent computer purchasers revealed that, at first, fewer hours were spent sleeping and socializing with family and friends. Mastering the machine or rooting out a program bug proved more exciting than talking across the dinner table or helping the kids with their geometry problems. While most had caught up on their sleep when they were re-interviewed two years later, they still devoted less time to family and friends.[10]

Children too find that computers can be the means for blocking out problems and feelings and offer escapes from personal interaction. The computer can't say "no," and the games played on them do just about whatever the player wants them to. Psychiatrists claim that adolescents find in the keyboard and screen "the acceptance and confidence they may not be getting elsewhere," even when it means ignoring others and avoiding intimacy.[11] The computer buff may be in sight of others, dazzled by the little green letters on the tube, yet not really "there" at all. The PC becomes the all-accepting, controllable friend. But time with the machine replaces time spent with flesh and blood friends, the opportunities for social growth.

The television, which also absorbs time and diverts time-use, has much the same effect as the PC does on family relationships.

Recently, twenty-two French families gave up their TVs as an experiment. The not-unexpected consequence? They used their time savings to rediscover the art of socializing with each other.

FROM BILL COSBY TO PECOS BILL

"We briefly kicked the TV habit (and), instead of hearing my husband yell, 'Would you turn that thing down?' I came home one night and actually heard him talking to our child, calling her by the affectionate name we had used when she was a baby. He was saying, "OK, Nucky, you've got a convex regular polygon, and it's got exterior angles equal to 120 degrees. What are its interior angles equal to? Meanwhile, I helped daughter Hannah write fourth-grade essays. We read stories on a whole range of mythological characters, from Big Foot to the Boogie Man. We began caring more about Brer Rabbit than Bugs Bunny, Pecos Bill than Bill Cosby, Brer Fox than Michael J."

—Alice Kahn[12]

Unless one is Lot's wife, a look backward is instructive. Consider post-prandial life of the no-tech family of yore. The evening meal (*sans* TV, of course) finished and the dishes washed and put away, mom, pop, kids, grandparents, cat and dog, etc. retired to the parlor to sit around a fireplace that burned real wood (how quaint!) and to chat, play, and generally entertain each other.

Technology soon overran this scene of sybaritic repose. Conversation had to cease out of respect for someone who decided it was time to play "Für Elise" on the piano (aha! the first technological intrusion). The record player, making its arrival next, silenced conversation for three inspiring minutes while all listened dutifully to John Charles Thomas sing "The Rosary," allowed it to resume once again during a brief intermission for winding up the spring and turning over the record, and then halted it for another three minutes out of respect for the unseen but certainly heard performer. Then along came the crystal radio. After carefully positioning the whisker in the proper spot on the crystal, everyone gathered 'round the earphone placed in a bowl. But no one dared talk: the fascinating voice wafting magically through the air was certainly more interesting than what anyone present might say. And we know the story from there.

With rising quality and falling prices for electronic technology, families began to commoditize every spare moment, not only their evenings together. Home technology came in the front door and at-home socializing went out the back. Now, the family was alone together.

While the dishes are being electrically scrubbed to an ever-increasing hygienic standard, each member of the family disperses to passively watch his or her particular rectangular tube in the privacy of his or her own rectangular territory. Junior goes off to play his Nintendo game, alone; Sis to watch ''Studs'', alone; dad to pound out tomorrow's staff memo on his PC, alone; mom to watch a videotape of ''Divorce Court'' automatically recorded that afternoon, alone.

Primitive interaction gives way to technological interaction. Person-to-person mode yields to man-machine mode. It is as if the miraculous machinery speaks to us, jealously asking, which will it be, me or *them?* We know the answer: me. Every advance in technology seems to further the distance separating individual from individual, making each (*i.e.,* us) increasingly independent of each other. The only person left with whom to interact in this electronically commoditized age is, alas, the repair person who comes to fix the broken gadget.[13]

As time grows more scarce and valuable, the markets expand for the **T**-saving, **S**-boosting gadgets. And the *BB* factor encourages us toward activities with growing **S/T**s, those that tend to be the ones which please us, rather than the activities which please others. At risk are the actions that serve the common good, such as our willingness to volunteer, to vote, and to be polite.

SAYING ''NO'' WHEN WE SHOULD SAY ''YES''

Are more people attending PTA meetings, soliciting donations for museums, working on fund-raisers, serving on neighborhood improvement committees, and volunteering more time to other organizations that serve the public good? Overall, the proportion of Americans who volunteer is falling and the major drop-outs are those in the gender and age groups experiencing the biggest time squeezes. In 1988, the most recent year for published figures, 47 percent of women volunteered their time and talents in some capacity, down from 56 percent in 1981; the corresponding drop for men and women 25 to 44 years old was from 59 to 49 percent.[14] If present rates of decline continue, volunteering will have all but disappeared in fifty years.

Even the Boy Scouts of America are feeling the pinch of time scarcity. Both the satisfaction gained from helping the legendary old lady across the street and the time required to perform the good deed have seemed impervious to change, while **S/T**s have risen for activities that compete for a youngster's time. Indeed membership has dropped off. In 1946, one in three young men of eligible age proudly wore the Scout uniform. Today's figure comes to only one in five.[15] The crisis in membership includes the leaders as well as the led. Nearly five hundred fewer adults today are willing to give evenings and weekends to Scout activities than they were in 1970.[16]

The American Heart Association has found the secret of keeping its corps of volunteers happy and growing. AHA's volunteer staff has grown by 50 percent in only three years. Good intentions and a noble cause, once seen as the prime motives behind volunteering, are less the *sine qua non* today, for the Association ruthlessly weeds out the non-performing deadwood among its volunteers, and "outplaces" (to use the polite term) them. As for the livewood, the organization has redefined the aims of volunteering by making the time spent "meaningful." Meaningful means that the experience not only must serve a useful social purpose but must reward participants for their contributed time.[17] Therein lies the secret to success: *personal* rewards boost the **S** of volunteering.

Exactly what those personal rewards might be surfaces in research done on why, and for how long, people volunteer. Organization analyst Jone Pearce first asked volunteers in human service organizations why they had signed up. Heading the list were the usual lofty reasons like helping others and contributing to society. But the longer they worked, the more that personal motives came into play. In fact, the steadfastly faithful die-hards were driven not by abstract notions of doing good but by such practical and personally rewarding aspects as socializing with co-workers, acquiring skills, and gaining experience.[18] Even though altruism may have prompted an initial commitment, participants often discovered later on that only the personal pay-offs made the donated time worthwhile. Thus, if non-profit and social service organizations are to survive, opportunities must be found to satisfy volunteers' more selfish motives.

Technically a duty, jury service has nonetheless taken on the character of a voluntary activity, particularly because so many people get excused for reasons of "inconvenience" rather than true hardship. If the court system is to work, juries must be made up of true cross-sections of the community. Yet, because the time commitment can be formidable, busy people are begging off in increasing numbers, and getting away with it. Someone has observed that the fundamental flaw in this system is that your fate is in the hands of a dozen people who weren't smart enough to get out of jury duty. Those in search of an excuse might try something like this one which got relief for its too-busy author: "I am a 68-year-old retired man taking care of an 86-year-old lady who wishes to marry me. She has stumbled into a gopher hole feeding her chickens and does not walk very well. But her health and outlook on life have greatly improved since I began taking care of her and her chickens."[19]

GOVERNMENT OF, FOR, AND BY THE FEW . . . AND FEWER AND FEWER

Americans' obsession with politics amazed European observers of the nineteenth century. The most observant of all, de Tocqueville, claimed that politics were "the only pleasure an American knows,"[20] and the voting statistics supported his point. In the latter part of the century, 80 percent of eligible voters turned out to vote.[21] Then the turnout rate nosed downward. With only half of eligible voters bothering to go to the polls in the 1988 presidential election, non-voters constituted the largest political party. Meanwhile, the turnout rate exceeds 90 percent in Italy, 80 percent in West Germany, the Netherlands, and Scandinavia, and 75 percent in France and Great Britain.[22]

Could Americans be voluntarily self-disenfranchising because they refuse to spend the time informing themselves on the issues at stake and going to the polls to register their preferences? When taken seriously, preparing to vote intelligently is a time-consuming task bearing meager personal rewards. As we might expect, the degree of economic prosperity also affects voter turnout. With full employment, time is particularly valuable; with high unemployment, many people have little to do. During the Great Depression of the 1930s, voter turnout edged up at least partly because voting didn't "cost" much in time given up. With the return of prosperity, and rising employment, income, and time value, however, voter turnout declined. (One personal cost paid by non-voters is a possible loss of friends, at least if the friends are poets. One of those, Ogden Nash, wrote, "People on whom I do not bother to dote, are people who do not bother to vote."[23])

High-income earners, who of course also prize their time highly, must be among those on whom the celebrated poet does not bother to dote. A recent election day survey showed that, compared to an overall one-in-three of the eligible-age population who turned out to vote, 27 percent of those with $40,000 to $75,000 incomes bothered to cast ballots, and only 7 percent earning over $75,000 did so.[24]

There is no reason to believe that voter turnout rates have yet reached a nadir. Voter turnout has dropped, and will likely continue to drop, as long as there are too many other things to do on election day.

Harken to the words of educator Robert Maynard Hutchins who once warned that, "The death of democracy is not likely to be an assassination from ambush. It will be a slow extinction from apathy, indifference, and undernourishment,"[25] the consequence—we are compelled to add—of the *BB* factor.

LOVE THYSELF

In her haste to skip out on settling her hotel bill, an elderly woman left behind a steam iron, a car tire, and a bag of cement, belongings that were returned to her when she showed up some months later to pay up.[26] Carelessness and hurriedness go hand in hand. Add another parallel, rudeness. Politeness, like irons, tires, and cement, is likely to be left behind too when we hurry.

Rudeness, to most, is a vice; to a few, a virtue. The late Alice Roosevelt Longworth, who shocked diners at the White House by eating asparagus with glove-clad fingers, had no doubts about the matter. Near death, she roused herself to reprimand a guest for politeness that was excessive by her standards: "I will not have good manners in my house."[27] What was *passé* in Ms. Longworth's time may be *de rigueur* today. Common courtesy becomes an oxymoron.

In Victorian times, referring to legs as "legs" was judged rude. They were limbs and decorum necessitated hiding piano limbs with drapery. Occupying a seat that still carried the residual warmth of a previous sitter was considered offensive. As recently as a few decades ago, about the rudest thing a school kid could do was to chew gum. Only the most boorish male failed in his duty to hold the door open for a woman. And it was a most ungallant fellow indeed who neglected offering an elderly person his seat on the bus. It was a time when theaters still conspicuously posted signs guaranteeing that such boorishness exceeded the limits of tolerance:

> Coughing, Sneezing, or Spitting Will Not Be Permitted in the Theater . . . In case you must Cough or Sneeze, do so in your own handkerchief, and if the Coughing or Sneezing Persists Leave the Theater At Once. GO HOME AND GO TO BED UNTIL YOU ARE WELL. If you have a cold or are coughing and sneezing DO NOT ENTER THIS THEATER.[28]

Gone are such warnings. In their place are the graffiti that convey messages in mysterious symbols, and the patrons' once-forbidden sneezes and coughs strategically timed to coincide with quiet moments during concerts, plays, movies, and lectures. No doubt about it, churlish behavior is on the rise and may even have become the accepted standard. Courtesy is time-expensive, discourtesy is time-cheap. In the meantime, decorum and deportment have all but vanished from the vocabulary. We're too busy for such niceties, and so is everyone else.

As the code of deportment, a casualty of the *BB* factor, grows shorter by the minute, the list of grievances against rude others, another manifestation of the *BB* factor, grows longer.

YOUR TIME IS MY TIME

Everyone has a favorite story about how they've been done in by someone: by the plumber who arrives to fix your faucet three days after the scheduled appointment made two weeks before, by the fellow who lets the door slam in your face as you struggle along behind him loaded down with three full suitcases, by the secretary at the other end of the telephone who puts you on hold never to return to the line, by the guy hovering over the public phone who appears to have taken up permanent residence in the booth, by the group parading arm-in-arm down a narrow sidewalk who force you into the gutter, by the postal clerk who insists that there is no place called Germany and besides it's too much effort to consult his big fat book that tells how much it costs to send a postcard to that city, by the family seated in the row behind at the movies who insist on discussing a better film they saw last week (for them, a synchronic use of their time; for you, an unwanted distraction), or by the salesman who when asked why he didn't say thank you for your purchase replies, "why should I when it's written on your receipt?"

It takes longer to hold the door for someone than to go through first, to offer your place in the supermarket check-out queue to a shopper with only two items in their basket compared to your twenty-two, to yield the right-of way to pedestrians or other drivers at rush hour, to inquire seriously about a friend's state of

INDIGNATION VS. HAVING A GOOD TIME

"Let people push you around. The person who says, believes, and acts on the phrase, 'I ain't taking any shit from anybody' is a very busy person indeed. This person must be ever vigilant against news vendors who shortchange him, cab drivers who take him the wrong way around, waiters who serve the other guy first, florists who are charging ten cents more per tulip than the one down the block, pharmacists who make you wait too long, and cars that cut you off at the light: they are a veritable miasma of righteous indignation and never have a minute to relax and have a good time." —Cynthia Heimel[29] health, especially when you really don't care how sick they've been, to take care not to poke others in the eye with your umbrella, or to preface a request with "please" and follow a favor with "thank you."

To be rude takes less time than to be courteous. Technology has done little to change that sorry fact. On the one hand, equipping home and office with the latest machinery has made us dependent on repair people who, with their claims of special expertise, believe that they can afford to deal rudely with their befuddled customers. On the other hand, technology has made it somewhat easier to avoid the rudies. Why do we often observe long lines waiting to use a bank's automated teller when there are no lines waiting for the human version? Because the machine won't give a rude response: it will never reply "there you go" instead of "thank you," and "no problem" instead of "you're welcome."

As adviser on matters of behavior, Abigail Van Buren writes, "If a person is kind, or generous, it's an event."[30] Such events seem more commonplace in the nation's rural towns and the Deep South where people cling more tenaciously to the vestiges of gracious behavior. Time there is more elastic, and one can "afford" to devote more of it to graciousness. Rampant rudeness seems to be mainly an urban phenomenon. That would be expected, for in the big cities where people lead more harried lives, time apparently counts for more. A feature article in *Time* devoted to the disappearance of ordinary courtesies, drew most of its examples from metropolitan America.[31]

The Problem: Rudeness on the Road

The automobile is a veritable laboratory on wheels for discovering people's reactions to the *BB* factor. One not-very-surprising discovery made in that laboratory is that, as time becomes more scarce, drivers are inclined to speed up.

People do seem to be driving faster these days, not only because Congress increased legal speeds, but simply because speeding gets you there quicker, albeit at greater risk to self and to others. The 1974 oil embargo that fueled a fuel crisis prompted lawmakers to cap speeds at 55 mph. At first the new limit was observed, but not for long. In 1974, 65 percent of drivers exceeded the maximum, and the fraction rose steadily until a dozen years later it had topped

76 percent, a proportion that rendered the limit virtually meaningless and suggested that enforcement officers might have become more sympathetic to the majority's desire to save precious time by faster driving.[32]

Speeding is one discovery; rudeness, another. The *BB* factor has turned the streets a little meaner. The auto allows the real you, clad in steel rather than in social strictures, to emerge. The steel shield of the car's body that offers protection from aggression allows drivers to be more ruthless, more indifferent to the welfare of others, more aggressive, and at once more protected from their aggressions. Whether it's running a red light, creating gridlock by inching into congested intersections, tailgating the driver ahead, weaving from lane to lane, hogging the fast lane, neglecting to flash when changing lanes, failing to yield the right-of-way, or making left turns when it is dangerous to do so, motorists are finding ways of getting there more quickly, but at the frustration of other drivers. According to the Rev. Ian Gregory, president of the Polite Society, Newcastle-under-Tyne, 47 percent of auto accidents reported for insurance damages are the result of rudeness.[33]

Coast-to-coast surveys—one taken in New York City and another in Los Angeles—disclose the pervasiveness of roadway rudeness. "Anarchy rules the streets," concluded a team sent to six busy midtown Manhattan intersections by the Automobile Club of New York in 1987 to observe driving habits. On each of the street corners, traffic laws were broken an average of 274 times an hour. Motorists routinely jumped red lights and blocked crosswalks, bicyclists regularly rode in the wrong direction, and pedestrians jaywalked with abandon.[34]

The next year Los Angeles, not to be outdone by New York, sent investigators out to survey rush-hour traffic behavior at nine local intersections. The investigators tallied up 272 drivers who ran red lights and 428 who made illegal left-turns. A spokesman summed up the situation neatly: "we've just got too many people in too much of a hurry to get someplace."[35]

The Solution: Shoot 'em!

In the early days when automobiles were rattly flivvers, drivers customarily tipped their hats when passing each other on the road.[36] In the era of the *BB* factor when automobiles are Challengers, Chargers, Cougars, or Cutlasses, quaint greetings have given away to more lethal media of exchange. Again we turn to Los Angeles for inspiration.

Long known for their frontier ways and for confronting complex challenges straight-forwardly, Angelenos hit on a solution to the problem of roadway rudeness. True to the traditions of the Wild West, it was the quick-draw. In the space of a few short weeks during a recent hot summer, freeway vigilantes took their revenge on drivers who were too busy to be polite. The freeways became war zones. Seventy shootings were reported during an action-packed ten-week period, all prompted by drivers' anger with motorists' discourtesy.[37]

No vigilante was to upstage one Charley Tom Lee, Jr., 25, however, whose freeway frenetics climaxed the dramaturgy. According to press accounts, Mr. Lee, the driver of a 40-foot tractor-trailer loaded with a cargo of ironing boards, rammed some twenty-four cars at speeds ranging up to 80 mph, leaving a thirty-five mile swath of destruction. "Those people who would get out of my way, I wouldn't hit," explained Mr. Lee in parsimoniously describing his special mode of dealing with rudeness. "But if they wouldn't get out of my way, I would hit 'em."[38]

Responses to highway rudeness of course are seldom so violent as those of the freeway vigilantes or so creative as Mr. Lee's, but violent they are nonetheless. Surveys by psychologist Raymond W. Novaco show how enraged drivers periodically transform their vehicles into weapons. Over 40 percent of males and up to 21 percent of females sampled had chased annoying drivers, finds Novaco, and other aggressive behaviors, such as throwing objects, shouting or yelling, and deliberately riding someone's bumper, bumping or ramming others (though undoubtedly with less panache than Mr. Lee) were reported to occur "with worrisome frequency." For some, abusive behavior was a more than sometime thing. Nine percent said that they registered their disdain digitally on a weekly basis.[39] Father, forgive me, for I gesture obscenely once a week.

If that's not enough, consider the results of another driver survey which found that 12 percent of the men and 18 percent of the women believed that they could "gladly kill another driver."[40] Those in search of less violent alternatives will find solace in an old adage, "time wounds all heels."[41]

Alice Roosevelt Longworth, Wherever You Are, You Would be Proud!

Real courtesy, the opposite of rudeness, might be defined as the caring for another person, rather than just the courtesy bred out of fear and deference. Our norms for demonstrating that care for others seem to have become more lax as we have shifted the ways we spend each twenty-four hours toward activities that favor us rather than others. Among the others are youngsters and oldsters.

15:00

YOUNG FOLKS IN TROUBLE, OLD FOLKS DOING WELL

"The first half of our lives is ruined by our parents, and the second half by our children."

—Clarence Darrow[1]

In the beginning, there was the Void (Chaos) out of which Earth (Ge) was created. Ge in her turn gave birth to mountains, sea, and sky (Uranus). Ge then mated with her son Uranus, a union that produced a dozen Titans, of whom Cronus (Time)(!) (=Saturn) was one. Uranus somehow put the later children into his wife, Gaia, giving her, to no one's surprise, great pain. Only Cronus dared to come to her aid and, hidden, castrated his father Uranus, when the latter came to mate again with Gaia. Cronus, after disposing of his father's naughty little bits, became the ruler. Carrying on the incestuous traditions the family was becoming noted for, Cronus then married his sister Rhea. Forewarned that he, like his own father, was to be overcome by his own sons, Cronus hastily ate all of the children that were born to him by Rhea. Without taking care what or whom he swallowed, Cronus consumed Demeter, Hades, Hera, Hestia, and Poseidon.

This grim little myth drawn from the distant past, first, tells us that time (Cronus) eats kids, and, second, explains the merits of doing away with our kids when they get in the way. Neither the fact nor the advice are altogether far-fetched, for contemporary parents are using their time today in ways no less destructive. "The Breakfast Club," a modern version of the ancient Greek tale, tells how.

In the 1985 movie, five teenagers in trouble—"a brain, a basket case, a princess, a juvenile delinquent, and a jock," as the film's preview describes them—are thrown together for a weekend group therapy session to try to answer the question, why did they go wrong? After painful hours spent exploring every possibility, they finally hit on the answer: they don't know their parents. And their parents haven't taken the time to get to know them. Had the troubled teenagers merely found a scapegoat for shortcomings that were really their own fault?

NEGLECTED CHILDREN

Kids are in deep trouble these days. "Many observers consider today's children to be worse off than their parents' generation in several important dimensions of physical, mental, and emotional well-being."[2] Violence and accidents, now accounting for nearly two out of three deaths among those under age 10, have replaced natural causes and disease as the chief source of child mortality. "External causes" distinguish the reasons for child mortality from deaths of those in any other age bracket.[3] Between 1960 and 1980 their rates of delinquency, alcohol and drug abuse, and illegitimate births more than doubled, the proportion murdered quadrupled, and the suicide rate skyrocketed to become the second leading cause of adolescents' dying.[4]

Researchers set out to uncover the reasons. First, was the cause an increase in poverty? No. Although poverty has increased in recent years, during the two decades studied, 1960–80, the proportion in poverty dropped 5 percentage points. Second, was it family size? No. The proportion of large families declined by 7 percentage points. Third, was it the parents' education? No. The proportion of children raised by parents with low education dropped by half. Fourth, was it the quality of education? No. School expenditures per pupil (in real dollars) and the proportion of teachers with high degrees doubled, and class size fell. Fifth, were there fewer parents then to nurture more children? No. The number of children dropped by 830,000 and the adult population rose by 48 million.[5]

Further detective work uncovered a single main factor: "the declining commitment of parents." Fewer hours were made available to children. "It appears that parents are becoming available at times convenient to the parents, not at times when the child has the most need for attention."

Responsibilities to young children have not kept women out of pink-collar jobs. Today, two in three married women 20 to 34 years of age work for pay and about nine out of ten working women in that age bracket expect to become pregnant.[6] In 1960, 39 percent of mothers with children under 18 worked in the labor force; in 1991, the proportion was 67 percent. The up-trend is likely to continue. Women now make up close to half the labor force, and the Labor Department predicts that in the 1990s women will fill 60 percent of all new jobs and, by the year 2000, there will be an equal number of men and women in paid work.[7]

With more and more women working outside the home, fewer hours are left for the children. The number of traditional families, with husband employed and wife working at home, declines by nearly 300,000 each year. The number of working couples with kids has been increasing by 5 percent a year until today three in four dual-earner families have children.

Behind these calm words, courtesy of the Census Bureau, lurks a social transformation. The Silent Revolution, as the rush of women into paid jobs is dubbed, has been a revolution as much in concept as in numbers. Consider what the revolution was against. As the editor of *Popular Science Monthly* put it a century ago:

> Birds often plunge into the watery deep, and fishes sometimes rise into the air, but one is nevertheless formed for swimming and the other for flight. So women may make transient diversions from the sphere of activity for which they are constituted, but they are nevertheless formed and designed for maternity, the care of children, and the affairs of domestic life. They are the mothers of human kind, the natural educators of childhood, the guardians of the household, and by the deepest ordinance of things, they are this, in a sense, and to a degree, that man is not.[8]

Women lost their allegorical wings and fins with the mechanization of housekeeping tasks, the growing acceptance of family planning, and the civil rights and feminist movements of the 1960s. Stagnating incomes and wages during the next decades pushed many mothers into the work force in order to maintain family living standards. Widowhood, divorce, and pregnancies outside of marriage prompted an increasing number of other women to assume the sole breadwinner's role.

Not only were the conditions right, but most women *wanted* to work for pay. Paid work not only brings economic independence, they believed, but a fulfillment not available to those who slave at housework. When asked if they would keep their jobs even if family finances were not an issue, an overwhelming 82 percent of working mothers said they would, and, among nonworking women, fully 71 percent said they would prefer to be working.[9] Only one woman in five would willingly sacrifice income for more free time and those who were employed wanted to keep things that way, even if it meant sacrifices at home.[10] Women pulled between the urge for paid jobs and unpaid household responsibilities are understandably frustrated. Fully a third report feeling "a lot of stress" in balancing obligations to work and family.[11] In more and more cases, the jobs win the tug-of-war, leaving in its wake stressed mothers and neglected children.

Today's mom must juggle everything from arranging baby sitters to cooking dinner. Women who forsake unpaid work in the household for paid work in the labor force must instantly find thirty to forty additional hours a week for the job. Other activities must give way. Time spent in domestic duties drops by nearly half and leisure time by one-fourth. But time with kids is the major loser. The reduction amounts to a whopping 69 percent! That means that, for every hour mom spent with the kids before she got a job, she now spends only 19 minutes.[12] Gone is the image of Mommy at work in the kitchen watching over baby in the playpen. Today's Mommy is more likely working at a desk. And who is watching over baby?

Sacrifices in a working mother's care would be negligible if dad more fully shared household duties. This hasn't happened. For many men, careers, indifference, or "tradition" serve as excuses for neglecting children and domestic chores despite the blurring of men's and women's traditional roles. Only 15 to 20 percent of households divide the chores evenly.[13] If few dads are willing to do their share, farming the very young out to day care centers or baby sitters or older children may be the only alternative. Yet, as well as the alternatives may operate, they are poor substitutes for parents' time and loving care.

Dedicated parents who willingly give their time to nurturing, guiding, and supervising children quickly learn that those tasks take as long today as they ever did. Technology helps little if at all.

Television as a parental surrogate helps, but not much. Neither does a home computer, even one loaded with action games. Gadgets have done much to remove dust and dirt from floors and dishes, but cannot remove the loneliness of children left unattended—and to them, unwanted and alone—at home. Social critic Amitai Etzioni puts it simply: "If you want to have children, take care of them, dammit, instead of buying another VCR."[14]

"Lack of parental supervision" was targeted by 72 percent of Americans as the reason for teenage violence.[15] That belief seems to be well founded. One scary report, *High Risk: Children Without a Conscience,* contends that lack of parental care from birth on is a major cause for the growing numbers of child psychopaths.[16] Neglected children are at high risk for delinquency, crime, and violence. "A workaholic parent," claims one expert, "is just as abusive as one who physically abuses his children."[17]

The evidence leads to a discouraging conclusion. Because time caring for children fails to offer the rewards of time working for pay, and it cannot be perfectly substituted for or commoditized, time spent nurturing children loses, as the *BB* factor wins.

We have returned full circle to "The Breakfast Club," with an explanation behind the five troubled teenagers' discovery. The working family of the future faces the daunting challenge of juggling job and family obligations. This challenge is yet to be met, for a majority of young working parents report child care as their leading problem and half of working women and one in three men feel the frustration of having "no time for spouse or for children."[18]

Challenges they are for the future, but in the meantime we must worry about the outcomes of spending too little quality time with children. And formidable are those outcomes.

PARENTS TOO BUSY

Things have changed from those days when dad left home in Westchester (or New Halcyon) at 6:30, caught the train for his job in New York City, and returned home twelve hours later. First, these days both mom and dad are on that train. Second, their children are latchkey kids, so named because they need keys to let themselves into their empty homes after school. They are perhaps the first generation in history to be raised by fathers *and* mothers who work. There are a surprising number of such children—more than 40 percent of Americans under age 13.[19]

George Bernard Shaw used latchkey to signal self-reliance in a 1905 play, "Major Barbara": "Your independence is achieved: you have won your latch key.' "[20] But whether today's kids thrive on such independence is quite a different matter. The freedom afforded children by the time their parents commit to work has consequences ranging from rudeness to suicide. *In loco parentis* has taken on new meaning for latchkey kids.

Rudeness Begins at Home

Not only are adults more rude, as time scarcity takes its toll, but so are their offspring. Young people are the worst offenders when it comes to discourtesy, claims the author of the syndicated "Dear Abby" column, because "the parents say they're too busy or it's too much work to teach polite behavior." It all begins at home, says Abby. "The common amenities take time. They tend to slow a person down."[21] A psychiatrist puts it more academically: "The ability of kids to absorb parental norms has been compromised as mom and dad are out of the house more."[22]

But the problems of today's youth run deeper than mere rudeness. Rising rates of teenage suicide, alcohol and drug abuse, crime and delinquency all attest to an increasingly serious problem. Three in four adults are convinced that life as a child today is worse than when they were young, and "the troubles of young people have been largely tucked out of sight, in a kind of massive studied avoidance." Barely half believe that most youngsters have loving parents or are "basically happy."[23] Few parents are taking the time to hug their kids today.

School Drop-Outs Too Begin at Home

Remember when the worst thing a pupil could do was to "horse around"? A CBS report compared the top seven problems reported by schools today and fifty years ago. Talking out of turn, chewing gum, making noise, running in the halls, cutting in line, violating the dress code, and littering topped the list of major infractions in 1940. How innocent seem those pranks! Forty years later, the top-seven consisted of drug abuse, alcohol abuse, pregnancy, suicide, rape, robbery, and assault.[24] What went haywire?

From pioneering work completed in the mid-1960s, James S. Coleman discovered that student achievement depended more on family environment than on any other factor, including the quality of the school. When Professor Coleman recently returned to his laboratory to restudy achievement and drop-outs, he found that the explanation still worked. Comparing students' progress in over 1,000 public and private high schools, he uncovered two key factors. Greater parental support and more authority went hand-in-hand with higher math and verbal skills, and lower drop-out rates. Greater support means a more direct and effective connection between family and school, and between parent and child that reinforces children who are at risk of dropping out. More authority means that the parents backed up the school's demands for giving the students more math, English, and history courses. The schools made tough demands on the students and the parents enforced the demands.

Parents are at once cause and cure. "Schools have never been very successful with weak families," says Coleman. "These days many more families have become weak, either because they are single-parent families or because both parents are working and the family cannot devote sufficient time and attention to children." Drop-outs can be blamed on "the absence of close relations with adults who can provide aid when needed."[25]

For a happy contrast, consider Japan, where drop-out rates are near zero and, by no coincidence, mothers lavish the needed aid on their children. The cause-effect reasoning goes beyond nurturing and success in school achievement, right to the heart of Japan's economic miracle.[26] Workers have wrought that miracle because of school-learned virtues of discipline and perseverance. The responsibility carried by mothers, and the nurturing environment they provide, in turn explain success in school. From day one in grade one, Japanese children begin to learn group skills that prepare future workers for harmonious employer-employee relationships. Innate ability matters less in Japan than does single-minded effort, a fact that forces students to work with incredible diligence. While it is the student's single-mindedness that ultimately pays off, it is the Japanese mother's single-minded dedication of countless hours, and the shaping of her own life around her children's success in school, that gives the necessary incentives.[27] The causal chain is completed: credit Japan's economic miracle to the time and effort of caring mothers.

The Tragedy of Teenage Suicide

Several years ago the nation was stunned by the news that four teenagers in Bergenfield, New Jersey, had locked themselves in a garage, turned on the engine of a car, and died. The four who took their lives had dropped out or been suspended from school, for undisclosed reasons. But apparently those were not the real causes underpinning the self-initiated tragedy.

Bergenfield, a middle-class town across the Hudson River from Manhattan, was regarded as a model community boasting thirty-two juvenile-assistance programs ranging from Youth Environmental Services to Adopt-a-Cop. But community programs are not parental surrogates. So said the head of the town's youth counseling program: "As a community, we can provide shops, public schools, social services, and sidewalks. But there are other things that are equally important, notably the home environment." Added the director of the County's Adolescent Suicide Awareness Program: "The dropouts don't have a natural support system at school—and frequently not at home either."[28]

Teenagers who go home to empty homes are far more prone to turn to drugs and alcohol. Regardless of their sex, race, family income, school achievement, participation in sports and other extracurricular activities, or stress level, latchkey kids are twice as likely to use alcohol, tobacco, and marijuana as those youngsters who are cared for by adults after school. And the longer they spend alone, claims the discoverer of that fact, the greater the risk of substance abuse.[29] Substance abuse exacerbates the suicide problem in dual ways: it may be the kids' reaction to their elders unwillingness to give time, which is symbolic of love, and may provide the courage required to follow through with a suicide threat—as an attention-getting, *time*-getting device—that, under normal circumstances, would never be carried out.

Rather than carrying out an impulsive, unpredictable action, the person bent on suicide contemplates the intended-to-be-fatal act for some time, all the while transmitting warnings of the pending disaster. Investigators studying twenty-one youthful suicides disclosed emotional disorders that went unrecognized and untreated, signals that watchful parents might have intercepted before the final, fatal act.[30] But the elders were too busy.

> "The reason these children become suicidal in their late teens and early twenties is that they encounter severe difficulties in becoming independent. A child who has never felt secure and adequately cared for does not know how to become a good parent to herself or himself. These young adults become easily overwhelmed by their own feelings. They feel hopeless and blame themselves for their difficulties. They feel intense guilt and shame. . . . [Their] depression is frequently masked, expressed only through a smiling, overly compliant manner or through acting out self-destructive behaviors such as alcohol and drug abuse, antisocial acts, and abusive sexual relationships."
>
> —Joan Rothchild Hardin[31]

Suicide appears to be a larger problem in middle- and upper-class families, who most strongly feel the pressures of time. The rate among those under age 25 is twice as high among whites as African-Americans and higher among African-Americans than Hispanics. Moreover, the incidence of suicide seems to be lowest in countries better known for family-centeredness and a relatively carefree approach to time-management, and less known for economic prosperity. Mexico, the Philippines, and Egypt are among the nations with the lowest suicide rates.[32] Is it mere coincidence that rich Americans—and perhaps the Japanese too—seem to place job before family? Apparently, the higher the parents' income and time value, the easier parents make the division between work for pay and work for the kids. A survey of households whose incomes hovered around $200,000 a year makes a telling point. Career success was their priority. "Two-thirds of respondents said they strongly felt the need to be successful in their jobs, while fewer than half said they strongly felt the need to spend more time with their families."[33] Those priorities may explain the surprising discovery that latchkey kids, and teenage suicides, are more likely to come from higher-income areas of town,[34] and the homes of those most prone to the *BB* factor.

"I LOVE MY CHILDREN DEEPLY, BUT . . ."

A good deal is written and said about how the disintegration of the American family imperils children. High and rising rates of separation and divorce leave children in the breach. The new work ethic has bred the delinquent parents who claim to love their children deeply, but also believe that they should be "free to live their own lives even if it means spending less time with their children." Two in three so qualify their love, and the proportion is trending upward.[35]

W. C. Fields, when asked, "How do you like kids?" replied, "fried." If the consequences of time sacrificed from child care are as horrendous as portrayed here, apparently two-thirds of parents like their kids the same way.

Children estranged from families, homes, and traditions that anchor the troublesome years of adolescence may go to extreme ends to find the stability, reassurance, and affection that oftentimes only parents can give. The symbolic aspect of time commitment to helping and caring also matters. Children quite perceptively index their relative worth by the amount of "quality" time their busy parents willingly relinquish from competing activities in order to spend with them. The less time spent doing other things, the more the child feels he or she is worth. A former president of the American Association of Suicidology notes that "American parents spend less time with their children than those of almost any other nation of the world," and adds

> The attitude of many American parents is that their children are an inconvenience, an impediment to freedom or success. . . . The adolescent who is neglected or unheard may see attempting suicide as the only way to get attention. Occasionally this attempt may turn out to be lethal.[36]

Parents can reorder their priorities, and that means choosing to use time in different ways, giving the time and effort to the kids they have brought into the world. It is not that parents don't *want* to spend more time with their children—although 81 percent of adults believe that parents spend too little time with their children, nearly 60 percent said they want more time for the kids[37]—it is that they simply *don't* spend the time. And if parents are unwilling to activate their desire to give the quality time, it may fall to institutions, the school and church, to teach a course of instruction they forsook three or four decades ago, but that parents have forsaken today: concern for others, helpfulness, consideration, generosity, understanding, learning to listen, respect for diversity, social ethics, and a sense of community at local and global scale, and the other aspects of life that foster responsible child development. Failing that, increasing work opportunities for women, an almost inbred male aversion to serving as stand-ins for now-absent mothers, and the desire to live lives freely regardless of the consequences for children, all point to more kids being in more trouble tomorrow.

As the quality of life declines among our youth, however, it rises by leaps and bounds for those at the opposite end of their life cycles. The aged are indeed better off than ever before. Ironically, this success is due to the same reasons as the social pathologies of their distant juniors. Time, and the way it is valued and used, explains much of the difference.

WHY TODAY'S ELDERLY ARE SO WELL OFF

More than age separates the young and the old of today. Well-being does too. Although the young may never have had it so bad, their grandparents are doing very nicely, thank you. For one thing, most of the 30 million Americans over 65 are happy, and happier certainly than today's youth. Only about half of youngsters aged 18 to 24 express satisfaction with life, in sharp contrast to three-fourths of the elderly who are that contented.[38] There is good reason for this, for the elderly are far better off than kids—better off, in fact, than they have ever been.

Asked about the age factor, aging Senator Russell Long retorted, "I still have a lot of snap in my garters."[39] If Sen. Long is typical of his elderly compatriots, he should add, "and a lot of money in my pockets."

Seniors can boast the highest income growth rate, the highest after-tax income per head, the highest household net worth, and the lowest poverty rate of any age group in the country.

- Their incomes are rising *seven times* faster than the incomes of all others.[40]
- The over-65 group has twice the discretionary income per capita of those aged 25 to 34, yet pays only 14 percent of income in taxes, compared to 22 percent nationwide.[41]
- Americans over 50 hold 70 percent of the total wealth of U.S. households.[42]
- Since 1970, the fraction of oldsters who are poor has been cut in half. The proportion in poverty today (12 percent) falls below the national average (13 percent), and well below the poverty group of youth (19 percent).[43]

Not only are today's older Americans wealthier, but healthier than ever before, and longer-lived. With a bonus of eleven years added to the life-span since World War II, more golden years remain for living out lives of leisure. Better financial circumstances and better health increase the quality of that quantity. Their superior financial position allows the aged to retire early for a welcome respite after years of labor. In 1950 nearly half of all men 65 and older continued to work, as against one in six currently.[44] Those who have quit work early are glad they did so. A skimpy 12 percent said they want to go back to work.[45] As a press account observes, "The Flesh is Able, the Spirit is Weak."[46]

And how are people of age using their increased time, good health, and freedom from economic woes? They drive their own cars, trek around the world, and go to the movies on half-price tickets. The vast majority live in the community, not nursing homes, and most of these occupy their own debt-free homes. The independence they have won is as personal as it is financial. No longer need they be a care to their offspring, as so many were in days not long past; no longer need they look forward to growing older in the homes of their children, often unwanted and unloved dependents.

Dependency is not a happy state. The time required to care for an elderly person is a hefty burden, one that often must be borne by sons and daughters least able to assume it. Forty-four percent of care-giving daughters living with dependent mothers hold paying jobs and one-fourth have a young child of their own at home.[47] Care-givers' out-of-pocket costs mount up quickly. Equipment must be rented for the infirm, the home modified, and special diets provided. The average burden of providing care for an unimpaired elderly person exceeds $200 a month (in 1990 prices) but, for the greatly impaired, costs sky-rocket to $1,100, with family and friends bearing the great bulk (at least 70 percent), and charities or public agencies footing the rest of the bill.[48] On top of that, care-givers must assume less obvious personal costs of work opportunities foregone, social activities given up, and privacy lost. The overall time requirement may add up to the equivalent of holding down a full-time job.[49] All told, supporting an elderly person can be devastatingly expensive.

When the elderly can live out their golden years in the dignity that economic independence provides—which is what survey after

survey shows the vast majority of oldsters want[50]—their offspring too can live independent lives freed of the time-consuming tasks of caring for elderly parents—and that's what *they* want. Separated spatially as well as by age, elders and kin can enjoy intimacy at a distance. For good reason, young and old alike have joined forces to fight for that autonomy. And they have won the battle.

THE GUILTY "IN-BETWEENERS"

While the quality of life deteriorates for youngsters and improves by leaps and bounds for oldsters, what about the actions of the care-giving generation in between? These people, in the middle-ages of their lives, respond most to the *BB* factor.

Young and old alike have won independence if only because of the indifference of the in-betweeners, the pivotal group much concerned with allocating its own time in the most personally rewarding ways. Parents do not want to spend time taking care of the kids or their elders if doing so requires sacrificing activities with higher **S/T**s. Because caretaking resists commoditization, the **S/T**s of these selfless efforts have risen little, if at all, and caring for Moms, Dads, Bobbys, and Sues has become time-minus in the minds of many in the harassed middle years.

All sides cheer the independence of the 65-plus group. So broad is the support for social security, for example, that "reform" of the system has remained off limits to political discussion. Advocates representing the in-betweens and the elderly have won the aged a disproportionate share of public benefits.[51] All told, the benefits seniors receive are over five times their relative importance in the total population, and account for seven times the amount of taxes they pay! Is it any wonder that, in a comparatively brief span of time, their economic status has soared, and the vast majority have achieved their sought-after economic freedom?

All well and good, but giving also requires taking. Giving the elderly subsidies and other benefits requires taking them from others. The losers, in this case, are children. Government expenditures on the elderly range anywhere from three to ten times more for the old folks than for the young,[52] an imbalance that raises serious issues of intergenerational inequity.

While the oldsters have boisterous constituencies, the organized voices for youngsters are mere whispers in comparison. Recent political history tells the story. Much attention was focused on the family in the late 1970s, but since then emphasis on the need for child-care facilities for working mothers' offspring has deteriorated, publicly sponsored lunch programs for poor children have been trimmed back, and the real value of payments made to aid dependent children has eroded. For good reason, nearly two out of three believe little is being done to deal with the worsening problems of the young.[53] In government-spending circles, the elderly occupy the limelight and the kids are out there somewhere in the dark. And the in-betweens, prompted by their concern for scarce time, support these shifts.

Money, perhaps the most impersonal of all resources, bought the aged their independence, and bought time for their offspring on whom they once depended. Money cannot buy the kind of care that kids need: the care that requires their parents' time. Not coincidentally, those who are to blame for the kids' problems and for the seniors' success constitute the same generation, the in-betweeners. In both cases, the *BB* factor must be held accountable.

16:00
THE DISSERVICING OF AMERICA

"By and by, God caught his eye."
—David McCord, "Epitaph on a Waiter" [1]

How ever did the Duke and Duchess of Windsor cope during the abdication? Compared to the army of 300 servants at Sandringham, a meager cadre of only eighteen were at their beck and call during those days that England's ex-King Edward and Wallie Simpson spent in the little Bois de Boulogne palace. Clearly, making the most of their faithful servants' precious time now mattered more than ever.

They had been given careful instructions. Butlers were ordered to squeeze the toothpaste on to the brush, to unroll the toilet paper and cut it into little squares, and to remove the bed sheets for a daily ironing. The *sous-chef* sorted out the salad leaves and matched them for size. The footman served the pugs their daily ration of *petit beurre* biscuits in solid silver bowls, and each night arranged the pets on the Duchess's bed.[2]

Grandeur such as this belonged to a past age, and a life-style accessible to only the privileged few. A generation later, we live in the lean, clean, tidy post-industrial age of information and ideas. Household servants have gone the way of the sixth toe, yet we have more "servants" available to us, and their services are accessible to rich and poor alike.

They are the service workers who sell us TV sets and repair them, who mend our marriages and help us across life's hurdles, who teach us and advise us on legal problems, who heal our bodies and psychoanalyze us, who serve up Big Macs at the counter and wash dishes in the kitchen, who design our homes and fix the faucets, who defend us at the bar and in the Persian Gulf, who advise us which appliances to buy, and who sit all day at computers manipulating odd little symbols. These are the workers who produce not a product, but "convenience, security, comfort, and flexibility," items that "cannot be inventoried."[3] The category even includes the president of the U.S. of A.

Currently, three out of four workers produce those items instead of growing crops, mining minerals, or making goods, the staples of a bygone era. In the decades since World War II, the service sector has accounted for most new employment, and an astonishing 97 percent of the new hires created during the current decade will be for the production of "convenience, security, comfort, and flexibility."[4] As the numbers of service workers have grown, however, the overall quality of their work has eroded. The *BB* factor helps to account for that seeming contradiction.

The number of workers who produce goods, rather than good deeds, has declined even though their output, measured in terms of production per working hour, has risen. The reason: in goods manufacture, the energy of machines is performing the routine, repetitive tasks that once required the energy of human beings. Rendering services is a different matter. The machinery has yet to be invented for human-oriented jobs like performing brain surgery, selling makeup in the department store, mediating troubled relationships, delivering sermons, or even for matching the salad leaves.

Not only has productivity in services remained low, but the *quality* of output remains low, and seems to be in steady decline. Providing quality service is on the wane: a time-minus activity, one where gazinta **S/T** fails to keep pace.

Americans are dazzled by speed. Domino's Pizza, Federal Express, Jack in the Box, McDonald's, Martinizing, Polaroid, and 7-Eleven have built corporate empires on the quest for quickness. Surveying the listings in one metropolitan telephone directory—a veritable thesaurus entry for the word fast—turns up Fast Start Auto Insurance, Instant Wedding Chapel, One-Hour Eye Glasses, Presto Cleaners, Prompt Rubbish Disposal, Rapid Mortgage, Speedy Graphics, Swift Cleaners, and Quick and Dependable Eviction Service.

Speeding up the delivery of professional services presents more challenges. Yet there are ways to do it. Take psychiatry, a procedure that once took longer than an archaeological dig. So time consuming was the process of mending the mind, so expensive was it, and for many so dull talking endlessly about one's ego and id, that 80 percent of patients in therapy dropped out in under a half year.[5] Time was too precious (not to mention money).

Short-term treatment is the answer. Quick-therapy with treatments running to months, not years, has replaced the tradition of painfully digging to expose the roots of the problem. After all, Freud cured Gustav Mahler's impotence in four hours, the time that it took the father of modern therapy to discover that a mother fixation repelled his patient from his celebrated wife Anna.

In the late '60s encounter groups, nude therapy, transactional analysis, and primal scream therapy collapsed the years of psychoanalysis into months. More streamlining has trimmed the time requirement further. Today's crowd signs up for therapeutic experiences that stop short of taking the patient back to birth. Co-counseling, in which unlicensed people counsel each other, lasts around eighteen weeks. Cognitive therapy, a routine that focuses on a person's thought patterns and garbled beliefs, not on deep-seated conflicts or relationships with parents, may require as few as six sessions. Transpersonal therapy, such as meditation, pilots its followers through a rite of passage from a toxic situation and toward an innerlife, a voyage that lasts as little as six transcendental weeks.

Besides instant psychotherapy, electronic tellers, computerized reservations and ticketing, instant check-in and -out, and automated record-keeping are among the innovations meant to speed up the delivery of services to consumers and deliver them at higher quality. Yet, something is wrong. Very wrong. Too many consumers claim that they receive bad service. If the complaints have merit, the service economy's rapid growth has left a trail of ashes and bad will.

ASHES AND BAD WILL

Everyone has a favorite tale about how someone did them at the store or at home by service people who failed to take the time to care. Repairmen arrive days late, or not at all. Sales clerks talk on the phone to their boyfriends or girlfriends while customers wait. Waitress Vera tells you that waitress Irma will take over while she goes on her break, then vanishes altogether. Gas stations can't fix flats. Postal clerks haven't heard of Germany.

That has not always been so. A brochure for the Hotel Terminus, a turn-of-the-century Parisian hostelry linked by footbridge to the train platforms of Saint-Lazare Station, boasted a convenience of service that wisely took account of a tourist's tight time budget:

> I walk straight into the *Hotel Terminus,* giving my luggage chit to the porter, and already I'm in bed. On departure my ticket is brought to my room, my luggage registered without my having to leave the entrance hall. Amply warned, I reach my compartment in my slippers, directly by the footbridge. Thus I've saved time, money, and trouble. Whereas I came once to Paris, so now I'll come twice.[6]

Or consider the instructions in a 1929 employee's guide, published by one of the nation's most up-scale department stores, in a day when clocks ran slower:

> . . . "Say 'We, not I; patron, not customer; and approve, not OK.' "
> . . . "We never appear impatient."
> . . . "We give directions graciously and, whenever possible, escort the patron at least part of the way to the next section which she wishes to visit."
> . . . "We ask if we can be helpful when we see a patron who appears to be confused or to be having difficulty with packages."
> . . . "We step aside politely to permit our patrons to enter and leave the elevator before us."
> . . . "Even if we are unable to supply our patron's requirements, we can make a friend . . ."[7]

Such care for their customers'—the *patrons'*—welfare is a concern of the past, for salespeople today disregard the second rule in their hurry to "serve" the next patron, even if doing so means sacrificing the opportunity to make a friend.

We decry the lost art of serving. A recent *Time* magazine feature, "Why Is Service so Bad?" prompted the largest reader response of any story the magazine had published, even larger than the reaction to feature stories on Oliver North and ethics. The avalanche of more than 1,000 letters, commented *Time*'s editor, "reflected a sense of things falling apart."[8]

While the decline of services is rooted in large part in the attempts of service providers to use *their* time more efficiently, the consumers' chief gripe is about "anything that wastes *my* time." So concludes the *Wall Street Journal*'s 1989 "American Way of Buying" survey. Whether it was "waiting in long lines while other service windows or cash registers stay closed," or "staying home for delivery or salespeople who fail to show," or any of a series of other irksome experiences, being forced to wait was more prominent in the gallery of consumer complaints than any other gripe.[9]

Indifferent service abounds in large part because customers don't censure it. The White House Office of Consumer Affairs discovered that 96 percent of angry customers do not complain directly to the offending company. Instead, they simply take their business elsewhere and broadcast their dissatisfaction to friends.[10] Complaints directed to the guilty party not only benefit the complainer, but other customers too if the guilty change their ways. Because talk is cheap and writing is expensive, filing a complaint requires more time than customers are apparently willing to take.

When people were asked to rate some of the major products and services they shop for, over half expressed indignation about lawyer's fees, 50 percent believed that hospitals gave poor value for the money, and appliance repairs were rated far down the scale. Good buys included *products* such as men's and women's clothing and shoes, home furnishings, and restaurant meals.[11] A pattern emerges: goods are a far lesser source of discontent than are services. Those working in health care fields and the airline industry—to take two instances—are not exempt from that criticism.

Changing Goals for the Medics

Two patients in three maintain that doctors are too much interested in making money and too little interested in spending sufficient time with patients, says the American Medical Association.[12] The one in three who disagree probably see a practitioner much like one described by journalist Martha Fay as "admired for his time-consuming thoroughness. A proper checkup by Henry Horst Ludemann is a thing of beauty," she writes, "and the fact that it is often not completed in less than two hours is simply one more proof to the 61-year-old Ludemann's devoted patients that the regard they feel for him is reciprocal. In thirty-three years of practice, the courtly, German-born Ludemann—considered by patients to be one of their own—has refined his examiner's art into a symphony of tests mechanical, tactile, and gently inquisitorial. 'I'm criticized by my associates for taking so much time,' says Ludemann, whose days practicing in Westchester County routinely stretch to 10 p.m. . . . 'But I can't do it any other way. I hate to think that because I didn't do something, a patient will suffer.' Indeed, any patient who cherishes the childhood memory of the family doctor standing beside the sickbed will believe he has found heaven in Henry Ludemann's patient, capable hands."[13] But Dr. Ludemann is an old-fashioned practitioner, whose numbers are limited, as are his days.

Altruism motivates many who are attracted to the health-giving professions, as to volunteering. But, over time, the goal of helping others seems to give way to more personally rewarding goals. Like making money, for example.

Entering medical students may plan to set up practices in towns where doctors are scarce, but the prospect of earning higher incomes lures them to the cities. Veterinary school students who initially aim to enter rural large animal practices, on graduation head off for the city to set up more lucrative small animal practices. Once on the job, nurses motivated to enter the profession "to give service," soon come to place a higher value on less idealistic rewards like "social interaction."[14]

Turbulence Ahead for the Airlines

Bumpings. Overbookings. Cancellations. Delays. Lost luggage. Refunds not received. Surly flight attendants. Tiny seats with no leg room. Pitiful little in-flight snacks. "Down" computer ticketing systems. The well-known horrors of air travel have replaced house prices as the favored topic of social conversation. It began with moves initiated in the late 1970s to open up competition among the airlines.

Deregulation brought more flights at bedrock fares, which in turn boosted the number of passenger trips. Today's average American flies somewhere two times a year, a remarkable statistic since it seems unnatural for people to fly at all. Compared to a decade ago, twice as many people are flying, and traveling twice as far.[15] And enjoying it less.

For carriers, deregulation brought new competition. In trying to keep fares down, the airlines had to economize somewhere. Reducing maintenance jeopardized safety. Cutting advertising budgets threatened market shares. Workers could be laid off, or—the chosen option—workloads could be increased. Working personnel harder left less time for providing passengers with the amenities they had grown accustomed to. In the reallocation of personnel time and effort, consumer services became a casualty of the *BB* factor. Today, it is consumer-be-damned.

Of all the charges made against the airlines, costly and exasperating delays or "schedule irregularities" (a neat euphemism) head the list. The number of hours spent waiting in the airport, fidgeting and fuming for a delayed take-off, could equal the number of hours aloft. As performance records worsened, the airlines discovered that angry passengers could be as turbulent as a thunderstorm. Grievances more than tripled in number in one recent year alone.[16] The nature of the suffrages covers a broad range, but the fastest growing concerned passenger service, with the number spurting upward five-fold.[17] The consequences of economizing on the time spent catering to the customer were all too apparent.

DOES MECHANIZATION MATTER?

With electronic assists banks make quick loans, airlines dispense tickets in the twinkling of an eye, car rental agencies offer instant check in, and hotels advertise instant check out. But the intrusion of electronic gadgets that contribute to the servers' feelings of powerlessness may explain their increasing indifference to the quality of what they were hired to provide across the counter, personally and without the intermediation of a machine. The new gadgetry, aside from explaining quality changes, may even excuse them. After all, mechanical failure can easily take the blame for personal deficiencies: "Sorry, I can't help you. The computer is down."

But this is a poor excuse for poor service. To see why, we need to look no further than Japan, where technology is a fact of life.

Where Customers, Not Goods, Come Back

Although fewer people bow on meeting than in times past and flower arrangement has become a bit more casual, the dazzling technological advances that have paralleled Japan's miraculous transformation from an isolated nation into a major industrial power seem not to have compromised its tradition of service. Even Japan's highly automated society has not forgotten the human ingredient.

Never mind that signs in Western languages are little known. Ask someone on the street, anyone, and directions are given cheerfully and carefully (even by those with only five minutes to get from the parking lot to the doctor's appointment). Need a train ticket but thoroughly befuddled by the maze of undecipherable directions at the station's complicated vending machine? No matter. A push of the small red panic button summons a smiling face behind a tiny window in the machine and the person behind the face produces the ticket.

"A certified cynic, I went with plans for a story on all the things there that don't work," writes *New York Times* reporter Clyde Haberman, on returning from a five-year assignment in Japan. "I never gathered enough material." One thing that *does* work is the people. And they take great pride in their work. "Just about any Japanese you meet—from the tatami maker to the old man polishing brass-lined steps in the department store—believes that a job worth doing is worth doing well." Salespeople are no exception.

Providing retail customers with good service requires committing time to knowing the merchandise, learning how to demonstrate it convincingly, evaluating alternative makes and models, and answering customers' queries competently. As product cycles grow shorter, and the time interval shrinks between the introduction of new models, keeping abreast of the merchandise becomes a time-consuming chore. Japanese salespeople seem more willing to make that effort than their American counterparts. Shopping for an appliance in the U.S. has few joys. If the clerk just happens to know the relative virtues of a particular line, something always seems to stand in the way of a demonstration: the cord is missing, the instruction book has been swiped, or the thing fails to operate. Tourists to Tokyo's booming Akihabara district know that there they will find as broad a selection of electronic equipment as anywhere in the world, and get expert advice on any device from an unfailingly polite clerk anxious to make a sale. "Sales clerks *run* to bring the customer what he wants."[18]

In Japan, deliveries are made and repairmen arrive at the appointed hour, not "sometime in the afternoon." Jobs are finished on schedule. A train arriving a minute late in the tiniest village is cause for a national investigation. Exults journalist Haberman in his eulogy to Japanese efficiency: "In five years, I never rode a Tokyo subway train that was late."[19]

SERVICE AT THE SERVICE STATION

"At what used to be called a service station (in the U.S.), the attendant, who sits behind bulletproof glass, can do nothing to help a novice learn the new greasy, smelly routine of pumping his own gas. Memories flood back of the typical Tokyo station, where a horde of neat, well-mannered, and expert attendants take charge of the car, fill it up, wash it, and check the tires. Then they doff their hats, shout their thanks, and stop traffic so the customer can drive away."

—Edwin M. Reingold[20]

American banking customers have taken to automated tellers with such enthusiasm that they will queue outside for the machine while the tellers inside wait for business. The impersonal machines do what clients want, and without incompetence or insult. In Japan, where electronic tellers are well known, most people still prefer the human equivalent for they know that service will be competent and polite. A row of cashiers greets the morning's first patrons, bowing and wishing them in unison a cheerful *ohayo gozaimasu*. The arriving customer simply hands the forms for the transaction to a receptionist who passes them along to clerks for processing. Then, instead of standing in line, the customer sits comfortably, sips tea, and watches television or reads a newspaper until the transaction is completed. Far-sighted bank managers provide spectacles for near-sighted clients who forget their own.

Public telephones are equipped with scratch paper. Not only is that convenience absent from the American phone booth, but often the phone is too, with only a few dangling wires remaining as a grim reminder that another public device has been ripped off by a vandal who had a different idea of how to reach out and touch someone.

That said, we return to the original question. Has automation alienated Japan's service workers? In three words, it seems not. Somehow, in Japan, serving others has retained a high **S/T**, even in the face of automation, rewarding to the server and to the served. Even technology that threatens the workers' very livelihood has failed to blunt the quality of service.

Give Japan a ten on a scale of ten for the quality of service rendered, and heed the words of a Japanese industrialist who encapsulates the whole issue in one well-phrased sentence: "It is about selling products that do not come back, to customers that do."[21]

Back home in the U.S., service quality continues on its downward course. One wonders if things can grow worse. Imagine, if you will, the intersection of typical American Middletown, perhaps New Halcyon where the Gnomons live. At the curb, beside a trashed fire hydrant, a tourist loaded down with luggage asks a

cabby, "can you take me to Main Street?" and is answered, "where's THAT!?!" An idle street cleaner discards his own cigarette in the gutter so that he will have more work later on. The owner of Speedy Flower Delivery sends off a teenage delivery boy on a tricycle. Upstairs a bewildered client of Bob's Travel Agency is advised to "take a hike." A bookshop patron is vicariously overheard asking, "where can I find Shakespeare?" to which an indifferent clerk replies, "he doesn't work here." Inside a restaurant, waitress Vera throws the disgruntled customer's order at him; after all it *is* a fast food establishment. And so it goes as disservicing overtakes America.[22]

THE PATHOLOGY OF SERVICE WITH A SCOWL

To Adam Smith, service providers were no more than "menial servants." Bootblack, lawyer, physician, public official, and university professor (which included Mr. Smith) alike were "unproductive of any value." By this the father of classical economics meant that these workers, though occupying "some of the most respectable orders in society," produced no value for their labor (Karl Marx, please note). Yet with three out of four workers today dedicated to occupations that presumably generate convenience, security, comfort, and flexibility (there they are again, the euphemisms) rather than a tangible output, Smith overlooked the key fact that services, intangible as they are, are as essential to society as are goods. The problem is less the service workers' apparent lack of productivity, but that the quality of their work seems to be so low, and so rapidly declining.

Does Commoditization Excuse Bad Service?

The commoditization that was meant to improve the quality of services during the era of the "information explosion" has only worsened the problem. Take, for example, the automation of office work, that set of labor-intensive, time-consuming, frequently wasteful processes involved in originating, manipulating, and disseminating information.

Since the dawn of the information revolution in the mid-'50s, the number of "professional and technical workers" and "managers and administrators''—in short, ''knowledge workers''—has exploded. Ditto the ranks of clerical workers, but unlike the other high-growth information occupations, computers have automated the particularly repetitious aspects of their jobs.

To computerize clerical work required breaking down tasks into standard components in much the same way, and for the same purpose, that Henry Ford standardized parts and operations in automobile production. Achieving standardization, however, requires countless standardized internal communications. In a word, paperwork. Many of the hoped-for gains were illusion, for communications became more complex, not more simple. Information requirements grew like Topsy. Authority Paul Strassmann claims that every communication or transaction with a customer generates up to forty internal messages to keep the many functional units up to date with sales. The sales department must be notified of course, but so must inventory, and don't forget credit and invoicing, and consumer relations. Oh yes, and marketing must know too, and quality control. And the R&D people. Maybe even the people on the janitor's Christmas card list. The cheap and simple task of processing a customer order has now become costly and ungainly.[23] The computer, instead of creating the envisioned paperless office, has simply flooded the office with paper.

Because servers are so preoccupied with internal company procedures, less and less time remains for them to serve clients. The action shifts backstage from the counter and the distance between served and server widens. With automation taking the fun out of dealing with the customer, is it any wonder that the quality of services declines?

How to Buy a Vacuum Cleaner

''Sears recently advertised a special sale on its new top-of-the-line vacuum cleaners. I called our local Sears to buy one. The sales clerk had never heard of the product and was unaware of the advertised sale. I asked to speak to the boss, who said that the product was not in stock nor did she anticipate receiving it. She suggested that I call around to other Sears stores to find one. I suggested that she do the calling for me, but she said she was too busy for that kind of service. Undaunted, I asked for the customer service department. A representative there offered to order the vacuum cleaner but said I would have to drive to a distant Sears warehouse to pick it up. With my blood pressure rising, I asked to speak to the store manager. He said he would look into the situation and get back to me. Four days later, a sales clerk called, inquiring if my wife might be interested in buying a vacuum cleaner.''

—Robert E. Kelley[24]

Do Poorly Served Servers Poorly Serve the Served?

In a system so complex, yet tidy, a minor mishap causes all hell to break loose. When every breakdown or flawed instruction unleashes a flood of new paperwork, as for the hapless customer, well. . . . Errors or unique cases may cost up to fifty times as much as the standard transaction for which an automated system was designed, resulting in ever-larger computer programs and ever-thicker procedure manuals. The buck passes in ever-widening circles. Employers put the blame on staff shortages and low-quality personnel, salespeople blame short-sighted management and technical breakdowns, management experts blame ignorant customers for not knowing or insisting on their rights.

Who really has responsibility for this sorry state of affairs? Everyone who works for someone else knows that the boss sets the tone for the entire organization, and that style trickles down through the whole hierarchy. Subordinates tend to mimic the boss's behavior. As management treats employees, so employees treat customers: employees treated indifferently by management treat their customers indifferently. The executive who deals disrespectfully with a middle manager can expect the manager to act accordingly toward the next employee down the line, and the domino effect continues all the way to the bottom rung, to the person who must deal with the customer. Those on the bottom rung who face clients across the counter, in the check-out line, on the phone, or in the reception, have ''no one else to dump on. Since he has no one to abuse inside the organization, he treats customers as if they were the ones on the next rung down.''[25] So the responsibility for poor service may be traced to the inner workings of the company, and to the bosses who fail to take the time to adequately train, inspire, and motivate those in their charge. And to listen to them.

The average U.S. employee submits .14 suggestions per year, while in Japan, the annual average is twenty-five per person. Three times as many suggestions are followed in Japan, compared to the U.S.[26] In other words, Japanese business managers are more willing than their American counterparts to listen to their employees and to countenance and respond to criticism, a factor that goes far in explaining the higher quality service one expects, and receives, in Japan.

RESERVICING AMERICA

A first step in reversing the decline is recognizing the importance of service. Eighty-six percent of Fortune 500 senior executives did just that when they ranked "quality of customer service" as "extremely important" and above ten other items including growth, productivity, and company reputation. As quality has eroded, that recognition has grown in importance. Three years earlier only 68 percent ranked service quality as high.[27] But such a commitment is hollow unless translated into action.

The next step is making that translation. Recognizing that price-conscious buyers are also service conscious, Nordstrom's department store has turned service into an art form. The retailer is trying to recapture that share of the buying public who no longer shops for pleasure. And there are many of those. A third of shoppers admit that they "do not enjoy at all" window shopping or browsing, and wouldn't waste even an hour at it. In six years, the amount of time the average consumer spent shopping in a mall fell by 24 percent.[28] Nordstrom's reputation for old-fashioned service, from a sales force that writes customers thank you notes and even makes house calls, shows up in their booming business: sales doubled and net income tripled in less than four years.[29]

Another answer is simply to ignore the problem and let the market take its course. Dissatisfied customers will take their business elsewhere. In fact, seven in ten customers who switch to a competitor cite poor service, not price or quality, as the reason.[30] Motivated by profit and market share, some businesses will work to restore lost customers' confidence. Ford Motor Company found out how loudly the market spoke when it discovered a 23 percentage point difference in the level of repurchases between its customers who were very satisfied with their dealers' service and those who were very dissatisfied.[31] In a few short years, Eastman Kodak's rating among the "most admired corporations" plummeted from fourth to seventieth, and photo finishing sales slid from $200 million to $60 million.[32] Rising customer discontent with service, particularly photo finishing, was a major factor, and the market responded.

Self-imposed penalties are another avenue toward restoring customer confidence. For example, a Detroit bank that pays a customer $10 per error on a checking account statement picked up some 15,000 new checking accounts and $65 million in deposits within two months.[33] Airlines that tender ticket discounts, frequent flier miles, and free drink vouchers find that such "apology kits" help to diffuse the anger of delayed passengers. Manufacturers provide toll-free telephone lines, open around the clock to answer consumers' questions about their products. But such "cures" are mere band-aids. Restoring the services sector to good health will require stronger medicine.

Lacking such remedies, consumers will continue to seek their own solutions, avoiding the occasion of the offense. As the **S** of shopping drops, consumers are coming to rely on substitutes for indifferent, inept clerks and tellers. Some of the substitutes like electronic tellers, teleshopping, and mail order catalogs have the added advantage of saving **T**. Or customers will take their business to dealers who take the time to provide quality service. Or they will do the job themselves.

Self-service came into being as a cost-saving innovation. In the 1930s depression, A&P advertised cheaper groceries to customers who helped themselves. These days, do-it-yourself is growing, not as a way to economize on costs, nor as a hobby, but as a refuge from deteriorating service. Whether it is self-service gas pumps and car washes, self-service salad bars, self-service tellers, or self-service airline ticketing, many have discovered they *can* do the job better and quicker than professional servers. All done in minutes. No waiting. Just pay and leave. Says Columbia University Professor John O'Shaughnessy, "People want the personal element removed from transactions, the same way they want cancer removed from cigarettes."[34] Two decades after machine-banking first appeared, nearly 70,000 self-service tellers were in use. The proportion of gas customers who pump themselves has skyrocketed to 80 percent.[35]

A short digression about relative wages—ours, as "do-it-yourselfers," versus theirs, as "pros"—shows why desperation, not the economics of the situation, is prompting self-help. It works this way. The decision to call in a plumber to fix a leaky faucet, a carpenter to repair a cupboard, or an electrician to fix a short-circuit depends on our ability and willingness to pay the "pro" to do the job. That, in turn, depends on how rapidly their time value increases compared to ours. If our wage, and time value, rises by say 10 percent during the year, and the plumber's hourly rate goes up by only 5 percent, a call to the professional makes more sense than doing it ourselves—unless (an important *unless*) painful experience has taught us that such rank amateurs as we can do the job better. Whatever the case, let the data speak for themselves.

In twenty years, average wages of auto mechanics, carpenters, electricians, and plumbers have risen only 73 to 80 percent as rapidly as wages in general.[36] If relative wages—theirs vs. ours—mattered, we would be using professional services *more,* and self-serving *less.* That is not the case. We are relying more on self-service. With the declining quality of service provided by plumber, carpenter, electrician, and the many others who supposedly "service" our needs, we have taken over their duties out of desperation, a factor that has little to do with relative wages.

There will always remain services that we amateurs can never provide on our own. Perhaps we can preach a sermon as well as the minister, or psychoanalyze ourselves to our satisfaction, but the day is far removed when we can self-perform brain surgery. It is not that we have not tried to move in that direction. For example, the Tapeworm-Trap (Patent No. 11,942) was invented for "removing worms from the system, without employing medicines, and thereby causing much injury." After fasting long enough to make the worm hungry, the do-it-yourself patient swallows a trap that has been baited and attached to a string. If all goes as planned, "the worm seizes the bait, and its head is caught in the trap," which the patient withdraws from his stomach "by the string which has been left hanging from the mouth, dragging after it the whole length of the worm. . . .'' (the rest of the description is better left to the reader's imagination).[37]

This and the three previous chapters have shown how the *BB* factor takes its toll on other-serving activities like voting, volunteering, being courteous, helping neighbors, caring for youngsters and oldsters, and providing service. When we allocate time with the intent of choosing and scheduling activities in ways that yield the larger satisfaction compared to the time spent, activities that serve others tend to get lost in the shuffle. And the larger community is the worse off for it.

Yet another, more subtle link must be forged between the *BB* factor and that community of others. The *BB* factor also jeopardizes time spent thinking, and taking time to be careful, activities vulnerable to crowding out because their **S/T** ratio fails to rise as rapidly as other activities. Crowding out these activities has major consequences in the public realm, as will be shown in the next chapters.

With time value rising, we spend less time studying and learning, making choices informed from an exploration of many alternatives, voting for the right candidate rather than the one who pleases most on television. Pressed by the *BB* factor, we fail to take time to take care. With time pressures mounting, the obvious and quick-and-easy solution becomes the preferred solution. In studying and learning, in making key decisions, in making political choices, there is no time to search among the array of possibilities for the *best* solution.

We become increasingly dependent on information provided by others and probably less careful about its accuracy. As Adam Smith reasoned 200 years ago, because no one can learn everything in a lifetime, we must become specialized and expert in a few areas of endeavor that interest and benefit us the most. That reasoning holds no less true today, only there is much more to learn. With an expanding stock of specialized knowledge, our dependency on others' talents and expertise also increases.

17:00

TIME FOR THE MATTERS OF THE MIND

"Three minutes' thought would suffice to find this out, but thought is irksome and three minutes is a long time."
—A. E. Housman[1]

It was a great day in 1946 when scientists at the University of Pennsylvania plugged in the great machine. Ten thousand vacuum tubes glowed just like they were supposed to, and the thirty-ton "Eniac" sprang into being. From that day on, the computer was heralded as the premier device to aid, and perhaps even to *replace,* thinking and decision making. If the computer could arrive at an answer faster and more accurately than the human mind, then it must be able to think. So it was believed.

If indeed computers can aid—possibly replace—human thinking, then with computers invading nearly all business firms, government agencies, and homes, the quality of decisions should have increased. Indeed there is evidence that people are spending less time thinking these days, an activity that computers may be successfully invading. As for the quality of decisions, however, that's a trickier issue to sort out.

ARE PEOPLE SPENDING LESS TIME THINKING?

The perceptive Professor McKean, who informed earlier chapters with his wisdom on the social consequences of time scarcity, has this sobering news about the possibilities of machinery simplifying thinking. Says he: "While capital equipment makes increasing amounts of information 'available,' man's brain as such is no more productive than in earlier epochs, and time spent in just plain reading, pondering, and decision making is increasingly expensive.''[2]

How many recall that the advent of the big computer brought with it dire predictions that this was the end of good thinking? How often is the computer blamed for a breakdown in decision making—even getting an airplane ticket—when, instead of bemoaning the technical failure, a bit of careful and creative thought could deal with the problem? According to the *BB* factor, time spent thinking would give way to other activities that are more satisfying (higher **S**) or can be done more quickly (lower **T**). And in fact there is evidence indicating that people seem to be giving less time to pondering, cogitating, ruminating, reading, and other matters cerebral. Perhaps technology has made that time-saving possible and boosted the efficiency of thinking. Perhaps, too, people simply don't want to think. But there's good reason to believe the *BB* factor makes thinking time-minus, crowded out by more rewarding alternatives.

Any precise measurement of the time spent thinking is probably suspect. We think while we brush our teeth, drive our car, or carry on a conversation. If asked what we are doing, even if we are deeply absorbed in thought, the answer would be ''can't you see I'm brushing my teeth, driving my car, or talking with you?'' But there are surrogate measures that hint at how often and when we think. The time spent reading is one of them. Another is the choice of a career that requires a lot of thinking compared to one that emphasizes the ''doing'' part.

Engineering, we are told, is a profession that stresses the ''doing'' of things, rather than the thinking about them; philosophy is the polar opposite. ''Gimme a job. I'll do it. Gimme a problem, I'll solve it,'' say engineers; philosophers would prefer pondering the problem. That, according to those who teach engineering, fairly accurately describes their profession, and the type of training that students receive for professional certification. An administrator at the Massachusetts Institute of Technology asks, ''are we trying to cram so much information into the engineering students that they do not have time to think?''[3] Probably so, for one of the glories of an engineering education is that it is so tightly engineered that no time remains for thinking. The bottom line tells the story: the number of applications that engineering schools receive has been on the rise for many years as enrollments in the more thoughtful disciplines, for example the humanities, have declined.

American publishers turn out 100 new titles a day. Yet, it is one thing to buy a book, another to read it. How many of us buy a book for its title or cover, with good intentions to read it, but discover on dusting the bookshelf ten years later that it remains unread? The fact that statistics tell us that more books are published each year says little about whether people are spending more time reading. "The pleasure of buying books lies not so much in reading them as in having them available," points out Staffan Linder in *The Harried Leisure Class.* "People are buying books as they buy pictures—to glance at."[4] Also, the types of books people buy, as noted earlier, have changed in favor of the practical rather than the thoughtful treatises—easy reading instead of the tough stuff.

Intellectual Jacques Barzun claims that reading habits have shifted from real literature in favor of fugitive materials, the "printed matter that has escaped hard covers and quite often has no covers at all." These are the dozens of specialist magazines, with "a wad of articles and ads that equals a book in length and has first claim on attention, because it feeds an existing passion, because it offers variety in small premasticated portions."[5] Add to these the proliferating and often unsolicited political weeklies, bulletins, newsletters, journals, trade magazines, corporation reports, organization newsletters, inserts in bank statements and phone bills, neighborhood Blah-Blahs, and the daily reading quota is full. The soft stuff that has pushed out the hard is a menace "not just to the reading of books but to leisure, sanity, and the pursuit of happiness," moans Mr. Barzun. "I fully expect that the Man in the Moon will shortly say to himself, 'I run an old and respected institution; we have done good service over the years helping to keep the tides going up and down; I'd better start issuing a small—um—newsletter, *The Lunar Month,* to explain to our many well-wishers how things look from this vantage point."[6]

Although the efficiency of reading has remained little changed, if a picture is worth a thousand words, the comics must cram information into the mind more quickly than line after line of conventional text. Perhaps that logic explains the boom in an industry that takes in over $300 million annually.[7] The oldies like

Archie, Jughead, Veronica, and Captain Marvel are still on the newsstands, but joined by a host of others with such captivating titles as *Bizarre Sex, The Fabulous Furry Freak Brothers, Good Jive, Leather Nun, Weirdo, Wonder Wart-Hog, Young Lust,* and *Zap,* for readers of more specialized taste. So lucrative are they that writers and artists are paid as much as $200 per page, up from a mere $35 two decades ago.[8]

Comic books and ephemera may be invading reading time, but analyst Curtis B. Gans claims that television is replacing reading altogether. If "the average American spends more than six hours a day watching TV, eight hours a day working, two hours commuting to and from work, an hour and a half eating, and eight hours sleeping, there is precious little time left for such things as reading and discussion."[9] Turning back the clock to explore the changing ways that news makes its way into the human mind drives home the point.

Newspapers obviously keep up with the news—that's their business—but the mechanism that gets the news from the printed page into the reader's brain is as primitive today as it ever was. The radio, by making the news flow into ears instead of eyes, found a better way. As they came into widespread use, radios quickly invaded the territory of newspapers to become the chosen information source. Then came television with programs that were more fun and took less effort to absorb than those of either medium it replaced. The eyes once again became the organ of reception. Moving from stage to stage in the evolution of the media saved time in transmitting information from producer to consumer.

As television watching grew, newspaper reading declined. Since 1950, the number of papers received per capita has shrunk by 25 percent, and the number of hours spent watching television has expanded almost 60 percent. Each year the proportion of adults reading a daily newspaper drops by one percentage point as former readers turn to the tube as the apparently more time-efficient medium for being informed and entertained.[10] Besides it's easier. It takes time to learn how to read but anyone can operate a TV. The kids don't have to be taught how to watch it. Just turn it on and they'll watch it, and watch it, and watch it.

Different people favor different media. An investigation of the associations linking television viewing to a host of social factors discovered that computer users tend both to be infrequent televiewers and to be antisocial.[11] The computer buffs encoding data, manipulating symbols, and predicting outcomes are imaginative people who spend their time at the machine for proactive, creative tasks. For them, the time spent with a computer has a higher **S/T** than time spent socializing with friends or watching television.

Youngsters who use computers must rely on their self-creativity and imagination, but those who play the video games regularly are a different breed altogether. They prefer spending a lot of time in front of the TV and palling around with their chums, but the more they play the less they read and use their imaginations. "Children who have inactive imaginations may prefer video and arcade games, which are more reactive activities and provide all the pictures," concludes telecommunications analyst Debra A. Lieberman from a study of 546 California school-age children.[12] Games that substitute electronic creativity for self-generated creativity transport kids temporarily from life's problems—a quick fix of sorts from the horrors of the world around them—and provide a programmed version of the fantasy life they lack. Although telecommunications researchers believe the games themselves may not be harmful, the experts advise parents to "be more concerned with what the kid is dropping to compensate for time spent with the game."[13]

Television and video games are not the only source of competition for kids' time. Many of them, like the rest of us, maintain frantic schedules. As with us, their choice of projects to fill the twenty-four hours in a day leaves little time for creative thinking. "Schedules and supervision replace spontaneity and freedom," declares one report from the field; "lessons, not make-believe, are the rule."[14] Kids carry executive Day-Timer calendars to keep track of their fast-track activities. With both parents holding jobs, the after-school schedule keeps them busy. Flute lessons on Monday afternoons, ballet on Tuesdays, Scouts on Wednesdays, gymnastics on Thursdays, orchestra on Fridays, soccer on Saturdays, and finger-painting on Sundays. Of all this frenzy and over-programming, child psychologist Bruno Bettelheim writes, "They are deprived of those long hours and days of leisure to think their own thoughts, an essential element in the development of creativity.''[15] No time left for fun. No time to be creative. No time to listen to the birds sing.

Matters of the mind are easily squeezed out. Perhaps the handicapped of the future will be the hard-of-thinking.

DO PEOPLE WANT TO THINK?

Probably so. Most people want to spend time pursuing matters of the mind, whether doing so involves thinking the great thoughts or simply day dreaming. Yet, finding the time to think has always been a challenge since the activity can be so easily crowded out. Instead of composing that difficult letter, figuring out how to deal with troublesome Aunt Harriet, or writing that feature story about the Gnomons that the world has been waiting for, we can always find an excuse to use the hour or two doing something else. The pencils need to be sharpened, the cat played with, the weeds pulled in the garden, the closet sorted out, or Norman's appointment made at the barber.

The celebrated Pope Gregory XIII, patron of timeologists, discovered (or, pronouncing *ex cathedra,* just decided) that there were a few seconds more each year than his forebears had reckoned. Although there is no record that this breakthrough was greeted with excitement, if it had been made today, in an age when time is far more valuable, the discovery would certainly have been cheered enthusiastically. The Roper organization ''discovered'' the same, but did so hypothetically in one of its polls. ''If you had four extra hours every day to do whatever you wanted to do,'' they asked 1,992 Americans, what would you do with them? The answer: reading.[16] The urge was there, but the time wasn't. It works both ways: reading ranks as an important activity to take on when time becomes available; when time becomes scarce, it is quick to go.

Americans aren't alone in their attitude toward reading. Confirming the Roper Poll results was a four-nation study of ''point time elasticities'' for employed men. Point time elasticities are ratios that measure the sensitivity of activities to a change in time availability. Of ten major activities studied, matters of the mind (termed ''study and participation'') ranked head and shoulders above any of the others as the first activity that would be cut down on when time grows scarce, well ahead of non-work travel, housework, and leisure, which came up second, third, and fourth in the rankings.[17] Thus matters of the mind are quick to be jettisoned from the schedule when time gets scarce.

These important findings have short- and long-run implications. In the short run, suppose a conference is canceled, freeing a few hours or perhaps a day. What to do with the time? The activity with the highest time elasticity—"matters of the mind"—would have first claim on the windfall. Most people would use the time for thinking or reading or studying.

The same logic works when time suddenly "disappears." If a family emergency interrupts the daily routine, the first activity to give would be the one with the highest time elasticity, for it ranks as the most vulnerable to the changing availability of time. It is, of course, "matters of the mind." The longer run interpretation, more our concern here, leads to the same conclusion. As time becomes ever tighter, the first activity to be crowded out is "matters of the mind."

Creative thinking, and invention as its most productive outcome, needs committed time. Yet creativity requires more than simply organizing time well. The fragile time needed to probe the minds' deepest recesses must be carefully protected: time free from the mundane details of life, ranging from genuine worries about job security to trivia like answering telephones.

The increasing competition for our time, particularly the distractions of mundanery, threatens the quality of thought and, with it, the quality of decisions made for ourselves and others. With few exceptions,[18] research done against a deadline rarely produces significant findings, for discovery is frequently an accidental event. The intellectual passion of individuals, rather than imposed deadlines, coax forth most technological triumphs. Time for discovery must be marshaled carefully.

Some find it impossible to be creative or to think deeply as a strictly solo endeavor. Justice William H. Rehnquist "began to realize that some of my best insights came not during my enforced thinking periods in my chambers, but while I was shaving in the morning, driving to work, or just walking from one place to another."[19] Without an agenda. Others require doing one thing at a time. Yogi Berra, the "uncut diamond of the baseball park," once asked O. J. Simpson, "how can you think and hit at the same time?" And the famous running back replied, "thinking is what gets you caught from behind."[20] For many, like Mr. Simpson, thinking is solo activity done at the right time and place, with the world of distraction closed out.

- Author William Faulkner got the privacy so crucial to his craft by removing the door knob, and taking it with him, when he retreated into the study of Rowan Oak, his antebellum Oxford, Mississippi home.[21]
- J. D. Salinger's watchful neighbor reports that the elusive and excessively private author of *The Catcher in the Rye* rises at about 5 a.m. and then walks "down the hill to his studio, a tiny concrete shelter with a translucent plastic roof," where he remains in total seclusion for 15–16 hours typing.[22]
- Writers are not alone in their quest for times and places freed of distraction. Art historian Leo Steinberg, one of those few chosen to win a coveted genius grant from the MacArthur Foundation, announced what he would not do with the handsome award. "I will not break my habit of living without a TV set and tuxedo." Nor would he give up his regular train commute from New York to Philadelphia, where he teaches at the University of Pennsylvania, because "I relish that hour and a half on Amtrak without telephone interruption. I have time to think. It's like taking a cruise."[23]

Remember Peter Paul Rubens, our seventeenth-century painter-hero who became rich and famous doing a zillion things at once while transferring voluptuous three-dimensional nudes onto two-dimensional canvas? Reports have it that his was a well-oiled (pardon the modest pun), calculating attitude toward painting, with the clock pacing his multifarious other activities. "He rose daily at four in the morning, and unless prevented by gout made it a rule to hear Mass; thereafter he set to work, invariably with a hired reader who read a chosen book aloud, usually Plutarch or Seneca, (then) undertook something else to relax his mind." Despite a frenzy of activity, and no doubt because of it, the artist had trouble finding a way to preserve time for reading or for reflecting or thinking deeply. Writes a biographer of Mr. Ruben's *vita activa,* "it is hard to know whether he was ever faced with soul-searching moments in his life, since his response to every problem or event appears to have been one of action, and not of reflection."[24]

Presidents, faced with making the most important decisions of any chief executives, are no less prone to allowing routine duties to crowd out the higher-order tasks. Senator-emeritus Barry Goldwater recalls that "Ike told me one day that he had signed 1,300 signatures. Now that takes all day. So when do you have time to sit down and worry about the world?"[25] Presidents are not alone. Ranking clerics apparently face the same sort of problem. A report on the power structure of the American Catholic Church, one of the best managed of all organizations, tells how archbishops have become mired in administrative trivia, with no time to worry about the world—this one or the next.[26]

A long-standing debate between Washington and the telecommunications industry has raged around whether radio and television stations should be required to offer programs that serve the public interest but nevertheless attract fairly select (read: small) audiences. In the early 1980s, the Federal Communications Commission started eliminating government guidelines mandating that broadcasters air newscasts, public affairs events and analysis, and educational children's shows. Because sponsors were difficult to find for the type of telecasts that forced people to think, the programs began to disappear. Apparently the losses have not been deeply felt, for people really didn't want to watch this type of programming anyway. Instead, according to the ratings, they preferred game shows like "Wheel of Fortune," cartoons, and beauty contests, all far more fun and requiring absolutely no thought whatsoever.[27]

For those propelled on the Wheel of Fortune, heady pursuits like thinking have become a casualty of time crunch. Some of them, unlike Messrs. Faulkner, Rubens, Salinger, and Steinberg, search for, and easily find, excuses to interrupt cerebral activity.

Business people who interrupt meetings to make phone calls, who regularly patrol the corporate corridors to discover "what's up," who start fidgeting when a conference lasts more than a half-hour all show the symptoms of people "for whom interruption has become the quickest way to scratch a mental itch, and a way to excuse themselves from thinking seriously about a subject for longer than five minutes."[28] "These are the people who taste something but don't eat," says psychiatrist Edward Stainbrook. "There's this constant search for arousal; they want to keep constantly on a high of doing something new." Interruption satisfies the craving for constant distraction—an excuse for not getting the job done on time—and for a circuit-breaker to the routine of tackling issues that demand long and deep pondering. With novelty winning out over substance, assigning tasks to "busy" interruptaholics assures that more problems will be created than solved.[29]

THE CURSE OF INTERRUPTAHOLISM

" 'His day is random,' says one bemused colleague. 'He will walk into a meeting and disrupt it until something else catches his fancy and then he'll go off and do that. Some days, he sits by the phone and just calls. . . . I don't think he spends more than five minutes at a time on any task. The lure of the unknown—who might be on the phone or tapping on his office door—often seems to interest him more than whatever he's doing at that moment. You don't have a conversation with him, you exchange data bursts."

—Michael Schrage[30]

"The pleasure derived from time spent in developing the mind and spirit is in fact very little dependent on goods," writes Linder. "For this reason . . . [it] is quite simply an inferior activity."[31] To use our parlance, thinking is time-minus because it cannot be easily commoditized. How discouraging. After all, wasn't the wizardry of the electronic age meant to do everything from aiding scientific advancement to liberating us from those mundane chores that interrupt thought?

CAN MACHINES THINK?

We have come a long way since that landmark day in 1946 when the Eniac came to life. The next year, AT&T's Bell Labs figured out how to replace vacuum tubes with transistors, and, in 1955, how to fit four transistors on a tiny chip of silicon.[32] The computer age had arrived. Costs and prices tumbled. Speed and versatility soared. Producers and markets boomed. With the power of machines doubling every two years or so,[33] a future when machines actually thought grew closer. And "the main event is yet to come," predicts a researcher at the Institute for the Future.[34] Will that event be the long-expected computer invasion of the human mind, with electronic technology taking over thinking and freeing our time for other pursuits?

Computers: The Hoped-for Automatic Thinkers

Today with more than 110 varieties of the magical machines worldwide (and half of them are in the United States), the computer has displaced much of the drudgery that typified business operations a few decades ago. Although the modern work place has been transformed at a scale rivaling that of the Industrial Revolution itself, the chores the computers replaced were routine. Humans, if they tried to perform the tasks that have been relegated to computers, would quickly ossify. Alphabetically listing the words in this book, and tallying how many times each was used, would take weeks. A desktop PC could accomplish the task in about a minute and, in the process, locate typos and misspellings and humbly suggest alternative terms.

Computers also help with editing by finding synonyms, catching sexist words, flagging clichés, and by spotting bad grammar, inadvertently repeated words, or too-often repeated words, and too-long sentences (like this one). But does Hal the Computer, equipped with the most advanced software, *think* about words better than you, me, and all our English comp teachers combined? No. Even Hal would admit that, if he had a brain like ours.

The properly programmed machine that made the alphabetical listing, simply triggers switches according to carefully worked-out rules. Without any understanding of *why,* the computer follows orders in much the same way that the television changes channels without knowing which has the better program. Whether the mini-est desktop version or the biggest mainframe, the computer doesn't think at all; it doesn't even think as well as pets Felix and Fido, and has no more intellectual depth than a light bulb. Thinking is left to the user holding the fond hope that, in obeying his instructions, Hal will respond in friendly ways. Computers are tools that serve the primarily venal ends of their craftsperson-users.

What the computer does have to offer is speed, if only for repetitive functions. Storing the word *time,* for example, requires translating the term, via a series of minuscule electronic switches, into a pattern of ons and offs, a lengthy operation but one that the computer finishes in the twinkling of an eye. Some of the seemingly simplest operations, done by a human even without thinking, require the computer to flip millions of switches. "In steps undertaken per result obtained, the digital computer makes an abacus look high-tech. But the computer sprints like nothing else under the sun."[35]

Sprinting makes computers great for writing. At the touch of a button or two, they vomit out reams of words. But will Hal ever be able to read, or to input an author's thoughts directly into the machine, let alone write for the writer?

For twenty-five years, technicians have been trying to teach computers how to read. It is proving difficult. The human eye easily identifies different type faces, varieties of paper, and graphics. The computer, so far, has balked at recognizing these differences. Indeed, electronic readers can scan printed pages, take an electronic picture, break up the image into a series of dots, and store that information. Software then takes over to interpret the patterns and transform them into letters, words, phrases, sentences, and all the other components of text. The mistakes, though, are many. Computers get misled, for example, by the difference between number 1 and letter l, and number 0 and letter O.

Those problems will be worked out with time and imagination but, tougher yet, and perhaps impossible in our lifetimes, is teaching the computer to write like writers write or to think like thinkers think. If computers can't, will robots be the little engines that could?

Robots: The Machines That Go Bump in the Dark

Scientist Hans Moravec believes that the answer is Yes. "Today our machines are still simple creations, requiring the parental care and hovering attention of any newborn, hardly worthy of the word 'intelligent,' " explains the robotocist. "But within the next century they will mature into entities as complex as ourselves, and eventually into something transcending everything we know—in whom we can take pride when they refer to themselves as our descendants."[36] Someday our descendants may be able to take over thinking. They will no longer need us. But not for awhile; in the meantime, they *will* need us and it will be up to humans to do the thinking—imperiled as that activity is by the *BB* factor.

The optimistic futurists of the 1950s, glowing with understandable excitement, envisioned a World of Tomorrow where robots could take over mundane activities from humans. They could clean our houses, balance our checkbooks, and mix our martinis. They could run our lives if we would let them. These singular feats would be accomplished by the magic of computers with their mind-like powers, mated to robots with their physical stamina. True marriages of brain and brawn. Best of all, computerized robots could think for us, and at least make the decisions that took up our time, freeing that time for the fun things in life.

The forecasts were premature. So far, robots have come to be used for doing exceedingly dull and repetitious jobs, or tasks that would imperil humans. They do as they are told without getting bored. With infinite precision, they repeat the same chore—like painting automobiles moving along an assembly line—twenty-four hours a day with a few minutes for the nourishment of repair. Willingly and without complaint, they take on dangerous jobs and go where humans fear to tread. They descend mine shafts and scale buildings, probe the ocean's depths and wander around in nuclear power plants. They repair ships, fix underwater utility cables, maintain offshore oil platforms, and find leaks in dams. They dispose of toxic waste and bombs, load ammunition, douse fires, and hoist loads several times their own weight.

We owe them much. But they're not very bright. So far they can't be programmed to avoid bumping into things when cleaning a floor. Advanced and useful as they are, robots are still a long distance from the R2D2s or C3POs that served human masters as servants and friends in the movie "Star Wars," for such machinery can perform these remarkable feats only with human intervention and human control.

While robots will probably never look or behave like honest-togoodness people, future versions may have more attributes similar to their human counterparts. "They are likely to have greater sensor capabilities, more intelligence, a higher level of manual dexterity, and a limited degree of mobility," according to one report. "There is no denying that the technology of robotics is moving in a direction to provide these machines with more and more capabilities like those of humans."[37] But do those capabilities, including "more intelligence," also include thinking? Perhaps. But perhaps, also, artificial intelligence will arrive at that capability sooner.

Artificial Intelligence: The Brain in a Box

Blazing speed and the capacity for storing mountains of information are the chief claims of the biggest supercomputers on today's market. Because they save **T**, call them Type-**T** machines to distinguish them from gadgetry of a different order, Type-**S** please, that have shown vague traces of human-like reasoning. Not surprisingly, the latter type increase **S**.

Scientists have worked at their benches since the 1950s to advance the frontiers of computer research on both fronts. Scientists working on the Type-**T** supercomputers push for more raw power and lightning-fast speed. The group writing programs that explore the mysteries of the mind seek to imbue the Type-**S** machines with human capacities for thought; for them, speed *per se* is of less importance than the tougher challenge of mimicking human beings' decision-making powers. Substantial progress can be reported on the Type-**T** front, far less for the Type-**S** marvels.

Each has reached a different stage of development. Type-**T**s can now produce graphics for TV commercials, assess brain functions, and analyze structures of hypersonic planes. Speed is gained simply by hooking together a battery of the machines in parallel. But they don't think. Soon they *would* be able to think, claimed Alan Turing, the brilliant British mathematician. Computers would be programmed so that an interrogator would have a 70 percent chance of knowing whether he was talking to a person or a machine.

Artificial intelligence, as this Type-**S** technology is dubbed, deals with matters of judgment far too subtle for conventional data processing, however powerful. In the beginning, the artificial intelligence community believed that the mind could be broken down into functions, and the functions broken into functions, until each one had become so simple—and mindless—that a brain in a box could do the job. Emphasizing software rather than hardware, instructions rather than machinery, and smartness rather than speed *per se,* the systems raised **S** rather than **T**.

A quarter century of research produced "expert systems." Using information input into them, expert systems calculate the costs, benefits, and risks of various decision options, and perform such practical tasks as plotting an investment strategy and predicting a customer's credit-worthiness. At best, this Type-**S** technology can diagnose the ailments of an automobile or of a human or of another computer, but it remains for the decision-maker armed with that advice to figure out the remedy.

These successes of the 1970s heightened expectations for the fledgling industry. As progress was made, visionaries in the early 1980s advanced their predictions another notch. Possibly the future foretold the prospect of truly delegating to these wise machines all the tasks of making key business and government decisions, delegations that would improve the quality of the decisions and free up the decision-makers' time. With slow progress, however, the state of the art has not arrived at that ultimate possibility, and many believe that it never will. Something will always slip through the crack between the model and the real world. At least the marketplace believed so.

Progress on the high speed Type-**T** supercomputer has been rapid, and sales volumes have grown explosively. Computers of the **S**-type, however, languish as the optimistic expectations of recent years fade.

In 1991, Turing's prediction was put to the test. MIT computer scientist Joseph Weizenbaum's succinct statement summarized the outcome: "The test will show how near we are to where we started—how little we've progressed in the past twenty-five years."[38]

Is the failure of computers to achieve thinking capacity due to technological failings? Or is artificial intelligence an impossibility? If reality cannot be formalized, or reduced to dimensions that a computer can manage, artificial intelligence may indeed be impossible. Although research continues in the hope that thinking-capability is theoretically possible, and expert systems notwithstanding, scientists have simply not yet been smart enough to invent machines smart enough to think, and to free up time for other pursuits. Until that day comes, thinking will remain an item on our "to-do" list.

WHY DON'T COMPUTERS WORK AT HIGH ALTITUDES?

Electronic technology, and the most powerful decision-support systems, have improved the productivity of many private firms and public agencies, but have failed to achieve the ultimate goal of replacing the mind. No matter how complete, the battery of doodads at the executive's beck and call—faxes, word processors, microcomputers, electronic mail, photocopiers, optical disks, spreadsheets, computer graphics, and enhanced telephones—don't approach doing what the brain does or doing it as well, and proving in the process that electronics are a poor substitute for gray matter. Tough decisions must still be made in old-fashioned, non-electronic ways.

Thinking and seeing require far more neurons than computers have transistors. If jobs as menial as cleaning an office or home stymie even the most advanced robots, can computers be expected to make complex decisions, to "see," and to take over the work of brains? Not likely. In order just to see, the human brain makes 100 billion computations a second, a speed 1,000 times that of today's fastest computer![39]

Richard Dawkins explains it all for us. The brain that reads these words has some 10 million kiloneurons, says the British zoologist. "Many of these billions of nerve cells have each more than a thousand electric wires connecting them to other neurons. At the molecular genetic level, every single one of more than a trillion cells in the body contains about a thousand times as much precisely coded digital information as my entire computer." So, in terms of capacity, the brain wins hands down over the computer.[40] If that isn't convincing enough, please note that the entire semiconductor industry annually produces as many bits of memory as there are synapses in the brain; that means that the computer industry's output is the equivalent of one human brain each year.[41]

Thus, the prospects for automating thinking remain dim. In

support of their claim that productivity will remain low in activities requiring large components of thinking, Professors William Baumol and Edward Wolff maintain that because "it is still very difficult to substitute capital for mental activity, it will always require the same amount of time for one person to produce one new idea."[42] In short, because of the difficulty of commoditizing thinking, it is time-minus.

For these good reasons, the use of computers in business has been limited to the lower echelons of management, with executives remaining computerphobes. Shoshana Zuboff points out in *In the Age of the Smart Machine* that office technology has successfully de-skilled workers at most levels, except at the very top of the managerial ladder.[43] In the same way that production line jobs have given way to automation, the most routine office tasks have given way to electronic computers. The machinery that aids the making of decisions at the higher altitudes of the hierarchy simply doesn't exist. "True expertise is a subtle phenomenon—and one that rarely can be replicated in the pre-programmed 'rules' that enable a software to simulate the thinking of its creators."[44] That is the expertise required of administrators who daily confront the challenges of planning, policy making, and oversight. And that is the work, in short, of those who use the documents and forms rather than those who produce them.

Learning to use the devices requires a substantial commitment of executives' time, and theirs is the most expensive of any in an organization. That fact of life in this electronic age also helps to explain why computers have not permeated the top echelons of management. Executives in the halls of power find the keyboard, long familiar to their secretaries, as foreign as Farsi. Male executives are more likely to have touched a secretary than a keyboard. Word processing requires keyboard knowledge, plus familiarity with programs that are constantly changing. For executives who have spent their time in a more abstract world far removed from computers, the long and arduous chore of learning a skill that the underlings already know well is a blow to their pride. As a training director for a major investment firm puts it, senior executives "never, never, never have the amount of time to spend in training that the regular professionals do."[45]

THE CURSE OF TRAINING TOP MANAGEMENT COMPUTERPHOBES:

MicroMentor, Inc., a major training concern that offers customized sessions for training executives to use computers for business problems, finds its educational challenge so great that it has developed a unique lexicon to describe the typical types that it must deal with. "There are 'puppydogs,' who slap away at the keys without apparent purpose. There are 'delegators,' who sit back, arms folded, and suggest a key for someone else to hit. There are the 'hover' types, whose fingers move ever closer to the keys but never quite get there, almost as though the keys were hot. Worst of all are 'cellists.' The allusion is to a Woody Allen movie that shows a cello teacher saying that some students have no concept of the instrument, followed by a shot of someone holding a cello up to his mouth and blowing into it."

—Paul B. Carroll[46]

The evidence shows up top managers for what they are: computerphobes. Workers whose tasks are routine make much use of the gadget, but executives whose problems are apparently too tough for computers rarely use them. Up to 81 percent of lower-level clerical, secretarial, and technical workers currently use a computer, but only one in three executives do.[47] That's why computers don't work at high altitudes.

The *BB* factor puts the quality of private and public decisions at risk in several ways. First, the tasks of thinking and pondering necessary to arrive at a careful decision have historically resisted automation. Yet, as the complexity of decisions has increased, so has the number of alternative solutions to a problem. Pressured by time, the top executive can explore fewer of those options.

Second, to save precious time, executives delegate to subordinates those burdens that, with less time pressure, they would shoulder themselves. Less time, more delegation. Top managers come to rely on staffs of subordinates who do the myriad things executives *could* do (except operate a computer) if they had the time. As hierarchies expand in size and complexity, so do the amounts and types of information. More top decisions come to depend on the focused and digested information supplied by subordinate specialists further down the organization chart, and the opportunities multiply for delivering information of lower quality.

Yet, by definition, only one person perches on top of the organizational pyramid: that person who must arrive at the decision served by the data transmitted from below. The wisdom of the ultimate decision relies on the quality of that information. Technology has done little to help the executive think through the decision, the most important task of all. As economist Marc Roberts reminds us: "For everyone, but especially for those [busy people] at the top of large hierarchical organizations, no one else's time is a perfect substitute for one's own."[48]

If all of this theory makes sense, then there should be evidence of increasingly sloppy decision making, particularly as it affects others than the decision-makers themselves. There is, unfortunately, substantial evidence that points in this direction. That evidence emerges in subsequent chapters. The next takes up where this leaves off: with the question of computers and organizational "altitude."

The devices that electronically automate thinking may not have reached very high into the uppermost strata of most corporate organizations, but other electronic assists have permeated to the very highest echelon of government. For proof, we need only examine the executive habits of a recent ex-occupant of the oval office.

18:00

WHO RUNS AMERICA?

"Politics—the gentle art of getting votes from the poor and campaign funds from the rich, by promising to protect each from the other."

—Oscar Ameringer[1]

Weekends were often spent at the getaway retreat on the West Coast. His work day followed a somewhat-less-than-standard nine-to-five regime, punctuated by naps, rides, and a daily hour exercising in the gym. "Business" dinners were tolerated as part of the routine. The evening in the cozy private apartment upstairs for watching old flicks on television—the activity that a biographer claims absorbed more of his time than anything else—fittingly climaxed a leisurely day.[2] During the White House days, Ronald Reagan knew how to make the best use of his time—and the best use of electronics—toward personally rewarding ends.[3]

Would one expect a president who "made a mockery of workaholism"[4] to be a great thinker? Matters of the mind, so time-minus are they, never seemed to get in the way. With his staff—his "mice"—keeping him informed, he could spend his time in other pursuits. "When he does look at a newspaper, the President's habit is to read the comics first," reports a former mouse.[5] TV often preempted the drudgery of reviewing reports. That too was up to the staff. "National security advisers read him documents aloud, got his approval, and initialled them on his behalf."[6] Detail was to be avoided, for his eyes quickly glazed over.

With this vague and impressionistic grasp of issues, Mr. Reagan will perhaps best be remembered for his many gaffes. One was the potentially lethal blunder when he announced to the press that a certain variety of missile could be recalled in the event of a mistake, when in fact the missile could not be recalled at all. Tilt! When called on the error, he admitted that he had "goofed someplace."[7] The press made much of the blunders in the beginning, but so numerous became the factual and statistical errors in the President's responses to questions that their newsworthiness disappeared. Then came the mega-gaffe of all, the one that remained to haunt him, and the rest of the world, for many years after he left the White House.

The Irangate fiasco brought into sharp focus most of the criticisms of this disconnected President: his failure to read, his impatience with detail, his forgotten facts, his dependence on staff. And he didn't take time off from watching television long enough to read official documents, for he apparently "never bothered to look at the critical decision paper of January 17, 1986, that formally authorized the arms-for-hostages deal."[8]

During one particularly crucial dress rehearsal for a meeting with the press, aides playing the roles of reporters asked him whether third countries were involved in the secret U.S. arms sales to Iran. He gave the wrong answer, not once but twice. "No, no third parties were involved." Aides reminded him that Israel's role in the debacle was well known, and it was time for a retake. Once more: "Were third countries involved in the arms sales to Iran?" "No, no third parties were." Oops again. More tilts. The curtain rose on the press conference and, predictably, he was popped *that* question and (predictably?) denied that the U.S. had condoned shipments from third countries. Prepared by extensive briefings for a later meeting with the media, the now well-rehearsed Chief Executive admitted he was not aware, until reading the Tower Commission Report, that the weapons sales had "degenerated" into an exchange of arms for hostages. Responding to a query why the President had earlier denied Israel's involvement in the Iranscam arms sale "when you knew that was not true," he admitted it was "just a misstatement that I didn't realize that I had made."[9]

Could innocent absent-mindedness excuse the gaffes? Or did Mr. Reagan regard doing his homework as a waste of time when other activities beckoned? To historian Barbara Tuchman, it was not absent-mindedness.

> The report of the Tower Commission concluding that Mr. Reagan is a hands-off President is widely accepted because it fits, and because of the statement let slip by Secretary of State George P. Shultz during the hearings that he obtained an interview with Reagan when the President "happened to be in Washington." This stays with me as the single most memorable remark of the hearings.[10]

Clearly, minding the affairs of state had little appeal to the holder of the highest public office in the western world. If he had kept abreast of key events and issues—as tiresome as time spent in those pursuits may be—he might have prevented the messiest scandals in recent decades and saved a terrorism policy from serious compromise. Failure to attend to such matters, however, meant a diminished place for this President in history and an administration that produced more investigated and indicted officials than any in American political history.

Others elected to high office may take their jobs more seriously but the formidable demands placed on politicians' twenty-four-hour days can just as easily squeeze out their time for pondering difficult public issues. Such thoughtful pursuits are as vulnerable for them in the pressure cooker atmosphere of Washington, and as time-minus, as they are for the Chief Executive. A journalist assigned to the Capitol Hill beat explains why the politician's clock runs so fast today:

> Days are a kaleidoscopic jumble: breakfasts with reporters, morning staff meetings, simultaneous committee hearings to juggle, back-to-back sessions with lobbyists and constituents, phone calls, briefings, constant buzzers interrupting office work to make quorum calls and votes on the run, afternoon speeches, evening meetings, receptions, fund-raisers, all crammed into four days so they can race home for a weekend gauntlet of campaigning.[11]

As schedules fill up with the speeches, meetings with constituents, quick briefings, and sessions on the floor, the time for thinking evaporates. "A senator or congressman has to be so many things to so many people now," notes veteran congressional observer Roger Mudd, "that they don't have an hour in the day any more to sit down and collect their thoughts."[12] The avalanche of mail received by congressmen indexes the exponential growth of such intrusions on politicians' time. Mail volume to the House of Representatives soars by 16 million pieces *per annum*. Each member of the House currently receives an Everest-high stack amounting to well over half a million pieces a year.[13]

Activities from answering correspondence to pondering issues inevitably get shunted off to others. When the boss hasn't the time to do it himself, he buys time by delegating to an underling who takes on the job even it means that the task gets done less well. The delegates may be staff members, including speech writers and "programmers," or lobbyists and political action committees fronting for "special interests," all of whom supply digested information for the politician. And indigestion for the public.

HOW POLITICIANS "BUY" TIME: BACK-STAGE IMAGE-MAKING

Politicians, it is widely believed, are elected to office for the quality of mind they bring to bear on critical policy matters. They are judged on their ability to make informed decisions for their constituencies, based on informed analyses of the policy options. Today, tyrannized by overly full schedules, politicians increasingly rely for these virtues on their staffs and the others to whom they delegate, officially or not, information gathering and analysis. If the speech writers and programmers accurately make the thought-to-word transformation, all to the good. If the lobbyists transmit objective, impartial information, all to the good. Both are big "ifs" worth careful examination.

Ghostwriters to the Rescue

"What would you do if you became President of the United States?" When the apparently perplexing question was put to him in the 1988 campaign debate, Mr. Quayle might have responded with greater assurance had he given more thought to the intriguing possibility that, at some time or other, must have occurred to him (just as it had crossed the minds of most of us in our wildest flights of fancy). "Delegate, delegate, delegate" might top the list of must-dos. Delegate to others to free up time for the key tasks. One of those delegations might have been to a speech-writer to script his thoughts and to answer tough questions like what he might do if he became President.

Speech making is one of the politician's most demanding and time-consuming tasks. Presidents Ford, Carter, and Reagan each averaged a speech a day during their tenure in the White House, with Mr. Ford setting a record for 682 public addresses in 1976. The demands for public appearances by the Chief Executive have not abated. By one calculation, the number of speeches delivered by presidents multiplied between 1945 and 1975 by almost six times,[14] and the demand for ventriloquists to put words in their mouths increased in tandem.

With the media's insatiable appetite for new material, few who are able to write their own speeches have the time for it. Prior to radio and television, politicians could recycle a stock speech, delivering it to different groups in different places at different times. In the pre-electronic era, a William Jennings Bryan could handily cross the nation, repeating time and again his celebrated Cross of Gold speech. Today, with the media transmitting the message to a national audience in the millions, a speech is only good for a one-night stand. With an increased demand for new speeches, contemporary audiences are more likely to hear words penned by a backstage crew hired for that purpose than the speaker himself.

A ghostwriter's speech is likely to be quite different from the words the speaker would craft. Speech writers assume the power of transforming the politician's thoughts into words, and even of framing policy in the words they cause him to utter. To Ernest Bormann, who analyzes speech making and speech writing, ghosting is "deception."[15] Walter Lippmann, who equated the practice with ghosting love letters or prayers, left no doubt where *he* stood on the morality of such delegations. "Those who cannot speak for themselves are, with very rare exceptions, not very sure of what they are doing and of what they mean," complained the celebrated commentator. "The sooner they are found out the better."[16]

Finding them out is easy when it becomes patently clear that the speaker has just seen the text for the very first time, or, in its delivery, becomes thoroughly bewildered by ideas that are clearly not of his or her own invention. In a talk delivered well before the advent of the TelePrompter, a baffled Warren G. Harding exclaimed, "Well, I never saw this before. I didn't write this speech and I don't believe what I just read."[17] A candidate running for a Senate seat in the mid-'50s ended his speech with the postscript: "And now I'd like to say a few words of my own."[18]

Of course, most of us are on to the speech-writing trick. Bill Moyers, one of Lyndon Johnson's chief speech writers, maintained that it would be hypocritical for politicians to presume the public believes they wrote their own speeches. "It is asking the public to be more of a boob than it is."[19] Nevertheless, the scripted speech poses the danger that the magic of the words becomes policy, and when the words are from another author, so is the policy. One of Mr. Truman's ghosts apparently spoke from experience when he declared that, "A speech writer can't help but be a policy maker . . . When he writes, he makes policy."[20] Such are the risks politicians take when, in response to the *BB* factor, they willingly delegate.

Programmers in Action

Whereas a speech writer's task is to save politicians' time (to reduce the **T** of the job, to recall a now familiar symbol), "programmers" are employed to enhance the politicians' image and performance by tailoring both to certain acceptable norms, and in so doing to raise the **S** of the activity. Although their reason for being differs, the consequences of programming are much the same as the consequences of ghostwriting. By transferring certain functions of the office, delegations of this sort transform the boss's image from the natural to the artificial.

Stay close to the people you are ruling, advised Niccolo Machiavelli. Politicians a half-millennium later follow Mr. Machiavelli's advice by staying close to the television cameras. That proximity requires help from staff programmers, usually known by the politer titles of "consultants," "political advisers," and "political technicians" or, as CBS anchorman Dan Rather labels them, "media mercenaries."

Whatever the moniker, the programmer's job description goes beyond mere public relations and the cosmetic qualities of personal appearances. Pulling their wires from offstage, programmers run the person who runs the country. And powerful they are. As

Martin Schram points out in *The Great American Video Game,* political success turns less on the candidates' policies than on the media managers' manipulative skills.[21]

H. L. MENCKEN ON W. G. HARDING'S SPEECH MAKING

"It reminds me of a string of wet sponges; it reminds me of tattered washing on the line; it reminds me of stale bean soup, of college yells, of dogs barking idiotically through endless nights. It is so bad that a sort of grandeur creeps into it. It drags itself out of the dark abysm of pish, and crawls insanely up to the topmost pinnacle of posh. It is rumble and bumble. It is flap and doodle. It is balder and dash."

—H. L. Mencken[22]

Chief executives, like President Harding, might have put a programmer's skills to good use, had programmers existed in those days. It fell to Ronald Reagan, however, to test and prove those skills. The former screen actor, who came to know the value of a back-lot production crew during his Hollywood years, transferred such talents from the movie set to the White House. Aides, under the First Lady's watchful eye, choreographed Mr. Reagan's every move. "Every moment of every public appearance was scheduled, every word was scripted, every place where Reagan was expected to stand was chalked with toe marks," recalls the former White House Chief of Staff. Just as a well-rehearsed actor need not concern himself with matters of the mind, a well-programmed president required little time for critical policy decisions. So it was believed. What mattered, alleges Donald Regan, was how an event would play in the media with "theatrical effect as the primary objective."[23]

"The idea that you can merchandise candidates for high office like breakfast cereal," declared Adlai Stevenson in 1952, "is the ultimate indignity to the democratic process."[24] Indignity it may be, but that is how today's candidates for public office market themselves. The television appearance has replaced the whistle-stop. Computerized polls have supplanted the platform. With apologies to Mr. Machiavelli, the advent of time-efficient electronic election merchandising has moved the politician one giant step away from his constituency.

In an era of high-valued time, the successful campaign is a high-tech one which projects image instead of issue, and does it quickly rather than thoroughly. Thus, the *BB* factor favors seasoned performers over seasoned statesmen. Little wonder that a former actor, comfortable with the tricks of performing before a lens, swept to the Presidency in large part on the strength of his "communication skills"; and that two charismatic preachers, Pat Robertson and Jesse Jackson, emerged as serious contenders in the 1988 race, although neither could claim political experience. Incorporating show-biz gambits into his public relations, distancing himself from the press and the public by throwing up an electronic *cordon sanitaire,* and limiting himself to tightly directed public appearances, Mr. Reagan convinced the public that he deserved to be crowned The Great Communicator. And his show that played to strong box office for eight years snapped, crackled, and popped, just like breakfast cereal!

HOW POLITICIANS "SELL" THEIR TIME

"The jet airplane wrecked everything," grouses Rep. Morris Udall. "It used to be a big deal when a constituent came in. You stopped whatever you were doing and hailed this traveler from far-distant Arizona. Now, hell, they come in here by the jetload every morning, educators and businessmen and whatever. Your day is full with Arizona people coming to see you."[25]

As understandable as the Congressman's lament may be, receiving the constituencies from back home is one of the duties elected politicians get paid for. Increasingly, however, politicians also get paid for meeting with constituencies who are not their electors. They are the political pressure groups that make contributions to politicians in two legal but ethically dubious ways. Lobbyists and political action committees (PACs) buy votes for legislation favorable to their cause and, via their special pleadings, supply digested information gratis. Contributions in both forms are welcome for they conserve the politicians' time: the dollars save time otherwise required for tapping funds from the more traditional sources such as the party and political supporters; and the digested information, biased to be sure, saves time otherwise required for research and analysis in order to arrive at an informed policy position on their own. Time is money, for contributions from pressure groups augment both the politicians' financial budgets *and* their time budgets.

Why PAC Contributions Are Time-Efficient

Says Congressman Jim Leach (R.-Iowa), who refuses to take PAC campaign money: "We have $10 or $20 receptions throughout the district. We have hog roasts, we have barbecues in which we seek small contributions. But it's very time-consuming and difficult as contrasted with the people around Washington. Every night of the week, here, there's a reception at the Capitol Hill Club for candidates, and they can raise $10,000 to $15,000. That takes me three weeks. Twenty events."

—Philip Stern[26]

Representative Wayne Owens, on returning to the House after he had relinquished his seat in 1974, was asked to identify the major change in Washington during his twelve-year absence. "The place is more bombarded by sophisticated lobbying techniques," he observed. "Basically every group you can think of has developed a Washington office or a national association aimed at presenting their case to Congress."[27] True, Mr. Congressman. In 1961, only 365 lobbyists were registered. The 1986 investigation of Michael Deaver—remembered as the once-Presidential-aide-turned-lobbyist who boasted of consuming a quart of scotch and three rolls of breath mints a day during his White House service (but was still convicted of perjury)—revealed that the number had skyrocketed to 20,400. That statistic—which provoked Senator Howard Metzenbaum to exclaim that "Washington has become a sinkhole of influence peddling"—has continued to grow until today there are 43 lobbyists available to offer advice and money for *each* member of Congress.

If lobbying ranks as a leading growth occupation, the PAC ranks as a leading growth institution. In 1974, 608 business, labor, and other interest groups funneled funds and information to Capitol

Hill. By 1988, the number had reached 4,268. Between those election years, contributions to the campaign coffers of candidates friendly to their interests soared seventeen-fold.[28] Until ways can be found to curb the abuses, to send the sly lobbyists and the wily PACmen packing, the lawmakers—and in fact the nation they serve—will remain vulnerable to the desires of the few.[29]

Politicians who delegate matters of the mind do so at large potential risk to the common good. Nevertheless, politicians continue to employ the speech writers who ghost the politicians' words that become position and policy, and the programmers who script the politicians' public appearances and their images. And the politicians continue to cater to the special interests of the lobbies who provide them with digested information and policy positions. Delegations, often made as responses to increasingly precious time, distort the politicians' image, skew the democratic process, and bias legislation.

TRADING IN POLITICIANS AT THE GONG SHOW

Electronic age technology has radically transformed the political campaign and moved the venue for campaign speeches from the train platform into the television studio. Once upon a time, politicians whistle-stopped their way across the nation, delivering stump speeches from coast to coast. Harry Truman is remembered for his "give 'em hell" whistle-stop tours, and a virtually unknown Jimmy Carter campaigned from farm to farm and house to house in an effort that got him nominated.

Audiences once met, over coffee and cookies served in a church basement, a touchable flesh-and-blood three-dimensional candidate. Today's audiences confront, over beer and popcorn served in the living room, a two-dimensional remote-control image electronically sprayed onto a cathode ray tube. The thunderous applause that once rewarded a politician's inspiring live performance has given way to the button pushed in a media laboratory signifying a "focus group's" approval of something-or-other said by a candidate's filmic screen-projected picture.

Scarce time, no less than technology, has transformed the political campaign. Political speeches delivered in the nineteenth century were a real event. People arrived from miles around to hear William Jennings Bryan, Henry Clay, Fighting Bob La Follette, and Daniel Webster hold forth in two- to three-hour monologues that dealt systematically and exhaustively with the issues that mattered. Each contender in the celebrated Lincoln–Douglas debates devoted an hour-and-a-half to a single topic: the future of slavery.[30]

Radio, and later television, shrank the acceptable length for speeches and, not coincidentally, the opportunities for voter enlightenment. Radio's advent cut the political speech to an hour. By the 1940s, the acceptable norm of half an hour still left enough time to lay out the substantive issues. With the emergence of television, the standard was cut further by the discovery that a half-hour speech drove viewers to other channels. Even the quarter-hour political talk, too long for the time-harried, eroded to the five-minute speechlet and further in the 1970s to the commercial spot abbreviated to sixty seconds, and finally, in the 1980s, to the seventeen-second snippet.[31]

The Hit-and-Run Speech

"Speakers in the golden ages of American, British, Roman, and Greek oratory routinely laid out the range of policy alternatives for examination, scrutinizing each in turn. Only after showing the flaws in the alternative options, weighing the objections to their proposals, and arguing the comparative advantages of the course they favored did they conclude. Such speeches demonstrated that the speaker commanded the facts of the situation, understood the alternatives, and could defend the choice of one over the others. . . . By contrast, contemporary political discourse tends to reduce the universe to two sides—one good, one evil—when in fact there may be four or five sides, each with its own advantages and disadvantages. After drawing simplistic and often false dichotomies, contemporary speech tends to canonize one side and anathematize the other. In the golden ages, speakers lovingly explored the range of available evidence. Today, speeches argue by hitting and running."

—Kathleen Hall Jamieson[32]

As the nature of political discourse shifted to accommodate the shrinking amount of time politicians and their audiences would give to a single event, complexity gave way to over-simplification, argument gave way to assertion, story gave way to headline, analysis gave way to synthesis, context gave way to one-liner, and the nuance gave way to the obvious. And the issues vanished somewhere in the ether separating candidate from voter.

HOW THE NON-ISSUE POLITICAL CAMPAIGN EMERGED

The quadrennial presidential campaign affords an unrivaled opportunity for the public to take stock, reflect, and learn: an opportunity to review the past, assess the present, and project the future. The tragedy of recent presidential campaigns is that the participants in that orgy of opportunity failed to show up for the party.

With political communication framed into public pronouncements squeezed down into thirty- (and seventeen-) second commercials, campaigns inevitably became superficial. Arriving at acceptable solutions to complex problems requires meticulous research, careful pondering, and thorough debate. Specificity takes time. Too much of it. Shrouded in vagueness and obscured by the fog of personality, trivia wins handily. And, it's quick. Just like reading the headlines.

The pronouncements of recent campaigns included the predictable bromides of "vision" and "leadership," but it was unclear just what the visions were of and who was being led where (and, of course, when). Since politics, like nature, abhors a vacuum, what rushed in to replace the deep issues requiring lengthy explanation were the "tissue issues" that didn't. Personality replaced platform, appearance replaced intellect, character traits replaced leadership skills, and past personal deeds replaced administrative experience. The tissue issues, televisually conveyed, give voter-televiewers their quick-fix and allow them to get on quickly with something else, or to change channels. Simple, short, satisfying. Few tissue issues have greater appeal than scandal.

While the practice of parading candidates' foibles of character before the voter is a hallmark of political history, the difference today is in the importance accorded scandal versus substance.

Scandal has become strategy. On today's political battlefield, probing an opponent's private past, rather than his private mind, may cost the opponent more votes.

The 1988 primaries produced the now nearly forgotten tidbit about Gary Hart's alleged dalliance with a Donna Rice, and in 1992, it was Bill Clinton's alleged affair with a Gennifer Flowers. To be sure, voters are entitled to certain information about the character of the candidates, and the candidates must be prepared for the invasive questions that reveal behavioral flaws; but how do such revelations help the voter assess the candidates' fitness for public service? Did FDR's affair with Lucy Mercer diminish the quality of his Presidency? Such intrusions into private lives discourage many otherwise qualified contenders—who would rather leave family skeletons in the closet—from applying for the job, leaving as our leaders only the bland. More importantly, the gossipy little bits dredged up from such probings divert the voters' attention from the big bits that matter.

Side-by-side with the boudoir tissue issues were the cosmetic tissue issues. Notwithstanding Adlai Stevenson's concerns about marketing candidates like breakfast food, the appearance of the package may count for politicians just as it does for cereal. But the evidence is mixed. The camera was generous to John F. Kennedy, whose charm slid through the lens and directly into the American consciousness, but Richard Nixon fared badly. "Who can forget Nixon's darting, shifty eyes on the tiny screen?" asks political historian Arthur Schlesinger.[33] Mr. Carter, despite a bumbling television personality, also won, and one media representative has speculated that Mr. Bush might have been "the most tele-repellent candidate ever."[34]

With the voters' attention riveted on matters of physical appearance and personal scandal, little time remains for matters that matter: discovering what the contenders for election think about the key issues of the moment and the future, how they handle themselves in crises, whether they have the knack for appointing well-qualified advisers and whether they listen to them, how they deal with erring or insubordinate subordinates, . . . or what they would do if, by some sudden twist of fate, they were propelled into the presidency of the United States of America?

HOW TO WIN AT TRIVIAL PURSUITS

The *BB* factor has propelled the American political system—perhaps our most sophisticated contribution to civilization—from one in which great men debated important issues to a sport in which trivia wins the game.[35] It was inevitable that issues would disappear as the media responded to viewer's demands to minimize the amount of **T** given to coverage of political events and to candidates' speeches; but the substitution of the trivia offered media and candidate alike the opportunity for maximizing the **S** of time given to winning that game.

News stories, like fish, are good for no more than three days. The modern version of the political journalists' traditional three-day rule is the phrase suitable for stopwatch timing. Surely not three days in length, nor three hours, and not even three minutes, the "sound bite," the whiz-bang, quick-as-a-flash (but oh-so-carefully-engineered) synoptic statement, collapses **T** and augments **S** to yield maximal impact in minimal time. Those mini show-and-tells, so it is believed, help time-oppressed viewers inform their vote. With picto-bites as the show, and sound-bites as the tell, the media fervently hope that political coverage might even garner Nielson ratings up there with "L.A. Law" and "Oprah Winfrey."

When viewed side-by-side with sponsor's commercial advertisements, rather than against the background of history or of larger questions, quick political advertisements easily mislead by diverting the televiewers' attention and minimizing the substan-

ADVICE TO THE TEFLON CANDIDATES

Refuse to discuss issues publicly, urges syndicated wit Art Buchwald. If Gary Hart followed the sage advice, he might respond to a question about an embarrassing issue like the deficit situation with, "The country's deficit happens to be a private matter between myself and my wife. Why don't you ask me serious questions about Donna Rice?"

—Art Buchwald[37]

tively serious. Maybe that is the goal, for sound bites juxtaposed with commercials "tend to give the viewer the belief that political problems may be ameliorated as quickly as aspirin relieves headaches."[36] That's the appeal of the Teflon candidates.

Picto-bites, side-by-side with sound-bites, further enhance the time-efficiency of the seventeen-second spot. Visiting a flag factory symbolizes patriotism. Riding in a tank wearing a helmet symbolizes a tough defense posture. Sinister criminals marching through a revolving door symbolize an opponent's weak stance on crime and punishment, just as a garbage raft floating in Boston harbor symbolizes his lack of concern over environmental degradation. An arm-waving preacher-turned-candidate suggests just about anything the viewers want to make of it. And it continued in 1992. Remember Jerry Brown burning bound volumes of the tax code to underscore the simplicity of his proposed flat tax on income, and Paul Tsongas's dive into the pool to reassure prospective voters that his victory over cancer had not left him enervated? Such are the symbols that shape the vote.

Television, with a punch that mere words lack, biases the viewers toward the visually obvious and intriguing, the surface quality rather than the substance. In the face-to-tube confrontation, the televiewer can arrive instantly at a judgment. But the judgment may be just a tad superficial.

To sum up, issueless campaigns meet the needs of time-harried voters who increasingly respond to messages minimal in content and maximal in punch. Politicians, competing for votes in this age of electronic electioneering, are criticized for preferring slogans over solutions, scandal over substance, ambiguities over specifics, inspirational words over technical terms, tissue-issues over real issues. They do it because it works; the media analysts tell them so. Telegenicity, personal character, and manner matter more than the content of whatever messages are conveyed. As the real issues vanish from the political dialogue in a cloud of electrons, we are rapidly becoming a nation of nonvoters not voting for non-issue candidates. Is it any wonder that the sound-bitten fail to go to the polls?

IS TV TO BLAME?

Something has gone very wrong with political discourse. Campaigns no longer grapple with compelling public issues. The televiewing voters, in their demand for instant gratification, have become apathetic. They are too busy even for the political discussions—if that is what they can be called—which take place in televised bursts of a few seconds. Yet modern electronic communications offer the potential for bringing to the public individuals and events both immediately and intimately.

Television gives a closer-up view of the politicians than ever before possible, "a proximity otherwise reserved for infants, lovers, and actors in mouthwash ads."[38] Television lets viewers measure candidates in "those intangible, up-close-and-personal ways that the newspaper page can never fulfill," claims *Chicago Sun-Times* editor Martin Schram.

In an earlier day, with the radio in command, up-closeness was manufactured in the minds of the listeners who, seated around the set, mentally transformed into visual images the speaker's words and countenance. With more effort required of the listener, it was easier to reflect on those words, savoring their meaning, and assembling the message. Today with the television assaulting eye and ear, messages do not permeate the mind so deeply and no mental transformation is required. Perhaps that is one reason why the messages seem, or *are,* more superficial. And more devious. "You can feel the candidates in your living room," says a ranking GOP political strategist. "And that's good for him, because it keeps people from looking at his record."[39] Even TV's greatest detractors agree that the medium, with its power to shape voter's perceptions and to distract from the record, has the power of making or breaking candidates. After all, if it can make Oliver North a national hero, there's no telling what it can do if it tries even harder.

Certainly the politicians who budget over half of their campaign financing for video advertising believe that the media wield the power to make or break. Although total campaign spending has increased nearly fivefold since 1972, expenditures for campaign ads on television have multiplied tenfold. In 1974, 30 percent of the average campaign budget was spent on video commercials; it is 55 percent today. In the five most costly senatorial campaigns, televised advertising cost a mere 12¢ per vote in 1974; ten years later a vote cost $3.54![40] Increased spending apparently paid off. The proportion of voters who said that campaign ads helped in choosing between candidates in 1988 was twice that in the 1984 Reagan/Mondale campaign.[41] Moreover, as pollster Louis Harris notes, the "Bush commercials have worked and the Dukakis commercials have not,"[42] and we know who won that contest. Place Mr. Bush beside Mr. North in the list of celebrities "made" by TV.

But it would be unfair to blame the press entirely for vaporizing the political issues in a mist of superficiality. While the medium can shape the message, just as the middleman can shape the product passed from wholesaler to retailer, it is the customer who ultimately determines what is produced. The candidates follow suit, responding to "customer"-viewer demands. The televiewer-voter apparently wants the sort of data that the candidates are willing to transmit, and the medium serves merely as go-between.

Although daily tube-time is higher than ever, that is not to say that viewers are willing to spend the increased time allocation watching serious fare like political news and features. In fact, to the contrary, apparently the only way to capture and sustain interest in such programs is to reduce their **T**. Watchers exercise their inalienable right to veto a political speech by zapping it from the airwaves. Armed with a weapon appropriate to the electronic age, the remote-control clicker, the viewer takes charge. Speech too long? Zap!

When it comes to televised political conventions, three out of four surveyed will watch highlights only, and comparatively few will couch-potato their way through live, gavel-to-gavel coverage.[43] By delegating the tasks of editing reportage to highlights, time-short viewers confer on the media the power to influence what they see and hear in much the same way that time-short politicians confer on special interest groups the power to influence what they learn about issues. In the same poll, a majority believed that "TV news wields too much influence in a Presidential election campaign" and that "the networks are politically biased in their campaign coverage." Still, to save time, televiewers, like politicians, are willing to put up with digested information.

The drastic decline in speech length and news coverage, and the no-less-radical shift in content, is simply a response to the unwillingness of television audiences to tolerate the former alternatives in its haste to get on with something else. The medium responds when the consumer-audience speaks, regardless of whether viewers ''speak'' by changing the channel to a game show or soap opera, or simply by pushing the ''off'' button in order to do something totally non-televisual.

While the electorate is undeniably influenced by what the medium conveys to them, the relationship is reciprocal. People don't have to put up with what they don't like, especially from a medium that relies on viewer audience for its support. Says David Burke, the president of CBS News, ''I fault us [TV] for being [like the public] . . . not as willing as we should be, perhaps, to put on the hair shirt and say: 'Look—sit down, I'm going to talk to you for a while about the Federal deficit and you're going to like it.' Well, they won't. They'll turn it off.''[44] Zap!

19:00

"WE APOLOGIZE FOR ANY INCONVENIENCE WE MAY HAVE CAUSED"

"Professionals built the Titanic, amateurs built the Ark."
—Anonymous[1]

Headlines scream of bridges collapsing, of buildings falling down, of ships sinking, of planes crashing, of oil rigs blowing up, of space shuttles exploding. In the final analysis, human failure is to blame, and at the root of human failure is the unwillingness of responsible people, responding to the *BB* factor, to take the time to take care.

Why? The *BB* factor explains it.

As activities shift toward the self-rewarding and away from the other-rewarding, decisions that affect others get slighted. Often the decisions are made by those who hold positions of power, and power means the ability to rule the destinies of others. When the decisions are thoughtless and careless (remember: thought and care take time!) innocent others "out there" bear the unfortunate, perhaps calamitous consequences.

DISASTER HERE AND THERE: THREE MILE ISLAND AND CHERNOBYL

The trigger that activates a chain of events ending in disaster may be as apparently innocent as hurrying a routine test to completion so that workers can get home to bed. No catastrophe in recent history tells that story more persuasively than Chernobyl. But disaster can also strike closer to home and, as the Three Mile Island tale tells, for much the same reason. Underpinning it all is the *BB* factor that distracts people in power from their responsibilities for the safety of others.

- Beyond the headlines of April 26, 1986, a horrified world read the story of an accident that would go into the record as the worst in the history of the harnessed atom. A pair of violent explosions had ripped through Unit 4 of the Chernobyl nuclear energy complex in the early hours of that fateful day. The radioactive cloud that rose high into the air spewed poisonous radiation around the globe and jeopardized hundreds of thousands of lives, among them the 300 killed (and an estimated 100,000 who would subsequently die), the hundreds hospitalized, and the untold numbers exposed to elevated cancer risks. Post-Chernobyl analyses made much of the inferiority of the technology. The reactor was known to be vulnerable to meltdown at low power. ''But only if all the safety systems are shut off,'' insisted nuclear scientist Valery Legaslov, a principal investigator of the accident.[2] And that is exactly what *had* happened, as the world's leading nuclear scientists were stunned to learn when they convened in Vienna for a post-mortem of the disaster. Reactor operators ''ignored both established rules of procedure and clear signs of developing trouble as they *rushed to complete a planned test* on one of the reactor's turbines. . . . The basic motivation for the behavior of operating personnel was an effort to finish the experiment faster.''[3] The quicker the test could be completed, the quicker they could get home after a long day at work.
- Although the headlines were smaller, the Three Mile Island nuclear accident near Harrisburg, Pennsylvania, America's version of Chernobyl, could have been just as dangerous. For weeks, TMI's troublesome valve had misbehaved. Contrary to company instructions, the valve should have been closed under those conditions, but negligence ruled and the valve was not repaired.[4] That the valve was stuck open, and allowed cooling water to escape, was known, as indicated by gauges which showed temperatures well above the allowable maximum. Operators ignored or misinterpreted those and additional danger signals, such as a rise in containment pressure, that appeared in the course of a test.[5] Then followed the string of events leading to meltdown.

Though separated in time and space by seven years and 4,500 miles, the incidents at TMI and Chernobyl invite comparison.

TMI's core melted down, as did Chernobyl's, and both disasters cost dearly in money terms. Both reactors were "very sensitive," or, in nuclear-speak, "responsive to perturbations," but the Russian model was considered the inferior. No deaths, injuries, or lingering contamination, however, have been attributed to TMI; the Chernobyl radiation release was a million times the magnitude of TMI's.[6]

The comparison shows that Russians have no monopoly on sloppy actions when the *BB* factor bids people in power toward reckless actions. At Chernobyl the operators ignored clear warnings from various sensors and, to accelerate the test, but contrary to regulations, even pulled out power control rods that could have saved the day. At TMI they refused to believe the temperature readings and turned off high-pressure injection pumps that were automatically activated when pressure in the reactor dropped to a dangerous level. And operators in both scenarios purposefully defeated the emergency safety systems as expedients.

"It is with human error that the major blame for both accidents apparently lies," concludes scientist John F. Ahearne in no uncertain terms. "Mechanical systems were defeated by operators who did not understand what they were doing."[7]

These were the failures of men, not of machines. Whether it was managers who failed to take the time to ensure that the procedural rules were carried out, or supervisors who failed to take the time to train employees thoroughly, or operators who "rushed to complete a planned test" in order to get on with something else, the roots of the problem lay in an eagerness to achieve quick results, to hurry decisions, to ignore responsibilities—failing in the process to take time to take care.

REACTORS BLOW UP AND BUILDINGS FALL DOWN

Things go wrong in the building and operating of structures, just as they do in the building and operating of nuclear reactors.[8]

- The worst construction disaster in U.S. history occurred on July 17, 1981, at Kansas City's almost-new Hyatt Regency Hotel, killing 114 people and injuring 200 others. As 2,000 party-goers danced below, a pair of double-decked open ''skywalks'' arching through the hotel's four-story-high atrium crashed to the floor, hurling dozens to their deaths and crushing many others under debris.

- After a heavy snowstorm in 1978, the 1,400-ton roof of the Hartford Civic Center Coliseum collapsed. Had it fallen but a few hours earlier, the structure would have trapped some 5,000 sports fans.
- A three-lane one-hundred-foot-long section of the Mianus River Bridge near Greenwich, Connecticut, fell on June 28, 1982, dropping three vehicles into the water below. Five years later, during heavy flooding, a supporting pier gave way and the Schoharie Creek Bridge in New York State collapsed. Both disasters claimed thirteen lives.

When the smoke has cleared after a structure has tumbled down or a reactor has blown up, the inevitable question arises: ''What caused it?''

Forensic engineers called to the scene of the fallen skywalks in Kansas City determined that the fault lay in a single badly rendered design detail. Original plans called for hanging each skywalk, one over the other, from the ceiling on forty-five foot rods. Because of the difficulty of installing rods of that length, the builders opted for two sets of shorter rods, one set for suspending the upper ramp from the ceiling and another set for supporting the lower ramp from the upper ramp. The engineers apparently failed to realize that the change order doubled the stress on the upper walkway, which gave way, leading to the collapse of the entire structure.

The Hartford collapse post-mortem revealed that several of the steel bars supporting the roof buckled under the added weight of the snow and ice, setting off a domino effect. In a matter of seconds, others did the same, shifting their loads to other rods, and down came the roof. The designers, said the investigators, failed to specify adequate bracing and a backup system for structural support in case of the failure of any part.

Inferior design, compounded by poor maintenance, precipitated the Mianus River Bridge collapse. The fall of the Schoharie Creek Bridge was blamed on builders' shortcuts. The post-disaster probe cited poor maintenance and inadequate inspections and found that the builders, in rushing to finish construction, had neglected to follow plans that called for shoring up the pier footings with heavy rocks. "In the last analysis," says engineer Mario Salvadori, "all structural failures are caused by human error—that is, lack of knowledge or judgment."[8]

DIMENSIONS OF CARELESSNESS ON LAND, AT SEA, AND IN THE AIR

"We can't help you at the moment because our computers are down."

"We regret that the flight will be delayed due to a technical problem."

Businesses, including the airlines, have learned that customers and passengers groan less when interrupted service or delay is attributed to an object rather than to a person. The failings of an inanimate (and inoperative) object are excusable, but the failings of an individual are not. Even if fault rests with the individual charged with keeping the object in working order, blaming the "thing" for the difficulty is better PR than blaming the negligent operator. Nonetheless, technical problems are ultimately human errors. For better or worse, the individuals who could have prevented the problem remain accountable.

- The Pentagon's official report of the 1988 Persian Gulf incident concluded that "human error was primarily responsible." The sophisticated radar equipment on board the cruiser Vincennes—which shot down an Iranian jetliner resulting in 290 deaths—"functioned well."
- The series of explosions that ripped through Occidental Petroleum's Piper Alpha North Sea production platform in 1988 cost the lives of two out of three of the platform's crew of nearly 200 men and the loss of equipment valued at upward of $1 billion. The odor of gas was detected, apparently reported, but, according to investigators, ignored. The source of the leak was a missing valve. Supervisors neglected to tell the shift on duty that the valve had been removed.[10]

Deregulation of the airlines in the late 1970s not only increased competition in the skies, but also carelessness. In the fare wars that followed, cost cutting took the form of ''deferred maintenance,'' often a euphemism for no maintenance at all. Mechanical failure and the deterioration of aging parts were to blame, so it was said, when roofs, wing-panels, and cargo doors mysteriously dropped off planes in flight. But human failure lurked in the background.

Accusations filed against a major carrier at the height of the rate wars suggested that the airline encouraged mechanics to skip normal equipment-installation tests, and reported that fuel leaks were ignored or plugged with unauthorized sealers, all so the planes could take off on schedule. Investigators also alleged that mechanics had the incentive to complete work quickly, for management had set performance goals that paid bonuses for getting planes ready faster.[11] The planes may have gotten there faster, but at high risks.

Failure to take the time to maintain equipment with care is one source of safety risk. Taking the time to operate it with care is another. Overall, two out of three jet transport accidents, and 80 percent of accidents taking place during final approach and landing, are attributed to mistakes made by flight crews.[12]

Behind those mysterious doors that shield flight crews from passengers, an investigation launched by the Federal Aviation Administration, the government regulator of air traffic and safety, discovered a circus of errors. One airline's pilots had landed on the wrong runway, in the wrong city, inadvertently shut down both engines of a two-engine plane during take off, and nearly collided with a jumbo jet after straying sixty miles off course. In criticizing pilots for the ways they managed their time aloft, the investigators pointed out poor crew discipline and coordination, and communication breakdowns, citing specific instances where pilots arrived at the aircraft without enough time to perform preflight duties in an orderly manner, confirmed the air traffic controllers' instructions when the co-pilot was not listening, rolled the plane away from the gate with passengers still standing in the aisle, and made company-related calls or PR announcements to passengers at low altitudes—all flagrant abuses of accepted safety procedures and approved ways of using their time.[13]

Hardly had the FAA filed its report when a tragic accident—the second worst air disaster in U.S. history—ratified its conclusions.

A transcript of conversations from the cockpit voice recorder showed that Northwest Airlines Flight 255, which crashed near Detroit Metropolitan Airport, taking 156 lives, got in trouble almost immediately after takeoff. Pilot error was to blame, said the National Transportation Safety Board's charge. Specifically, the pilot had neglected to deploy the wing flaps that give the plane additional lift on takeoff. During the taxi for takeoff, the jet missed "Charlie," its assigned taxiway. Here is what was said:

> Co-pilot: Where's Charlie at?
> Captain: Right at the end of this ramp—no that's Bravo—no, it is Charlie.

The co-pilot failed to set his radio frequency to establish contact with the control tower. As the jet taxied, a startled controller radioed, "who's the Northwest . . . just going by?" While the co-pilot dialed to the proper frequency, he and the pilot, distracted and (in the words of the official report) "worried about meeting a demanding schedule,"[14] skipped mandatory checks to be completed during taxi, a list which includes verifying that the wing flaps and slat are properly extended.

The jet roared down the runway, the captain pulled the nose up, and the aircraft started to rise. Within seconds, however, the pilot's control column began an ominous rattling that signals insufficient lift and impending stall. Then came a second warning, this one from a recorded voice chanting "stall, stall, stall . . . " The left wing, rocking from the stall, collided with a building and spun the plane to the ground.[15] One of the chief investigators maintained that the crew members, who had worked together for about a week, had grown complacent. " 'The more you do it, the more comfortable you feel with it,' he said, adding that such shortcutting isn't infrequent in today's 'high-tempo operations.' "[16]

Failing to maintain and to operate planes with care are two dimensions of human failure which may lead to potential tragedy. Sometimes, however, sheer negligence or stupidity is at fault. Two cases illustrate downright indifference to the welfare of innocent others. They are similar in that those holding responsible positions chose to divert time from their jobs in ways that earned them higher **S/T**s.

On June 28, 1988, after a three-and-one-half-hour delay due to air traffic congestion, a DC-9 jet took off from Rome loaded with 103 passengers bound for Reggio Calabria in Italy's "boot." At 12:49 a.m., as the craft neared its destination, the control tower radioed that the airport would close at 1 a.m. and urged the pilot to hurry up. Sixty seconds from touchdown, the controllers, determined to close up shop and head home, broke radio contact and plunged the field into darkness. It was precisely 1 a.m. and the controllers had kept their promise. The pilot, who quickly pulled the plane up and landed at an airport 100 miles away, saved the day.[17] Punctuality has its price.

The calamitous grounding of the oil tanker Exxon Valdez off the Alaskan coast in 1989 wreaked environmental havoc from Prince William Sound to locations as far as 700 miles away, polluted 300 miles of shoreline, and took the worst toll on wildlife of any industrial accident in history. Was technical failure—weak radar, as first alleged—responsible for the tanker impaling itself on a reef, rupturing its hull, and spewing some 10 million gallons of oil into the water? No, said the federal grand jury, in handing down a five-count indictment and fining the world's largest oil company $640 million in damages. The charges alleged that the skipper was below in his quarters imbibing when he should have been at the bridge guiding the ship and that corporate management was negligent in employing crew members known to be "physically and mentally incapable of performing the duties assigned them."[18] Human error, not technological fault, was responsible.

The story behind the explosion of the Challenger space shuttle illustrates how decision-makers at the highest levels, in their rush to accomplish a major feat and to maintain a schedule of accomplishments, raise risks to unacceptable levels. That is a fourth source of human error. Challenger, like the Piper Alpha episode, illustrates a fifth source as well. Risk compounds when key actors in a hazardous drama fail to take the time to communicate especially critical information, a function that may be relatively low in **S/T** for them. For others, it is quite a different matter.

CHALLENGER'S ILL-FATED LAUNCH[19]

All was in readiness for lift-off. All except the weather. Florida was in the throes of an unexpected cold wave. Weather forecasters predicted temperatures on the pad at 20° to 30° below normal, a new record low for any previous launch. Technicians were worried about the forecast and data that showed how the effectiveness of the now-infamous O-rings—the rubber gaskets that sealed the booster joints—could diminish at low temperatures. Engineers who worked for the booster's manufacturer, Morton Thiokol, unanimously recommended that the National Aeronautics and Space Administration postpone the launch.

Despite the warnings, lift-off went ahead right on schedule. Seventy-three seconds later a fiery white-and-yellow explosion consumed space shuttle Challenger and its crew.

Not surprisingly, the inquiries following that event on January 28, 1986, focused on technical matters. A "burnthrough" in a solid rocket casing was believed to be at fault. A seal in a solid-fueled booster failed, allowing hot flames to escape and ignite an adjacent liquid-fuel tank. The explanation seemed plausible, for seals had partially eroded on thirty-two joints during previous shuttle flights. NASA had been warned of a potential catastrophe, studied the problem, but apparently took no further action.[20]

There had been repeated warnings of trouble starting with the discovery in another shuttle flight—one in 1981—that seals had eroded, allowing hot gases to escape. NASA recognized that backup gaskets could dangerously erode and, in the arid language of government-speak, formalized the potential risks as "loss of mission, vehicle, and crew due to metal erosion, burnthrough, and probably case-burst resulting in fire and deflagration."[21] In 1985, Thiokol, with similarly suitable phrasing, argued that action should be taken "to reduce criticality." Because the action could not be taken earlier than months after Challenger was scheduled to lift-off, that would have meant another postponement after what had already been a series of delays. Nonetheless, it was widely believed that, with the weather cooperating, safety risks would be minimal. The gaskets *should* hold. But they didn't.

Blame was put on the little O-rings. It was believed that the unusually low temperature on the launch pad made the first gasket so stiff that it failed to seat properly and seal the joint. After the coldest previous launch, in 1985, came the discovery that a gasket had badly eroded and its backup was charred.[22] But never mind—back to launch-control. . . .

In the few last hours of the lives of Challenger and its seven crew members, senior NASA executives were busy overseeing final preparations. Four of them knew about Morton Thiokol's recommendation to postpone. However, none of the four—who had direct responsibility for the booster program's success or failure—took the time to inform the others in the control room of Thiokol's worries.[23] The "others" included the three principal agency officials who had the power to halt the launch. The worst fears were realized only hours later.

The tragedy proved that, once again, to err is human.

PULLING THE PLUG ON THE PLANET

Human error has been held accountable for blown-up reactors, fallen-down structures, crashed aircraft, spilled oil, and failed space shuttles. So far there have been no accidental nuclear wars, but should such mishaps occur human error will be a likely cause, for insufficient time has been given to training those who manage crisis operations during a threatened nuclear attack—in short, the

individuals whose very actions may govern destiny.

Of all disasters, nuclear war ranks as the ultimate. Paul Bracken's book, *The Command and Control of Nuclear Forces,*[24] tells how it *could* happen in the future, just as it nearly *did* once in the past.

In 1956, during a particularly tense period in the Middle East, early warning radar picked up unidentified aircraft flying over Turkey, and a hundred Soviet fighters cruising in Syrian airspace. A British bomber in the area was downed as a Soviet naval fleet moved from the Black Sea toward open water. Washington, reacting to what appeared to be the beginnings of a major superpower confrontation, quickly put the nuclear forces on alert.

The confrontation turned out to be only a case of misinterpreted signals. The aircraft over Turkey were swans, there were far fewer planes over Syria than the radar had indicated, mechanical trouble had downed the British plane, and the Soviet fleet was moving into position for a routine maneuver. When the truth became known, the alert was promptly called off. Patently erroneous as it was, however, the information could have sparked retaliation and a nuclear holocaust.

That cool heads prevailed may in itself have been accidental. In an era when the number, power, speed, availability, and accuracy of nuclear weapons have multiplied manyfold and political tensions and terrorism have escalated, cool-headed arms control experts fear that benign events at the height of a crisis could precipitate accidental war, if the time isn't taken to be *very* careful.

Is there good cause for their concern? After all, in a real crisis, wouldn't the President be instantly supplied with the best information available, and wouldn't decisions be made in the framework of overall policy goals with appropriate actions chosen from a menu carefully prepared by the National Security Council's experts? In a word: No, says a discouraging *Science* analysis of crisis management in the highest places.[25]

Richard Beal, since 1982 the White House senior director for crisis management systems and planning, identifies the key problem as the failure of those at the highest echelons of government to spend time planning for trouble. A top U.S.-Soviet crisis specialist recalls being called to the White House during a major emergency, and "all of a sudden realizing that there are no rules, no books, and no procedures. One of your first thoughts is to ask the President, but the President doesn't know; he only knows what the staff tells him.''[26] And who tells the staff what to tell the President?

What they tell him should be a cause for concern, for crisis decision-makers are unable to treat emergencies systematically due to their ''lack of a sense of history,'' alleges Mr. Beal. Those who hold the fate of the nation, indeed of the world, have neglected to spend the time to learn their history lessons, and to generalize from those events. Crises are ''so well documented as idiographic events that very few people, including crisis decision-makers, can treat them in any generic sense, and therefore they are lost for what to do to control or manage or attempt to influence significantly most of the crises they are confronted with. [This] means that every single one of them begins anew with an empty yellow pad.'' With a less-than-sanguine view toward the future, Mr. Beal concludes by bringing us full circle to a point made in an earlier chapter: that technological innovation does pitifully little to assist decisions at the top. ''The American government will spend literally billions of dollars developing information for the bottom and nothing for the top. . . . By top, I mean the National Security Council, the President, and other people.''[27]

MOTHER NATURE, MEET FATHER TIME

The causes? Were machinery and materials to blame for these debacles, or can blame be laid at the doorstep of that most complex machine of all, the human being?

Can we blame the people promenading on the skywalks in Kansas City, the evacuees from Chernobyl, the motorists crossing the bridges in New England? Or the snow piling up on Hartford's Coliseum roof, or the sea otters paddling around in the oil slick off the Alaskan coast? They must be judged innocent.

Can we blame the volatile reactor at Chernobyl; or the malfunctioning valves at Three Mile Island, and Piper Alpha; or the rods supporting the Hyatt's skyways and Hartford's roof; or the steel in the bridges that cross Mianus River and Schoharie Creek; or the oil that gushed into the pristine waters of Prince William Sound; or Challenger's O-rings that refused to seat properly? Perhaps machinery and materials failed, but the underlying causes run deeper.

Or, can we blame those who were supposed to devote sufficient time and effort to designing and engineering the failed projects, to operating and maintaining the failed equipment and structures, to supervising and training the careless operators, and taking the time to do so in ways that bring no harm to others? Failure on any and all of these counts can be chalked up to human, not mechanical, shortcomings.

Were the engineers, apparently oblivious to stress requirements, at fault for the collapsed ramps and roof in Kansas City and Hartford? Did supervisors act responsibly when they failed to communicate their knowledge about the missing valve at Piper Alpha? Or the NASA officials who failed to inform the control room about the O-ring manufacturer's serious concerns in the short hours before the Challenger lift-off? Did officials at Chernobyl and TMI who neglected to train operators in the rudiments of reactor technology and emergency procedures, and to develop and enforce appropriate operating rules, fail in their duties? The answers are clear.

And there is the additional human failure, even more closely linked to the *BB* factor, of people in positions of great responsibility who flagrantly abuse the right to allocate their time in ways that provide *them* with high rewards at the risk of innocent others. At Chernobyl, the guilty were the operators who disengaged safety systems in order to prevent delaying the test (and their timely return home). At Schoharie Creek, the guilty were the contractors who, in rushing the project to completion, neglected to shore up footings. At Reggio Calabria, the guilty were the air controllers who, anxious to finish their workday, doused the landing lights as the plane approached. At Valdez, the guilty were the corporate officers who failed to ensure that qualified personnel were in charge of the oil tanker. As for Challenger, the guilty were the decision-makers who knew the risks, yet hurried to get the spaceship aloft lest the record and "production" schedule be compromised. And if the ultimate disaster strikes, a major share of blame can be placed on the crisis manager's aversion to time spent planning.

The euphemism "human failure," in these gruesome instances, merely blankets a multitude of sins ranging from sheer stupidity to the selfishness and carelessness that come from the impatience to get on with activities that yield higher **S/T**s for the guilty ones making the choices, but disaster for innocent others. Hurry, for there are better things to do. Finish the task at hand quickly, or don't do it at all. To hell with the consequences.

Mother Nature has arranged for most disasters to be either of two types. Epic disasters, like nuclear war, will happen only very rarely but produce horrendous outcomes. Others, like denting a fender, occur frequently but are of comparatively little consequence. Although no data are available to prove that the *number* of low-probability/high-consequence disasters—like Chernobyl or Valdez—have increased, there is little doubt that the *consequences* of major disasters have. Half a century ago, an assembly line worker asleep on the job could wreck most of the day's production; today, a nuclear power station worker asleep at the switch could destroy most of the planet. Disabling the safety equipment on the conveyor belt could endanger many workers; disengaging the apparatus at the power station could endanger most of the world's population.

Analysis and risk-reduction techniques can lower the chances of accidents. Analysis will show the possibilities for cutting occurrence probabilities, and risk-reduction strategies can be implemented appropriately. As applied to materials, risk analysis leads to better predictions than when applied to human beings, whose behavior is far trickier to predict, if it can be predicted at all.

Enter Father Time. Electronic wizardry has raised the accuracy of risk analysis and lowered the chance of mechanical failure. Computers aid the designers and engineers in making calculations, the manufacturers in controlling quality, and the supervisors in monitoring equipment use. High powered computers can test the strength and reliability of O-rings, structural supports, and valves, or estimate the chances that safety systems will fail or that reactor cores will lose all cooling water. These are feasible tasks compared to the challenge of predicting human behavior when crisis looms.

No matter how thoroughly the machinery and materials have been tested in the manufacturer's laboratories, however, critical moments arise in their use. We know that, in an emergency—the most time-pressured case of all—the probabilities of judgmental error increase, even though the probabilities of machine or material failure remain unaffected. The decisions, in such cases, are forced on humans, not on inert objects that fail to arrange their molecules in the correct order. At those tense moments humans must intervene and decide how the materials should be used and the machines should be operated.

Can we predict whether technicians will disable safety devices in an emergency, whether supervisors will adequately train and monitor operators, whether life-threatening information will be passed on to those who need to know, whether the hundreds of human agents involved in every phase from first-designs to the ultimate users will make sure that the gadgets behave as they are meant to, whether the operators will interpret the computer print-outs carefully, whether operators will react appropriately to the readings on the monitoring gauges, whether people will "turn the dials" in the correct directions when the worst fears are realized? In short, can humans in critical positions be counted on to take the time when activities with higher **S**, or perhaps lower **T**, bid? Yet, until these questions can be answered, human action and reaction will remain unknowns in the equations that predict disasters with small chances of occurrence and, regrettably, large consequences. We can only speculate, with alarm, that the *BB* factor causes a larger chance of harm, and should our fears be realized, be prepared to apologize for any inconvenience our negligence may have caused.

20:00
WASTE-MAKING HASTE

"All haste is from the devil."
—Medieval Latin proverb

If the aphorism, Haste Makes Waste, is truly axiomatic, then *increasing* Haste also Makes for *increasing* Waste. When producers hurry products through production and onto the store shelves, mistakes will be made. Accidents that are "their" fault increase. When consumers hurry products from the store to home, mistakes will be made. Accidents that are "our" fault increase too. As hurry increases, so do the unpleasant consequences.

As time becomes more scarce, we are less willing to spend as much time as we once did to acquire information, just as there seems to be more information to acquire. Unfortunately, there's no real short-cut to gaining knowledge. So we make the inevitable choice: less time acquiring, assimilating, and applying information. Yet, knowledge—call it know-how if you will—prevents making mistakes. With less knowledge, we make more mistakes, and more mistakes mean more harm to others.

The professionals on whom we rely for informed decisions are expected to *have* the latest knowledge and to *use* it to (our) good advantage. Not only does the gaining of knowledge seem to be time-minus, but so does putting knowledge to good use. That generalization takes on special meaning when those affected are those in whom we put our trust. When the distracted doctor prescribes the wrong medication; the thoughtless lab technician decides a test is positive when it is really negative; or the bored quality controller overlooks the flaw in a car rolling down the assembly line, decisions are being made that affect the rest of us, for better or for worse. In these cases, it's for the worse: a patient suffers bewildering effects from taking a wrongly prescribed medication, another patient has unnecessary surgery, a car breaks down in a congested intersection.

It boils down to a matter of time and trust. Can we be expected to take the time to learn enough to diagnose our own illnesses, to analyze lab specimens, to check the quality of our recently bought car? No, we leave it to the experts. We trust that they have taken the time to acquire and use the knowledge required to do their jobs well. In the age of the *BB* factor, and an age of exploding knowledge, that trust may be misplaced.

CAVEAT EMPTOR *IN THE MARKETPLACE*

As goods producers grow increasingly careless, we will more often read news accounts of how the auto manufacturers must recall X million cars due to faulty brakes, exploding engines, faulty seat belts, leaking fuel pumps, or sudden and unexplained acceleration.[1] As services producers grow increasingly careless, we will more often read of heart transplants gone awry, of erroneous lab tests failing to detect preventable illnesses, and of soaring medical malpractice costs. And we will read about new federal and state regulations and agencies organized to protect consumers from the producers' haste-making waste, and from the consumers' own carelessness.

Mistakes are bound to increase in a world made increasingly complicated by the parallel explosions of knowledge and the technology required to store, categorize, and access it. With only limited time to consider the potentially damaging consequences of each decision and to acquire an expanding fund of facts and information on our own, we have become increasingly dependent on the specialized knowledge of experts. The experts may be counselors, legal and medical specialists, even travel agents, or those working for agencies like the Food and Drug Administration or Federal Aviation Administration, upon whom we rely for testing and certifying the reliability of new drugs that we consume and the safety of airplanes that we fly.

In recent years, malpractice and product liability cases have skyrocketed in number due to increasing miscalculations, mistakes, and mismoves. There must be good reason why apparently injured Americans more and more turn to the courts for remedies. There may be good reason to file suit when more and more products are put on the market, or actions are taken, that injure the innocent. Whatever the exact reason, the evidence on runaway litigiousness is staggering.

- Product liability suits filed by plaintiffs in federal district courts have increased in number by more than eight-fold since 1974, to reach an all-time high exceeding 17,000 in 1988.[2]
- The number of personal injury lawsuits filed between private parties in federal courts has risen more than 50 percent, to over 40,000 annually, just since 1980.[3]
- In 1976, the average physician could expect to face a malpractice suit just once in a forty-year career; eight years later, the chance had risen to a case once every six years.[4]

What are the consequences of this liability "crisis"? To be sure, the injured get compensated for damages (definitely not a plus for the defendants) and the lawyers get their fees (definitely not a plus for non-lawyers). More importantly, if the system performs as designed, guilty producers of flawed goods and services learn the virtues of taking time to take care. Until we learn those virtues, litigation is bound to increase, the courts' dockets will become even more congested, and consumers will pay higher prices that reflect the costs of litigation and malpractice insurance passed on to them. Without the threat of suit for careless actions and misdeeds, we would all behave even more carelessly as we let the *BB* factor take its course.

Yet no threat of litigation can ever conclusively certify complete safety. There will always be the lurking chance of an error. Errors are also made by purveyors of health services, whether they are the physicians or the labs that provide the technical data for diagnoses.

DANGER ON-STAGE AT THE DOCTOR'S OFFICE

Readeth what the Bible saith: "He that sinneth before his Maker, let him fall into the hand of the physician" (Ecclesiasticus, 38:15).

Those who have sinned and indeed fallen into the physicians' hands (is there one among us who hasn't?) are aware that practitioners of the medical arts may be no less guilty than producers of goods for failing to take adequate time to take adequate care. Blunders in the doctor's office injure, even kill, patients. The case of the surgeon who, upon finishing the surgical procedure, fails to take the time to look around inside and remove instruments before sewing up the patient, is classic. British data indicate that those cases are on the increase. The number of known incidents where instruments, needles, forceps, and the like were left inside surgery patients went up from fifty-two a year in the 1960s to an annual average of seventy in the late 1970s.[5]

Whether called "adverse medical outcomes," "potentially compensable events," "therapeutic misadventures," or—by a term that few outside the profession can be expected to pronounce, let alone understand—"iatrogenic incidents," medical mishaps caused by doctors, paramedics, nurses, hospitals, and labs seem to be on the upswing. The list includes drugs misprescribed and faulty diagnoses hastily made by medics, hospital infection caused by negligent supervisors, careless use of medical devices by care-providers who failed to read the directions thoroughly, and improper monitoring of IVs or of radium treatments by technicians busy doing something else. All obviously are related to the *BB* factor.

Keeping current with the drugs produced by the pharmaceutical companies takes time—lots of it, considering the pace of new discoveries. The importance of keeping current with the newest and latest was underscored in a 1988 Harvard Medical School study which pointed out that nearly every prescription written that year by physicians who completed medical school in 1960 was for a drug about which those physicians had received no formal education.[6] How then do physicians keep up to date? Busy physicians do their homework—in their case, mainly keeping up on the medical research literature—much as busy politicians do theirs. Pressed for time, they are open to shortcuts, and these come in the form of lavish sales inducements from the pharmaceutical industry. Just as PACs have become a major source of information—digested and biased—for politicians, the pitches of drug merchants have become a chief source of information—digested and biased—for physicians. The risks for the quality of decisions are no different.

Promotional tactics that run the gamut from a gift of a stethoscope for a medical student to a weekend skiing trip for an intern to frequent flyer points for a practicing physician who prescribes a beta-blocker for a patient, sway the physicians' decisions about the best drugs to prescribe. The time-pressed practitioners' recommended treatments become based on the salespeople's pitches and the manufacturers' advertisements, rather than on the reasoned judgments based on doing their own homework. A major pharmaceutical house "used continuing-medical-education credits as the carrot on its stick in marketing a new antihistamine," thus saving physicians the time needed to earn such credits for retaining their medical licenses. "When the marketing is successful, doctors may never review the scientific literature on a drug. To promote their products, the drug companies spent more than $5,000 on each of the country's 479,000 doctors in 1988, for a total of about $2.5 billion."[7] And the patient pays more for drugs, and has cause to worry more about the quality of the diagnosis.

Poor doctor-patient communication is one root of the malpractice problem. Because physicians spend less than two minutes of a twenty-minute session giving information, "60 percent of patients leave a doctor's office confused about instructions on medication, and more than half of new prescriptions are taken improperly or not at all," says Marshall Becker at the University of Michigan's School of Public Health.[8] U.S. doctors write an average of eight prescriptions per adult per year. But seldom does the hurried physician tell the patient more than "take one tablet twice a day" (how can *one* tablet be taken *twice* a day?). The patient has a vague idea what the drug is intended to remedy, but little knowledge about how it works or about its side effects. The Food and Drug Administration discovered that 70 percent of patients said their physicians didn't tell them about side effects. Medical specialists fear that, in the future, "doctors will have less time than ever to discuss treatments with their patients, including potential side effects."[9]

That doctors spend insufficient time thinking and communicating about their patients' symptoms is reflected in the increasing number of malpractice cases reaching the courts. Only about one injury in five can be blamed on a procedure performed improperly. The most common type of injury claimed came from decision-making errors that "result in inappropriate treatment or in misdiagnosis." Write the researchers who uncovered that fact, "In most cases, the claim is not that the doctor *did* something wrong, but rather that he or she *thought* something wrong."[10] With doctors giving insufficient time to the thinking rather than to the doing, thinking surfaces once again as time-minus.

Another investigation uncovered 4.65 episodes of malpractice per 100 hospital admissions.[11] Yet another claims that the deaths of one in four of 182 patients admitted for heart ailments, stroke, and pneumonia were preventable. Because the physicians failed to take sufficient time, "some patients had inadequate initial work-up of their condition," and doctors should have been more aggressive in their treatment, intervening with drugs or surgery to avert the fatal attacks.[12]

The incidence of malpractice, as large and frightening as it seems to be, is even larger than the sobering statistics reveal. Patricia M. Danson, an expert on malpractice, reports that many acts of malpractice are missed because few patients injured in a negligence incident—only about one in ten, in fact—file a claim.[13] For that reason, it may be cheaper for doctors to buy insurance to cover themselves than to spend more time on each patient and problem. Physicians buy personal time when they insure themselves and, to the extent that the costs of the premiums are passed on in higher fees, patients and health insurance programs become the unknowing donors of a gift of time! In the process, care gets crowded out—a time-minus activity for the physicians.

Perhaps Billy Bones in *Treasure Island* was correct in believing that "doctors is all swabs." And so was Sir Anthony Carlisle, who once remarked, in somewhat more elegant prose, that "medicine is an art founded on conjecture and improved by murder."[14] Scary as the scene on-stage at the doctor's office may be, it is worse in the labs.

MEANWHILE, BACKSTAGE AT THE LABS . . .

Twenty cents of every medical care dollar goes for lab tests, whether electrocardiograms or CAT scans, blood cholesterol and white cell counts, or readings on diabetes and genetic flaws. Some

19 billion tests are performed each year, amounting to eighty tests "for every man, woman, and child, which surely makes Americans among the most analyzed people on the planet."[15]

Dazzling advances in computerized testing have made them possible. But are all these tests yielding information as accurate as it is exact? Although filled with numbers, lurking behind the detailed printouts that give that much desired sense of exactitude is human error: the failure of overworked and undertrained lab technicians to take the time to do the job well.

Sloppy lab work and doctors' mistakes lead to results that are often wrong or misinterpreted. Tests may actually harm patients by failing to detect serious illnesses or by indicating disease when none exists. For example, a positive Pap test in a negative case may force a patient to have a hysterectomy when one is unnecessary. A woman with cervical cancer who tests negative may die from a disease that, when caught early, minor surgery can often correct.

- Nearly half of 5,000 laboratories asked by the College of American Pathologists to test a sample for cholesterol missed the result by over 5 percent, an unacceptably large error.[16]
- About one in six labs tested by the Centers for Disease Control failed to correctly identify several common strains of bacteria and one in seven failed to classify fungal growths accurately.[17]
- One in ten hospital labs inaccurately measured blood platelets, a simple and common test of a patient's ability to form blood clots.[18]
- Doctors' office labs overlooked 18 percent of salmonella infections, and hospital labs missed 12 percent.[19]
- The Pap test, one of the most unreliable of all clinical lab procedures, misses between 20 and 40 percent of cancerous and precancerous specimens.[20]

Every year some 7,000 of the 60,000 women who develop cancer of the cervix die from the disease. The Pap smear, the major test that has been credited with sharply reducing deaths from the malady, has become an indispensable part of women's health care. Yet, if this common and curable disease is easily detected, why does the high mortality rate persist?

Investigative reporter Walt Bogdanich decided to find out, and his reports not only won him a Pulitzer Prize but prompted Congress to investigate medical tests with an eye to improving regulatory policy. What emerged from Mr. Bogdanich's visits to labs, inspections of records, and interviews with personnel was an indictment of an "industry kept afloat by overworked, undersupervised, poorly paid technicians."[21]

For the Pap, human hands and eyes do what machines do for most other tests. The work is tedious and, if done properly, time consuming. Technicians may earn as little as forty-five cents to do an analysis for which a patient is billed thirty-five dollars. Pay is based on the number of samples processed, a practice that encourages screeners in so-called Pap-mill labs to rush through the analysis. To add to the incentives for haste, many labs let their employees leave for the day when they have reached their quotas. If labs held to a maximum of 12,000 slides a year—the recommended norm—the average worker would take home under $6,000 per annum. At that low pay, many lab workers need to supplement earnings by overtime work or by moonlighting at other labs; and with all the extra work, the error rate mounts.[22]

Erroneous laboratory research may not be as dangerous as incompetent surgery, for patients' physicians frequently catch lab errors. Due to their own sloppy methods of taking samples, however, or their sloppiness in interpreting results, physicians must share the blame. Although the testing technology is dazzling, even presumably foolproof computerized results still require human interpretation and a decision whether the test is positive or negative. Yet physicians presume that if the glitzy equipment works, it will give a correct result. Not necessarily so.

About half of laboratory errors can be blamed on the methods health care professionals use to obtain Pap smears.[23] Taking the specimen is a simple procedure that involves smearing cells from the female genital tract on a glass slide which is then sent to a laboratory for analysis. Physicians often become bored with the routine procedure, and careless in taking the sample. Explains a spokesman for the American College of Obstetricians and Gynecologists, "It's possible that some people who take Pap smears get a little casual about it as the years go by."[24]

Manufacturers who are too busy become careless, and more reluctant to spend increasingly expensive time on assuring quality control and safety. Accidents that are ''their'' fault increase. As with any interesting issue, there are two sides. Consumers who are too busy also become careless, and reluctant to spend time searching for the best products and assuring the best, and safest, buy for the money. When the *BB* factor beckons, accidents that are ''our'' fault increase too. Before discussing remedies to the problems of *others* doing us in, consider how, by our hurriedness and harriedness, by our failure to take time to be careful, indeed by our own hand, *we* can do ourselves in.

21:00

MEA CULPA: THE CUSTOMER MAY NOT ALWAYS BE RIGHT

"Nullius Poeniteat . . . Festina Lente" (May no hour cause thee to regret it . . . hasten slowly)

—sundial inscription

Innocent consumers may not always be so innocent. By *their* carelessness, consumers can compound the injury created by producers' carelessness. The carelessness of producers of goods and services—whether a manufacturer, a physician, or a lab technician—results from their failure to take time to be careful. Consumers, when *they* fail to take time to be careful, also create risks. Care requires finding out all that needs to be known. That is a daunting task: a fine idea in theory but one that fails in practice when the *BB* factor urges haste, constraining the search for the best and safest. When it comes to making a purchase, there simply isn't time enough to explore the pros and cons in the vast assortment of items crowding the dealer's shelf. As the choice of offerings grows, the risk compounds in tandem, for a thorough search becomes increasingly time consuming. As a result, consumers are increasingly unable to ensure the reliability and safety of their purchases.

Advertising serves a time-stressed society in at least two ways. Of course ads try to motivate us to buy. But, by telling us what is available, ads also serve to save our time searching for just the right thing. As the *BB* factor gives that time-saving function new meaning, advertising budgets expand: in forty years, expenditures expressed in inflation-adjusted dollars have nearly quadrupled.

So that advertising can fulfill its informative function, we must assume that the sales pitch is accurate. To ensure this, we pay the government to enforce truth-in-advertising laws, and to test and certify potentially dangerous products, and to supervise their manufacture. If this fails, we can . . . ahem . . . sue. The system—the advertising industry, the government agencies, and the court—save us the time we would otherwise have to spend searching for the best and safest goods and services on the market. But how well does this system work, in fact?

HOW (AND WHERE) CONSUMERS GO WRONG

Although government tries to guarantee that manufacturers adhere to minimal standards of quality and safety, they cannot protect us from the hazards of reacting too quickly, and sometimes impulsively, in our purchasing habits. The effort required to think through shopping decisions, to carefully consider the growing range of choices, and to choose the best is just as vulnerable to the *BB* factor as is any activity requiring thought.

The *BB* factor stimulates compulsive and impulsive buying—the extremes of perverse shopping behavior—and it discourages the more rational shopper from taking the time to get the best buy. The working woman, for example, increasingly relies on brand names because comparison shopping takes too much time. For them, and for the rest of us, shopping has taken on a certain mindless quality. "People are going into debt in incredible levels without making rational decisions about how and why they are spending money," explains a psychology professor. The number of compulsive shoppers "is much, much larger—a national problem," warns an advertising professor.[1] As the extremes of perverse shopping behavior become the norm, so does the importance of providing consumers with cautions to moderate their hasty decisions at the store.

Failing to Read the Label

Rather than prohibiting substances or uses outright, the law instructs producers to furnish risk-related data about their products through standardized descriptions and warning labels that enable consumers to make their own risk assessments. Each pack of cigarettes, for instance, must carry a warning that the contents pose a significant hazard, and, for smokers who wish to pick the level of their poison, a description of the brand's tar and nicotine content. Desirable as they seem to be, instructions and cautions on labels don't matter much. Consumers—like sheep being led to the slaughter—are more likely to ignore warnings on potentially dangerous products. People don't take the time to read and heed.

At least that is the conclusion reached by researcher Roger L. McCarthy after sifting through some 400 studies that deal with the effectiveness of product warning labels.[2] Most people don't even see them.

- One hundred high school and college students were asked to drive nails with a hammer. Glued to each hammer was a label warning them not to use the hammer. All the students followed the instructor's directions; all ignored the printed warning. During interviews after the experiment, none even recalled seeing it.[3]
- As part of an intensive effort by the Consumer Product Safety Commission to reduce power lawnmower accidents, users were provided with danger stickers and detailed fact sheets, supplemented by posters and radio and television spots. Monitors discovered that the campaign was a flop. Why? Because users failed to heed the warnings, and perhaps even to read them.[4]
- Researchers who stopped and interviewed motorists after passing "curve" signs discovered that "such signs attracted little *conscious* attention." In other words, most drivers hadn't noticed them.[5]
- Fifty expectant mothers were divided into two groups and asked to install an infant restraint—"Infant Love Seats" as they are called—in a car according to instruction labels. One group's instructions included cautions, the other's did not. There was no difference in rates of errors made, suggesting that the warnings had been ignored.[6]

Despite the fact that there are over 300,000 smoking-related deaths per year, and smoking remains the nation's number one preventable cause of death and disease, federally required health warnings on cigarette packages apparently have no deterrent value. Groans the Federal Trade Commission: "the current health warning is rarely noticed and is not effective in alerting consumers to the health hazards of smoking."[7] It's simple: in the era of the *BB* factor, such admonitions are likely to go unheeded.

Failing to Take a Stitch in Time

Not only do people seem unwilling to prevent potential personal disaster by reading warning labels, they are also unwilling to take the time to prepare for potential disasters of such magnitude as fire and earthquake.

Fires kill more Americans than all other natural disasters put together and cost society $30 billion annually. Every year 6,000 Americans perish in fires and ten times that number are injured seriously enough to require medical attention. Canada and the United States register the two highest fire death rates in the world, with the U.S. figure double the world average.[8]

Fire rates are lower in countries where the time is taken to reduce risks. In Britain, with rampant pyrophobia, the BBC announcer closes each broadcast day by reminding television viewers to disconnect the set from the mains. Every outlet has a switch and school children are instructed to turn off electrical devices at that source. In Japan, where disaster-preparedness has become almost a national pastime, fire engines answering alarms are accompanied by loudspeaker-equipped PR cars which lecture the bystanders on the merits and methods of fire prevention. Fire safety programs are routinely televised. In Nagasaki, a third of housewives belong to fire prevention leagues which are responsible for spreading fire safety information to their friends and neighbors.[9] Unfortunates whose homes catch fire are socially ostracized, and public pressure often forces them to move to other neighborhoods.

To these people a stitch in time saves nine. Americans apparently prefer the nine. It is not that we are not fire-conscious, but that we have come to depend on technology to deal with the problem rather than taking our own time to minimize risks. "Americans tend to assume that fires are unlikely and that if they do occur, smoke alarms and sprinkler systems will save them. They tend to be blasé about fire safety, bored with fire drills and routine fire awareness programs," says a prominent fire consultant.[10] More precisely, Mr. Fire Consultant, for Americans preparedness and prevention take too much time.

Earthquake preparedness is no better. Sixty-one percent of Americans are fatalistic about the "Big One," believing that earthquakes would cause widespread loss of life and property whether we prepare for them or not. "Household preparedness is dismal," concludes a major study of preparedness in earthquake-prone California.[11] The researchers announced to a less-than-stunned world that about half of those surveyed had a working flashlight, battery radio, and first-aid kit somewhere in the house, but only one in ten had bought them in anticipation of the big shake. Even fewer had taken specific emergency measures like storing food and water, or rearranging cupboard contents to prevent objects from falling. Virtually no one reported being a dues-paying member of a neighborhood preparedness organization.[12]

Matters are different in other earthquake-prone areas. The Japanese are more willing to spend time getting ready for the worst. Department stores have disaster sections that vend a wide variety of emergency foods, tools, and earthquake prediction devices. The favored predictor is a catfish that many families keep in a bowl on their TV. When the fish gets nervous, it's believed, a quake is imminent.

JAPAN PREPARES FOR THE BIG ONE

At an earthquake-preparedness drill, "schoolchildren ran through tunnels of smoke with handkerchiefs over their faces and grandmothers shot fire extinguishers at collapsing plywood buildings. [Overhead] the air force pushed boxes of medical supplies out of planes and staged rescue attempts from helicopters. [The] Emperor surveyed the damage on his horse. At one of the drills, everyone who stepped up to a simulated bedroom window, flung it open and yelled 'Earthquake! Put out flames!' was given a printout showing the decibel level of the warning."

—David E. Sanger[13]

Americans, it seems, are unwilling to spend time getting ready for disaster, or any sort of contingency. In terms of the *BB* factor, taking precautions has a low **S/T**. A survey of the chief executive officers of the largest American corporations bolsters the point. Although 90 percent of the CEOs believed in the inevitability of emergencies, only half said their firm had formulated plans for dealing with a crisis like fire or earthquake. Yet contingency plans pay off. Crisis management expert Steven Fink reports that crisis-stricken companies with crisis management plans recover from the acute stages of their crises and return to business as usual two and one-half times faster than those lacking plans.[14]

WHAT CAN BE DONE

The *BB* factor shares blame for the growing numbers of product liability cases, medical malpractice incidents, and faulty medical tests. In post-tragedy investigations, the operative term "human failure," rather than technical breakdown, pops up too often to be ignored. Calling it carelessness—the unwillingness to devote enough time to a decision, an inspection, or a thought—is merely a synonym. Too-much-else-to-do crowds out carefulness, whether by producers or by consumers.

The public and private costs of bad decisions run staggeringly high. To the extent that they result from failing to take-enough-time-to-do-it-right, mistakes are bound to increase as the value of time increases. Many of the most costly mistakes could have been avoided if thinking and decision-making were not time-minus activities squeezed out by the *BB* factor.

The remedies are not simple. Until technological breakthroughs either make thinking and careful decision-making somehow high in **S/T**, or mechanize those peculiarly human activities altogether (insuring that only the "right" decisions are made), we will continue to rely for remedies on the "market," public action via new rules and regulations, or private action via the courts.

When market forces work in the right direction, negligence costs a company some of its market share. That is one form of justice which encourages producers to be more watchful in the future.

If the markets for physician care were efficient, sloppy practitioners would go out of business. Given enough data, patients could choose their doctor on the basis of his success as a diagnostician who made few, and perhaps no, errors. But few patients have access to such data.[15] Until that information becomes widely available, choices will continue to be based on slim or no evidence of a doctor's worth, and patients will usually know whether their doctor is careless only when it is too late.

When the market is as porous as it is for medics, a defensive posture is called for. Second opinions from other doctors, though requiring more of a patient's time, are one defense against shoddy medical practice and lab procedures. "Grill the doctor about each test," patients are advised. "Ask if the lab is accredited by the government or a professional group, refuse procedures that seem unneeded and insist on a retest when in doubt."[16] If prevention fails, the only cure may be that American standard: a lawsuit.

The threat of huge damage judgments should serve to induce manufacturers and service providers, including physicians, to measure their actions more carefully. That threat seems to work. Two in three corporate leaders surveyed said that the principal impact of product liability suits has been to force companies to take greater care with their products.[17] The threat of medical malpractice litigation has apparently encouraged health-care providers in the same direction. Following an eleven-year climb, the rash of lawsuits that added $12 billion a year to the nation's health bills leveled off in 1989. Then, malpractice claims dropped. Physicians and hospitals began tightening up on procedures, and presumably taking more time to get things right.[18]

In America, perhaps more than in other countries, private action seems to be the favored way to recover or prevent the costs of bad decisions. But when the markets and the courts fail to provide adequate remedy, it falls to the guardians of the public safety to expand their watchdog functions. New regulations must govern the use of safety apparatus until fail-safe mechanisms are invented to prevent careless operators from overriding them. New proficiency-testing programs to reduce the errors made in medical laboratories seem almost inevitable. Operating procedures, such as the safety checking routines followed by pilots during take-off and landing, will be stiffened.

Public action has certain advantages over individual, private recourse. For one thing, it is far more time-efficient for the Consumer Product Safety Commission, the Food and Drug Administration, the Occupational Safety and Health Administration, and the Department of Transportation to test and certify merchandise than for us to test each item. For another, if they do their work well, the regulators will protect us from unscrupulous manufacturers and vendors.

That government oversight worked in the past is evident in the data on safety in the work place. Work-place safety improved in the years after 1970 when the Occupational Safety and Health Administration started up operations. Job-related illnesses and injuries declined from 11 percent of full-time workers in 1973 to 7.6 percent in 1983; then the rate bounced back up to 8.3 in 1987.[19] Poor enforcement and reduced funding during the Reagan years were blamed for the turn-around. Consumer protection also virtually disappeared from the public agenda during these years but there seems enough evidence to restore it to the list of priorities.

New and more careful forms of regulation may be necessary, but protection of this sort requires expanding the bureaucracy and the red tape that binds it together. New operating rules and regulations, and the new agencies established to enforce them, sweep broadly, imposing restrictions on the safe as well as the unsafe, and costs on the innocent and the guilty alike. Taxpayers shoulder the burden of enforcement costs, and those who are regulated must tolerate the hassles of conformity. Whether the burdens require filling out reporting forms, satisfying inspectors, or retooling products and services, each takes time.

Which brings us back to our point of departure. Carelessness casts a broad net. The consequences of some failing to take the time to take care affect the many. Perhaps all of us. Until the incentives and technologies are discovered for restoring carefulness, we will have to depend on expensive alternatives. Taking action will involve an increasing number of cases in already overburdened courts to right the wrongs of bad decisions. Taking action will expand the public regulation of producers, and of consumers. Taking action will mean a growing number of regulations designed to protect us, and a lengthening roster of public servants charged with the onerous task of enforcing them.

Readers who believe this is a happy book just because earlier chapters were silly can ferret for their optimism elsewhere. They are reading the wrong book.

Man's tenure is merely a minute to the Earth's day, but the environmental crisis has lodged that vast day in our minds. Preserving that day will require an all-out struggle against environmental degradation. It will require deferring pleasures that we have grown accustomed to. Short of that, the only path to survival may be living out our lives huddled in rockets speeding toward Mars.

Our willingness to lengthen our time horizons by deferring pleasure will shape the nation's future, as I argue in the final chapters. Americans have set aside too few of the financial resources required to sustain future growth and maintain rank in world markets. We are losing that game, too. Many of our concerns about personal futures, the nation's future, or the planet's future reduce our understanding of the worth of time future relative to time present.

22:00
TIME FUTURE

***"Modern technology
owest ecology
an apology."
—Alan M. Eddison[1]***

The newsreels of old reminded us that "Time Marches On!" and someone-or-other observed that "time flies like an arrow, and fruit flies like bananas." A moving belt, time marches (and flies) in only one direction. Time's arrow points straight ahead, right to the future. If this were not true we could relive the past, correct past errors, and revel once again in glories long gone. If time were reversible

- we could disinvent the nuclear bomb
- buildings destroyed during the heyday of urban renewal would rebuild themselves
- great oil paintings would have disappeared back into the tubes
- the pages of books like this would once again become trees in far-off Finland
- Saddam Hussein wouldn't exist
- we could have love affairs without offending our mates because we wouldn't have met them yet.

According to Albert Einstein, all of that is possible, and it doesn't require running the movie backward. A limerick sums up the renowned scientist's "special theory":

> There was a young lady named Bright,
> Who traveled much faster than light.

She started one day
In the relative way,
And returned on the previous night.[2]

Outrageous as it seems, Prof. Einstein claimed that whatever traveled faster than light, like Ms. Bright, went backward in time. And if, on her journey, fast Ms. Bright were unlucky enough to fall into a black hole, time might slow down or stop altogether! Even scarier is economist Clifford Sharp's calculation: "a forty-year journey away from earth and then back to this planet during which we were accelerating at the same speed as the pull of earth's gravity would return us to an earth 48,000 years older than the one that we left forty years before."[3]

Because time is a moving belt, the present instant is a fleeting thing destined quickly to become history. That very assertion, dear reader, *was* read in a moment now past. The present, for that reason, is an ambiguous concept. The minute a thought which was future has become present, it has already become past.

Although little can be done about yesterday, and the present scarcely exists, much can be done today about tomorrow. We decide today to divide our time and energy between activities that

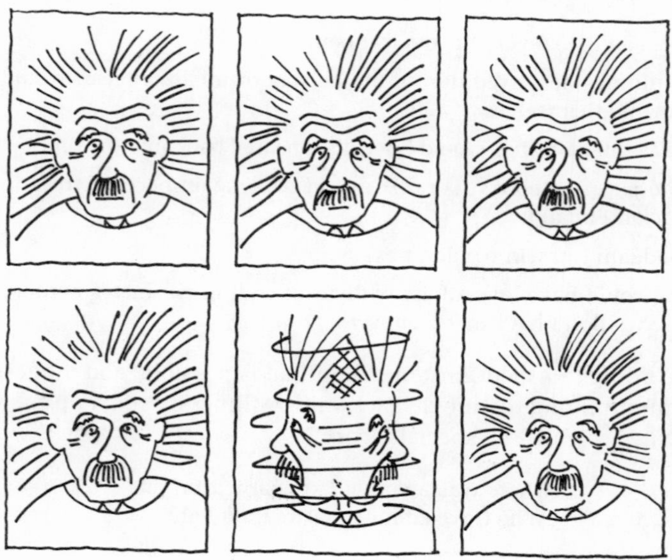

give us immediate pleasure and those that yield their rewards sometime in the future. Deciding whether to go to school, to change jobs, to maintain our homes, to bet on a horse, or to give up smoking are decisions made now with payoffs expected in the future.

Some of the most bizarre decisions are made with an eagle eye on the future. Technology makes possible freezing the sperm of those who insist on reproducing later, or freezing one's own blood for future surgery comfortable in the knowledge that the eventual transfusion is contamination-free. Some people with terminal illnesses believe that cryogenics allows them to freeze themselves until that day when medications are discovered for a cure.

The Ultimate Gift

"Saul Kent wanted to bestow the ultimate gift upon his 83-year-old mother: a new life. So when Dora Kent was near death, Saul, 48, took her to the Alcor Life Extension Foundation in Riverside (CA). There, her head was cut off and frozen in liquid nitrogen. Called cryonics, the process is based on the hope that someday scientists will be able to attach the head to a new body." The county coroner ruled the event homicide.

—*Time.*[4]

The decision to invest today in tomorrow, whether that investment is in upgrading skills, maintaining homes, freezing blood or relatives, or a host of other future-oriented decisions, turns in large part on whether we are willing to postpone benefits that we might otherwise enjoy now. The rate of *time discount,* as economists call it, is the curious device that collapses future to present. It is a "discount" because it measures how much we are willing to discount rewards received in the future compared to rewards received today.

Those with high time discount rates spend for the moment because they place great importance on the present. These "present-oriented" folks are unwilling to sacrifice current satisfaction in favor of longer-run, future considerations. Those so possessed require immediate gratification, like overeating tonight without worrying about tomorrow, or devouring the frosting before the cake.

The "future-oriented," on the other hand, willingly invest current resources in the future, even the long-range future. They will make sacrifices in today's quality of life in order to assure a higher quality of life in distant years. Low time discounts are associated, for example, with farmers who buy fertilizer today to increase crop yield, or with those of us who unwrap Christmas presents slowly. These are the types who, with long planning horizons, defer gratification for a rainy day.

A long planning horizon requires a certain amount of optimism about the future. If there were no future, there would be no reason to postpone pleasure and there would be good reason to eat, drink, and be merry, for tomorrow we die. There are equally good reasons for believing in the future, for such hopes yield rewards. For example, an optimistic attitude both eases rehabilitation from surgery and sustains sobriety in recovering alcoholics, some researchers say. Patients who recuperate faster from coronary bypass surgery have made plans and set goals for their recovery period.[5] By strategic thinking, they reckon their futures. Stress studies identify successful copers as more forward-looking, approaching life and its problems rather than avoiding them.[6] In brief, those who cope well with the present have a vision of the future and the way their time will be used.

SAVING THE PLANET'S FUTURE

Just as the quest for economic growth has done little to expand the amount of free time for enjoying the good life, the single-minded pursuit of growth also has failed to conserve many exhaustible resources for future generations. Our haste to exploit resources as a means to double per capita gross national product every generation (a feat requiring a 3 percent annual rate of economic growth) was a major ingredient in the recipe for eco-catastrophe. Grow now, raise the quality of life today, and to hell with the future, we once thought. But no more. For that transformation to take place, time future had to matter as much as, or more than, time present.

In fact, it does seem we are valuing the future more these days; or, in other words, our collective time discount seems to be falling in certain respects. Given our knowledge of the reckless ways that our forebears raped the landscape, we are coming to learn how to occupy the land today in ways which benefit those who will occupy it tomorrow. We now preserve historical artifacts so that unborn generations can enjoy the symbols and accomplishments of a past age, and we search for ways to ration exhaustible resources so that our children and theirs can also use them. We have said, in effect, that it is important for the next generations not to be deprived of the features of an increasingly endangered natural and man-made environment which have enriched our lives, and we have begun to translate that far-sighted belief into action.

The Positives

In many respects, society has faced up to the issue of vanishing resources. Some could dismiss Earth Day—the birthday of the environmental movement—as fad and the Club of Rome's gloomy predictions of a resourceless future as overblown, but the oil shortage following the 1973–74 Arab oil embargo quickly collapsed future to present. Regardless of whether we needed oil to fuel the furnaces of our homes or to power the internal combustion engines of our cars, the vague specter of an enduring resource shortage then became a hard reality. As we waited in the gas line, the thought crossed our minds that there might be something after all to the dire warnings by those prophets of doom, the environmentalists. Perhaps society and economy were dependent on a limited and exhaustible quantity of resources. Perhaps resources that lived and breathed and allowed *us* to live and breathe were vanishing. Perhaps past actions had failed to take sufficient account of the future. *Perhaps our time discount was too high.*

Just as we learned that the reserves of oil were dwindling came the discovery that the same was happening to the reserves of amphibians, birds, fishes, mammals, and reptiles populating land and sea. All told, the list of endangered and threatened species in the U.S. now comes to 462.[7] Close to home, varieties of life such as the California condor, the Florida panther, the El Segundo Blue butterfly, and fresh water mollusks, and in far-away places, the African rhino, wild cats, the scimitar-horned oryx, and the black woodpecker are threatened with disappearance altogether. Heroic efforts saved the American alligator, the red wolf, and the bald eagle (all are now doing well, thank you very much). Recently, the obituaries were written for the Palos Verde blue butterfly and the dusky seaside sparrow, the latter a casualty of Cape Canaveral's development. And the spotted owl in the Pacific Northwest faces a similar fate. Our children and grandchildren will never again see these creatures in the flesh, and the secrets for fighting diseases or improving crops that genetic materials such as these might reveal will never be known. It took awhile for the consequences of resource exploitation to become apparent, but happen it did.

Past losses and projected future losses roused us to action. Or at least raised our level of concern. A 1989 poll found that an astonishing 80 percent of those surveyed believed that "protecting the environment is so important that requirements and standards cannot be too high, and continuing environmental improvements must be made regardless of cost." That proportion has risen steadily since 1981, when only 43 percent believed as strongly.[8]

Our environmental innocence lost, we have come to behave better toward the world around us. For one thing, we have learned to take better care of the built environment, no less threatened with extinction than the natural environment. Historical buildings and structures of intrinsic architectural merit, built to serve an earlier age, have been added to the list of endangered objects and activities deemed worth protecting from the bulldozer.

The lone surviving Art Deco office building, neo-Baroque movie palace, or Victorian mansion in a town has been rescued by policy which argues that preserving endangered resources, whether natural or man-made, serves the public interest. Generous public subsidies, mixed with a healthy dose of courageous risk-taking by visionary private entrepreneurs, are transforming our private real estate into quasi-public realty and saving yesterday's built environment for tomorrow.

The positive side of the environmental ledger includes many other entries. Water use per person has dropped from an all-time high in 1975, water quality has improved, and sewage treatment has expanded. Air pollution emissions fall as abatement expenditures rise. Recycling has mushroomed; since 1960 the amount of material recovered from municipal solid waste has tripled.[9] This is only a beginning.

Complacency is misplaced, however. Today's prophets of doom warn of the effects of acid rain, a depleted ozone layer, disrupted food chains, chemical poisons, shrinking water tables, polluted water and air, mounting industrial and nuclear waste piles, and genetically altered plants running amok. These are just the sideshows, with the greenhouse effect and a nuclear winter ranking as the leading contenders for total planetary destruction. Who knows which scenario in the unfolding environmental crisis will kill us, or at least ruin our day?

The Negatives

The column of negatives on the environmental ledger—like the evil genies that flew from Pandora's box—is lengthy and growing. Despite recycling, the garbage piles continue to grow. The volume of detritus has doubled in twenty-five years. So has the production of synthetic organic pesticides.[10] Acid rain kills trees and whole forests. Algae fed by pollutants destroy marine ecosystems and kill fishes. Pesticides poison the lakes and the aquatic life that live in them. Factories dump toxic wastes into rivers and streams, imperiling drinking water supplies. Underground aquifers are being pumped dry. Smokestacks disgorge noxious gases into the atmosphere. Four decades of nuclear weapons production have polluted air, soil, and water with arsenic, cesium, chromium, mercury, PCBs, plutonium, strontium, and uranium (in short, radioactive waste). Automobiles guzzle irreplaceable oil resources and foul the air.[11] Worldwide, carbon emissions from fossil fuels have tripled since 1950.

Of all the items on the environmental agenda, none is more troubling than the notion that exhaust fumes are converting the planet into a slowly warming oven. A land area the size of New York State has been deforested in Brazil's Amazon region, fueled by the industrialized nations' appetite for beef, coffee, and wood. Carbon dioxide given off by burning the Amazon forest, added to emissions of industrial and automobile gases, has produced the global pollution that promises to become the most threatening environmental issue of the twenty-first century.

The theory holds that carbon dioxide and other "greenhouse" gases released by fossil fuel burning linger in the air and trap heat instead of allowing them to escape into space. The planet's average temperatures will warm up by as much as eight degrees. The heat will reach perilous levels within a century and set in motion a string of disasters. As the polar ice cap melts, the sea level could rise 250 feet, leading to salinized farmland, violent storms, and widespread drought, and decimating the world's flora and fauna. The rising water level would inundate Rio's beaches, Venice's canals, the Maldive Islands, the Nile Delta, much of the populated or fertile growing area bordering coastlines, and major ports the world over.

Extending our planning horizon into the future by lowering humanity's time discount rate may be the only way to compromise our predatory relationship with nature, and restore the equilibrium to an acceptable balance. Toxic wastes, acid rain, and the other pollutants that poison water, land, and atmosphere can be contained only by paying a high price today for pay-offs accruing in the distant tomorrow. The next generations will reap the benefits if research discovers alternatives to fossil fuels, but the present generation will pay the substantial front-end costs of the search. Imposing a "sin" tax on coal, for example, would encourage manufacturers to switch to cleaner fuels like methane, but would raise costs to consumers by drastically lowering industrial efficiency (much as a sin tax on disposable diapers would reduce household efficiency). Conversion to state-of-the-art technologies such as ceramic gas turbines for auto engines, more efficient turbines for electricity generation, gas-fired heat pumps, and surface wave fluorescent lights will cut carbon dioxide emissions but raise operating costs.[12] Toughened federal standards for automobile fuel economy, and government-sponsored inducements to make electricity production by utilities more efficient and reduce its consumption by homes and businesses, will run into the trillions of dollars. The U.S. share, by one estimate, could "rival the current level of military spending."[13]

SAVING OUR FUTURE: THE TIME OF OUR LIVES

Preserving the earth is one thing, preserving ourselves is another. For many centuries, the search has been on for the legendary fountain of youth that would stop the biological clock at, say, age 25. When life spans averaged only twenty-two years, as in ancient Rome, the demand was brisk for the services of a physician named Galen who advised inhaling the breath of virgins as a means to forestall death. Pope Innocent II is said to have sipped the blood of boys as a rejuvenating tonic and, more recently, fresh cells from unborn lambs have been injected into luminaries the likes of Konrad Adenauer, Charlie Chaplin, Winston Churchill, Christian Dior, the Duke of Windsor, and Pope Pius XII.[14] Deoxyribonucleic acid (DNA) may hold the hope for tinkering with the biological clock, for some believe that cells will stop aging if the DNA sends messages to repair itself. When cells stop aging, then *we* stop aging. The possibility challenges death itself.

Until virgins' breath, lambs' cells, and DNA become proven elixirs, we will have to content ourselves with more traditional remedies that have bought time, not by expanding daily hours beyond a finite twenty-four, but by learning to live longer and linger later. On that count, our scorecard is impressive. In the U.S. today, a newborn girl can expect to live seventy-nine years, and a boy seventy-two years, a bonus of five years over those born three decades ago.

Medical advances, better health care, and more healthful lifestyles have all helped to extend life. Years can be added by spending time in certain less hazardous ways, for example:

- In twenty-five years, the death rate from cardiovascular disease has been cut nearly in half as people have forsaken smoking, cut down on fat in their diets, and taken up regular exercise routines.
- People learned that those who wear seat belts cut in half their risk of dying in an auto accident. Since 1981, when states began enacting mandatory seat belt–use laws, the proportion of drivers who buckle up has jumped from 11 percent to nearly 45 percent, and the Harris Poll reports that every year another 6 percent of front seat occupants wise up.[15]
- Research linking suntans with wrinkles and, worse yet, skin cancer has shown that a healthy tan may be a misnomer; "library pallor," as its replacement is called, is in and, at pool parties these days, sun screens are passed around like gin and tonics.

Exercise and diet pay off too. Now, seven in ten adults exercise weekly, compared to only about five in ten a few years ago. Average cholesterol levels dropped from a dangerous 240 to 215 as many people switched from fatty foods like hamburgers and potato chips to the low-fat, low-cholesterol, and low-sugar foods recommended by health experts.[16] But of all the changes, perhaps kicking the smoking habit has paid the largest health dividends.

In 1492 Christopher Columbus discovered tobacco, among other things, when he became acquainted with natives who "drank smoke." As people the world over began drinking smoke, death rates from lung cancer and heart disease soared. The incidence of fatal heart attacks among middle-aged men rose steadily until the mid-1960s, then leveled off and started to decline.[17] Not coincidentally this was about the time that people in large numbers became aware of the harm done by cigarettes.

The smoking rate for the general population has fallen off 40 percent since the mid-1960s[18] when the first shots were fired in the war on smoking, and since the early '80s, about two million Americans have kicked the habit each year. The battle is yet to be won: 54 million Americans smoke over 520 billion cigarettes each year and risk turning up as one of the 400,000 annual cancer fatalities, a toll larger than deaths caused by alcohol, auto accidents, cocaine, fire, heroin, homicides, and suicides combined.

Forsaking "smoking materials," as they are referred to in airspeak on planes, pays big time dividends. Consider the arithmetic. If each cigarette shortens life by 5.5 minutes, as has been estimated,[19] smoking sacrifices 2.9 trillion minutes of life each year. By collectively giving up the habit, in one year Americans would add 5.5 million years to their collective lives (or 15,000 years for every day they smoke).

The smoking rate correlates with the values people put on their lives: the higher the value, the less likely they smoke. Forecasts put the smoking rate in the year 2000 at 30 percent of people with less than a high school education, but only 10 percent among college graduates.[20] Higher income, better educated people—those most prone to the *BB* factor—are less likely to smoke and more likely to quit if they do smoke.

The worship of health has become a fact of life. For it is one of the few, proven ways to extend the time of our lives.

We live in an increasingly imperiled natural and man-made environment. The reckless actions of the past that despoiled lakes, destroyed forests, allowed erosion to devastate the land, and punched a hole in the earth's protective shield overvalued the importance of the present. The ominous consequences of those actions may doom the future of the ecosystem for all unless ways are found to lower the time discount, and raise the value of time future compared to time present.

Individuals, operating in their own interest, have taken steps to "buy" time by extending life itself. The elixirs—whether giving up smoking, taking the time to fasten-up, or dieting for better health—require forsaking current for future pleasure. Taking those oftentimes painful decisions required individuals to lower their time discounts—the worth of time future compared to time present.

As the world struggles to preserve its fragile environment, and we struggle to preserve our personal futures, the nation faces problems severe enough to shake the very foundations of the political system which governs it. Those problems too involve the worth of time future relative to time present.

23:00

SAVING THESE UNITED STATES OF AMERICA

"Old Time is still a-flying:
And this same flower that smiles to-day,
To-morrow will be dying."
—Robert Herrick[1]

As the year 2000 rapidly approaches, the air of millennial doom hangs heavily. Something has gone wrong with the systems that govern. Eastern Europe has turned upside down and socialism has come under fire in China and what used to be the Soviet Union. In America, many are questioning the efficacy of capitalism. The U.S. has lost its position as the world's leading economic power. The public debt grows larger, the quality of the labor force declines, innovation lags, and incomes and productivity stagnate.

Although their lofty, Heavenly perch distances Adam Smith (1723–90) and his friend Carla Marks (1899–1971) from such issues, both are still much concerned with the problems of a world they left some years ago. Shall we eavesdrop on their conversation?

LESSON 1 WITH THE SMITH-MARKSES: THE PROBLEM VIEWED DIMLY

ADAM SMITH: Come in Carla. Pull up a cloud, and sit down.

CARLA MARKS: *(pulling up a cloud and sitting down)* Lousy what's going on down below, isn't it? And they haven't got the foggiest idea what to do next. I suppose *you* do, though. You always do.

SMITH: Of course. It all has to do with time discounts. Spending too much today. Setting aside too little for tomorrow. As simple as that.

MARKS: *(with just a trace of sarcasm in her voice)* My stars! Tell me more.

SMITH: Listen carefully . . . for once. The huge trade and federal deficits are hooked up directly to the high time discount that discourages people from saving. It works this way. Scarce savings raise interest rates. There are three effects. Firstly, the pricey interest rates attract foreign capital. Secondly, they discourage investment. And thirdly, investment goes to projects that pay quick and certain profits rather than to long-term projects like research and development, and educating and training the work force. Now, since such investment is needed to keep industry up-to-date and globally competitive, the productivity growth is low by international standards.

MARKS: What do you mean by productivity, Smitty?

SMITH: That's the value of what the average worker produces each year. With low growth in productivity, American-made goods can't compete in price and quality with goods made abroad where productivity has risen faster. And as imports have risen compared to exports, foreign debt has soared. Since you have to pay for everything (or at least *they* must), when the debt comes due, money flows out of the country, there is less to go around at home, and standards of living fall. Put another way, a country that is less productive than its global trading partners must compete by paying lower wages at home and that translates into a lower living standard for labor.

MARKS: It's like a family living too high on the hog, isn't it? Pray tell, why are Americans buying so much from abroad?

SMITH: Because foreign-made goods are cheaper and higher quality, and the reason for that goes back to productivity. Offshore producers have won the competitive edge by raising productivity faster. They make the investments necessary to increase productivity because borrowing costs them less.

MARKS: You've said that before.

SMITH: I know, but I'm summarizing just to hammer home the point and introduce another.

MARKS: You weren't a professor for nothing, you sly old devil.

SMITH: May I proceed?

MARKS: Please do. I won't interrupt.

SMITH: The internationalization of capital has also changed how and where business is conducted. We often prefer foreign-made goods because of their superior quality, but the service that is a part of the package may be *vastly* superior.

MARKS: Is that why we see names like Fuji film, Barclays and Mitsubishi Banks, and Lloyd's appearing on the skylines of our cities?

SMITH: They have succeeded in invading U.S. markets because of their greater know-how. They know how to provide the kinds of services that Americans once, but no longer, provide. You see, it all goes back to the savings rate, the willingness of people to set aside part of their incomes they otherwise could spend today. Those savings, whether in institutions or even in stocks and bonds, become available to industry to invest. You can do only two things with the money you earn—spend it today, or save it to spend tomorrow. When people spend too much currently, too little is left for saving. And that's just what they're doing.

MARKS: I don't see why they should save at all. Why not spend, spend, spend?

SMITH: Spend, spend, spend is what's gotten the nation in trouble. Two hundred years ago I wrote about how we are creatures with inextinguishable wants that are played out in the marketplace; we worship in the cathedrals of mass consumption.

MARKS: You're mixing metaphors again.

SMITH: *(Oblivious, Smith goes to a bookshelf, finds* The Wealth of Nations, *rifles through the pages until he comes to pp. 324–25).* Here it is. . . . *(Reads:)* "the desire of bettering our condition . . . comes with us from the womb, and never leaves us till we go into the grave. In the whole interval which separates those two moments, there is scarcely perhaps a single instant in which any man is so perfectly and completely satisfied with his situation, as to be without any wish of alteration or improvement."[2]

MARKS: Heavens, I'm glad *we're* past that phase up here.

SMITH: *They're* not down there. In the throes of satisfying their personal gratification, an overriding dedication to materialism, hedonism, . . .

MARKS: Oh, cut it out, lamb-chop.

SMITH: But it's true! It's true because of American's high time discount.

MARKS: I hope you've got some facts and figures to back up all of that fancy theorizing.

SMITH: I do, but let's put it off till tomorrow.

MARKS: I can't wait.

LESSON 2: THE SHORTFALL IN INVESTMENT

SMITH: You've brought along your harp.

MARKS: I did, muffin. I have to practice. If you don't mind, I'll strum and pluck while we talk. *(Begins strumming and plucking harp.)*

SMITH: Splendid. I approve wholeheartedly of your synchronous use of time. Now, where were we? . . . *(No response, except some tuning up of the strings)* . . . I just wanted to know if you'd remembered. Well, *I* have. This is evidence day, a time for the facts and figures behind the theory that runs from the time discount to chaos of international scope. Consider that America has lost its dominant position as a world leader, and growth industries like microelectronics, robotics, and auto manufacturing have been lost to Japan and Asia's other miracle economies, and even to Europe's venerable industrial nations. Yet investors in nations where people save more—and have lower time discounts—saw the States as a good place to invest partly because interest rates were higher, and that means that the cost of capital was higher, and . . .

MARKS: . . . cost of capital, cupcake?

SMITH: That's how much businesses must pay for the funds needed to finance a project, like buying a new piece of equipment that increases productivity by boosting labor's output. At any rate, pricey capital attracted foreign investors like flies to honey. Encouraged by high returns, they rushed in with their capital to fill up the thirsty reservoir. That fact accounted in large part for the massive investments from abroad in Stateside enterprise and real estate, for to lend foreign capital in America was to make more than lending at home. And America was seen as a safe place to sock away capital. All well and good, but sooner or later the Piper must be paid. When the bill comes due, the U.S. must pay the interest on its borrowings, and those payments go abroad instead of staying in the country. With less and less to go around at home, the standard of living falls. Argentina, Brazil, Mexico, and Venezuela, the four biggest debtors in the Third World, made that discovery in the 1980s when their income per person shrank under the weight of extraordinary debt burdens. Though the U.S. standard of living is unrivaled in the world, it has declined compared to other industrial nations since 1970[3] and may go the way of Latin America.

MARKS: What can Americans do to prevent that from happening, my chocolate cake?

SMITH: It depends in large part on productivity, and Americans are doing poorly on that count. So you see, over the long haul, rising productivity determines how well people live. If productivity doesn't grow, wages don't grow. In fact, wages corrected for inflation haven't grown since 1973.

MARKS: Whew, that was complicated. But, cookie, what's the problem with our productivity?

SMITH: Too little investment. Overall growth in productivity requires investment in physical capital and in education. "People with better tools and equipment produce more," as one economist puts it. "People with better education think of ways of improving either the tools or the way they are used."[4] Most investments take a long time to pay off and Americans haven't the patience these days to wait. The people in your United States seem to have forgotten the truism that investment is the engine of economic growth.

MARKS: And why, cream puff, have Americans invested so little?

SMITH: As capital gets more expensive, less will be borrowed for investing, even when investment is necessary as a means to remain competitive. Since savings feed the capital supply, when savings are scarce, capital costs dearly.

MARKS: And why are savings scarce, dare I ask, dear professor?

SMITH: To save requires a low time discount rate—we keep returning to that point, don't we?—for we must be willing to defer the pleasure of spending the money until some day in the future. *(Aside, to audience:* Ah! Time intrudes into the logic. As it always does.)

MARKS: We? You mean them. *We* don't have to worry about complexities like that anymore.

SMITH: Happily, no. But *they* do. Expensive capital is causing American business to invest in quick-payback projects. Take the case of the declining steel industry that failed to invest in the new technologies required to upgrade its production. When the basic oxygen furnace and continuous casting came on line for modernizing operations, scarce capital deferred their adoption. These were long-run investments and the decision-makers were concerned about short-run profits.

MARKS: No long-term projects on the must-do list. Right, my Scottish scone?

SMITH: "Time-expensive" projects don't make the list. The Japanese take the opposite tack. "You may never be able to compete with us," says Messrs. Akio Morita and Shintaro Ishihara in *The Japan That Can Say "No."* "We are focusing on business ten years in advance, while you [the United States] seem to be concerned with profits ten minutes from now."[5] They're correct. For example, four in ten U.S. companies extract their profits from investments in technology within three years. The Japanese give projects more time—five, six years, and more—to become profitable.[6] Yet, the MIT Commission on Industrial Productivity discovered that "successful firms both in this country and abroad tend to accept longer payback periods and see innovation as part of their competitive edge."[7] But American business doesn't undertake the investments with long payback periods when capital costs are high. You, my dear, are a case in point. How long did it take you to learn the harp before you had the courage to play in public? How much do you practice before a concert? There's the quality issue too. You could play *Chop Sticks* even without practicing. But learning Ravel's *Introduction and Allegro* requires hours. You're not playing *Chop Sticks,* are you?

MARKS: No. And I'd better get to work. I've got a few notes to learn for the recital. Can we carry on tomorrow? *(Exits with harp.)*

LESSON 3: THE CONSEQUENCES OF UNDERINVESTMENT

(Marks arrives, again with harp in tow.)

SMITH: Have you learned your notes?

MARKS: Yes, and fingered my passages. The Allegro is tough going, but I love fast movements. Today, let's talk about speed. Are Americans speedy, love-dove?

SMITH: Compared to their competitors who have learned the secrets of shortening product-development cycles, no. The Japanese and Koreans are able to plan, design, and build a new blast furnace for producing steel in two to three years, compared to four or five years in the U.S. Japanese auto makers take about 3.5 years to get cars from conception to the showroom. American companies take over five years. That puts the Japanese manufacturer a year and a half closer to the consumer.[8]

MARKS: Why are they speedier, honey-bun?

SMITH: Developing tight and cordial linkages with suppliers and distributors removes bottlenecks, ensures flexibility, stimulates innovations, improves quality, and speeds things up. Close contacts with customers are essential to know today what customers will need tomorrow; close contacts with suppliers are essential to make sure orders arrive on time.

MARKS: Why can't Americans do that?

SMITH: Developing long-term commitments and loyalties takes time, and is slow to pay off. Hence, American business firms tend to deal with customers and suppliers at arms length.

MARKS: Examples please, gum-drop.

SMITH: Honda discovered the importance of these linkages when it mounted its hugely successful campaign to penetrate the U.S. auto market. Between 1965 and 1980, the fifteen-year period when it geared up for the big shove, Honda's return on assets dropped sharply from 9 to 3 percent, so vast were the sums they were spending up front to promote their product and establish distribution channels. By the mid-1980s, Honda's return had gone back up to it's initial level and the $400 million company had grown into a $20 billion enterprise. Linkage-development cost dearly in the short run but soon paid off handsomely.

MARKS: How about another for-instance?

SMITH: Take NEC, the giant Japanese electronics firm. Before starting production, Chairman Koji Kobayashi took his time to carefully sort out the distribution channels—a very different approach from strategies pursued by American firms when they launch a new product line. Before introducing his microcomputer, Mr. Kobayashi spent a year developing personal contacts with software developers, retailers, and users. By learning the marketplace, he gained first-hand knowledge of potential suppliers and customers. He set up demonstration centers to feature his equipment. The centers sell no computers, but merely teach prospective customers about NEC products. Customers then buy at discount stores. The novel approach enables NEC to distribute through simple retail stores and requires minimal technical know-how of its sales personnel. A long time horizon, coupled with a commitment to spend money up front and get things right from the beginning, paid off handsomely. The firm now claims over 70 percent of Japan's personal computer market.[9]

MARKS: *(sneaking a quick glance at her watch)* Haven't we strayed just a bit from the major issue, capital costs, and how they are affected by the time discount rate?

SMITH: We have. That will head tomorrow's agenda. Agreed?

LESSON 4: WHY CAPITAL COSTS SO MUCH

MARKS: The topic of "expensive capital" brings us back to our starting point. Right, buttercup?

SMITH: Right, as always. Time plus the time discount enter as a key explanation. When the time discount is high, savings are low, and borrowing capital is costly. That's the situation America faces today.

MARKS: What's it like in other nations, dew-drop?

SMITH: Elsewhere, capital costs less. Large American firms may pay two to three times for capital what Japanese firms pay. For good reason, pricey capital forces a shorter time horizon on the U.S. firms compared to their major competitors in Japan.[10] We talked about that a couple of days ago.

MARKS: Right.

SMITH: And capital is pricey when savings are short.

MARKS: You've said that before, sugarplum.

SMITH: For many years, Americans' rate of savings has been lowest among the advanced countries. The Belgians, Canadians, French, Japanese, and West Germans save at over double the rate of Americans.[11] And matters are getting worse. Truly, the 1980s was the spree decade. The net U.S. savings rate since 1982 has been under one-third of the 1950–81 average[12] and consumer debt has grown by $2.60 for every $1 increase in total output. That's just the opposite of countries with lower time discounts, where output exceeds consumption.[13] Such irresponsible behavior initiates a vicious downward spiral. The Americans' penchant for overspending for today and undersaving for tomorrow depletes the pool of capital for investment, increases the cost of investment, and discourages the investment that improves labor productivity. As productivity falls, so do wages. Eventually there is less to spend and save. So the cause of the problems is largely the low savings rate or, in now familiar terms, too high a value on spending money today, or too large a time discount.

MARKS: There it is again. Why don't Americans sock away more dollars?

SMITH: They are too much concerned with time present and too little concerned with time future: a key that unlocks the problem of their deteriorating world economic position.[14] It's as simple as that.

MARKS: I hope you have some ideas for solving the problem that you have so elegantly set out. I hope . . .

LESSON 5: SOLVING THE PROBLEM

MARKS: O ye Father of Political Economy, tell me and tell Heaven, and shout to Earth below how you would curb the Americans' urge to splurge!

SMITH: That will take time. (*again, an aside:* But one high in **S/T**.) Let's start straight away. Encourage saving for tomorrow by discouraging consumption today. A sharp rise in savings is the *sine qua non* for maintaining both U.S. standing in the world economy and the quality of life.

MARKS: Easier said than done, O purveyor of the blessed and magical balm. How do you propose translating this apt bit of knowledge into action?

SMITH: To make consumption less attractive requires persuading the public to sacrifice some current for future pleasures. A revealing poll finds that three in four consumers have satisfied most material wants.[15] Perhaps we are reaching the point of satiation . . . *(Suddenly a stentorian voice is heard from above. Lo! It is John Stuart Mill speaking from a neighboring—and higher-placed—cloud)*.

MILL: . . . That's my line. I said it years ago. I maintained that human needs for material things were limited. If I'm correct, Mr. Veblen's wrong.[16] And you know where he is!

SMITH: Where? *(Mill, unhearing, and having spoken his piece, drifts away on his cloud)*.

MARKS: *(to Smith:)* Rumors have it that Mr. Veblen's not among us fortunate ones. Alas, he's gone to his reward in the *other* place.[17]

SMITH: At any rate, if most have fulfilled their material wants, as Mr. Mill said, why do they keep borrowing like mad to buy when they could delay some gratification?

MARKS: Beats me. But you should know, prof.

SMITH: One belt-tightening remedy would be a national sales tax. Like the value-added tax levied in Europe, it would tax consumption.

Taxing consumption, but not the rest of income, would encourage households to spend less and save more. Tax increases, though politically unpopular in the short-term, would also reduce the federal deficit and cut costs of capital.

MARKS: Taxes! Why not think positively, O harbinger of happiness and respite?

SMITH: Favoring saving is the other side of the coin. The federal tax structure could be changed. Subsidies like the favorable treatment of Individual Retirement Accounts and investment tax credits that encouraged people and businesses to invest in the future could be reconsidered. Proposals like the Family Savings Account, which allows a family to set aside income in a long-term savings account that pays tax-free interest, could stimulate personal saving. More favorable tax treatment for profits distributed as dividends and less favorable treatment for interest expenses (which encourage borrowing) are other possibilities.

MARKS: O savior of princes and others, you made a big thing of my investment in learning to play the harp well? Shouldn't we be investing more resources into training workers and educating children, even those who don't want to learn the harp? Can you say something profound about that?

SMITH: Of course. If productivity is to rise, we must discover how to upgrade labor, too. That's not an easy task since costly capital doesn't favor human resources investments because they take too long to pay off. Still, today's productivity depends on humanware investments made in the past. Unless workers' capabilities can be upgraded and they can be trained to adapt to the technologies and more flexible factories of tomorrow, your industrial muscle will grow even flabbier and the world will pass you by. Over 40 percent of jobs created in the U.S. through the end of the century will be "high skill" jobs, as against just 24 percent of existing jobs. Twenty-three million Americans are now considered functional illiterates.[18] With so many new workers lacking even the most basic skills, doesn't it seem obvious that employers and government must worry about training and retraining?

MARKS: How about kids in school? After all, they're tomorrow's workers. Shouldn't the battle to improve global competitiveness be waged in the classroom as on the factory floor?

SMITH: Performance in the three R's is worsening, as so many surveys show.[19] The drop in skills in recent years, as measured by the fall in test scores, costs the economy over three percent of its real gross national product.[20] The fact that skills have dropped so drastically, and pulled down productivity growth with it, indicates underinvestment in schools and skill-building. The time has come to regain the vision of your nation's founding fathers who saw education as an instrument for democratization and the fuel under the national melting pot.

MARKS: Let's get back to consumerism, O charmer of the outward hatchments of the soul. It makes people happy to buy things, doesn't it?

SMITH: The people in the industrialized countries, particularly the profligate Americans, are commoditizing like crazy. They seem to have to as a way to raise the **S** of their activities, of making the most of their time, as we know from observing the Gnomons in New Halcyon. Americans wouldn't demand phone answering machines for their BMWs, word processors for their homes, Rolex watches for telling time, $80 athletic shoes for running, and the other talismans of the moment, if there weren't good reason. The demand for these and other goods operates with particular vitality when time is an underlying cause. Time scarcity is partly to blame for "now nowism" isn't it?

MARKS: O perpetrator of the magnitude of greatness, do you think your advice will help restore the economy to world preeminence?

SMITH: Let me summarize with this: stimulate the savings that stimulate investments that stimulate productivity, for high savings and high economic growth go hand-in-glove. We need to take very seriously the findings and recommendations of the experts who discovered that "the most successful firms have a long-term outlook, emphasize research, stress quality, have a strong market orientation, and work closely with potential customers."[21] These are the strategies that we have discussed and they all get short shrift when the rate of time discount, and the cost of capital, are high. America's continued failure to invest in its future, spending too much instead on defense and consumption, will cause the nation to slip from hegemony. Continuing along that path, the nation is destined to be overtaken by those with a different set of priorities. I once said, "there is a lot of ruin in a nation." I still believe it. Shall we conclude on that somber note?

24:00
TIME'S UP

***"What is this life, if full of care,
We have no time to stand and stare?"
—William Henry Davies[1]***

To most of us, time—like the mercy of God—passeth all understanding. Even to the venerable scholar, St. Augustine, time was a mystery. "What is time?" he asked himself. "If no one asks me, I know. If I want to explain it to a questioner, I do not know."[2] The tortured ponderings of scientists, philosophers, theologians, and people of other stripe have led them but a short distance from St. Augustine's question. Comparing the ultra-abstraction of time with more concrete notions of space, interpreting time as a fourth dimension, contrasting physical with mental time, or ignoring "now" and explaining time as the interval between momentary states of mind only seemed to amplify the confusion. Even clocks that "told" time told little about its meaning, only that time marches on. In the final analysis, we were content to conclude that God only knows what time is. Time defied definition, like hunger or gravity, a mystery to be experienced but not comprehended. Or was it?

The concept of *what time is* bewildered, so utterly confoundingly abstract it was in the *absolute*. However, in *relative* terms—like past, present, and future—time took on meaning for all. History, it is understood, enlightens the past for the benefit of the present. The future, it is also understood, takes on meaning with an appreciation of the long-term consequences of current decisions. The periodic rebuilding of a celebrated Japanese shrine snaps together both past and future in the instant of a single event. Perhaps time could be controlled by being "stopped."

How to Stop Time

"The way to stop time, the Japanese discovered, is by letting it have its own way. Just as the shape of nature is observed, revered, so is the contour of time. Every twenty years—and for over a thousand years—the shrine at Ise is razed and a new one is erected on an adjacent plot reserved for that purpose. After only two decades, the beam-ends barely weathered, the copper turned to palest green, the shrine is destroyed. Only twenty generations of spiders have spun their webs, only four or five generations of swallows have built their nests, not even a single blink has covered the great staring eye of eternity—yet down come the great cross-beams, off come the reed roofs, and the pillars are carted off to be reused in other parts of the shrine grounds. On the adjacent plot is constructed a shrine that is in all ways similar to the one just dismantled. More, it is identical. Something dies, something is born, and the two things are the same. This ceremony, the *Sengushiki,* is a living exemplar of the greatest of religious mysteries, the most profound of human truths. And time at last comes to a stop. Forever old, forever new, the shrines stand there for all eternity. This—and not the building of pyramids or ziggurats, not the erection of Empire State Buildings or Tokyo Towers—is the way to stop time and thus make immortal that mortality which we cherish."

—Donald Richie[3]

In other ways too, relative time carries more meaning than absolute time. We may not know what Time is, but all of us know what Too Much Time and Too Little Time are. And changes in too much or too little both fall within our realm of comprehension. We know too the consequences of a surfeit or shortage of this presumably most fixed of all resources. We easily grasp what is meant by a surfeit of time—"whatever will I do with it; I'm so bored"—because at one time or another we have all experienced it. Or of time-shortage—"however will I get everything done; I'm so busy."

Expanding time provokes worries about how to put the surplus to good use. Shrinking time—the central concern of this book—evokes concerns about how to get by with the lesser amounts. Most of us belong in the latter camp, fretting over having to make do with what seems to be an ever-shortening day, week, and year. With so many more things to do, time passes too fast. We suffer the curse of the *BB* factor, our mantra in this book. Although twenty-four hours indeed remain twenty-four hours, the scarcity of time comes from the ever-enrichened menu of options from which to choose, not from the fact that enjoying any one of the options takes longer than it did "before."

Faced with ever more options, we become perplexed. It would be easier not to have to choose among a growing number of different activities, but choose we must when finite time imposes unyielding limits. Squeezing a new activity into the daily routine requires finding out how to tease more time-efficiency from the schedule of "to-do's," or paring the list. Either way, "time-minus" activities become less important in our lives, and eventually they yield to the "time-plus" activities which assume greater importance. It has been this book's focus to identify which activities gain and which lose, and the consequences for us and for the societies in which we live.

To recall: The winning activity appeals because the amount of satisfaction (**S**) gained from the amount of time (**T**) expended to produce the satisfaction increases faster than the **S**-relative-to-the-**T** of alternate time-uses. By the same token, the losing activities drop out because their **S/T**s fall, or remain unchanged, or at least fail to rise as rapidly as for alternate contenders.

The highest-ranking activities are those that individuals undertake primarily for personal reward. *Self-serving activities* like eating out, exercising, personal care, home entertainment, and attending certain arts activities like high-tech musicals make the time-plus list. Innovations and inventions—sometimes quite bizarre—seem to have saved sex, though the future of romance is in doubt. Other activities are abandoned in the reshuffling because methods and commodities are yet to be discovered that will enhance them. The *BB* factor also explains the impending demise of some forms of entertainment and of religious endeavor. These too must be relegated to the time-minus column.

The most serious effect of increasing time scarcity—the *BB* factor for short—is the threat it poses to the activities that serve others, close and distant alike. Scarce time is better used, so the self-interested among us will admit, for serving oneself rather than others. Little did a teenage business tycoon, who runs a home-based bicycle repair shop in upstate New York, realize that he spoke (more generally than grammatically) for perhaps the majority when he claimed that he was so busy he hadn't "enough time to find the people to give to."[4]

When time grows short, self-serving wins out over other-serving. For that reason, the list of time-minus other-serving activities is far longer than the list of time-minus self-serving activities (and one searches in vain for any time-plus other-serving activities at all). Many traditional forms of leisure, courtesy, socializing, volunteering, voting, and caring for others fall into the time-minus column. Providing quality professional and personal services, for example—and thinking, too—are on the wane. The decline in some other-serving activities poses personal risks, especially the lack of care given to careful decision-making in private and public realms, engineering and design for safety, and certain professional actions taken to minimize the risk to innocent clients, whether they be doctors' patients or airline passengers. Such is not as matters *should* be. Such is, however, the way matters *are*.

Time-budget data collected periodically since 1965 by John Robinson show similar trends. As the 5,000 Americans surveyed became more time-pressed, Professor Robinson discovered, the personally rewarding self-serving activities gradually replaced the other-serving. Those whose lives are most hectic devote a greater proportion of time to washing and grooming themselves, to active sports participation, to attending certain arts events, and to engaging in organizational functions—"with the exception of attending church services." They meanwhile commit fewer hours to dining with the family at home, to writing letters or reading, and to involvement in social activities like visiting friends or relatives and partying.[5]

Alienation is one inevitable result of our increasing aversion to allocating time to the service of others. Choosing to distance oneself from others fates a deepening sense of detachment. Pollster Louis Harris finds that indeed to be true. "In the frenetic environment into which most Americans are now thrust, where the pressures are immense to get many things done in too little time, it is obviously difficult at best to feel a sense of having deep roots, of belonging, and of making a contribution to the larger community in which one lives," he writes. "A substantial 60 percent of the adult public felt this sense of alienation, up sharply from only 29 percent who felt that way twenty years ago."[6]

The feasts of consumption that we gorge on have not only shifted our time uses toward the self-satisfying and away from the other-satisfying, they have also shortened our time horizons. With our predilection for counting today for too much and tomorrow for too little, we have put aside too few of the financial resources required for investment in the future. The nation suffers from the lack of resources required to sustain future growth and maintain rank in world markets, a risky position in a hypermodern world of global interdependence. In a few short years, our relative share of the world economy will be less than half what it was forty years ago, a slip from prominence that endangers the quality of life for a population that still boasts the highest standard of living in the world.

The United States may be the richest country of all, but if Americans refuse to postpone more of today for tomorrow, they will never be able to replenish the dwindling pool of savings and mobilize the long-range resources required to boost productivity and maintain position as a technological giant; or to finance the education that will equip labor for productive roles in an environment of unprecedented competitiveness; or to rebuild the network of bridges, dams, highways, harbors, railroads, sewage systems, tunnels, waterways, and other elements of the nation's infrastructure; or to mount an effective war on drugs or rebuild cities and industries; or to protect the planet against acid rain, toxic wastes, the depletion of the ozone layer, and other scourges on the environmental agenda. Achieving those goals will require people to sacrifice the rewards of immediate consumption, and business to sacrifice the higher returns on short-term investments.

At least as menacing as the threat to environment and nation is the peril that time reallocation creates for the welfare of society and ourselves as individuals. This is a more subtle danger, but more intractable. It is far easier to mobilize the powerful tools of public policy to boost the savings rate, accumulate capital, and generate the resources to deal with deficits, than it is to alter the self-serving actions of a society relentlessly bent on reallocating time in the name of personal efficiency. To make the point, let us return full circle to the beginning of this book.

For good or bad, it was widely believed that economic development would ineluctably lead to new-found freedoms. Mankind's pursuit of money, that "disgusting morbidity," as John Maynard Keynes termed it, would give way to his "permanent problem—how to use his freedom from pressing economic cares, how to occupy the leisure . . . to live agreeably and wisely and well."[7] History has borne out a part of Lord Keynes's prediction. In little more than a half century, the American standard of living has trebled, consumption has risen by even more, and people are borrowing like crazy in order "to live agreeably," which is to say, to buy what they might easily postpone. With affluence, mankind has awakened to the luxury of finding the best ways "to occupy the leisure." So it is believed.

Americans' confidence in future progress has flowed from the belief that the parade of technology, marching in lock-step with economic development, has fueled—and will continue to fuel—material growth, and underwrite sweeping social progress. We have something of a technological fixation. To be sure, the benefits of a profoundly enhanced capability in science and technology are visible in every corner of human life: in agriculture and food supply, in medicine and public health, in transportation and communication, on television and in print, in home and work place, in city and countryside. "No previous generation has had so much of the world at its doorstep," remarks Louis Harris, "so many opportunities to travel to places other generations never dreamed of visiting, such affluence as Americans have today."[8] Technology has become an article of faith.

In the past several decades, a growing awareness of the downside of technology has shaken that faith. The blind embrace of technology has brought side-effects like resource depletion, environmental degradation, new forms of disease, and the awesome risks of weapons technology. In more subtle ways, technology has also altered social and human relationships, diminishing their importance by decreasing the time given them.

Many Americans believed that dramatic developments in technology would eventually usher in an age of utopia. Innovations have raised the **S** and lowered the **T** of some activities, but not all. Technology can do little if anything to speed up a Mahler symphony or a church service, or to enhance them very effectively. But technology can speed travel, create more vivid home entertainment, and even build up our bodies quickly and effortlessly. Yet the obsession with technology has been worked out unevenly. Self-serving activities have prospered and displaced the many other-serving activities that seem less amenable to the layering-on of technology. Can technology augment the joys of volunteering, aiding the aged, or most of a host of other activities that largely serve others, distant or near?

Let's look at some of the individual choices made at the behest of the *BB* factor. Notice how the very technologies and goods that bought us new time move us toward social isolation:

- We prefer watching a film alone on the VCR to watching it in a cinema with others.
- We prefer viewing political campaigns on a television screen rather than in person at a rally.
- We prefer speaking over the phone rather than talking face-to-face, and a short message left on the answering machine beats a conversation.
- We prefer working at home, hooked up only electronically to the office where other people are.
- We prefer transactions with the electronic bank teller rather than with the human equivalent behind the counter.
- We prefer making our purchases from mail-order catalogues to buying in a crowded shopping center.
- We prefer solo exercising in a technologically advanced home gym instead of with others at the neighborhood "rec" center or the health club.
- We prefer playing games with computers rather than with companions.
- We prefer the sharp anonymous retort rather than asking rude others what irks them.
- We prefer seeing a psychiatrist counseling patients on the afternoon soap opera to helping friends with their problems.
- We prefer a good cry alone rather than on the shoulder of a friend.

These preferences toward which we are shifting, in tandem with the parade of new technologies, give cause to social historian Barbara Ehrenreich's observation that, over the years, American culture has moved "toward a moral climate that endorsed irresponsibility, self-indulgence, and an isolationist detachment from the claims of others—and endorsed these as middle-class virtues and even as signs of 'health.' "[9] Some would question the state of health. Analysts point out how often they hear patients with laments like, "we don't socialize as much as we used to." "Parties? They're almost things of the past." "I'm so lonely. Why am I so depressed?"[10]

We have turned away from emotionally fulfilling activities like interactions with friends that knit together the social fabric for support, because they are non-commoditizable aspects of life. We turn toward the television, the computer, and the other products of the electronic era that enhance time expenditure and spread couch-potato blight. We would rather interact with machines than with a natural and social environment that resists commoditization. Our preferences have been revealed:

- We prefer watching TV to watching a sunset.
- We prefer hearing music in the background rather than sitting down and really listening to it.
- We prefer dashing between car and take-out restaurant to grab hot dogs and videos to dashing down the street or around the block.
- We prefer walking on an electronic treadmill to walking in the park.
- We prefer driving a car to walking . . . anywhere.
- We prefer a short to-the-point sound bite rather than in-depth reporting.
- We prefer instant foods to those prepared with care.
- We prefer buying fully developed plants at a nursery to sowing seeds and watching them grow.
- We prefer just about anything to taking time to ponder our lives.

In short, we prefer the commoditized and time-efficient alternative, even when (and maybe because) it requires an isolated detachment from the claims of others. Pity that that is so, for some aspects of life—perhaps the most important ones—cannot be improved by commoditization, nor can they be compressed in time.

Someone who asked the secret of the lush lawns at Versailles was told that the answer was simple: they only required daily watering for three hundred years. Watching sunsets, strolling in the park,[11] wandering in the mountains, basking at the beach, making and keeping friends, love affairs, cooking gourmet meals, contemplating the meaning of life—in short, listening to the birds sing: these are the casualties of the *BB* factor.

Readers who come to this story from the political right will decry the loss of social values, the flight from family life, the unmet

obligations to children and to elders, the eroded responsibilities to neighbors and clients, and the loosened bonds of authority that are the outcomes of choices made in the name of time-efficiency. In a similar spirit, those in the leftist camp will find fresh evidence supporting their case against a capitalist system which offers a relentlessly enlarging cornucopia of material temptations that bid away time resources otherwise spent in volunteering for the common good, in discharging the obligations inherent in a democratic society to vote intelligently, and in fostering the other norms of social responsibility that also seem to be the consequences of self-interested choices motivated by time-efficiency. Those in the political middle may simply remind readers of both persuasions that these are the outcomes of choices made by individuals who seek to enhance the use of their time in the most personally rewarding ways. With a shrug of their shoulders, they will claim: we brought it on ourselves.

The question that all of us must address, whether on the right or left or in the middle of the road, is whether the relentless pursuit of time-efficiency is really worth the consequences. Surely the capitalist system that produces the goods that help us rationalize our time commitments is bigger and richer as a result. We must at least *think* that *we* too are better off, or else why would we demand those goods, and shift time-uses accordingly? Is society better off after we have made our time-reallocations? As technology shifts activities from other-serving to self-serving, others—ranging from our close friends to the nation—must lose out. That, if true, supports the view of those social critics who lament the rise of self-indulgence and isolation. And for the gloomy prognosticators' predictions of national decline.

As we move from the 1990s and on into the '00s, it seems inevitable that time scarcity will continue on its course, pointed in the direction of the activities that serve *us* rather than *them,* and which sever the connections between ourselves and others. As time marches toward the millennium, we wonder. . . .

Those who occupy that future will look back and ponder the apparent insanity of their forebears who watched a sunset, strolled aimlessly in the park, dined leisurely with the family, played with their kids, chatted with an elderly relative . . . and listened to the birds sing. In their primitive way, they resisted the temptations to layer onto these most precious of endeavors the technological wonders that had become commonplace in the now-present, but were certain to become the primitive artifacts of a future society.

They enjoyed their leisure unaided by a radio playing in the background. They basked at the beach without a boom-box. They thought a complicated issue through to its conclusion unaided by a computer. The letters they wrote to nearly forgotten friends were delivered by a human being, not by a fax machine. They visited with their neighbor without aid of a telephone. They hiked, not drove, through the countryside. They spent the weekend just reading for the pleasure of it, rather than watching the flickering images on a television. They spent an evening at home helping the kids with their math lessons, rather than writing memos on their PCs. They left home without presetting the timer on the microwave oven, without filling the automatic dog/cat feeder, without arming the burglar alarm, or without triggering the phone answering machine. What a curious lot of have-nots they were. We have no time for those uncommoditized down-scale time-costly pursuits. Perhaps, we wonder, there was something to it (even though the *BB* factor denies it). Perhaps, someday, we will return to their ways. Perhaps.

Time will tell.

NOTES

Introduction

1. Staffan Linder, *The Harried Leisure Class*. New York: Columbia University Press, 1970.

1:00. Gifts of Time

1. *Richard II*, V.v.49.
2. Suzy Menkes, *The Windsor Style*. Topsfield, MA: Salem House, 1987.
3. N. John Hall, *Trollope: A Biography*. New York: Clarendon/Oxford, 1991.
4. Jean Roy, notes for *Messe Solennelle*, by Gioacchino Rossini. New York: Musical Heritage Society, no date.
5. James MacLachlan, "What People Really Think of Fast Talkers," *Psychology Today, 13*, 6 (November 1979), pp. 113–17.
6. "A 20% speedup means that a 36-second commercial can be made that will run in 30 seconds—and 6 seconds is worth $20,000 on a popular evening program." MacLachlan, pp. 116–17.
7. Paul J. Bach and James M. Schaefer, "The Tempo of Country Music and the Rate of Drinking in Bars," *Journal of Studies on Alcohol, 40*, 11 (November 1979), pp. 1058–89.
8. Peter Holland, "Whistling All the Way Home," *Times Literary Supplement*, December 8–14, 1989, p. 1364.
9. "Please Turn Off the Dog," *Time*, February 29, 1988, p. 70.
10. The visitor was Otto Sperling, a Danish doctor; from Christopher Brown's review in *The Times Literary Supplement* of Christopher White, *Peter Paul Rubens*. New Haven, CT: Yale University Press, 1987.
11. A. E. Brown and H. A. Jeffcott, Jr., *Absolutely Mad Inventions Compiled from the Records of the United States Patent Office*. New York: Dover, 1932, pp. 46, 47.
12. As proof of how frantically joggers and others seek synchronic time-use devices, consider the fact that the Walkman sold under a billion units in 1980, its first full year of production, and over 10 billion in 1988.
13. A. Szalai, *The Use of Time*. The Hague: Mouton, 1972.
14. Walter Kerr, *The Decline of Pleasure*. New York: Simon & Schuster, 1965, p. 136.
15. N. R. Klenfield, "Conquering Those Killer Queues," *New York Times*, September 25, 1988, pp. III1, 11.
16. Lawrence Wright, *Clean and Decent*. New York: Viking, 1960, p. 169.

17. Brown and Jeffcott, pp. 48–49.
18. Frederick A. Bushee, "Social Organizations in a Small City," *The American Journal of Sociology, 51,* 3 (May–July 1945), pp. 216–26.

2:00. Machinery of Time

1. *Proverbs of Hell.*
2. G. J. Withrow, *Time in History.* Oxford: Oxford University Press, 1988, p. 105.
3. M. Drayton, "Of His Ladies Not Comming to London," in J. W. Hebel (ed.), *Works.* Oxford: Oxford University Press, 1932, iii, p. 204.
4. Withrow, frontispiece.
5. Arthur M. Schlesinger, Jr., *The Cycles of American History.* Boston: Houghton Mifflin, 1986, p. x.
6. Henry Adams, "The Rule of Phase Applied to History" (1909), in *The Tendency of History.* New York, 1919, p. 167; cited in Schlesinger, p. x.
7. A. E. Brown and H. A. Jeffcott, Jr., *Absolutely Mad Inventions Compiled from the Records of the United States Patent Office.* New York: Dover, 1932.
8. Editors of *Consumer Reports, I'll Buy That!* Mount Vernon, NY: Consumers Union, 1986, p. 46.
9. Clifford Edward Clark, Jr., *The American Family Home, 1800–1960.* Chapel Hill: University of North Carolina Press, 1986, p. 135.
10. Hans P. Moravec, *Mind Children.* Cambridge, MA: Harvard University Press, 1988.
11. Editors of *Consumer Reports,* p. 37; and Hans Fantel, "Digital Finds," Home Design, *New York Times,* April 12, 1987, pp. 46–47.
12. *Statistical Abstract of the U.S.,* various years; and Dealerscope Merchandising, *68th General Statistical and Marketing Report, II,* April 1990.
13. "All in the American Family," *Time,* June 13, 1988, p. 74.

3:00. The Value of Time

1. *London Assurance.* London: S. French, 1841, p. i.
2. *Walden.* Boston: Houghton Mifflin, 1893.
3. 1991 Hilton (Hotels) Time Values Survey, "Time: The Currency of the '90s," press release, March 12, 1991.
4. And this age group showed the largest *increase* in feeling rushed. John Robinson, "The Time Squeeze," *American Demographics,* February 1990, pp. 30–33.
5. Jeff Biddle and Daniel Hamermesh, *Sleep and the Allocation of Time.* Working Paper 2988. New York: National Bureau of Economic Research, 1989.
6. Dennis Kneale, " 'Zapping' of TV Ads Appears Pervasive," *Wall Street Journal,* April 25, 1988, p. 27.
7. Spokesman for the Florida Department of Citrus; quoted in "Chilled Orange Juice Overtakes Frozen Concentrate," *Wall Street Journal,* March 12, 1987, p. I1.
8. The NPD Group's National Eating Trends Service.
9. (No title), *Wall Street Journal,* July 10, 1986, p. 1.
10. *Statistical Abstract of the U.S.,* 1990, Table 400, p. 234.
11. For those who want to economize further on time, a videotape—the "Video Dog"—guarantees the "experience of owning a pet without the

mess and inconvenience'' ($19.95); the ''Video Baby'' is available at the same price.

12. ''An End to Free Phone Information,'' *Business Week,* June 22, 1974, p. 57.
13. Yet, the time savings to the public would be offset in part by the losses to census users who would have less information to work with. Constance Holden, ''Census a Public Burden?'' *Science,* August 21, 1987, p. 839.
14. Alice Kahn, ''Trampled in the Rush to Relax,'' *Los Angeles Times,* April 27, 1988, p. V1.
15. David Herbert Donald, *Look Homeward: A Life of Thomas Wolfe.* Boston: Little, Brown, 1987, pp. 61, 73.
16. Sen. David Durenburger; quoted in Hedrick Smith, *The Power Game.* New York: Random House, 1988, p. 21.
17. Amanda Bennett, ''Early to Bed . . . ,'' *Wall Street Journal,* March 20, 1987, p. 22D.
18. Time for those pursuits was scarce, for the average lawyer puts in a forty-seven-hour week, with Saturdays frequently spent in the office. Rosslyn S. Smith, ''A Profile of Lawyer Lifestyles,'' *American Bar Association Journal, 70* (February 1984), pp. 50, 52, 54. Apparently alcoholism goes in tandem with workaholism, at least for lawyers, for their alcoholism rate is nearly double that of the general population, and divorce rates and health problems run high. Paul Ciotti, ''Unhappy Lawyers,'' *Los Angeles Times,* August 25, 1988, p. V1.
19. Kazuko Fujimoto, ''Working Their Way to a Sudden Death,'' *Japan Times,* December 5, 1990, p. 16. The incidence of heart attacks among Japanese managers nearly quadrupled during the oil crises of 1974 and 1979. In 1987, the Japanese press published the death notices of a dozen CEOs of major companies—up by three times the number of the previous year. Although the immediate causes were officially listed as stroke, heart attack, ulcer, and pneumonia, it was widely believed that the real cause was *endaka,* the strong and rising yen that reduced exports abroad and threatened profits. Life in the executive suite suddenly became extraordinarily stressful as corporate leaders pushed themselves beyond their limits in the frantic search for ways to reverse sagging sales and exports. *Time,* August 3, 1987, p. 46.
20. According to a 1987 survey by the American Medical Association; cited in Ann Japenga, ''Endless Days and Sleepless Nights,'' *Los Angeles Times,* March 6, 1988, pp. VI1, 14.
21. James Barron, ''Making Sure Doctors Get Enough Sleep,'' *New York Times,* May 22, 1988, p. E7.
22. Joseph E. Hardison, ''The House Officer's Changing World,'' *New England Journal of Medicine, 314,* 26 (June 26, 1986), p. 1713.
23. Barron, p. E7.
24. James Robert Wendt and Lester J. Yen, ''The Resident by Moonlight,'' *Journal of the American Medical Association, 259,* 1 (January 1, 1988), pp. 43–44.
25. According to Aviation Safety Reports filed with NASA; R. Curtis Graeber and others, ''Aircrew Sleep and Fatigue in Long-haul Flight Operations,'' *Proceedings of the 40th Annual International Air Safety Seminar,* Arlington, VA: Flight Safety Foundation, 1987, p. 52.
26. National Transportation Safety Board; Cynthia F. Mitchell, ''Firms Waking Up to Sleep Disorders,'' *Wall Street Journal,* July 7, 1988, p. 25.

27. William Stockton, "Pilots' Fatigue Termed Threat to Safe Flying," *New York Times,* June 5, 1988, p. Y15.
28. W. F. Cock, "The First Operation Under Ether in Europe," *University College Hospital Magazine, 1* (1911), pp. 127–44; and P. Flemming, "Robert Liston, the First Professor of Clinical Surgery at UCH," *University College Hospital Magazine, 1* (1926), pp. 176–85; in Richard Gordon, *Great Medical Disasters.* New York: Dorset, 1983, p. 19.
29. Gordon, p. 21.
30. Robert Kanigel, "Angry at Our Gods," *Columbia, 14,* 1 (October 1988), p. 32.
31. Meyer Friedman and Ray H. Rosenman, *Type A Behavior and Your Heart.* New York: Knopf, 1974, p. 60.
32. Friedman and Rosenman, pp. 59–60.
33. Friedman and Rosenman, pp. 68, 70, 72.
34. Larry A. Pace and Waino W. Suojanen, "Addictive Type A Behavior Undermines Employee Involvement," *Personnel Journal,* June 1988, p. 40.
35. Pace and Suojanen; cited in Amanda Bennett, "Type-A Managers Stuck in the Middle," *Wall Street Journal,* June 17, 1988, p. 17.
36. Joel E. Dimsdale, "A Perspective on Type A Behavior and Coronary Disease," *New England Journal of Medicine,* January 14, 1988, pp. 110–12.
37. Among the Type As surviving their first heart attack, only 2.5 percent died of heart disease within a year, and 8.5 percent of the Type Bs died of heart disease in less than a year. Dimsdale, pp. 110–12; D. R. Ragland and R. J. Branc, "Type A Behavior and Mortality from Coronary Heart Disease," *New England Journal of Medicine,* January 14, 1988, pp. 65–69.
38. Marilyn M. Machlowitz, "A New Take on Type A," *New York Times Magazine,* part 2, May 3, 1987, pp. 40–42.
39. Ragland and Branc, pp. 65–69.
40. Bill Smethurst; quoted in *Time,* March 16, 1987, p. 40.
41. *Chicago Tribune,* June 12, 1971, p. 10; cited in Barry Schwartz, *Queuing and Waiting*. Chicago: University of Chicago Press, 1975, p. 23.
42. Schwartz, p. 171.
43. Schwartz, p. 143.
44. Schwartz, p. 41.
45. Gordon, p. 19.
46. H. L. Mencken, *Prejudices: Sixth Series*. New York: Knopf, 1927, p. 90.
47. Jonathan Dahl, "For More Travelers it Pays Not to Fly," *Wall Street Journal,* January 4, 1989, p. B1.

4:00. The Paradox of The Good Life

1. *Clockwise*. London: Methuen, 1986, p. 58.
2. Cited in Norman Macrae, "The Next Ages of Man," *The Economist,* December 24, 1988, p. 5.
3. Sebastian de Grazia, *Of Time, Work, and Leisure*. Garden City, NY: Twentieth Century Fund, 1964, p. 59.
4. Benjamin Kline Hunnicutt, *Work Without End*. Philadelphia: Temple University Press, 1988, p. 45; and Witold Rybczynski's stylish celebration of leisure, *Waiting for the Weekend*. New York: Viking, 1991, p. 142.
5. Louis Harris, *Inside America*. New York: Vintage, 1987, p. 19.
6. George L. Church, "The Work Ethic Lives!" *Time,* September 7, 1987,

pp. 40–42; Peter T. Kilborn, "The Work Week Grows," *New York Times,* June 3, 1990, pp. E1, 3.

7. Or could the change be explained by the march of women into the labor force? The fact that most worked shorter hours than men would drag down the average, not raise it.
8. The statistics comparing work hours and real wages tell the story. The average hourly wage dropped 29 cents between 1973 and 1975, and the work week lengthened 2.5 hours. Then from 1975 to 1980, when wages fell by another 20 cents, the average worker put in an additional 3.8 hours each week. From 1980 to 1984, work hours went up by about 1 percent as wages went down in the same proportion. Finally, working hours dipped slightly in the next three years and the average wage rose by a negligible 1 cent. Over the entire fifteen-year period, the work week lengthened by 15 percent and real wages dropped by 10 percent. Economist Juliet B. Schor's analysis of lengthening work hours takes a different route but arrives at the same destination. Professor Schor shows how the doubling in productivity (worker's hourly output) since 1948 would allow workers to take the "productivity dividend" either as a paid sabbatical every other year, or cut their work week or work day in half. The catch is that they would have to accept their 1948 material standard of living to do so. Her evidence shows that workers declined that opportunity, choosing instead to sacrifice leisure for a productivity dividend paid in money. As a consequence, in each of the past twenty years, the average American worker added approximately nine hours to time spent on the job; and over twenty years, that adds up to another month's work. Juliet B. Schor, *The Overworked American*. New York: Basic Books, 1991, pp. 1, 2, 29.
9. As with most things as complicated as this, scholars fail to agree on what actually happens. From his examination of cross-sections of workers, Gary Becker concludes that, except among the better educated and highly skilled, when their wages rise, workers tend to work longer hours ("A Theory of the Allocation of Time," *Economic Journal, 75,* 299 [September 1965], pp. 493–517); on the other hand, Clifford Sharp finds from longitudinal data for British workers that fewer working hours accompany higher wages. (*The Economics of Time*. New York: Wiley, 1981, ch. 6). The latter squares with U.S. data that show, over the long haul, an inverse relationship between wages and hours on the job. As noted in footnote 8, hours worked (particularly overtime, moonlighting, and other forms of second-job holding) have risen since 1973 and real wages have fallen. These conclusions accord with Sharp's and Schor's findings.
10. Economist-readers may object to the use of the terms "balance" and "satisfaction" when equilibrium and utility are meant. Indeed, these rough synonyms are being used in place of the more technical jargon.
11. Balancing our time budget is much like balancing our household budget. The family financial budget is balanced with the help of borrowing, if necessary. Whatever the course of income, only so much of it is available to spend each week or month; similarly, our time budget makes available a fixed twenty-four-hour quota each day. We try to use our income in ways which yield maximal satisfaction, and similarly for available time. If we decide to spend less on one good in order to spend more on another, we do so comforted in the expectation that we are happier with the result; that is as true of the time budget as of the financial budget. We often shift expend-

itures when a new and better product comes on the market, and we shift time amounts when a new and better opportunity comes available. Because income is not easily expanded, buying the new product usually requires forsaking the opportunity to spend the amount on something else; and with the time allotment fixed, shifting to the new activity usually requires giving up another opportunity.

12. For economist-readers, that is $S = S(s_1/t_1, s_2/t_2 \ldots s_n/t_n)$, subject to the twenty-four-hour constraint. The objective is to maximize this equation that describes the allocation of our time-absorbing activities, where each activity's utility (or satisfaction per time-unit) is **S/T**; the ideal distribution has been reached when $dS_1/dT_1 = dS_2/dT_2 = dS_3/dT_3 = \ldots$.
13. David R. Roediger and Philip S. Foner, *A History of American Labor and the Working Day*. New York: Greenwood, 1987.
14. Data from Kenneth Jon Rose, *The Body in Time*. New York: Wiley, 1988, pp. 24, 35, 142.
15. Joan Quigley, *What Does Joan Say*. New York: Birch Lane, 1990, pp. 12, 171.
16. Martin Moore-Ede and others, *The Clocks That Time Us*. Cambridge: Harvard University Press, 1982, p. 320.
17. Jeremy Campbell, *Winston Churchill's Afternoon Nap*. New York: Simon & Schuster, 1986, p. 210.
18. Gina Kolata, "Heart Attacks at 9:00 a.m.," *Science*, July 25, 1986, pp. 416–18.
19. Paul Dean, "An Old Myth Comes Back to Capistrano," *Los Angeles Times*, March 14, 1987, p. V1.
20. John P. Robinson and Philip E. Converse, "The Impact of Television on Mass Media Usages: A Cross-National Comparison," in A. Szalai, *The Use of Time*. The Hague: Mouton, 1972, pp. 197–212. Technically, the relationship between ownership and utilization of television receivers is nonlinear and shaped like an inverted "U." No one watches television in countries where TV sets don't exist (with that, few will disagree). As ownership increases, however, the hours spent before the set also increase, but only up to a point. In countries where ownership nears 100%, televiewing tends to decline with increases in income and education.
21. Szalai, p. 114.
22. H.-M. D. Toong and A. Gupta, "Personal Computers." *Scientific American, 247*, 3, 1982, pp. 86–107.
23. These qualities help to account for the boom in mail-order buying. The number of catalogues mailed is up from 8.7 billion in 1983 to 13.4 billion in 1991, and the proportion who shop from catalogues has more than doubled in the same period; data from Direct Marketing Association and Simmons Market Research Bureau, cited in *Los Angeles Times*, March 21, 1992, p. D1.
24. E. P. Thompson, "Time, Work-Discipline, and Industrial Capitalism," *Past and Present, 38* (1967), p. 81.
25. Michael R. Kagay, "Personal Satisfaction Rises in U.S., Poll Shows," *New York Times*, December 25, 1988, p. Y10.
26. This generalization is subject to the qualification that the increase in **S** (or marginal utility) diminishes for all activities as the amount of time allocated to them increases.

II.

1. Data from *Statistical Abstract of the U.S.*, various years.

5:00. Rising Curtains, Falling Attendance

1. "The Academy of Drive-Time Radio," *(Los Angeles) Reader*, June 10, 1988, p. 8.
2. The data source in this section, unless indicated otherwise, is *Statistical Abstract of the United States, 1990*.
3. Jay Sharbutt, "Arts Poll," *Los Angeles Times*, March 16, 1988, pp. VI1, 8.
4. National Research Center of the Arts, an affiliate of Louis Harris and Associates, Inc. *Americans and the Arts*, V, New York: the author, January 1988, pp. 64, 69. Only in the categories of popular music and sports has support for more performances eroded.
5. Garff B. Wilson, *Three Hundred Years of American Drama and Theatre*. Englewood Cliffs, NJ: Prentice-Hall, 1973, pp. 7–8.
6. William J. Baumol and William G. Bowen. *Performing Arts—The Economic Dilemma*. Cambridge, MA: MIT Press, 1966, p. 23; and Abigail Evans, *The Impact of Labor Relations on Broadway Economics*, M.A. Thesis, Theater Department, Yale University, 1987.
7. When receipts are expressed in "real" dollars to take account of dwindling purchasing power (a dollar in 1985 bought only what 36 cents bought in 1970), for a starter, the growth in receipts over the fifteen-year stretch is reduced from 290 percent to a mere 41 percent. Next, when adjusted to a per capita basis, real box office receipts rose from $1.09 to $1.18. Finally, the average person spent $1.15 per $10,000 income for theater tickets in 1970, but only $.95 per $10,000 in 1985. In their comprehensive study of the performing arts in the early '60s, Baumol and Bowen arrive at a similar conclusion. After correcting their data as we have here, they find that "the amount spent on the arts has actually fallen by about one fourth since 1929" (p. 45).
8. Between 1980 and 1987, for example, admissions to events in all five of these major performing arts categories declined by 15 percent, or roughly 2 percent a year; in the more recent 1983–87 period, the rate of decline doubled to about 4 percent annually. National Research Center of the Arts, p. 4.
9. National Research Center of the Arts, pp. 69, 70. This is more than a short-term trend for, compared with a benchmark year a quarter century ago, attendance drops even more dramatically. The typical theater-goer attended 8.4 times during the 1963–64 season, triple the 1987 rate! Baumol and Bowen, p. 77.
10. The *number* attending, however, was up for dance, art museums, and the movies, and the *frequency* of attendance rose between 1980 and 1987 for the latter two categories.
11. National Research Center of the Arts, p. 63.
12. Meg Cox, "Skating Fast Toward Broadway," *Wall Street Journal*, March 16, 1987, p. 24; Jeffrey A. Tennanbaum, "British Master Tries American

Opening,'' *Wall Street Journal,* April 21, 1988, p. 28; and Peter Watson, "Lloyd Webber,'' *New York Times,* April 1, 1990, p. II1.

13. Baumol and Bowen, p. 162.
14. William J. Baumol and Edward Wolff, "On the Theory of Productivity and Unbalanced Growth,'' Discussion Paper Series No. 80-03, C. V. Starr Center for Applied Economics, New York University, New York, January 1980, p. 5.
15. League of American Theaters and Producers; cited in Peter Passell, "Broadway and the Bottom Line,'' *New York Times,* December 10, 1989, p. H1.
16. National Research Center of the Arts, pp. 8, 78. One-third so responded, and 59 percent said that they were hard pressed by the lack of time to attend more often. Unfortunately, the time-shortage question was offered as an alternate possible answer only in the most recent poll. However, if our theory is correct, the proportion choosing this response would increase with each subsequent survey.
17. Sharbutt, pp. VI1, 8.
18. John Henken, "The Philharmonic's Once and Forever King,'' *Los Angeles Times,* July 10, 1988, p. 3.
19. Calculated from 1980 and 1987 data in National Research Center of the Arts, pp. 69–70.
20. Fred Metcalf, *Dictionary of Modern Humorous Quotations.* London: Penguin, 1987, p. 181.
21. Ernest Fleischmann, "The Orchestra is Dead. Long Live the Community of Musicians,'' commencement speech delivered at the Cleveland Institute of Music (no date), p. 4.
22. Calculated from 1980 and 1987 data in National Research Center of the Arts, pp. 69–70.
23. Baumol and Bowen, pp. 255, 497. Adventurous programs are those that include a work which does not fall naturally into the "popular category (such as the symphonies of Schumann, Mahler, Bruckner . . .).'' Also, most music composed in the twentieth century is considered "adventurous.'' The other programs are "those devoted *exclusively* to the performance of familiar or frequently played works in the standard orchestral repertoire.''
24. Analysts who uncovered these results conclude gloomily that "audience size can sometimes be stimulated by means requiring sacrifices of principle, such as the avoidance of contemporary works, sacrifices which some organizations may be unwilling to accept.'' Baumol and Bowen, pp. 254, 257.
25. Robert S. Brustein, *Who Needs Theatre.* New York: Atlantic Monthly Press, 1987, pp. 218–19.
26. The interview is fictitious; the data, gathered from press accounts, are not, and Mr. Lloyd Webber is not responsible for their accuracy. The press, however, is.
27. Meg Cox, " 'Cats' Composer Hopes Theater Investors Will Greet His 'Blind Pool' with Rates,'' *Wall Street Journal,* April 13, 1990, p. B1; Mervyn Rothstein, "On Broadway, Spectacles Raise the Stakes,'' *New York Times,* January 8, 1989, p. II2; and Watson, p. II1.
28. Tennanbaum, p. 28; and Watson, p. II1.
29. Susan Sontag, *Notes on Camp.* New York: Wolff, 1969, p. 291.

6:00. The Mystery of the Empty Pew

1. Jeremy Rifkin, *Time Wars*. New York: Henry Holt, 1987, p. 124.
2. Max Weber, *The Protestant Ethic and the Spirit of Capitalism*. New York: Scribner's, 1958, p. 157.
3. " 'Jim and Tammy Show' Held 13th Spot among Religious Programs," *Los Angeles Times*, March 28, 1987, p. I29.
4. Rodney Stark and William Sims Bainbridge, *The Future of Religion, Secularization, Revival and Cult Formation*. Berkeley, CA: University of California Press, 1985.
5. Louis Harris, *Inside America*. New York: Vintage, 1986, p. 67.
6. According to the Gallup Poll, the proportion of American adults holding that belief rose from 78 percent in 1978 to 84 percent in 1988; cited in Russell Chandler, "Surveys Find a Gain in Faith, a Drop in Giving," *Los Angeles Times*, August 20, 1988, p. II7.
7. George Melloan, "God and Mammon," *Wall Street Journal*, August 30, 1988, p. 19. The growth in numbers of Catholics, fed in large part by immigration from the Latin countries, masks a drop in proportion from nearly 24 percent of the population in 1965. *Statistical Abstract of the U.S.*, various years.
8. "Unchurched" adults consist of those who either do not belong to a religious organization or do but have not attended services for six months, exclusive of religious holidays or other special occasions. George Gallup, Jr., and Jim Castelli, *The American Catholic People*. Garden City, NY: Doubleday, 1987, pp. 162, 166.
9. John Ronsvalle and Sylvia Ronsvalle, "Protestant Giving as a Function of United States Per Capita Income," paper presented at the 1989 Spring Research Forum, "Philanthropy and the Religious Tradition," Chicago, March 10–11, 1989, processed.
10. Andrew Greeley and William McManus, *Catholic Contributions*. Chicago: Thomas More Press, 1987, pp. 38, 45, 64.
11. But church leaders have been indifferent to the losses. "Any other human organization in which a loss of half of its income, more than $6 billion a year, had occurred would have engaged in intense soul-searching and policy reformulation." Greeley and McManus, p. 68.
12. General Register Office, *Religious Worship in England and Wales*. London, 1854; cited in Adrian Forty, *Objects of Desire*. London: Thames & Hudson, 1986, p. 109.
13. *Statistical Abstract of the United States 1986*, p. 51; and Harris, p. 67. Matters are no better in Britain where, on an average Sunday, only 119 adults out of an average parish population of 8,410 go to a service of the Church of England, the official faith; that's one in seventy. Attendance at normal Sunday services is declining at a rate exceeding 40,000 per year. The Archbishop of Canterbury's Commission on Urban Priority Areas, *Faith in the City*. London: Church House, 1985.
14. With defections and retirements reducing the number of active diocesan clergy, today's Catholic priest shepherds a flock nearly twice as large as his precursor did forty years ago. Dean Hoge, *The Future of Catholic Leadership*. Kansas City, MO: Sheed and Ward, 1987, p. 5.

15. John Deedy, *American Catholicism: And Now Where?* New York: Plenum, 1987, p. 131.
16. Hoge, pp. 228–29.
17. Katarina Schuth, *Reason for the Hope*. Wilmington, DE: Glazier, 1989, p. 123; Hoge, pp. 228–29.
18. *Official Catholic Directory*. New York: Kennedy, various years; Maura Dolan, "Many Nuns Now Forsake Convent," *Los Angeles Times*, August 16, 1987, p. I27; John Dart, "Retirement Funds Pleas for Catholic Orders Set," *Los Angeles Times*, November 18, 1987, p. I3.
19. Arthur B. Schlesinger, Jr., *The Cycles of American History*. Boston: Houghton Mifflin, 1986, p. 87.
20. Rudolph M. Bell, *Holy Anorexia*. Chicago: University of Chicago Press, 1985.
21. Harvey Cox, *Turning East*. New York: Simon & Schuster, 1977, p. 174.
22. Andrew Greeley's data; cited in Robert Suro, "Switch by Hispanic Catholics Changes Face of U.S. Religion," *New York Times*, May 14, 1989, p. 14. A 1986 Gallup Poll found that 19 percent of Hispanic Americans identified themselves as Protestant, up from 16 percent in 1972.
23. Richard Rodriguez, "Latin Americans Convert from Catholicism to a More Private Protestant Belief," *Los Angeles Times*, August 13, 1989, p. V1.
24. Wilhelm Schiffer, "New Religions in Postwar Japan," *Monumenta Nipponica 11* (April 1955), p. 114; Felix Moos, "Some Aspects of Park Chang No Kyo," *Anthropological Quarterly* (July 1964), pp. 110–20; both cited in Anson D. Shupe, Jr., *Six Perspectives on New Religions*. New York: Edwin Mellen, 1981, pp. 3, 15.
25. Mike Granberry, "Unarius Students Await Dawning of a New Age," *Los Angeles Times*, September 29, 1986, pp. V1, 3.
26. Jonathan Dahl, "Icons Shedding Tears Are a Mixed Blessing to Congregations," *Wall Street Journal*, January 30, 1987, p. 1.
27. Ari L. Goldman, "More than a Cathedral," *New York Times Magazine*, November 15, 1987, pp. 22–76ff; Russell Chandler, "Keeping the Faith at the Battlefront," *Los Angeles Times*, December 12, 1989, p. B3.
28. Paula Span, "And Now, a Word From . . . ," *Los Angeles Times*, January 23, 1988, p. II8; Aimee L. Stern, "Putting Faith in Madison Avenue," *New York Times*, December 27, 1987, p. F4.
29. "Since usurers sell nothing but the hope of money, that is, time, they are selling the day and the night," proclaimed the thirteenth century document, *Tabula Exemplorum*. "But the day is the time of light and the night the time of rest; therefore, they are selling eternal light and rest"; according also to Duns Scotus, c. 1260–1307, in his commentary on the *Sentences* of Peter Lombard; J. LeGoff, *Time, Work, and Culture in the Middle Ages*, trans. A. Goldhammer. Chicago: University of Chicago Press, 1980, n. 12, p. 290.
30. Andrew M. Greeley, *Crisis in the Church*. Chicago: Thomas More Press, 1979, p. 157.
31. Michael Novak, "Orthodoxy vs. Progressive Bourgeois Christianity," in Peter Occhiogrosso, *Once a Catholic*. Boston: Houghton Mifflin, 1987, pp. 127, 133.
32. "The Challenge of Peace: God's Promise and Our Response" (1983) and "Economic Justice for All: Catholic Social Teaching and the U.S. Economy" (1986).

33. *New York Times*/CBS poll taken in 1985; Joseph Berger, "Being Catholic in America," *New York Times Magazine*, August 23, 1987, p. 25.
34. Deedy, p. 19. Moreover, seven in ten Catholics believe that schools ought to establish direct links with family planning clinics "to make sure that young people learn about sex and birth control." Harris, p. 84.
35. Poll by Yankelovich Clancy Shulman, reported in Richard N. Ostling, "John Paul's Feisty Flock," *Time*, September 7, 1987, p. 48; the proportion in a 1985 *New York Times*/CBS poll was 15 percent; Joseph Berger, "Catholic Dissent on Church Rules Found," *New York Times*, November 25, 1985, p. A7.
36. Constance Holden, "The Vatican Weighs In," *Science*, March 20, 1987, p. 1455.
37. Yankelovich Clancy Shulman, for *Time*, p. 48.
38. Yankelovich Clancy Shulman, for *Time*, p. 48.
39. Yankelovich Clancy Shulman, for *Time*, p. 48. In a 1982 Gallup survey—that failed to distinguish between active and inactive homosexuals—39 percent accepted and 46 percent rejected homosexuality as an alternative lifestyle. Catholics showed a considerably higher tolerance than Protestants, of whom 28 percent accepted and 58 percent rejected gay lifestyles. Moreover, in a 1985 survey, over half of Catholics favored, and 38 percent opposed, legalizing relationships between consenting gay adults. The proportions among Protestants were 38 percent for legalization and 53 percent against. Gallup and Castelli, p. 63.
40. Larry B. Stammer, "Poll finds 2 of 3 Catholics in Favor of Women Priests," *Los Angeles Times*, June 19, 1992, pp. A1, 26.
41. As Catholics have become more liberal, the army of the faithful supporting women's ordination has won new recruits. In 1992, 67 percent favored ordaining women, up sharply from 29 percent who believed that eighteen years earlier. Gallup polls reported in Stammer. Vatican insistence on a male clergy rests on the tenuous grounds that, at the Last Supper when Jesus instituted Holy Orders, no females were present (not even as waitresses). True, but since the disciples were also Jews, consistency would oblige Rome to ordain only Jewish males, a ruling that would yield a double-barreled benefit by easing Judeo-Christian ecumenical relations and obviating the need for so many faith-to-faith dialogues.
42. One-forth of Catholics believed religion was "old-fashioned and out of date" and another 27 percent had "no opinion" on the matter; in contrast, only 15 percent and 23 percent, respectively, of Protestants so answered. Gallup Poll, reported in *Our Sunday Visitor*, January 27, 1985, p. 5.
43. By a large margin, the drop in importance assigned by Catholics was the largest of all denominations surveyed, and by 1984 was the lowest of all. Gallup and Castelli, p. 12.
44. Deedy, pp. 275, 276.
45. Dolly Patterson, "Peter F. Drucker: Managing Churches," *Crossings*, #13, 1989, p. 1.
46. Elizabeth McAlister, "Where's the Church?" in Peter Occhiogrosso, *Once a Catholic*. Boston: Houghton Mifflin, 1987, p. 261.
47. Gallup and Castelli, pp. 4, 5. The growth in socioeconomic status is even more impressive when the large numbers of recently arrived Hispanic Catholics are considered.
48. Gallup polls cited in Hoge, p. 54.

49. Yankelovich Clancy Shulman, for *Time,* p. 48.
50. Lenny Bruce, *The Essential Lenny Bruce.* New York: Ballantine, 1967, p. 57.

7:00. Chaste by Time

1. From an interview in the *New York Post,* 1975; cited in Fred Metcalf, *Dictionary of Modern Humorous Quotations.* London: Penguin, 1987, p. 14.
2. Staffan Linder, *The Harried Leisure Class.* New York: Columbia University Press, 1970, p. 85.
3. Linder, p. 84.
4. Albert B. Gerber, *The Book of Sex Lists.* Secaucus, NJ: Stuart, 1981, p. 23.
5. Florence Howe Hall, "Etiquette for Men," *Harper's Bazaar,* November 1907, pp. 1095–97.
6. Beth L. Bailey, *From Front Porch to Back Seat.* Baltimore, MD: Johns Hopkins University Press, 1988, pp. 3, 25.
7. Cynthia Heimel, *Sex Tips for Girls.* New York: Simon & Schuster, 1983, pp. 90–91.
8. Bailey, p. 30.
9. Maureen Daly (ed.), *Profile of Youth.* New York: Lippincott, 1949, p. 30; cited in Bailey, p. 30.
10. Art Unger (ed.), *Datebook's Complete Guide to Dating.* Englewood Cliffs, NJ: Prentice-Hall, 1960, p. 34; cited in Bailey, p. 55.
11. Daly, p. 30.
12. Allyn Moss, "Whatever Happened to Courtship?" *Mademoiselle,* April 1963, p. 151.
13. Moss, p. 151.
14. Bailey, p. 80.
15. Jack Shepherd, "The *Look* Youth Survey," *Look,* September 20, 1966, p. 48.
16. Bailey, pp. 141, 142.
17. Sebastian de Grazia, *Of Time, Work, and Leisure.* New York: Twentieth Century Fund, 1962, p. 325.
18. Shere Hite, *Women and Love.* New York: Knopf, 1987, pp. 89, 826.
19. Deidre Sanders, *The* Woman *Report on Men.* London: Sphere, 1987, pp. 69, 77.
20. Sanders, pp. 72–73.
21. In the late '80s, 29 percent of females aged 25–29 were never-married, compared to 10.5 percent in 1970; among males, the comparable figures were 42 percent and 19 percent. *Statistical Abstract of the United States 1989,* p. 43.
22. Hite, p. 324. A review of twelve years of data gathered by the National Opinion Research Center finds a weakened commitment to the wedded state. Women are getting less out of it (and perhaps putting less into it) than they once did. Norval Glenn and Kathryn Kramer, "The Marriages and Divorces of the Children of Divorce." *Journal of Marriage and the Family, 49,* 4 (November 1987), pp. 811–25. A survey by the Battelle Memorial Institute, done in 1985 for *Cosmopolitan* magazine, also concludes that marriage has become less central in women's lives; see S. D. McLaughlin and others, *The Changing Lives of American Women.* Chapel Hill: University of North Carolina Press, 1988.

23. Trip Gabriel, "Why Wed? The Ambivalent American Bachelor," *New York Times Magazine,* November 15, 1987, p. 24.
24. Bruce Weber, "Alone Together: The Unromantic Generation," *New York Times Magazine,* April 5, 1987, pp. 22, 58.
25. Edna Everage, *My Gorgeous Life.* New York: Simon & Schuster, 1991.
26. Sanders, p. 74.
27. James Thurber and E. B. White, *Is Sex Necessary?* New York: Harper, 1950, p. 140.
28. There is apparently some truth to the claim. When Ms. Sanders asked 5,000 men to guess how their partner rated their sexual prowess, more than three in four singles thought their performance rated "good" or "excellent," compared to just over one-half of marrieds. Sanders, p. 71.
29. Marabel Morgan, *Total Joy.* Old Tappan, NJ: Revell, 1976, p. 16.
30. Sanders, p. 100.
31. Sanders, pp. 146, 151.
32. Linder, p. 84.
33. Thurber and White, p. xv.
34. From a review by Jonathan Weiner of Mark Jerome Walters, *The Dance of Life.* New York: Arbor House/William Morrow & Co., in *New York Times Book Review,* March 27, 1988, p. 45.
35. James S. Gordon, *The Golden Guru.* New York: Viking/Penguin, p. 79.
36. Alfred Kinsey, *Sexual Behavior in the Human Male.* Philadelphia: Saunders, 1948, p. 580.
37. Alfred Kinsey, *Sexual Behavior in the Human Female.* Philadelphia: Saunders, 1953, pp. 350–51; Carin Rubenstein and Carol Tavris, "Special Survey Results," *Redbook,* September 1987, p. 149.
38. Rubenstein and Tavris, pp. 148–49.
39. "General Review of the Sex Situation," *The Portable Dorothy Parker.* New York: Penguin, 1973, p. 115.
40. Morgan, *Total Joy,* p. 212.
41. Sanders, pp. 95–96, 98.
42. Morgan, *Total Joy,* pp. 134–35.
43. Morgan, *Total Joy,* pp. 144–46.
44. According to Mary Ellen Donovan in a review of Barbara Ehrenreich and others, *Re-making Love.* New York: Anchor, 1986, *Los Angeles Times Book Review,* December 14, 1986, p. 2.
45. Sanders, p. 79.
46. Sanders, pp. 80–81.
47. Sanders, p. 103.
48. Sanders, pp. 182–83.
49. P. J. O'Rourke, *Modern Manners.* New York: Morgan Entrekin, 1983, p. 109.
50. According to IXL/IdealDial, Denver, annual revenues have risen from about $25 million in 1984 to $310 million in 1988. Michael W. Miller, "Talking Dirty," *Wall Street Journal,* August 5, 1988, p. 1.
51. Joann Ellison Rodgers, *Drugs and Sexual Behavior.* New York: Chelsea House, 1988, pp. 20–21, 51, 55, 57.
52. Louis Harris, *Inside America.* New York: Vintage, 1987, p. 151.
53. According to David Friedman, president of the Adult Film and Video Association; cited in "Porn: Fantasy Film Makers Face Reality of AIDS," *Los Angeles Times,* April 15, 1987, p. VI5.

54. Hairbrushing? The first in the set includes a beginner's set of instructions; available for $69.95 from Marksman Productions, PO Box 77836, Van Nuys, CA 91409.

8:00. Taking Care of Ourselves

1. Fred Metcalf, *Dictionary of Modern Humorous Quotations*. London: Penguin, 1987, p. 73.
2. Jean Anthelme Brillat-Savarin, *The Physiology of Taste* (translated and annotated by M. F. K. Fisher). New York: Limited Editions Club, 1949.
3. Editors of *Consumer Reports, I'll Buy That*. Mount Vernon, NY: Consumers Union, 1986, p. 69.
4. Editors of *Consumer Reports*, p. 179.
5. Claudia H. Deutsch, "Why Fast Food Has Slowed Down," *New York Times*, March 13, 1988, p. III1; "Women: Female Workers Spur Growth, Create Jobs," *Los Angeles Times*, September 12, 1984, p. I7.
6. Alix M. Freedman, "The Microwave Cooks Up a New Way of Life," *Wall Street Journal*, September 19, 1989, p. B1.
7. *Statistical Abstract of the United States*, various years.
8. NPD Group's National Eating Trends Service.
9. Alice B. Toklas, *The Alice B. Toklas Cook Book*. New York: Harper & Row, 1954, pp. 33, 102, 126, and 133.
10. Pierre Franey, *60-Minute Gourmet*. New York: New York Times, 1979; Pierre Franey, *More 60-Minute Gourmet*. New York: New York Times, 1981; Martha Stewart, *Quick Cook*. New York: Potter, 1983; Abby Mandell, *Fast and Flavorful*. Greenwich, CT: Cuisinart Cook Club, 1985; Emalee Chapman, *Fresh 15-Minute Meals*. New York: Dutton, 1986; Emalee Chapman, *Fast Italian Meals*. San Francisco: 101 Productions, 1983; Shinko Shimizu, *New Salads: Quick, Healthy Recipes from Japan*. New York: Kodansha, 1986.
11. Ruth Reichl, "Sign of the Culinary Times," *Los Angeles Times*, November 13, 1987, p. VI1.
12. Lawrence Sombke, "How Our Meals Have Changed," *USA Weekend*, November 11–13, 1988, pp. 4–5.
13. Bureau of Labor Statistics data.
14. Leonard L. Berry, "Market to the Perception," *American Demographics*, February 1990, p. 32.
15. Thomas W. Merrick and Stephen J. Tordella, *Demographics: People and Markets*. Washington, DC: Population Reference Bureau, 1988, p. 9.
16. Timothy K. Smith, "By End of This Year, Poultry will Surpass Beef in the U.S. Diet," *Wall Street Journal*, September 17, 1987, p. 1; "Consumer Spending Survey Updated," *Los Angeles Times*, July 5, 1986, pp. 1, 18.
17. U.S. Department of Agriculture; cited in Smith, p. 1.
18. Jacques Pepin, *Everyday Cooking With Jacques Pepin*. New York: Harper & Row, 1982.
19. Louis Harris, *Inside America*. New York: Vintage, 1987, p. 26.
20. Harris, pp. 26, 127. Data from the Atlanta-based Calorie Control Council's *National Survey* confirm the declining popularity of dieting: the number of dieters has fallen from 65 million to 48 million between 1986 and 1991.
21. Horace Fletcher, *The New Glutton or Epicure*. New York: Frederick Stokes, 1906, pp. 11–12. If these claims weren't enough, Fletcher added that he lost all "desire for wine and beer," not at "all a surprise to me, but it was

not an amazing surprise until one day one of my tramp guests came to me and said: 'Boss, this eatin' game is great; think of me with a dollar in my pocket and not wantin' beer.' '' Fletcher, *Fletcherism: What it Is*. London: Ewart Seymour, 1913, pp. 94–95.

22. Harvey A. Levenstein, *Revolution at the Table*. New York: Oxford University Press, 1988, pp. 89–90.
23. Francis Crowninshield, *Manners for the Metropolis*. New York: Appleton, 1909, p. 40; cited in Levenstein, p. 95.
24. Rupert Brooke, *Letters from America*. London: Sidgwick & Jackson, 1916.
25. Lesley Garner, ''A Snack Culture Eating Away at Our Dining Tables,'' *London Daily Telegraph,* September 28, 1988, p. 13.
26. John Elkins, ''Out of Time,'' *American Way, 20,* 24 (December 15, 1987), p. 18.
27. The Pillsbury Company, *What's Cookin'*. Minneapolis, MN: the author, 1988.
28. The Pillsbury Company, *What's Cookin'*.

9:00. Cleanliness, Fitness, and Beautifulness

1. *The Code of the Woosters,* New York: Doubleday, Doran, 1938, p. 251.
2. *Fot Magazine,* March 15, 1987, p. 46.
3. From a 1978 survey of 2,000 British subjects; reported in Lawrence Wright, *Clean and Decent*. New York: Viking, 1980, p. 191.
4. With 95.3 percent of households having a bathroom (up from 78 percent in 1970), Britannia ruled Europe, and perhaps even America, for the U.S. had a fractionally smaller share (94.6 percent) of homes so-equipped. Wright, p. 191.
5. Wright, p. 179; Alexander Kira, *The Bathroom*. New York: Bantam, 1977, pp. 20–21; and ''West Germany: Dirty Linen,'' *Time,* May 18, 1970, p. 30, cited in Kira, p. 21.
6. Kira, pp. 32, 33.
7. Wright, p. 191.
8. ''Lifestyles and the Family,'' *The Futurist,* November–December 1986, p. 57.
9. Phillippe Pons, ''Going into Battle . . . Against the Dreaded Four Ks,'' *The (Manchester) Guardian,* September 4, 1988, p. 16. Sales of the sonic-blocker run about 3,000 a month, with the government, aware of the possibilities for conserving water, a major buyer. Ron Iori, ''The Good, The Bad and the Useless,'' *Wall Street Journal,* June 10, 1988, p. 18R.
10. Pons, p. 16.
11. M. Langford, *Personal Hygiene Attitudes and Practices in 1,000 Middle-Class Households*. Ithaca, NY: Cornell University Agricultural Experiment Station Memoir 393, 1965, p. 63; cited in Kira, p. 287.
12. Kira, p. 287.
13. Wright, p. 73.
14. Kira, p. 8. There were many St. Gregory's. Gregory the Wonderworker (b. 213), Gregory the Enlightener (b. 240), Gregory of Nazianzus (b. 329), Gregory of Nyssa (b. 335), Gregory of Tours (b. 538), Gregory the Great (b. 540), Gregory of Utrecht (b. 707), Gregory the Seventh (b. 1020), Gregory of Sinai (b. 1290), and Gregory Palamas (b. 1296). (Note: dates are approximate.) The St. Gregory in question was probably one of these.

15. Kira, p. 199.
16. R. Fliess, *Erogeneity and Libido*. New York: International Universities Press, 1956, pp. 116–17.
17. Pons, p. 16.
18. Damon Darlin, "Japanese Take to High Tech in Bathrooms," *Wall Street Journal*, July 25, 1988, p. 15.
19. *American Health Magazine;* reported in the *Wall Street Journal*, June 22, 1987, p. 29.
20. David Brand, "The Price of Perfection," *Time*, July 25, 1988, p. 66.
21. "A National Obsession: The U.S. Turns On to Exercise," *Time*, June 16, 1986, p. 77.
22. Rose E. Frisch, "Lower Lifetime Occurrence of Breast Cancer and Cancers of the Reproductive System among Former College Athletes Compared to Non-Athletes," paper presented at the Annual Meeting of the American Association for the Advancement of Science, Boston, February 14, 1988; and R. E. Frisch and others, "Lower Prevalence of Diabetes in Female Former College Athletes compared with Nonathletes," *Diabetes, 35,* 10 (October 1986), pp. 1101–05.
23. Louis Harris, *Inside America*. New York: Vintage, 1987, pp. 4–5.
24. Kelly Brownell, "The Yo-Yo Trap," *American Health*, March, 1988, p. 81.
25. *The Sharper Image Catalogue*, November 1986, p. 68.
26. Barbara Pearlman, *Workouts that Work for Women Who Work*. New York: Doubleday, 1988.
27. The gym and the home are the first two.
28. Suzy Menkes, *The Windsor Style*. Topsfield, MA: Salem House, 1988, p. 147.
29. Kathleen A. Hughes, "Body Not Perfect? Nose Too Large? Chest Too Small?" *Wall Street Journal*, August 2, 1988, p. 1.
30. Not included in the list are chemical peels, collagen injections to smooth wrinkles, chin augmentations, forehead lift, and cheekbone implants . . . ouch. From data supplied by the American Society of Plastic and Reconstructive Surgeons, cited in Nine Green, "Costs, Effects and Risks," *Los Angeles Times*, December 22, 1991, p. A42. Tokyo's Jujin Clinic offers three additional surgeries: sweat glands can be removed for $2,000, surgery to "restore" virginity by sewing up the hymen is available at about $1,000, and shrinking the vagina to reduce the stretch from childbirth costs around $3,000. Leonard Koren, *283 Useful Ideas from Japan*, San Francisco: Chronicle Books, 1988, p. 68.
31. Richard Gordon, *Great Medical Disasters*. New York: Dorset Press, 1986, p. 188.
32. As described in Joyce Wadler, "Fat Begone!" *Los Angeles Times Magazine, IV,* 2 (January 17, 1988), pp. 8, 10, 11; Robin Marantz Henig, "The High Cost of Thinness," *New York Times Magazine*, February 28, 1988, pp. 41–42; and Ann Louise Bardach, "The Dark Side of Cosmetic Surgery," *The Good Health Magazine, New York Times Magazine, 2,* April 17, 1988, p. 25.

10:00. Housework

1. George Bernard Shaw, *Getting Married*. New York: Brentano's, 1920, p. 18.
2. Mrs. Orrinsmith, *The Drawing-Room*. London: Macmillan, 1877, p. 1.
3. Mrs. C. A. Riley, "Home," *The Family Circle and Parlor Annual 1851*. New York: Reed, 1851–52, p. 38; cited in Clifford Edward Clark, Jr., *The American Family Home, 1800–1960*. Chapel Hill: University of North Carolina Press, 1986, p. 31.
4. Alexis de Tocqueville, *Democracy in America I*. New York: Barnes, 1863, p. 70.
5. *Woman's Columbian Souvenir of Mitchell County, Iowa*. Osage, IA: Tuttle, 1893, p. 50.
6. J. Sherer, "The Management of the Home," *Family Friend, III*, 3 (March 1867), p. 203.
7. R. Brandon, *Singer and the Sewing Machine*. Philadelphia: Lippincott, 1977, p. 126. To back up this last claim, he offered easy credit with monthly payments as low as $3 to make his machine affordable to even the poorest householders. During the fifty years in which the sewing machine penetrated the home market, the price plummeted from $125, the cost of acquiring Singer's first "family machine," to a Sears Roebuck model available at the bargain price of $7.58. Adrian Forty, *Objects of Desire*. London: Thames and Hudson, 1986, pp. 96–97.
8. Adam Gowans Whyte, *The All-Electric Age*. London: Constable, 1922, pp. 232–33.
9. Elizabeth Banks, "The Educated American Drudge," *North American Review, 179* (September 1904), pp. 433–38; cited in Clark, p. 170.
10. Catherine E. Beecher and Harriet Beecher Stowe, *The American Women's Home*. Hartford, CT: Stowe-Day Foundation, 1975 (reprint of 1869 original), p. 318.
11. Gerald Carson, *Corn Flake Crusade*. New York: Rinehart, 1957, pp. 72, 162.
12. Harvey Levenstein, *Revolution at the Table*. New York: Oxford University Press, 1988, p. 163.
13. Meg Cox, "Staying at Home for Entertainment," *Wall Street Journal*, November 22, 1989, p. B1.
14. From ten to fifteen hours, according to John Robinson; quoted in Cox, p. B1. By 1987, the annual revenues from videocassette movies had eclipsed the receipts from first-run "theatrical playoffs." Jack Mathews, "What Your Entertainment Dollar Will Buy in 1997," *Los Angeles Times*, July 14, 1987, pp. VI1, 4.
15. Cox, p. B1.
16. From a survey by National Demographics and Lifestyle; cited in Terry Atkinson, "Video Days," *Los Angeles Times*, July 25, 1987, p. V1. Juliet B. Schor underscores the importance of television watching, and of other low-energy recreations for the stressed-out, noting "although it certainly isn't proof, it is suggestive that the globe's only other rich, industrialized country with longer (work) hours than the United States—namely Japan—is also the nation to watch more television." Juliet B. Schor, *The Overworked American*. New York: Basic Books, 1991, p. 161.

17. "Romantic Porn in the Boudoir," *Time,* March 30, 1987, pp. 40–41.
18. Stanley Meisler, "News, Games, Dating," *Los Angeles Times,* September 12, 1986, pp. I1, 14, 15; Beverly Beyette, "The Amazing World Beyond Your Phone," *Los Angeles Times,* September 28, 1987, p. V1.
19. Suzy Menkes, *The Windsor Style*. Topsfield, MA: Salem House, 1988, p. 88.
20. "Women: Female Workers Spur Growth, Create Jobs," *Los Angeles Times,* September 12, 1984, p. I7.
21. Shooting up from $2.6 billion to an estimated $10 billion; David Brand, "A Dashing Way to Dine," *Time,* September 18, 1989, p. 96.
22. Average household income of TV shoppers was $40,500 (about 50 percent higher than the national average) and 73 percent were women; Sydney P. Freedberg, "Home-Shopping Shakeout Forces Survivors to Find Fresh Approach," *Wall Street Journal,* November 4, 1987, p. 35.
23. Peter H. Lewis, " 'Electronic Cottages' Take Root," *New York Times,* October 16, 1988, p. F10; and Janice Castro, "Staying Home is Paying Off," *Time,* October 26, 1987, p. 112. Link Resources, a New York–based consulting firm, estimates the 1989–90 growth rate of stay-at-home workers at 38 percent.
24. Jack M. Nilles and others, "Telecommunications Substitutes for Urban Transportation." Los Angeles: University of Southern California Press, 1974, pp. 2–3.
25. "Telecommuters Work from Prisons in New York and California," *Wall Street Journal,* July 22, 1986, p. 1.
26. Faith Popcorn, "Eager," *The New Yorker, 62,* 20 (July 7, 1986), p. 22.
27. Elgin Stove Co., *Freedom from Kitchen Worries.* Elgin, IL: the author, 1938, pp. 6–7; cited in Clark, p. 208.
28. Hazel Kyrk, *Economic Problems of the Family.* New York: Harper, 1933, p. 99; also see Schor, pp. 86–88.
29. A Bryn Mawr College survey taken in the post–World War II years reported that women still devoted over eighty hours a week to child care, house cleaning, and meal cooking; cited in Clark, pp. 241–42.
30. Fred Metcalf, *Dictionary of Modern Humorous Quotations.* London: Penguin, 1987, p. 127.
31. To achieve that feat, rotate the garment 180° each day, then wear it inside out for three days; Damon Darlin, "Need Gifts for Man with Three Legs Who Has Dubious Taste?" *Wall Street Journal,* October 16, 1987, p. 1.

11:00. Time in Motion

1. John B. Jackson, "Truck City," paper delivered at a symposium on The Car and The City, University of California, Los Angeles, April, 9–10, 1988.
2. Jackson, p. 9.
3. David J. Solomon, "Sometimes it Seems People Are a Bit Obsessed with Convenience," *Wall Street Journal,* June 15, 1987, p. 36.
4. James J. Flink, *The Automobile Age.* Cambridge, MA: MIT Press, 1987; cost data from James J. Flink, "The Ultimate Status Symbol," in Martin Wachs and Margaret Crawford, *The Car and the City.* Ann Arbor: University of Michigan Press, 1992, p. 155; earnings data from U.S. Bureau of the Census, *Historical Statistics of the U.S.: Colonial Times to 1957,* Washington, DC: USGPO, p. 91.

5. *Automotive News;* cited in Paul Ingrassia and Gregory A. Patterson, "Is Buying a Car a Choice or a Chore?" *Wall Street Journal,* October 24, 1989, p. B1.
6. Richard Bauman, "Auto Inventions that Didn't Quite Make It!" *BPOElks Magazine,* no date, p. 37.
7. Federal Highway Administration estimate; cited in Gregory Witcher, "Smart Cars, Smart Highways," *Wall Street Journal,* May 22, 1989, p. B1. Gridlock on Washington's Capital Beltway costs employers as much as $120 million per annum in lost time. Martha Smilgis, "Trapped Behind the Wheel," *Time,* July 20, 1987, pp. 64–65. Even a five-minute delay per subway commuter going to or coming from work costs the New York City economy $166 million annually; Richard Levine, "Car Madness in Manhattan," *New York Times,* October 11, 1987, p. E6.
8. Travel time savings loom so large in traffic engineers' reckoning that such amounts account for the bulk of benefits (around 80 percent) ascribed to transport improvements. Changes in vehicle operating costs and accident rates account for the remainder; Clifford Sharp, *The Economics of Time.* New York: Wiley, 1981, p. 86.
9. I refer here, and later, to the time that commuters spend on the road. Although commuters may not see the time as costly *per se,* a very different sort of reasoning must apply to the movement of goods which obviously does entail costs that higher **S**s cannot compensate for. Therefore, the reasoning applied here, and the conclusions reached, apply only to the commute, not to all travel forms and purposes.
10. Yacov Zahavi, *Travel Time Budgets and Mobility in Urban Areas.* Washington, DC: U.S. Department of Transportation, Federal Highway Administration, 1974.
11. Indeed there appeared to be variations from place to place, but the differences were small enough to disregard (the standard deviation was only eight minutes). Neither the mode of travel nor wealth seemed to make much difference. "Workers in some of the more affluent countries, with faster transport facilities such as cars and electric trains at their disposal, spent nearly as long traveling to work as did those in countries where walking or cycling is more common." Sharp, p. 97.
12. The surveys were taken in 1934 and 1958; Ira S. Lowry, *Portrait of a Region.* Pittsburgh: University of Pittsburgh Press, 1963, p. 135.
13. Fast limited-access highways made it possible for commuters to achieve the American dream of free-standing, single-family, large-lot homes in the suburbs without necessarily lengthening the time of the commute to work. The trade-off between that choice and traveling a greater distance was first explained theoretically in William Alonso, *Location and Land Use.* Cambridge, MA: Harvard University Press, 1964.
14. Starr Roxanne Hiltz and Murray Turoff, *The Network Nation.* Reading, MA: Addison-Wesley, 1978, p. 478.
15. Hiltz and Turoff, p. 478.
16. Reyner Banham, *Los Angeles: Architecture of Four Ecologies.* London: Penguin, 1971, p. 222.
17. Well, perhaps a bit. There is a downside to commuting, particularly on congested roads. Studies show that some commuters suffer greater stress, higher blood pressure, higher work absence, negative moods, and other ills. Raymond W. Novaco and others, "Transportation, Stress, and Community Psychology," *American Journal of Community Psychology,* 7 (1979),

pp. 361–380; and Raymond W. Novaco and others, "Objective and Subjective Dimensions of Travel Impedance as Determinants of Commuting Stress," *American Journal of Community Psychology, 18* (1990), pp. 231–57. The relationship between commuter's **S** and time traveled is obviously nonlinear. At some point—perhaps around thirty minutes on a one-way trip—**S** declines and stress builds up. Were this untrue, there would be little justification for the billions of public dollars budgeted for urban transportation improvements.

18. Chris Maynard and Bill Scheller, *Manifold Destiny*. New York: Villard, 1989.
19. Invented by Joseph Grant in 1926; Bauman, p. 31.
20. Sinclair Lewis, *Free Air*. New York: Harcourt, Brace and Howe, 1919, p. 4.
21. Kevin Todd Berger, *Zen Driving*. New York: Ballantine, 1988.
22. David L. Lewis, "Sex and the Automobile," in David Lewis and Laurence Goldstein (eds.). *The Automobile and American Culture*. Ann Arbor: University of Michigan Press, 1983, p. 123–33; and Martha Smilgis, "Trapped Behind the Wheel," *Time,* July 20, 1987, pp. 64–65. Those in search of romance short of marriage may find it via the Freeway Singles Club, a mail-forwarding service whose 2,000 members advertise their availability by means of a decal stuck to their windshields.
23. According to projections for 1990; *Wall Street Journal,* October 29, 1986, p. 29.
24. *Statistical Abstract of the United States 1989,* p. 78.
25. *Allright Parking News,* Winter 1988, p. 4.
26. Based on 1975–87 data when the number of licensed motorists climbed 25 percent but auto ownership rose 30 percent; *Statistical Abstract of the United States 1989,* various tables.

12:00. Doing unto Others

1. John Kenneth Galbraith, *The Affluent Society*. Boston: Houghton Mifflin, 1958, p. 253.
2. The response to the Census forms mailed to all households hit an all-time low of 64 percent in 1990. A *New York Times* poll discovered that "too busy" was the main reason cited for non-response. Felicity Barringer, "Mixed Reception Likely to Greet Census Takers Today, Poll Finds," *New York Times,* April 26, 1990, p. A18. When the Census bureau statisticians analyzed the poor return rate, the only correlate they could find was the voter turnout rate. Felicity Barringer, "The Census, in One Not-so-easy Lesson," *New York Times,* April 22, 1990, p. 4.1. Perhaps the eligibles who failed to vote were also "too busy."

14:00. Undoing Others

1. Roland N. McKean, "Spillovers from the Rising Value of Time," in Thomas Schelling, "Symposium: Time in Economic Life," *Quarterly Journal of Economics, LXXXVII,* 4 (November 1973), p. 639.
2. Lois Pratt, "Business Temporal Norms and Bereavement Behavior," *American Sociological Review, 46* (1981), pp. 317–33; also Robert Fulton, "The Sacred and the Secular," in Robert Fulton (ed.), *Death and Identity*. New York: Wiley, 1965, pp. 89–105; David Stannard, *The Puritan Way of Death*. New York: Oxford University Press, 1977.

3. Paul Leinberger and Bruce Tucker, *The New Individualists*. New York: HarperCollins, 1991.
4. Louis Harris, *Inside America*. New York: Vintage, 1987, p. 237.
5. Harris, pp. 108–10, 112, 119.
6. Alexander W. Astin and others, *The American Freshmen*. Los Angeles: Higher Education Research Institute, University of California, 1991, p. 26.
7. Alix M. Freedman, "But It is the Good Life That Lures These Youths," *Wall Street Journal*, January 14, 1987, p. 23.
8. Harris, p. 148–49.
9. "Yuppie Politics," *ISR Newsletter*, Spring/Summer 1986, pp. 5–7.
10. Nicholas Vitalari, and others, "A Post Adoption Analysis of Computing in the Home," *Journal of Economic Psychology, 8* (1987), pp. 151–80.
11. Jim Lomax, director of psychiatry at Baylor University Medical School, Houston; quoted in Cynthia F. Mitchell, "The Electronic Interloper," *Wall Street Journal*, June 16, 1987, p. 29D.
12. Alice Kahn, "Drinking too Deep of TV's Elixir," *Los Angeles Times*, January 11, 1989, p. V1.
13. McKean notes, "If two persons spend an hour with each other, it is more expensive to both than it would be if hourly earnings were lower. If so, each of us is making it more difficult for each of us to get individual attention, which all of us, nonetheless, continue to crave. The result should be a proliferation of superficial commitments to other persons." (McKean, p. 639).
14. Independent Sector, *Giving and Volunteering in the United States*. Washington, DC: the author, 1988; Gilbert Fuchsberg, "Charities Are Stepping up Recruiting as Good Help Grows Harder to Find," *Wall Street Journal*, March 6, 1990, p. B1. Surveys conducted by the Census Bureau found a drop between 1974 and 1989 from 24 percent to 20 percent of the population volunteering; Bureau of Labor Statistics, "Thirty-Eight Million Persons do Volunteer Work," March 29, 1990. Although people are giving less of their time to charitable causes, they are giving more of their money. Giving USA, an organization that monitors charities, reports that annual donations now exceed $120 billion, three times the 1955 amount after adjusting for inflation. Felicity Barringer, "In the Worst of Times, America Keeps Giving," *New York Times*, March 15, 1992, p. E6.
15. *Statistical Abstract of the U.S.*, various years; the membership decline in the Girl Scouts is even more striking.
16. *Statistical Abstract of the U.S., 1990*, Table 401, p. 235.
17. Peter Drucker, "The Non-Profits' Quiet Revolution," *Wall Street Journal*, September 8, 1988, p. 26.
18. Jone L. Pearce, "Participation in Voluntary Associations," in David Horton Smith and Jon Van Til (eds.), *International Perspectives on Voluntary Action Research*. Washington, DC: University Press of America, 1983.
19. David Larsen, "Jury-Duty Excuses," *Los Angeles Times*, August 7, 1988, pp. VI1, 10.
20. Alexis de Tocqueville, *Democracy in America, I*. New York: Doubleday, 1986, ch. xiv; cited in Arthur M. Schlesinger, Jr., *The Cycles of American History*. Boston: Houghton Mifflin, p. 256.
21. Schlesinger, p. 256.
22. David Glass and others, "Voter Turnout," *Public Opinion*, December/January 1984.

23. Ogden Nash, ''Election Day is a Holiday,'' *Happy Days*. New York: Simon & Schuster, 1933.
24. From a *Wall Street Journal*/NBC poll; Arlen J. Large, ''Missing Persons,'' *Wall Street Journal,* ''Special Report on Politics '88,'' December 4, 1987, pp. 9D–10D.
25. Editorial ''Government of (Half) the People,'' *New York Times,* November 7, 1988, p. 24E.
26. Carrie Dolan, ''What do Travelers Lose?'' *Wall Street Journal,* January 23, 1989, p. B1.
27. Carol Felsenthal, *Alice Roosevelt Longworth*. New York: Putnam, 1988, p. 263.
28. Richard Gordon, *Great Medical Disasters*. New York: Dorset, 1986, p. 88.
29. Cynthia Heimel, ''Lower Manhattan Survival Tactics,'' *Village Voice,* June 7, 1983, p. 32.
30. ''Rampant Rudeness,'' *Wall Street Journal,* March 12, 1987, pp. I1, 26.
31. Stephen Koepp, ''Pul-eeze! Will Somebody Help Me?'' *Time,* February 2, 1987, pp. 48–55.
32. *Statistical Abstract of the U.S. 1990,* p. 610.
33. Reported on the BBC Morning News, October 9, 1988.
34. John J. Goldman, ''It's a Jungle out There, Auto Club Finds in Manhattan Traffic Survey,'' *Los Angeles Times,* March 14, 1987, p. I23.
35. Paul Dean, ''The End of Civility,'' *Los Angeles Times,* August 26, 1988, p. V2.
36. John B. Jackson, ''Truck City,'' in Martin Wachs and Margaret Crawford (eds.), *The Car and the City*. Ann Arbor: University of Michigan Press, 1992, p. 17.
37. Raymond W. Novaco, ''Automobile Driving and Aggressive Behavior,'' in Wachs and Crawford, p. 236.
38. Nieson Himmel and Carol McGraw, ''Trucker Rams 24 Cars in High-Speed, 35-Mile Freeway Trip,'' *Los Angeles Times,* May 19, 1988, p. II3.
39. Novaco, p. 246.
40. C. W. Turner, J. F. Layton, and L. S. Simons, ''Naturalistic Studies of Aggressive Behavior: Aggressive Stimuli, Victim Visibility, and Horn Honking,'' *Journal of Personality and Social Psychology, 31* (1975), pp. 1098–1107.
41. Attributed to Jane Ace; Fred Metcalf, *Dictionary of Modern Humorous Quotations*. London: Penguin, 1986, p. 219.

15:00. Young Folks in Trouble, Old Folks Doing Well

1. Fred Metcalf, *Dictionary of Modern Humorous Quotations*. London: Penguin, 1986, p. 185.
2. Victor R. Fuchs and Diane M. Reklis, ''America's Children: Economic Perspectives and Policy Options,'' *Science,* January 3, 1991, p. 41.
3. Data from the National Center for Health Statistics; reported in Alan L. Otten, ''Unnatural Causes Claim Lives of More Children,'' *Wall Street Journal,* February 13, 1989, p. B1.
4. Peter Uhlenberg and David Eggebeen, ''The Declining Well-Being of American Adolescents,'' *The Public Interest,* No. 82 (Winter 1986), pp. 25–38.
5. The last point, based on 1970–90 data, is made by Stanford economists

Victor Fuchs and Diane Reklis, who note "with many more adults available to provide and care for children, a substantial increase in the well-being of children might have been expected. Instead the reverse seems to have occurred" (p. 41).

6. U.S. Department of Labor, and a Census Bureau survey; Sara Rimer, "Women, Jobs and Children," *New York Times,* November 27, 1988, p. 1.
7. U.S. Department of Commerce, *Special Labor Force Reports,* Nos. 13, 130, and 134; Bulletins 2163 and 2307; in *Statistical Abstract of the U.S. 1989,* p. 386.
8. George Youmans, "The Higher Education of Women," *Popular Science Monthly, 4* (April 1874), p. 748; cited in Clifford Edward Clark, Jr., *The American Family Home, 1800–1960,* Chapel Hill: University of North Carolina Press, 1986, p. 104.
9. Louis Harris, *Inside America.* New York: Vintage, 1987, p. 92.
10. A survey of 60,000 households by the Bureau of Labor Statistics; cited in Cathy Trost, "All Work and No Play?" *Wall Street Journal,* December 30, 1986, p. 21.
11. Cathy Trost, "Men, Too, Wrestle with Career-Family Stress," *Wall Street Journal,* November 1, 1988, p. B1.
12. My correlations of the time-budgets (from A. Szalai and others, *The Use of Time.* The Hague: Mouton, 1972, p. 114) of employed men, employed women, and women not employed show that the ways employed women use their time more closely resemble the ways that employed men use theirs; correlations were lower between employed women and women not employed. The respective correlation coefficients are .976 and .825.
13. Harris, p. 98, reports 15 percent. Another study based on interviews with fifty two-job couples puts the proportion at 20 percent; Arlie Hochschild, *The Second Shift.* New York: Viking, 1989, pp. 3–4. And another shows an increasing domestic time commitment among males. John P. Robinson's time-budget surveys note that men are spending about 60 percent as much domestic work time as women, compared to 40 percent two decades ago. John P. Robinson, "Who's Doing the Housework?" *American Demographics, 10,* 12 (December 1988), p. 26.
14. Quoted in Michael D'Antonio, "Tough Medicine For a Sick America," *Los Angeles Times Magazine,* March 22, 1992, p. 36.
15. Yankelovich Clancy Shulman survey for *Time*/CNN; reported in Anastasia Touifexis, "Our Violent Kids," *Time,* June 12, 1989, pp. 52, 57.
16. Ken Magid and Carole A. McKelvey, *High Risk.* New York: Bantam, 1988. Among children who suffered neglect, 13 percent were arrested for a subsequent violent offense. Cathy Spatz Widom, "The Cycle of Violence," *Science,* April 14, 1989, pp. 160–66.
17. Randa Dembroff, an official of the Los Angeles County Bar Association; quoted in Touifexis, "Our Violent Kids," p. 57.
18. Seventy-two percent of males and 65 percent of females reported child care as a major problem, according to a survey by Work and Family Resources; cited in Trost, "Men, Too, . . . ," p. B1.
19. Jean L. Richardson, and others, "Substance Use among Eighth-Grade Students Who Take Care of Themselves After School," *Pediatrics, 84,* 3 (September 1989), p. 556.
20. William Safire, "Day Care, Child Care, Word Care," *New York Times Magazine,* May 29, 1988, p. 10.

21. (No author), "In the U.S. Today, 'Common Courtesy' Is Contradictory Phrase," *Wall Street Journal,* March 12, 1987, B15.
22. Quote from Ronald Pies, a psychiatrist at New England Medical Center in Boston; "Rampant Rudeness in the U.S. Today," *Wall Street Journal,* March 12, 1987, pp. I1, 26.
23. Harris, p. 113.
24. Reported on the CBS Evening News, February 9, 1987; cited in Magid and McKelvey, pp. 261–62.
25. James Coleman, "Educational Achievement," paper presented at a "London Conference on Educational Reform," Manhattan Institute for Policy Research and the London Center for Policy Studies, May 1988; and James S. Coleman, "Do Students Learn More in Private Schools than in Public Schools?" paper prepared for the Fifth Annual Critical Issues Symposium on, "Improving the Quality of Education in the United States," 1989, p. 20.
26. *Japanese Education Today,* Washington, DC: U.S. Government Printing Office, 1987; William J. Bennett (ed.), *A Report from the U.S. Study of Education in Japan*. Washington, DC: U.S. Department of Education, 1987.
27. Benjamin Duke, *The Japanese School*. New York: Praeger, 1986; and Merry I. White, *The Japanese Educational Challenge*. New York: Free Press, 1987.
28. (No author), " 'Model' Town Asks 'Why?' After Four Youths' Suicide," *Los Angeles Times,* March 13, 1987, p. I18.
29. Jean L. Richardson, and others, pp. 556–66. Richardson's research on 4,932 eighth grade students "indicated that self-care is an important risk factor for alcohol, tobacco, and marijuana use. Eighth grade students, who took care of themselves for 11 or more hours a week, were at twice the risk of substance use as those who did not take care of themselves at all."
30. Study by Mohammed Shaffi; cited in Constance Holden, "Youth Suicide," *Science,* August 22, 1986, pp. 839–41.
31. Letter from Joan Rothchild Hardin, *Science,* October 10, 1986, p. 127.
32. According to Michael Peck; Ursula Vils, "The Gathering Storm over Suicides among Teen-Agers," *Los Angeles Times,* March 23, 1987, pp. V1, 4.
33. Survey by Ernst & Young and Yankelovich Clancy Shulman; reported in "Careers Count Most for the Well-to-Do," *Wall Street Journal,* October 16, 1989, p. B1.
34. Jean L. Richardson, and others, pp. 556–66.
35. Daniel Yankelovich, *New Rules*. New York: Random House, 1981, p. 104. When opinion polls asked women whether they agreed with the statement, "When there are children in the family, parents should stay together even if they don't get along," 51 percent in 1962 and 63 percent in 1980 disagreed.
36. Pamela Cantor, "Teen-Age Suicide," *Los Angeles Times,* March 17, 1987, pp. V1, 8.
37. Report of the National Commission on Children; Dara McLeod, "Study Finds Americans Pessimistic on Status of Families," *Los Angeles Times,* November 22, 1991, p. A4.
38. Harris, p. 39.
39. "Era of the Geezer' Dawns as the Elderly Hit Campaign Trail," *Wall Street Journal,* July 31, 1986, p. 1.
40. Michael D. Hurd, "The Economic Status of the Elderly," *Science,* May 12, 1989, p. 660.

41. Unpublished 1984 Census Bureau data reported in Fabian Linden, "The 800 Billion Market," *American Demographics,* February 1986, pp. 4–5; Rita Ricardo-Campbell, *The Economics and Politics of Health.* Chapel Hill: University of North Carolina Press, 1982.
42. Ken Dychtwald and Joe Flower, *Age Wave.* Los Angeles: Tarcher, 1989, p. 268. The typical elderly household's wealth exceeds by $3,000 that of their juniors aged 45–54, and one elderly household in four can boast a median net worth of between $100,000 and $250,000; Bureau of the Census, *Household and Asset Ownership: 1984,* Series P. 70, No. 7, Table 5. The typical senior's asset holdings were larger than any other age group's, except for home equity, where they were exceeded by householders aged 55 to 64; "Insurance for the Twilight Years," *Time,* April 6, 1987, p. 53.
43. As of 1989; *Statistical Abstract of the U.S. 1990,* pp. 37, 460.
44. Data from the National Center for Health Statistics, Census and Bureau of Labor Statistics. Beth J. Soldo and Emily M. Agree, *America's Elderly, Population Bulletin, 43,* 3 (September 1988), p. 25.
45. Data from a National Health Interview Survey; cited in "The Flesh is Able, the Spirit is Weak," *Wall Street Journal,* July 9, 1987, p. 31.
46. "The Flesh is Able, the Spirit is Weak," p. 31.
47. Robyn Stone, and others, "Caregivers of the Frail Elderly," *The Gerontologist, 27,* 5 (October 1987), pp. 616–25.
48. Comptroller General of the United States, *The Need for a National Policy to Better Provide for the Elderly.* Washington, DC: U.S. Government Printing Office, 1977; 1977 data adjusted for price level changes to 1990.
49. Sandra Newman, *Housing Adjustments of Older People.* Ann Arbor: Institute for Social Research, University of Michigan, 1976, p. 32.
50. L. E. Troll. "The Family of Later Life," *Journal of Marriage and the Family, 33* (1971), pp. 263–90.
51. The elderly, representing 12 percent of the total population and paying only 10 percent of all income and payroll taxes, receive 68 percent of total government benefits, a figure that includes Medicare, Medicaid, food stamps, and housing subsidies. Census Bureau data reported in Robert Pear, "U.S. Pensions Found to Lift Many of Poor," *New York Times,* December 28, 1988, p. A1.
52. Robert Clark and Joseph Spengler, "The Implications of Future Dependency Ratios and Their Composition," in Barbara P. Herzog (ed.), *Aging and Income.* New York: Human Sciences Press, 1978. Census data report that per capita federal spending on children in 1984 was but 9 percent of the per capita spent on the elderly; Samuel H. Preston, "Children and the Elderly," *Demography, 21,* 4 (November 1984), p. 440.
53. Harris, p. 131.

16:00. The Disservicing of America

1. David McCord, *What Cheer,* New York: Coward-McCann, 1945, p. 354.
2. Suzy Menkes, *The Windsor Style.* Topsfield, MA: Salem House, 1988, pp. 7, 17, 35, 66.
3. James Brian Quinn and Christopher E. Gagnon, "Will Services Follow Manufacturing into Decline?," *Harvard Business Review, 64,* 6 (November/December 1986), p. 95.
4. Bureau of Labor Statistics projections; *Statistical Abstract of the U.S. 1991,* p. 395.

5. Robin Marantz Henig, "Less Can be More," *New York Times Magazine,* June 26, 1988, p. 33.
6. Jean d'Ormesson, and others, *Grand Hotel*. New York: Vendome, 1984, p. 65.
7. Jack Smith, "Serves You Right," *Los Angeles Times Magazine,* October 18, 1987, p. 6.
8. *Time,* February 22, 1988, p. 11.
9. David Wessel, "Sure Ways to Annoy Consumers," *Wall Street Journal,* November 6, 1989, p. B1.
10. Robert E. Kelley, "Poorly Served Employees Serve Customers Just as Poorly," *Wall Street Journal,* October 12, 1987, p. 22.
11. Louis Harris, *Inside America*. New York: Vintage, 1987, p. 356–58.
12. Robert Kanigel, "Angry at Our Gods," *Columbia, 14,* 1 (October 1988), p. 27. And the amount of time spent is declining. General practitioners spend less than seven minutes per office visit talking to their patients, down from eleven minutes in 1975. Sonia L. Nazario, "Medical Science Seeks a Cure for Doctors Suffering from Boorish Bedside Manner," *Wall Street Journal,* March 17, 1992, p. B1.
13. Martha Fay, "Why Your Family Doctor is a Group," *New York Times Magazine,* June 7, 1987, p. 16.
14. R. Corwin, "Self-Importance," *American Journal of Sociology, 66* (1961), pp. 604–15.
15. Morton Hunt, "Was Man Meant to Fly?," *New York Times Magazine,* November 1, 1987, p. 42.
16. Teri Agins and William M. Carley, "Delays, Bumpings and Lost Bags," *Wall Street Journal,* November 10, 1986, p. 23.
17. U.S. Department of Transportation data for a nine–ten month period; reported in "Consumer Complaints Against Airlines," *Wall Street Journal,* November 19, 1987, p. 33.
18. Clyde Haberman, "The Presumed Uniqueness of Japan," *New York Times Magazine,* August 28, 1988, p. 74.
19. Haberman, pp. 39ff, 74.
20. Edwin M. Reingold, "A Homecoming Lament," *Time,* February 2, 1987, p. 55.
21. *The London Times,* July 10, 1987, p. 1.
22. Based on a cartoon in *Time,* February 2, 1987, pp. 48–49.
23. Paul A. Strassmann, "The Office of the Future," *Technology Review,* December/January 1980, pp. 58–60.
24. Kelley, p. 22.
25. Kelley, p. 22.
26. James M. Kouzes, president of T.P.G.-Learning Systems; quoted in Charyll Aimee Barron, "Getting Serious About Service," *New York Times Magazine: The Business World,* June 11, 1989, p. 52.
27. *The Forum Corporation Corporate Strategy Study*. New York: the author, 1989, p. 8.
28. Hart poll for the *Wall Street Journal;* Francine Schwadel, "Shoppers' Blues," *Wall Street Journal,* October 13, 1989, p. B1; and Alix M. Freedman, "Most Consumers Shun Luxuries," *Wall Street Journal,* September 19, 1989, p. B1.
29. Francine Schwadel, "Nordstrom's Push East Will Test its Renown for the Best in Service," *Wall Street Journal,* August 1, 1989, p. 1.
30. *The Forum Corporation Corporate Strategy Study*.

31. Daniel P. Finkelman, "Quality is Not Enough," *New York Times,* May 14, 1989, p. F3.
32. Clare Ansberry, "Uphill Battle," *Wall Street Journal,* April 2, 1987, p. 1.
33. Phillip L. Zweig, "Banks Stress Resolving Complaints to Win Small Customers' Favor," *Wall Street Journal,* December 8, 1986, p. 27; Barron, p. 23.
34. Claudia H. Deutsch, "The Powerful Push for Self-Service," *New York Times,* April 9, 1989, p. III1.
35. Deutsch, p. III15.
36. *Statistical Abstract of the U.S.,* various years.
37. A. E. Brown and H. A. Jeffcott, Jr., *Absolutely Mad Inventions Compiled from the Records of the United States Patent Office.* New York: Dover, 1932, pp. 56–57.

17:00. Time for the Matters of the Mind

1. A. E. Housman (ed.), 1905 Preface, *Ivvenalis Satvrae,* London: Cambridge University Press, 1938, p. xi.
2. Roland N. McKean, "Spillovers from the Rising Value of Time," in T. C. Schelling, "Symposium: Time in Economic Life," *Quarterly Journal of Economics, 87* (1973), p. 639.
3. Dean Ann Friedlaender; quoted in William Booth, "Curriculum Changes Spark Debate at MIT," *Science,* June 19, 1987, p. 1515.
4. Staffan Linder, *The Harried Leisure Class.* New York: Columbia University Press, 1970, p. 104.
5. Jacques Barzun, "Give Her a Book? She *Has* a Book," *Columbia, 13,* 3 (1987), p. 29.
6. Barzun, p. 30.
7. Lisa H. Towle, "What's New in the Comic Book Business," *New York Times,* January 31, 1988, p. F21.
8. Towle, p. F21.
9. Curtis B. Gans, "Is TV Turning Off the American Voter?" *New York Times,* July 3, 1988, p. 24.
10. *Simmons Market Research Bureau,* and *Statistical Abstract of the U.S.,* various years.
11. Debra A. Lieberman, "Predictors of Computer Work and Computer Play for Children and Adolescents," paper presented at the annual meeting of the International Communication Association, Montreal, Canada, 1987.
12. Lieberman, p. 11.
13. Quoted in Carrie Dolan, "Parents Fear (Video) Games Turn Their Kids into Zombies," *Wall Street Journal,* March 8, 1988, p. 37.
14. Carol Hymowitz, "For Many Kids, Playtime Isn't Free Time," *Wall Street Journal,* September 20, 1988, p. 39.
15. Hymowitz, p. 39.
16. Reading, fixing up things around the house, and hobbies and interests were the three top choices in both the 1988 and 1978 polls, but reading moved from third place in 1978 to first place in the more recent survey; the importance that "influential Americans," whose time is likely to be even more scarce than the general public's, attached to reading was higher, suggesting that they spent less time reading. Tabulation prepared for the author from Roper Report 88-5.

17. Andrew S. Harvey, *et al., Time Budget Research*. Frankfurt: Campus Verlag, 1984, p. 128.
18. Such as the Manhattan Project, Bell Labs' work on the transistor, and the Apollo Program.
19. William H. Rehnquist, *The Supreme Court*. New York: Morrow, p. 273.
20. Quoted in Jack Smith, "The Meaning of Life," *Los Angeles Times Magazine*, May 21, 1989, p. 6.
21. "He complained, of course, that nobody understood the demands of creative writing (it 'was different from compiling a grocery list'), that interruptions and undue noise broke his concentration. When that happened, it was hard to get back into his story and characters. . . . Radio, doorbell, telephone—all were 'forbidden items.' " Stephen B. Oates, *William Faulkner*. New York: Harper & Row, 1987, p. 96.
22. Ian Hamilton, *In Search of J. D. Salinger*. New York: Random House, 1988, p. 167.
23. Quoted in the *Los Angeles Times*, July 18, 1986, p. VI1.
24. Christopher White, *Peter Paul Rubens*. New Haven: Yale University Press, 1987, p. 73.
25. Patt Morrison, "Goldwater, Without Regrets," *Los Angeles Times*, September 25, 1988, p. VI1.
26. Thomas J. Reese, *Inside the Power Structure of the American Catholic Church*. San Francisco: Harper & Row, 1989.
27. Bob Davis, "Broadcasters, Absent Regulation, Kill New Shows—But is That Bad?" *Wall Street Journal*, October 16, 1987, p. 33.
28. Michael Schrage, "A Road Map for those Driven by Distraction," *Wall Street Journal*, March 21, 1988, p. 22.
29. Schrage, p. 22.
30. Schrage, p. 22.
31. Linder, 1970, p. 95.
32. Editors of *Consumer Reports, I'll Buy That*. Mount Vernon, NY: Consumers Union, 1986, p. 126.
33. Andrew Pollack, "The Computer Age," *New York Times*, August 11, 1991, p. E.2.
34. Pollack, p. E.2.
35. Michael Albert, "Computer Phobo-mania," *Zeta Magazine, I* (January 1, 1988), pp. 90–96.
36. Hans Moravec, *Mind Children*. Cambridge: Harvard University Press, 1988, p. 1.
37. Mikell P. Groover, and others, *Industrial Robotics*. New York: McGraw Hill, 1986.
38. "Machines Who Think," *Science*, November 29, 1991, p. 1291.
39. Moravec, pp. 59–60.
40. Richard Dawkins, *The Blind Watchmaker*. New York: Norton, 1986, p. ix.
41. William M. Bulkeley, "Frontiers of Science," *Wall Street Journal*, November 10, 1986, p. IV4.
42. William J. Baumol and Edward Wolff, "On the Theory of Productivity and Unbalanced Growth," Discussion Paper Series #80-03, C. V. Staff Center for Applied Economics, New York: New York University Press, January 1980, p. 6, and fn. 5, p. 46.
43. Shoshana Zuboff, *In the Age of the Smart Machine*. New York: Basic Books, 1988, pp. 106–07.

44. David E. Sanger, "Computer Fails as Job-Killer," *New York Times,* October 11, 1987, p. XII5.
45. Paul B. Carroll, "The Tough Job of Training Computerphobic Managers," *Wall Street Journal,* June 20, 1988, p. 17.
46. Carroll, p. 17.
47. Tora K. Bikson and others, *Implementing Computerized Procedures in Office Settings.* Santa Monica, CA: Rand Corp., 1987, pp. 25, 42.
48. Marc J. Roberts, "On Time," in Thomas C. Schelling, "Symposium: Time in Economic Life," *Quarterly Journal of Economics, 87* (1973), p. 648.

18:00. Who Runs America?

1. Fred Metcalf, *Dictionary of Modern Humorous Quotations.* London: Penguin, 1986, p. 195.
2. Hedrick Smith, *The Power Game.* New York: Random House, 1988, p. 109; Lou Cannon, *President Reagan.* New York: Simon & Schuster, 1991, p. 56.
3. Those priorities became all too clear to James A. Baker, III, when, on the day of the 1983 economic summit, he realized the President had not read his briefing notes. When the Chief of Staff asked why, Mr. Reagan calmly answered, "Well, Jim, *The Sound of Music* was on last night." Cannon, p. 57.
4. Smith, p. 109.
5. Larry Speakes, *Speaking Out.* New York: Scribner, 1988.
6. Smith, p. 109.
7. Kathleen Hall Jamieson, *Eloquence in an Electronic Age.* New York: Oxford University Press, 1988, p. 219.
8. Smith, p. 109.
9. "Well, He Survived," *Time,* March 30, 1987, pp. 14–15.
10. Barbara W. Tuchman, "A Nation in Decline?" *New York Times Magazine,* September 20, 1987, p. 55.
11. Smith, p. 108.
12. Jamieson, p. 214. P. J. O'Rourke develops the point in *Parliament of Whores.* New York: Atlantic Monthly, 1991.
13. Smith, pp. 23–24.
14. Roderick P. Hart, *Verbal Style and the Presidency.* Orlando: Academic Press, 1984, pp. 2–3.
15. Ernest G. Bormann, "Ethics of Ghostwritten Speeches," *Quarterly Journal of Speech, 47* (1961), p. 263.
16. William Safire, *The New Language of Politics.* New York: Random House, p. 414.
17. Eric F. Goldman, "Party of One," *Holiday, 31* (1962), p. 14; cited in Lois J. Einhorn, "The Ghosts Unmasked," *Communication Quarterly, 30,* 1 (Winter 1981), p. 43.
18. The candidate was Douglas McKay; Peter Lewis, "Ghost Town," *New York Times Magazine,* April 10, 1960, p. 42; cited in Jamieson, p. 210. Dwight Eisenhower, himself a former ghostwriter, thanked one of his writers for a successful product with, "On every side I have had compliments concerning the content of the talk. I am sorry you could not take over also its delivery." Robert G. Gunderson, "Political Phrasemakers in Perspective," *Southern Speech Communication Journal, 26* (1960), p. 24; cited in Jamieson, p. 210.

19. Einhorn, p. 43.
20. Einhorn, p. 44.
21. Martin Schram, *The Great American Video Game*. New York: Morrow, 1987.
22. H. L. Mencken, *A Carnival of Buncombe*. Chicago: University of Chicago Press, 1984, p. 39.
23. Donald T. Regan, *For the Record*. San Diego: Harcourt Brace Jovanovich, 1988, p. 226.
24. Arthur M. Schlesinger, Jr., *The Cycles of American History*. Boston: Houghton Mifflin, 1986, p. 270.
25. Smith, p. 29.
26. Philip Stern, *The Best Congress That Money Can Buy*. New York: Pantheon, 1988, p. 117.
27. Jeffrey H. Birnbaum, "Congressman Who Returned after 12 Years Notes Changes Including More Lobbying, Budget Fights," *Wall Street Journal*, June 15, 1987, p. 48.
28. Edward Zuckerman, *Almanac of Federal PACs*. Washington, DC: Amward Publications, 1990, pp. 594–95; Federal Election Commissions Report on Financial Activity. Washington, DC: May 21, 1987, p. 54.
29. Even though recent legislation has in part curbed the financial abuses, the lobbies' information abuses remain to threaten the quality of public decision making.
30. Schlesinger, Jr., p. 270; Jamieson, p. 11.
31. Jamieson, p. 10. An analysis of network newscasts prior to the 1968 and 1988 elections discovered that in twenty years the average 'sound bite' fell from 42.3 seconds to only 9.8 seconds. Kiku Adatto, "The Incredible Shrinking Sound Bite," *New Republic, 202,* 22 (May 28, 1990), p. 20.
32. Jamieson, p. 11.
33. Schlesinger, Jr., p. 269.
34. Reporter Sidney Blumenthal; quoted in David Shaw, "Television: Candidates' 'Mine Field'," *Los Angeles Times,* August 15, 1988, p. 1.
35. Christopher Matthews, *Hardball*. New York: Summit, 1988.
36. Curtis B. Gans, "Is TV Turning Off the American Voter?" *New York Times,* July 3, 1988, p. 24.
37. Art Buchwald, "How Hart Can be the Teflon Candidate," *Los Angeles Times,* December 22, 1987, p. V2.
38. Jamieson, p. 62.
39. Roger Stone; quoted in David Shribman, "TV's Election Coverage Busily Skims the Surface While Bemoaning Candidates' Lack of Substance," *Wall Street Journal,* April 11, 1988, p. 48.
40. Gans, p. 24.
41. From a *New York Times*/CBS poll; Michael Oreskes, "TV's Role in '88," *New York Times,* October 30, 1988, p. 1.
42. Oreskes, p. 1.
43. From an Opinion Research Corporation/*TV Guide* poll; reported in Michael A. Lipton, "Campaign '88 and TV," *TV Guide,* January 23, 1988, pp. 2–7.
44. Quoted in Oreskes, p. 9.

19:00. "We Apologize for Any Inconvenience We May Have Caused"

1. Fred Metcalf, *Dictionary of Modern Humorous Quotations*. London: Penguin, 1987, p. 13.
2. Mike Edwards, "Chernobyl—One Year After," *National Geographic, 171*, 5 (1987), p. 634.
3. U.S.S.R. State Committee on the Utilization of Atomic Energy, "The Accident at the Chernobyl Nuclear Power Plant and its Consequences," draft report presented at IAEA Experts Meeting, Vienna, Austria, August 25–29, 1986 (emphasis added).
4. J. G. Kemeny and others, *Report of the President's Commission on the Accident at Three Mile Island*. Washington, DC: U.S. Government Printing Office, October 1979, pp. 46, 116.
5. M. Rogovin and G. Frampton, *Three Mile Island: A Report to the Commissioners and to the Public*, NUREG CR/1250. Washington, DC: Nuclear Regulatory Commission, January 1980, pp. 14, 17, 18; John F. Ahearne, "Letter," *Science*, October 9, 1987, p. 145.
6. Mathew L. Wald, "Ten Years after Three Mile Island," *New York Times*, March 23, 1989, p. C14; and Colin Norman and David Dickson, "The Aftermath of Chernobyl," *Science*, September 12, 1986, p. 1141.
7. John F. Ahearne, "Nuclear Power After Chernobyl," *Science*, May 8, 1987, p. 677.
8. The following paragraphs are adapted from Henry Fuhrmann, "Why Things Fall Down," *Columbia*, April 1988, pp. 31–36; Mario Salvador, *Why Buildings Stand Up*. New York: Norton, 1980; and Steven S. Ross, *Construction Disasters*. New York: McGraw-Hill, 1984.
9. Fuhrmann, p. 33.
10. Mark Douglas Home and Nicholas Schoon, "Rig Disaster Report Could Help Claims for Damages," *The (London) Independent*, October 1, 1988, p. 2.
11. Janice Castro, "Questions About Eastern," *Time*, August 24, 1987, p. 41.
12. Boeing Commercial Airplane Co., *Statistical Summary of Commercial Jet Aircraft Accidents, Worldwide Operations, 1959–1988*. Seattle: Boeing Commercial Airplane Co., 1989.
13. "FAA Criticizes Delta Pilots for Lapses in Crew Discipline," *Washington Post*, September 19, 1987, p. A1h.
14. Laurie McGinley, "Northwest Air Crash in Detroit Is Blamed on Crew Failure to Make Required Check," *Wall Street Journal*, May 11, 1988, p. 10.
15. William M. Carley, "In a Big Plane Crash, Cause Probably Isn't Everybody's Guess," *Wall Street Journal*, March 29, 1988, pp. 1, 21.
16. McGinley, p. 10.
17. Associated Press, "Runway Lights in Italy Turned Off as Jetliner Approached to Land," *Los Angeles Times*, July 2, 1988, p. I6.
18. Ronald J. Ostrow and William C. Rempel, "Exxon Indicted in Alaska Spill," *Los Angeles Times*, February 28, 1990, p. 1.
19. The section draws on an authoritative series of articles published in *Science*. M. Mitchell Waldrop, "The Challenger Disaster," February 14, 1986, pp. 661–63; Eliot Marshall, "The Shuttle Record," February 14, 1986, pp.

664–65; R. Jeffrey Smith, "Shuttle Inquiry Focuses on Weather, Rubber Seals, and Unheeded Advice," February 28, 1986, pp. 909–11; R. Jeffrey Smith, "Commission Finds Flaws in NASA Decision-Making," March 14, 1986, pp. 1237–38; and R. Jeffrey Smith, "NASA Had Warning of Potential Shuttle Accident," February 21, 1986, p. 792.

20. Smith, "NASA Had Warning of Potential Shuttle Accident," p. 792.
21. March 1983 memo; cited in Smith, "Shuttle Inquiry . . . ," *Science*, February 28, 1986, pp. 909–11.
22. Smith, "Shuttle Inquiry . . . ," p. 909–11.
23. Smith, "Commission Finds Flaws . . . ," p. 1237.
24. Paul Bracken, *The Command and Control of Nuclear Forces*. New Haven, CT: Yale University Press, 1983, pp. 65–67.
25. The remainder of this section is adapted from a lecture delivered by Mr. Beale at the annual meetings of the American Academy for the Advancement of Science, June 1983, and a *Science* interview at his desk, "balanced at one end by Excedrin and at the other by computer terminals"; reported in R. Jeffrey Smith, "Crisis Management Under Strain," *Science*, August 31, 1984, pp. 907–09.
26. Alexander George; quoted in Smith, "Crisis Management Under Strain," p. 908.
27. Smith, "Crisis Management Under Strain," pp. 908–09.

20:00 Waste-making Haste

1. To be sure, the rising number of recalls responds to new laws, yet the laws respond to the need for consumer protections from faulty products.
2. *Statistical Abstract of the United States*, various years.
3. *Statistical Abstract of the United States*, 1990.
4. M. J. Mullen in Hearings Before the Senate Committee on Commerce, Science and Transportation, 99th Congress, 2d Session, (March 4, 1986), p. 183; cited in Peter Huber, "Injury Litigation and Liability Insurance Dynamics," *Science*, October 2, 1987, p. 33.
5. *The Medical Defence Union Annual Report*, 1980, p. 20; cited in Richard Gordon, *Great Medical Disasters*. New York: Dorset, 1986, pp. 37–38.
6. Jerry Avorn and others, "Scientific versus Commercial Sources of Influence on the Prescribing Behavior of Physicians," *American Journal of Medicine*, 73 (July 1982), pp. 4–8.
7. Michael S. Wilkes and Miriam Shuchman, "Pitching Doctors," *New York Times Magazine*, November 5, 1989, pp. 88, 90.
8. Quoted in Ron Winslow, "Sometimes, Talk is the Best Medicine," *Wall Street Journal*, October 5, 1989, p. B1.
9. FDA study conducted in 1983; cited in Frank E. James, "Doctors Don't Tell All on Drugs' Effects," *Wall Street Journal*, May 20, 1988, p. 21.
10. Beverly C. Payne, quoted in *ISR Newsletter*, Spring/Summer 1986, p. 4; based on Payne, and others, *Malpractice Trends in Michigan*. Ann Arbor: Institute for Social Research, University of Michigan, November 1985.
11. California Medical Association; cited in Patricia M. Danzon, *Medical Malpractice*. Cambridge, MA: Harvard University Press, 1985, p. 21.
12. Robert W. Dubois and Robert H. Brook, "Preventable Deaths," *The Annals of Internal Medicine*, October 1, 1988, pp. 582–89.
13. Danzon, p. 19; Danzon concludes that, "Even assuming a doubling of

claims since the mid-1970s, it is almost certainly true that the cost of injuries due to malpractice far exceeds the cost of claims'' (p. 29).

14. Gordon, (no page).
15. Walt Bogdanich, ''Medical Labs, Trusted as Largely Error-Free, Are Far From Infallible,'' *Wall Street Journal,* February 2, 1987, p. 1; Denise Grady, ''Going Overboard on Medical Tests,'' *Time,* April 25, 1988, p. 80.
16. According to the reports that came back, the sample with a known cholesterol value of 262.6 milligrams per deciliter was variously tested anywhere from 101 to 524. Walt Bogdanich, ''Inaccuracy in Testing Cholesterol Hampers War on Heart Disease,'' *Wall Street Journal,* February 3, 1987, pp. 1, 22.
17. Bogdanich, ''Medical Labs . . . ,'' p. 1.
18. Grady, pp. 80–81.
19. Grady, pp. 80–81.
20. Walt Bogdanich, ''Lax Laboratories,'' *Wall Street Journal,* November 2, 1987, p. 1.
21. Bogdanich, ''Lax Laboratories . . . ,'' p. 1.
22. Bogdanich, ''Lax Laboratories . . . ,'' p. 1.
23. According to the American College of Obstetricians and Gynecologists; cited in Walt Bogdanich, ''Physicians' Carelessness with Pap Tests is Cited in Procedure's High Failure Rate,'' *Wall Street Journal,* December 29, 1987, p. 17.
24. Quoting Dr. John Graham, American College of Obstetricians and Gynecologists; cited in Bogdanich, ''Physicians' Carelessness . . . ,'' p. 17.

21:00. Mea Culpa: *The Customer May Not Always Be Right*

1. Betsy Morris, ''Big Spenders,'' *Wall Street Journal,* July 30, 1987, p. 1.
2. Roger L. McCarthy, and others, ''Product Information Presentation, User Behavior, and Safety,'' in M. J. Alluisi and others (eds.), *Proceedings of the Human Factors Society,* 28th Annual Meeting, Santa Monica, CA, 1984, pp. 81–85.
3. A. L. Dorris and J. L. Purswell, ''Warnings and Human Behavior,'' *Journal of Products Liability, 1* (1977), pp. 255–64.
4. L. C. Kerpelman, *Evaluation of the Effectiveness of Outdoor Power Equipment Information and Education Programs.* Cambridge, MA: Abt Associates, 1978; cited in McCarthy, and others, p. 84.
5. D. Shinar and A. Drory, ''Sign Registration in Daytime and Nighttime Driving,'' *Human Factors, 25,* 1 (1983), pp. 117–22; cited in D. P. Horst, and others, ''Safety Information Presentation,'' in *Proceedings of the Human Factors Society,* 30th Annual Meeting, 1986, p. 5.
6. G. E. McCarthy, and others, ''Measured Impact of a Mandated Warning on User Behavior,'' *Proceedings of the Human Factors Society,* 31st Annual Meeting, 1987, pp. 479–83.
7. M. L. Myers, *Staff Report on the Cigarette Advertising Investigation.* Washington, DC: Federal Trade Commission, 1981. When a group of adolescents were asked to examine magazine advertising for cigarettes, about half failed to look at the health warning and only a few of those who did actually read it were able to recall its message; Paul M. Fischer and others, ''Recall and Eye Tracking Study of Adolescents Viewing Tobacco Adver-

tisements," *Journal of the American Medical Association, 261,* 1 (January 6, 1989), pp. 84–94.
8. Gina Kolata, "Fire! New Ways to Prevent It," *Science,* January 16, 1987, p. 281.
9. Kolata, p. 281.
10. Philip Schaenman, president of TriData, an Arlington, Virginia, fire consulting firm; quoted in Kolata, p. 281. For example, 85 percent of all homes are now equipped with smoke detectors and some local building codes require home sprinklers.
11. Ralph H. Turner, Joanne M. Nigg, and Denise Heller Paz, *Waiting for Disaster.* Berkeley, CA: University of California Press, 1986, pp. 119, 175.
12. Possibly even these proportions are too high, for respondents may have tried to please interviewers by telling them what they wanted to hear. Turner and others, p. 180.
13. David E. Sanger, "Moving and Shaking the Tokyo Way," *New York Times,* September 4, 1988, p. Y3.
14. Steven Fink, *Crisis Management: Planning for the Inevitable.* New York: Amacom, 1986, p. 67.
15. Indeed, the data exist, but for patients to get access to it is a different matter. Because the information is tabulated, some doctors avoid high-risk assignments to keep their error rate low.
16. Denise Grady, "Going Overboard on Medical Tests," *Time,* April 25, 1988, p. 80.
17. Associated Press, "Study Says Safer Products Result from Fear of Suits," *Los Angeles Times,* January 5, 1988, p. IV20.
18. Milt Freudenheim, "Costs of Medical Malpractice Drop After an 11-Year Climb," *New York Times,* June 11, 1989, p. 1.
19. *Statistical Abstract of the United States,* various years.

22:00. Time Future

1. *Worse Verse,* 1969; cited in Fred Metcalf, *Dictionary of Modern Humorous Quotations.* London: Penguin, 1987, p. 247.
2. Originally published in *Punch;* cited in Richard Morris, *Time's Arrows.* New York: Simon & Schuster, 1985, p. 160.
3. Clifford Sharp, *The Economics of Time.* New York: Wiley, 1981, p. 1.
4. "How Mama Lost Her Head," *Time,* March 7, 1988, p. 25.
5. Michael F. Scheier and Charles S. Carver, "Dispositional Optimism and Physical Well-Being," *Journal of Personality, 55,* 2 (June 1987), pp. 169–210; and Michael F. Scheier *et al.,* "Dispositional Optimism and Recovery from Coronary Artery Bypass Surgery," *Journal of Personality and Social Psychology, 57,* 6 (December 1989), pp. 1024–40.
6. Stephen Kahn, director of the University of Chicago Stress Project; cited in Aubin Tyler, "Optimists Considered Better Equipped to Battle Stress and Win," *Los Angeles Times,* February 11, 1988, p. II4.
7. *Statistical Abstract of the United States, 1990,* p. 208.
8. *New York Times* poll; reported in "The Environment," *New York Times,* July 2, 1989, p. 1. As for the cost, the *Los Angeles Times* poll found that, by more than two to one, people felt that environmental protection was worth the cost even "if that means some people will lose their jobs and the government will have to spend a great deal of money." George Skelton, "Ameri-

cans Give High Marks to Quality of Life," *Los Angeles Times,* January 1, 1990, p. A28.

9. *Statistical Abstract of the United States, 1989,* pp. 199, 202, 204, 218.
10. Up from 648 million pounds in 1960 to 1,180 in 1986, with a sales value rising from $262 million to $4,234 million! *Statistical Abstract of the United States 1990,* p. 206.
11. "The average American car driven the average American distance—10,000 miles—in an average American year releases its own weight in carbon into the atmosphere." Bill McKibben, *The End of Nature.* New York: Random House, 1989, p. 6.
12. William Fulkerson, and others, "Global Warming," *Science,* November 17, 1989, pp. 868–69.
13. Peter Passell, "Cure for Greenhouse Effect," *New York Times,* November 19, 1989, p. 1.
14. Mark Christensen, "Forever Young," *Los Angeles Times Magazine,* June 21, 1987, p. 18.
15. Hilary Stout, "U.S. Health Habits Haven't Improved Over Past Two Years, Survey Indicates," *Wall Street Journal,* May 3, 1991, p. B8.
16. Jane E. Brody, "America's Health," *New York Times Good Health Magazine,* October 8, 1989, pp. 30, 42.
17. Data from the National Heart, Blood, and Lung Institute.
18. Marlene Cimons, "Smoking-Linked Deaths up Sharply in '85–88 Period," *Los Angeles Times,* February 1, 1991, p. A4.
19. Tom Parker, *In One Day.* Boston: Houghton Mifflin, 1984, p. 31.
20. John P. Pierce and others. "Trends in Cigarette Smoking in the United States: Projections to the Year 2000," *Journal of the American Medical Association, 261,* 1 (January 6, 1989), pp. 61–65.

23:00. Saving These United States of America

1. "To the Virgins, To Make Much of Time," *Select Poems from the Hesperides of Robert Herrick, Esq.* Bristol, England: J. M. Gutch, 1810, p. 60.
2. Adam Smith, *The Wealth of Nations.* New York: Modern Library, 1937, pp. 324–25.
3. C. Alan Gardner, "Policy Options to Improve The U.S. Standard of Living," *Economic Review (of the Federal Reserve Bank of Kansas City), 73,* 9 (November 1988), pp. 3–16.
4. Allan H. Meltzer, "If Middle Class is Falling Behind, Solution Lies in Higher Productivity," *Los Angeles Times,* December 8, 1991, p. D2.
5. Lawrence Summers, "What to Do When Japan Says 'No'," *New York Times,* December 3, 1989, p. F2.
6. A recent survey comparing time discounts of 200 corporate managers finds that the fraction of R&D invested in long-term projects by U.S. firms is less than one-half that of Japanese and about one-third that of European-based firms. James M. Poterba and Lawrence H. Summers, "Time Horizons of American Firms: New Evidence from a Survey of CEOs," unpublished paper; October 1991, p. 27.
7. MIT Commission on Industrial Productivity, *Made In America.* Cambridge, MA: MIT Press, 1989, p. 296.
8. MIT Commission . . . , pp. 37, 183, 301.
9. MIT Commission . . . , p. 267.

10. In 1985 "American firms had a real cost of funds of six percent; Japanese firms . . . only 1.5 percent. This means that a U.S. firm should be willing to undertake a project that lowers earnings by a dollar today and raises them by 1.2 constant dollars . . . only if the payoff comes in less than three years in the future. By contrast, a Japanese firm (paying 1.5 percent) should be willing to sacrifice a dollar now for 1.2 dollars 12 years in the future." George N. Hatsopoulos, Paul R. Krugman, and Lawrence H. Summers, "U.S. Competitiveness: Beyond the Trade Deficit." *Science,* July 15, 1988, p. 303.
11. In 1990, the average Japanese and German household saved 14 percent of its after-tax income, compared to the average American's 4.7 percent; and Japan's and Germany's investment as a proportion of gross domestic product, and their productivity growth, have far exceeded America's. Steven Greenhouse, "Attention America! Snap Out of It!" *New York Times,* February 9, 1992, p. 8F.
12. Hatsopolous, and others, p. 304; Henry J. Aaron, "Politics and the Professors Revisited," *American Economic Review, 79,* 2 (May 1989), p. 4. OECD data show that savings have dropped in all the industrialized countries since the 1970s, but nowhere as sharply as in the U.S.
13. With debt rising several times as fast as total output, "one dollar of debt expansion was financing only 38 cents of GNP growth, roughly half the average rate for the earlier postwar years." Lindley H. Clark, Jr., and Alfred L. Malabre, Jr., "Debt Stops Surging, Easing the Pressures on Interest Rates," *Wall Street Journal,* January 3, 1990, p. A2; Hatsopoulos, and others, p. 300.
14. "As long as the U.S. national saving rate remains far below that of all our major competitor nations, there is little chance for restoring America's international economic position." Hatsopoulos, and others, p. 299.
15. Hart poll for the *Wall Street Journal;* cited in Alix M. Freedman, "Most Consumers Shun Luxuries, Seek Few Frills but Better Service," *Wall Street Journal,* September 19, 1989, p. B1.
16. Mr. Mill (1806–73) no doubt refers to Thorstein Veblen (1857–1929), the iconoclast and identifier of "conspicuous consumption," who maintained that satiation had little meaning in a hedonistic society where people—"self-contained globule(s) of desire," as he put it—bought and bought to keep up with the Joneses.
17. For the record, Mr. Veblen was a practicing Lutheran.
18. Marj Charlier, "Back to Basics," *Wall Street Journal,* February 9, 1990, p. B14.
19. With half of all American high school students, by age seventeen, unable to use decimals and percentages, recognize geometric figures, and solve simple equations, it comes as no surprise that they came in dead last in an international math exam, and another ranking put American students near the bottom of a seventeen-country survey on high school sciences; A. N. Applebee, J. A. Langer, I. V. S. Mullis, *Crossroads in American Education.* Princeton, NJ: Educational Testing Service, February 1989, p. 21; and John Walsh, "U.S. Science Students Near Foot of Class," *Science,* March 11, 1988, p. 1237. Still another survey discovered that only 42 percent of seventeen-year-olds could read well enough to understand a 12th-grade history book or a newspaper editorial; Ellen Graham, "If Johnny Can't Read, the U.S. Can't Compete," *Wall Street Journal, Centennial Edition 1989,*

pp. A22–23; and Kenneth H. Bacon, "U.S. Survey of Schools Finds Little Gain in Reading, Writing Skills Since 1971," *Wall Street Journal*, January 10, 1990, p. A14.

20. John Bishop, "Is the Test Score Decline Responsible for the Productivity Growth Decline?" NYSSILR Working Paper No. 87-05, 1987; cited in Aaron, pp. 1–15.
21. MIT Commission . . . , p. 118.

24:00. Time's Up

1. William Henry Davies, *Leisure*. London: Poetry Book Shop, 1920.
2. Jeremy Rifkin, *Time Wars*. New York: Henry Holt, 1987, p. 2.
3. Donald Richie, *The Inland Sea*. London: Century Hutchinson, 1971, pp. 31–32.
4. Alex M. Freedman, " . . . But it is the Good Life That Lures These Youths," *Wall Street Journal*, January 14, 1987, p. 23.
5. John P. Robinson, "The Time Squeeze," *American Demographics*, February 1990, pp. 32–33. Prof. Robinson finds that the hurried spend more time, however, talking to people on the telephone, no doubt because that activity has been commoditized.
6. Louis Harris, *Inside America*. New York: Vintage Books, 1987, p. 125.
7. Norman Macrae, "The Next Ages of Man," *The Economist*, December 24, 1988, p. 5.
8. Harris, p. 125.
9. Barbara Ehrenreich, *The Hearts of Men*. Garden City, NY: Anchor/Doubleday, 1983, p. 169.
10. For example, Cynthia Russell, "Couch-Potato Blight," *Columbia*, April–May 1989, p. 40.
11. And, as Tom Lehrer might add, poisoning pigeons in the park; *Too Many Songs by Tom Lehrer*. New York: Pantheon Books, 1981, pp. 50–54.

INDEX